United Nations University Series on Regionalism

Volume 16

The United Nations University Series on Regionalism, launched by UNU-CRIS and Springer, offers a platform for innovative work on (supra-national) regionalism from a global and inter-disciplinary perspective. It includes the *World Reports* on *Regional Integration*, published in collaboration with other UN agencies, but it is also open for theoretical, methodological and empirical contributions from academics and policy-makers worldwide.

Book proposals will be reviewed by an International Editorial Board.

The series editors are particularly interested in book proposals dealing with:

- comparative regionalism;
- comparative work on regional organizations;
- inter-regionalism;
- the role of regions in a multi-level governance context;
- the interactions between the UN and the regions;
- the regional dimensions of the reform processes of multilateral institutions;
- the dynamics of cross-border micro-regions and their interactions with supra-national regions;
- methodological issues in regionalism studies.

Accepted book proposals can receive editorial support from UNU-CRIS for the preparation of manuscripts.

Please send book proposals to: pdelombaerde@cris.unu.edu and lvanlangenhove@cris.unu.edu.

More information about this series at http://www.springer.com/series/7716

Pierre Sauvé • Rodrigo Polanco Lazo
José Manuel Álvarez Zárate
Editors

The Pacific Alliance in a World of Preferential Trade Agreements

Lessons in Comparative Regionalism

Springer

Editors
Pierre Sauvé
World Bank Group
Geneva, Switzerland

Rodrigo Polanco Lazo
World Trade Institute
University of Bern
Bern, Switzerland

José Manuel Álvarez Zárate
Universidad Externado
Bogotá, Colombia

ISSN 2214-9848 ISSN 2214-9856 (electronic)
United Nations University Series on Regionalism
ISBN 978-3-030-08704-3 ISBN 978-3-319-78464-9 (eBook)
https://doi.org/10.1007/978-3-319-78464-9

Printed on acid-free paper

This Springer imprint is published by the registered company Springer International Publishing AG part of Springer Nature.
The registered company address is: Gewerbestrasse 11, 6330 Cham, Switzerland

Contents

Abbreviations

ACE	Economic Complementation Agreement (Acuerdo de Complementación Económica)
AEO	Authorized Economic Operators
ALADI	Latin American Integration Association (Asociación Latinoamericana de Integración)
APEC	Asia Pacific Economic Cooperation
APPRI	Agreement on the Reciprocal Promotion and Protection of Investments (Acuerdo de Promoción y Protección Recíproca de Inversiones)
ASEAN	Association of Southeast Asian Nations
BIT	Bilateral investment treaty
CAN	Andean Community of Nations (Comunidad Andina de Naciones)
CEAP	Consejo Empresarial de la Alianza del Pacífico
CELAC	Community of Latin American and Caribbean
CETA	Comprehensive Economic and Trade Agreement
ECLAC	Economic Commission for Latin America and the Caribbean
EU	European Union
FDI	Foreign direct investment
FNE	Fiscalía Nacional Económica
FTA	Free trade agreement
FTSW	Foreign Trade Single Window
GATS	General Agreement on Trade in Services
GATT	General Agreement on Tariffs and Trade
GDP	Gross domestic product
GLI	Grubel-Lloyd index
GPA	Government Procurement Agreement
GRULAC	Group of Latin American and Caribbean Countries
GVC	Global value chain
HDI	Human Development Index
ICA	Ingenieros Civiles Asociados
ICT	Information and communications technology
IIA	International investment agreements

IIL	International investment law
IIT	Intra-industry trade
ILAM	Integrated Latin American Market
IMF	International Monetary Fund
IOT	Input–output table
IP	Intellectual property
IPRs	Intellectual property rights
ISDS	Investor–state dispute settlement
ISP	Internet service providers
LAC	Latin America and the Caribbean
MFN	Most-favored nation
MILA	Mercado Integrado Latinoamericano
MNCs	Multinational corporations
NAFTA	North American Free Trade Agreement
OECD	Organisation for Economic Co-operation and Development
PA	Pacific Alliance
PAAP	Pacific Alliance Additional Protocol
PPH	Patent Prosecution Highway
PPP	Purchasing power parity
PTA	Preferential trade agreements
RCEP	Regional Comprehensive Economic Partnership
RTA	Regional trade agreements
SEA	Single European Act
SITC	Standard International Trade Classification
SME	Small and medium-sized enterprises
SPS	Sanitary and phytosanitary standards
TBT	Technical barriers to trade
TDLC	Tribunal de Defensa de la Libre Competencia
TiSA	Trade in Services Agreement
TPP	Trans-Pacific Partnership
TRIPS	Trade-Related Aspects of Intellectual Property
TTIP	Transatlantic Trade and Investment Partnership
UNCTAD	United Nations Conference on Trade and Development
US	United States
VCLT	Vienna Convention on the Law of Treaties
WEF	World Economic Forum
WTO	World Trade Organization

The Pacific Alliance in a World of Preferential Trade Agreements: An Introduction

The Pacific Alliance (PA or the "Alliance") represents the most recent, ambitious, and innovative effort at promoting deep trade- and investment-led integration and regulatory cooperation among a group of Latin American nations with a professed common interest in harnessing the full benefits of policies that engage the regional and world economies. Launched in June 2012, the Pacific Alliance comprises Chile, Colombia, Mexico, and Peru, with two countries – Costa Rica and Panama – currently seeking membership of the regional grouping. As a bloc, the PA constitutes the world's eighth largest economy and its seventh largest exporting entity. Within the subregion of Latin America and the Caribbean, the Alliance represents 36% of GDP, concentrates 50% of total trade, and absorbs 41% of foreign investment flows directed to the region. The Alliance's four founding members have a combined population of 212 million, a majority of which are under the age of 30. With an average per capita GDP of ten thousand dollars, it can be viewed as a convergence club among recent members of the OECD (Mexico and Chile) and members currently engaged in negotiating their terms of accession to the industrialized country grouping (Colombia and Peru).

The PA aims to build, in a participatory and consensual manner, an area of deep economic integration and to move gradually toward the free circulation of goods, services, capital, and persons among its members. Bringing together a group of like-minded countries that have long championed a trade- and foreign direct investment-driven growth model and enacted a wide range of pro-competitive reforms at the domestic level, the PA is notable for the high level of hard and soft law aims it pursues despite the low level of intra-regional trade and investment characterizing the regional grouping. Indeed, reflecting similarities in the commodity composition of trade among the Alliance's three Andean members – Chile, Colombia, and Peru and the distance that separates them from the PA's northern-oriented industrial behemoth (Mexico), the Pacific Alliance offers the paradox of a highly ambitious policy initiative among countries whose level of intra-regional trade – hovering as it does below 5% – ranks among the lowest of all major regional integration compacts.

A distinctive feature of the PA is how its members pursue their deep integration aims through means differing markedly from other integration efforts afoot in Latin America, such as the Common Market of the South (MERCOSUR), the Andean Community (CAN), or the Bolivarian Alliance for the Peoples of Our America (ALBA). Largely (and deliberately) eschewing the creation of supranational institutions, the Alliance's DNA can be described as being essentially pragmatic, flexible, goal-oriented, and member-driven, focusing on the identification and supply of a number of integration-promoting regional public good initiatives that can be derived from heightened forms of *inter-governmental* cooperation. It is telling in this regard that only two documents have been developed as foundational elements of the Pacific Alliance: (i) the *PA Framework Agreement* of 2012 depicting the parameters, institutional architecture, and rules governing the process of region-wide political and economic cooperation and (ii) the *PA Additional Protocol* of 2014, which governs the liberalization of cross-border transactions and covers a wider range of issues relating to trade in goods, services, investment, the mobility of people, and government procurement, among others. A 2015 amendment to the Protocol added a new chapter on "regulatory improvement" and updated previously existing chapters on technical barriers to trade (specifically on trade in cosmetic products), electronic commerce, and telecommunications services.

Because of its distinctive, targeted, and explicitly intra-governmental nature, and the like-mindedness of its members favoring closer engagement with the world economy and especially the deepening of trans-Pacific ties, the Pacific Alliance has generated considerable interest within policy and nongovernmental circles. No less than 52 countries are associated to the policy initiative in their capacity of "observer" states. Such a group currently includes Australia, Canada, China, France, Germany, India, Japan, New Zealand, Singapore, South Korea, Switzerland, the United Kingdom, as well as the United States.

The PA has recently embarked on a collective outreach process with Australia, Canada, New Zealand, and Singapore, with whom it has begun negotiations to conclude a preferential trade agreement which could be completed in the coming year when these countries become associated members of the PA. With the exception of Colombia, all other PA members and expected associated ones are members of the TPP, which should ease the negotiating process.

This volume, which draws on a conference held in November 2015 at Externado University in Bogota, Colombia, brought together leading scholars, practitioners, and officials from public, regional, and international organizations interested in a critical analysis of the Alliance, its distinctiveness, and likely future directions. The edited volume adopts a multidisciplinary lens, highlighting salient legal, economic, and global political economy dimensions of the PA process and journey. With a view to offering a critical and scholarly reading of latest developments in Pacific Alliance integration efforts to the widest possible audience within and beyond Latin America, English was the language of the conference papers.

The edited volume features contributions made by researchers from Bocconi University (Italy), the Economic Commission for Latin America and the Caribbean (ECLAC), the Inter-American Development Bank (IADB), the International Centre for Trade and Sustainable Development (ICTSD, Switzerland), the Munich Intellectual Property Law Center (MTIT, Germany), the Organisation for Economic Co-operation and Development (OECD, France), Universidad Centroamericana (Nicaragua), Universidad de Chile, University of Costa Rica, Universidad EAFIT (Colombia), Universidad Externado (Colombia), the University of Miami (United States), the University of Melbourne (Australia), Universidad Panamericana (Mexico), University of Perpignan Via Domita (France), Pontificia Universidad Católica del Peru (PUCP, Peru), Universidad de La Sabana (Colombia), as well as the World Trade Institute (WTI) at the University of Bern (Switzerland).

The edited volume brings together a set of papers initially presented at the conference. It is organized in two parts. Part I explores several core features of the Pacific Alliance and situates the regional grouping in a comparative context. It addresses key recent developments and future prospects, the growing insertion of PA firms in regional and global value chains, the challenges arising from integrating new members to the Alliance, as well as comparing the PA with the WTO and MERCOSUR processes, institutions, and substantive disciplines. Part I concludes by exploring what is needed for the PA to meet its deep integration objectives. Part II of the edited volume sheds analytical light on the evolving body of rules governing the integration process among Pacific Alliance members. This includes first generation issues that already form part of the PA rule book, such as trade in services, cross-border investment, electronic commerce, and dispute settlement, alongside newer, frontier issues, such as intellectual property protection, competition law and policy, and digital governance. A concluding chapter, based on a synthesis by the conference rapporteur, underscores the PA's achievements to date and identifies a range of forward-looking challenges confronting Alliance members, highlighting possible pathways for future development and a number of themes arising from the PA process warranting greater scholarly scrutiny.

Among these, the question of the optimal degree of institutionalization required to secure the depth of integration the PA members are seeking is of central importance. Experience in other parts of the world, notably under the North American Free Trade Agreement and the Association of South-East Asian Nations, has revealed a clear range of trade-offs and possible limitations when parties to a deep integration compact profess significant reluctance toward pooled regulatory sovereignty. At the same time, innovative implementation modalities, such as those adopted by ASEAN Member states to bridge development divides, have proven helpful to maintaining forward integration momentum amid considerable heterogeneity in income levels and capacity, particularly when combined with close cooperation with the lending and capacity-strengthening activities of regional and multilateral financial institutions.

A closely linked question concerns the extent to which a purely intra-governmental process of regional governance can supply (and fund) the regional public goods, notably the hardware of intensified physical and digital connectivity alongside the software of intensified regulatory cooperation, required to make a success of the PA. Equally important – and once more closely linked – is the question of how best to raise the (low current) levels of intra-regional trade and FDI in goods and services markets among PA members, without which sustaining the political and private sector commitment to the vision of a PA community may prove more challenging. Useful scholarship could also be directed to examining how closer trade and investment linkages between the PA and partners in the Asia-Pacific region will affect the structure of production and patterns of specialization in the PA. The coexistence of hard and soft law initiatives under the PA, one of the Alliance's most innovative features, raises natural questions of monitoring, compliance, and enforcement to which answers should be sought. Finally, there would be benefit in exploring whether and how the PA's interaction with a large and growing number of observer governments influences its agenda setting and policy priorities.

The editors wish to express their deepest thanks to the expert participants and institutions who attended the conference in Bogota and developed their conference contributions into chapters of this edited volume. Special thanks in particular are expressed to colleagues from the World Trade Institute at the University of Bern, Universidad Externado, the Ministry of Trade, Industry and Tourism of Colombia, as well as for the generous support provided by the Swiss State Secretariat for Economic Affairs (SECO) and its interest in academic diplomacy, which facilitated the participation of a number of experts whose conference contributions enriched our debates and subsequent edited volume.

Geneva, Switzerland — Pierre Sauvé
Bern, Switzerland — Rodrigo Polanco Lazo
Bogotá, Colombia — José Manuel Álvarez Zárate

Part I
Situating the Pacific Alliance in Comparative Context

Chapter 1
The Pacific Alliance: Building a Pathway to the High-Hanging Fruits of Deep Integration

Ana María Palacio Valencia

1.1 Introduction

As its members pursue deep regional integration, the Pacific Alliance (PA) faces the challenge of developing an institutional and legal architecture that can support the accomplishment of its goals in the long run. This chapter explores the development of such architecture by reviewing the legal instruments in place, the institutional setting, the activities already undertaken by the PA and the achievements of the integration scheme, together with the challenges that lie ahead.

To date, the academic literature has focused on the economic potential of the PA, the growing international attention paid to it, and the prospects for enhancing economic relations with the Asia-Pacific region (Abusada-Salah et al. 2015; George 2014). Commentators have examined the rebalancing effect that the PA has had in the region by reinvigorating the basic principles of open regionalism that must co-exist with the post-liberal regionalism of the past 10 years (Kotschwar 2013; Nolte and Wehner 2013). The early successes of the PA have also received attention (SELA 2013), but no comprehensive examination has yet been made of the role of institutions and law in consolidating the PA (Malamud 2012a; Seatzu 2015).[1]

The chapter first examines the legal instruments in place, setting out the basic organizational structures and commitments of the parties in relation to the integration scheme. It then reviews PA achievements to date. The chapter posits that the

[1] A couple of preliminary assessments have tackled the institutional design of the PA, stressing that developing a supranational regime is a prerequisite for success. Both take as a template the European Union, without giving careful consideration to the contextual and historical issues that have prevented proper implementation of supranational models of integration in Latin America, despite previous attempts within the framework of the Andean Community, the Caribbean Community and the Central American Integration System.

A. M. Palacio Valencia (✉)
The University of Melbourne, Melbourne, VIC, Australia

P. Sauvé et al. (eds.), *The Pacific Alliance in a World of Preferential Trade Agreements*, United Nations University Series on Regionalism 16,
https://doi.org/10.1007/978-3-319-78464-9_1

demands for further integration, in addition to the implementation of the current commitments by the PA – not only in the economic field, but also in other dimensions – will require adjustments to the current institutional and legal frameworks. The primarily intergovernmental nature of the integration scheme offers some flexibility for the process to grow, but this can come at the price of subjecting the PA to the uncertainties of domestic political dynamics and the shifting priorities of member states. Moreover, although the early harvest approach represents an understandable way to address the propensity for underperformance of previous Latin American integration schemes, it is likely inadequate to achieve consolidation. The PA's incipient DNA needs to be paired with an appropriate long-term development plan and examinations of how instrumental the current actions and achievements are in moving towards: deep integration, free movement of economic factors, growth and development, social equality and enhancement of the political and economic relations with the Asia-Pacific region.

1.2 Institutional Setting in the Pacific Alliance

1.2.1 Legal Agreements

The legal regime in place for the PA comprises pre-existing bilateral agreements between members, alongside a number of plurilateral agreements in force.

1.2.1.1 Pre-existing Agreements

The PA pursues deep integration[2] on the basis of existing commercial agreements (Lawrence 1996; Kuwayama 1999), through the homologation of such agreements.[3] Subsequent declarations by PA Heads of State have neither clarified the meaning or scope of the concept of homologation of existing agreements (Vieira 2015).

[2]The concept of deep integration, which traditionally refers to economic and commercial integration, was first used by Robert Laurence to distinguish between different types of regional trade agreements – shallow integration and deep integration. Shallow integration refers to agreements that deal with border issues preventing trade between two parties, while deep integration refers to agreements that deal with behind the border issues. They include disciplines such as services, movement of factors, harmonization of regulatory regimes, environmental standards, and domestic policies that affect international competitiveness. The first example of an agreement of the deep integration type in the Americas was the North American Free Trade Agreement (NAFTA) and academics have suggested that regional trade agreements North–South tend to follow a model of deep integration, while South–South agreements are primarily shallow in character. The PA challenges this proposition.

[3]The first presidential declaration mandates the ministers of foreign affairs and foreign trade of the member states to negotiate a draft for a Framework Agreement for the Pacific Alliance on the basis of the 'homologation' of the existing free trade agreements among the member states.

The Framework Agreement of the Pacific Alliance (the Framework Agreement) refers, in Article 8, to the relationship with other agreements, explaining that it neither replaces nor modifies the economic, commercial and bilateral integration agreements between the parties, nor the regional or multilateral agreements in force between them. Moreover, the Additional Protocol to the Framework Agreement of the Pacific Alliance (the Commercial Protocol) acknowledges the agreement of the parties on the co-existence of the Commercial Protocol and previous international agreements of which at least two of the PA member states are members. Thus, the function of homologation appears to be that of confirming or ratifying the rights and obligations of states in relation to each other in regard to pre-existing agreements. Compliance with this approach in practical terms has yet to emerge, since the implementation of the Commercial Protocol would potentially lead to the superposition of obligations found in several agreements and subsequent implementation rules (Tremolada 2014).

One of the conditions of the PA is the pre-existence of free trade agreements between the parties. This is also a requirement for candidates wishing to join the Alliance, according to Article 11 (1) of the Framework Agreement. As summarized in Table 1.1, the pre-existing agreements at the bilateral and regional levels include not only trade agreements but also the investment and taxation agreements already in place.

1.2.2 *Legal Instruments of the PA and Their Relationship with Pre-existing Agreements*

1.2.2.1 Legal Instruments

Two instruments establish the legal basis of the PA: the above-mentioned Framework Agreement, signed on 6 June 2012, and the Additional Protocol to the Framework Agreement of the Pacific Alliance, signed on 10 February 2014. The Framework Agreement entered into force on 20 July 2015, after ratification by Mexico, Chile, Peru and Colombia. The Commercial Protocol entered into force on 1 May 2016.

The Framework Agreement sets out the core features of the integration scheme in terms of its underlying principles, approach to regionalism, and objectives. These underlying principles encompass commitments to: democracy, the rule of law, the separation of powers, the constitutional order, and the respect for human rights and fundamental freedoms among the member states. The PA follows the approach of open regionalism, promoting the free movement of economic factors – capital, goods, services and persons – and identifies regional integration as instrumental to member states' insertion into the global economy.

The Framework Agreement sets out the following objectives:

1. constructing, in a participatory and consensual manner, a deep integration area to advance progressively towards the free circulation of goods, services, capital and persons;

Table 1.1 Pre-existing bilateral agreements between the Pacific Alliance member states

	Chile	Colombia	Mexico	Peru
Chile	–	ACE 24 1993, FTA 2009 ARPPI 2000 (not in force) FTA investment chapter 9 2009 Double taxation avoidance A 2009	FTA 1999 Strategic association agreement 2006 on political dialogue and cooperation FTA investment chapter 9 1999 Double taxation avoidance A 1999	FTA 2009 (substitutes ACE 38 1998) FTA investment chapter 11 Double taxation A 2004
Colombia	ACE 24 1993, FTA 2009 ARPPI 2000 (not in force) FTA investment chapter 9 2009 Double taxation avoidance A 2009	–	FTA 1995 Added investment chapter to FTA 2011 Double taxation avoidance A 2013	CAN 1967 and implementing decisions ARPPI 2010 (substitutes a 1994 ARPPI) Andean decision 578 on double taxation avoidance 2005
Mexico	FTA 1999 Strategic association agreement 2006 on political dialogue and cooperation FTA investment chapter 9 1999 Double taxation avoidance A 1999	FTA 1995 Added investment chapter to FTA 2011 Double taxation avoidance A 2013	–	Commercial integration agreement 2012 substituted the ACE 8 from 1987 FTA investment chapter 11 Double taxation A 2015
Peru	FTA 2009 (substitutes ACE 38 1998) FTA investment chapter 11 Double taxation A 2004	CAN 1967 and implementing decisions ARPPI 2010 (substitutes a 1994 ARPPI) Andean decision 578 on double taxation avoidance 2005	Commercial integration agreement 2012 substituted the ACE 8 from 1987 FTA investment chapter 11 Double taxation A 2015	–

2. boosting growth, development and competitiveness of the member states' economies with a view to improving welfare, reducing socioeconomic inequality, and enhancing social inclusion; and
3. becoming a platform for political articulation, economic and commercial integration, and projection to the world with emphasis on the Asia Pacific region.

The Commercial Protocol features the following core disciplines for the establishment of a free trade area among member states: market access (Ch. 3), transparency (Ch. 15),[4] rules of origin and related procedures (Ch. 4), trade facilitation and customs cooperation (Ch. 5), sanitary and phytosanitary measures (Ch. 6), technical barriers to trade (Ch. 7), government procurement (Ch. 8), and trans-border trade of services (Ch. 9), including general provisions and specific regulations on financial services (Ch. 11), maritime services (Ch. 12), telecommunications (Ch. 14), and electronic commerce (Ch. 13). The Commercial Protocol also features disciplines on investment, including provisions on dispute resolution and arbitral tribunals between a member state and an investor from another member state.[5] The Commercial Protocol establishes rules on the settlement of disputes between member states in relation to all matters covered in the Protocol. According to the Protocol, if disputes cannot be resolved through consultations or with the assistance of the Free Trade Commission (Ch. 17), they should be resolved ultimately through *ad hoc* arbitral tribunals. It stipulates general and specific exceptions to the core obligations. Finally, the Commercial Protocol includes general provisions on interpretation and compliance, its relationship with other international agreements, and prescriptions for the administration of the Protocol, led by a Free Trade Commission.

In July 2015, as a result of the continuing work of the technical groups, the parties concluded the first protocol modifying the Commercial Protocol to include: (i) an additional chapter on regulatory improvement, (ii) an annex to the chapter on technical barriers to trade (on the elimination of the technical barriers to trade in cosmetic products), and (iii) amendments to and new provisions of the Commercial Protocol on telecommunication services and electronic commerce.[6]

[4] In addition the Commercial Protocol includes various commitments on transparency across the disciplines including: Article 6.9, Article 7.8, Article 8.8 and Article 9.8.

[5] The arbitral procedures between an investor of one party and another party only apply in regard to the provisions of Section A in Chapter 10 (Investment). No other provisions of the Commercial Protocol allow for arbitration between parties other than the member states under the Protocol.

[6] In accordance with the Puerto Varas Declaration of the XI Presidential Summit, negotiations were concluded in 2016 on an additional annex to the Technical Barriers to Trade chapter that covers provisions regarding organic products and medical devices. The Cali Declaration of the XII Presidential Summit in 2017 also announced the conclusion of another annex on technical barriers to trade for food supplements.

1.2.2.2 Relationship to Pre-existing Agreements

The extent to which the web of pre-existing treaties co-exist with the Framework Agreement and later treaties and decisions developing and implementing it remains unclear. Two situations are foreseen in the medium run: (i) some of the provisions in pre-existing treaties will become obsolete because further commitments will be agreed upon in order to achieve deep integration, and (ii) the co-existence of agreements regulating the same subject matter will open the gate to inconsistencies that could result in future disagreements.[7]

The application of these provisions may not be straightforward in the case of incompatibility between the treaty establishing the Framework Agreement and pre-existing bilateral, regional or multilateral treaties.[8] On this particular point the Framework Agreement only includes preambular provisions asserting that PA members are aware that the integration process will have as a basis the economic, commercial and integration agreements in force between the parties at the bilateral, regional and multilateral levels. Moreover, the preamble reaffirms PA Members' rights and obligations under the WTO as well as those established in preferential trade agreements and integration agreements between the member states of the PA.

Situations of incompatibility between the Commercial Protocol and other pre-existing agreements need to be examined by resorting to Article 8 of the Framework Agreement, as well as Articles 1.2 and 1.3 of the Commercial Protocol. Yet even in such instances, the solution to incompatible provisions is not clear-cut. Article 8 of the Framework Agreement states that decisions by the Council of Ministers and agreements adopted within the framework of the PA will not replace or modify economic, commercial and integration agreements in force between the parties at the bilateral, regional or multilateral level. Article 1.2 of the Commercial Protocol specifies, in reference to the Framework Agreement and the intention of the parties, that pre-existing international agreements between the parties co-exist with the

[7] In cases of inconsistencies between treaties regulating the same subject matter, Article 30 of the Vienna Convention on the Law of Treaties (VCLT) will apply. This provision prescribes that:

2. When a treaty specifies that it is subject to, or that it is not to be considered as incompatible with, an earlier or later treaty, the provisions of that other treaty prevail.
3. When all the parties to the earlier treaty are parties also to the later treaty but the earlier treaty is not terminated or suspended in operation under article 59, the earlier treaty applies only to the extent that its provisions are compatible with those of the later treaty.
4. When the parties to the later treaty do not include all the parties to the earlier one:
   (a) as between States parties to both treaties the same rule applies as in paragraph 3;
   (b) as between a State party to both treaties and a State party to only one of the treaties, the treaty to which both States are parties governs their mutual rights and obligations.

[8] Note that the guidelines provided by the Directorate of Institutional Legal Affairs at the Ministry of Foreign Affairs of Colombia specify, as a matter of good drafting practice, that the agreement should establish the effect of the corresponding agreement on pre-existing agreements, for example through derogation, subrogation or declaration of pre-eminence of one over the other in case of incompatibilities (Ministerio de Relaciones Exteriores de Colombia).

Commercial Protocol. Article 1.3 makes a reference to the general rules on interpretation of international agreements, while the preamble emulates the content of the Framework Agreement preamble, reaffirming the preferential and integration agreements between the parties.

An uneasy harmony also results between the future rules adopted by PA bodies, comprising the legal regime of the PA and pre-existing legal regimes, and regimes that are continuing to develop such as the Andean Community of Nations (CAN). As mentioned before, the Framework Agreement only establishes that decisions by the Council of Ministers and 'other agreements' adopted within the PA will not replace the commercial, economic or integration agreements in force between the parties at the bilateral, regional or multilateral levels.

1.2.3 Overarching Institutional Architecture

At the institutional level, various bodies and technical groups operate within the PA. According to Article 4 of the Framework Agreement, the Council of Ministers represents the decision-making body of the PA. The ministers in charge of foreign affairs and trade in each member state make up the Council of Ministers responsible for implementing the Framework Agreement and the Presidential Declarations. Any decision of the Council must be approved by consensus. Functionally, the body beneath the Council is the High-Level Group (GAN), created through the Lima Declaration in 2011. Deputy Ministers of foreign affairs and trade constitute the GAN, whose primary role is monitoring the work of the technical groups and developing a strategy for the PA to manage its external relations. The Council of Ministers assumes a strategic and policy line function, whereas the GAN oversees the work of the various technical groups at the micro-level. Annex 2 of the X Presidential Declaration (Paracas Declaration) established the Council of Ministers of Finance to develop an agenda for economic and financial integration, reporting directly to the presidents.

Despite this formalized structure, in practice, the two main drivers of progress in the PA have to date been the presidents and the Council of Ministers, reaffirming the intergovernmental nature of the integration scheme. The presidents of the member states do not comprise a formalized body with functions assigned to it. However, they meet regularly every 6 or 12 months and issue declarations containing mandates that need to be implemented through the work of the Council of Ministers and the technical *ad hoc* groups.

The PA relies on a *Pro Tempore* Presidency that rotates each year among the member states. Government officials of each member state carry out the *pro tempore* presidential roles of an administrative nature such as organization of the meetings of heads of state, sessions of other institutional bodies and monitoring of progress in implementing presidential mandates. The *Pro Tempore* Presidency represents the PA by request of the parties, as prescribed by Article 7 of the Framework

Agreement. Around 20 technical groups are entrusted with developing the objectives and presidential mandates of the PA.[9]

Presidents of the national parliaments of the member states met in 2013 and constituted a Monitoring Parliamentary Commission of the Pacific Alliance (CISAP by the Spanish acronym), which held its first formal session in July 2014. The participation of national parliaments in the PA is in its early stages but signals a clear interest by national parliaments to support the PA process and enhance its political legitimacy. The Commission comprises at least six members of the national parliaments of each PA member state. Although its name suggests that it is a supervisory body, it is my view that the Commission is evolving towards a supporting role, with the ability to recommend measures to promote the development of the PA (Congreso de la República de Perú 2014). At the same time, the Commission aims to become a channel of communication with citizens. The Monitoring Parliamentary Commission of the Pacific Alliance does not aim to become a decision-making body within the PA in the medium-term.

A distinctive feature of the PA is the support that it has attracted from the business community of member states since the launch of the integration journey. This support was formalized with the establishment of a private body within the business sector – the Pacific Alliance Business Council (CEAP) – to promote the integration scheme.[10] The CEAP has championed an ambitious agenda for the PA that includes financial integration, taxation rules, insolvency regimes, trade facilitation, convergence, harmonization and equivalence in regulations covering various areas, such as technical regulations, and sanitary and phytosanitary measures, logistical competitiveness, education, public procurement, and entrepreneurship and innovation.[11]

---

[9]According to the XIth Presidential Declaration (Puerto Varas Declaration), two technical groups on Environment and Green Growth, and a Labour Group should be established. An additional subcommittee on the digital agenda has also been established together with a road map for its activities. Although the Labor Group, and the Environment and Green technical groups are incorporated in the institutional chart it is not yet clear what topics are being discussed or what the work programmes are for these two technical groups. Recently created groups include one on gender-related issue whose mandate is to develop a strategy for mainstreaming gender considerations into the work programmes of PA technical groups. There is also a technical group on cultural issues with an initial focus on the promotion of creative and cultural industries. In parallel, the Council of Ministers of Finance develops its agenda through additional groups on: infrastructure; financial integration; services trade; and catastrophic risks. Notwithstanding the establishment of all these working groups the PA is also undertaking works on fisheries and aquaculture, health and access to medicines, and consumer protection.

[10]The CEAP has representation in each member state and is formed by four business people per country. It has an advisory role, formulating recommendations to the governments and business unions about the PA including on how to enhance cooperation among the member states (CEAP 2012). It promotes common actions in the business community to encourage the development of third markets, especially in the Asia Pacific region.

[11]The CEAP Declaration of December 2014 includes recommendations that encourage further negotiations on capital markets integration and superannuation funds, as well as air services.

The CEAP serves as the main liaison point between the business and productive sector and government officials, identifying the primary concerns of major industry actors in each country.

The Commercial Protocol incorporates further bodies for the administration of the Protocol, including the Free Trade Commission, an intergovernmental body comprising public officials at the level of ministers of trade or economy. The Free Trade Commission oversees the work of the committees, subcommittees and technical groups created for the implementation of the Protocol. It has powers to adopt decisions on commercial matters such as tariffs to provide better access conditions.

From the review of the current institutional setting and the additional bodies operating now under the Commercial Protocol, several of the activities conducted through the *ad hoc* groups (Trade Facilitation, Government Procurement, Services & Capital) would be subsumed under the formal institutional structure of the Protocol. It will also be the case once the First Amending Protocol[12] enters into force with the Regulatory Improvement *ad hoc* group that will need to transition to a Regulatory Improvement Committee under the umbrella of the Protocol. However, PA members will likely need to make further readjustments to avoid institutional duplication and inefficiencies, as evidenced in Fig. 1.1.

Additional mechanisms to achieve coordination between the working groups will also be required, notably to manage inevitable overlaps between some of them.[13] Readjustments will also be required in relation to the pre-existing institutional setting of free trade agreements and other commercial agreements that provide for the existence of free trade commissions, together with several committees and working groups for the administration and implementation of those agreements. Duplication of efforts is inevitable, and progress in achieving deeper integration will lead some to become obsolete (Centro de Estudios Internacionales Gilberto Bosque 2014).

---

[12] It provides for the creation of a Regulatory Improvement Committee.

[13] For instance, although the Xth Presidential Declaration stipulates the creation of a working group on mining development, social responsibility and sustainability, the last two are also cross-cutting issues in relation to the promotion of investments in general, and, more broadly, are components of the sustainable development pursued by the PA. Activities in these two areas currently seem to be concentrated in the mining sector. Coordination will also be needed between the Technical Group on Services and Capital and the groups on Innovation, Education, and the Mobility of Persons, including with regard to cross-cutting issues with the SMEs Group and the Digital Agenda Sub-Committee.

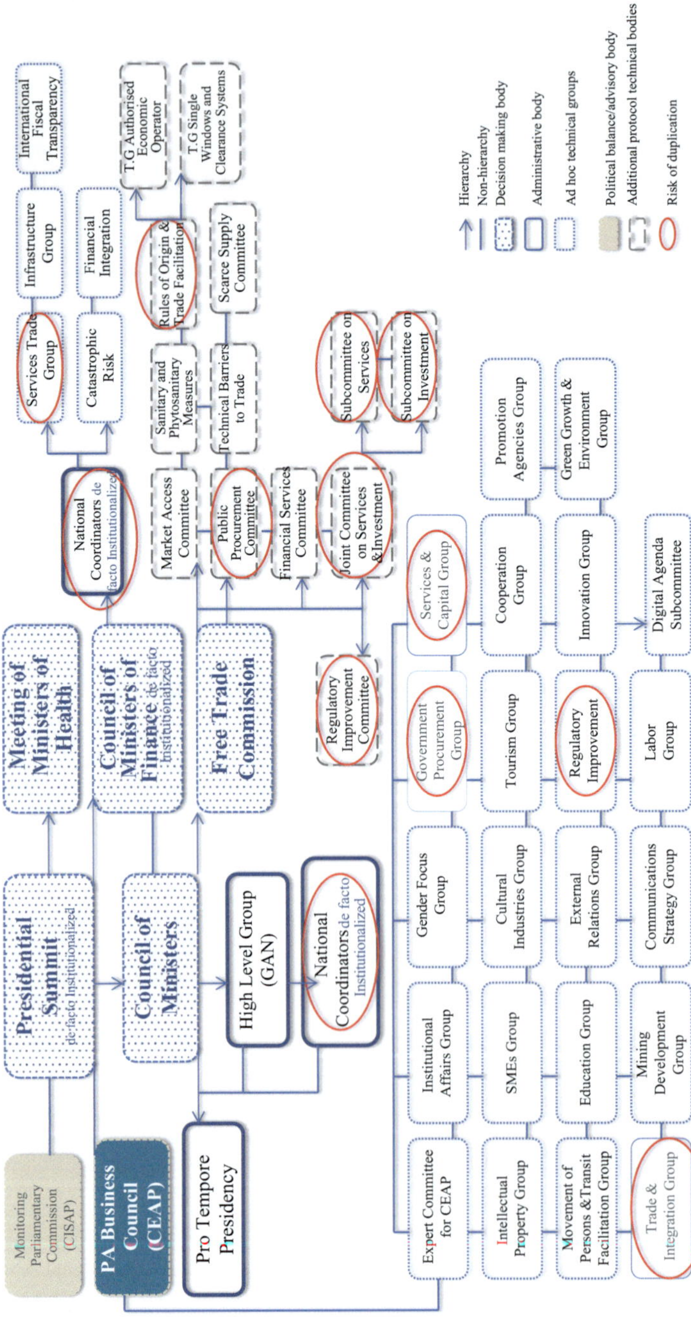

Based on A. Malamud 2003

Fig. 1.1 Institutions in operation after the amending protocol enters into force

1.3 Challenges Ahead

1.3.1 Early Harvest Approach

The PA pursues deep integration in an open, flexible and pragmatic manner with a view to reaping an 'early harvest'. This concept refers to the achievement of short-term and medium-term results by addressing the easiest hurdles first, primarily to create confidence in the project (Dade and Meacham 2013). Positive results have already been obtained, providing heightened international visibility and reputational externalities for the integration scheme (Secretaría Permanente SELA 2013). In doing so, the PA departs from previous integration efforts in the region whose progress has often proved unduly slow.

1.3.1.1 Advances in the Economic Sphere

In 2013, PA member states asserted in their VII Presidential Declaration (Cali Declaration) that customs duties for 90% of the goods traded among members would be eliminated at the moment the Framework Agreement entered into force in July 2015. In a later presidential declaration, the liberalization threshold for goods trade was raised to 92%, with a commitment to gradually reducing customs duties on the remaining 8%. Notwithstanding the total exclusion of sugar from the negotiations of the Commercial Protocol, the remaining 8% – mainly agricultural and animal goods (Perry 2014) – is subject to schedules of liberalization with a time frame ranging from 2 to17 years for total tariff elimination

Several studies have pointed out the early progress registered on goods trade liberalization (Abusada-Salah et al. 2015). However, upon closer scrutiny, it would appear that, compared to what was already liberalized under pre-existing trade agreements between the member states, the PA-induced gains are not as significant as they appear at first glance (see Table 1.2).

Assessing results in this area further needs to take account of PA rules of origin and the possibility of cumulation of origin rather than the actual levels of tariff reductions achieved through the Commercial Protocol. This may have a major bearing on the ability of PA firms to take advantage of regional value chains. At the same time, cumulation of origin should facilitate intra-industry trade across the PA. Progress has also been made on trade facilitation through the interoperability of national single windows, the online exchange of phytosanitary certifications, and the work plan for mutual recognition of authorised economic operators across the PA (Cali Declaration 2017).

Another PA project that has attracted significant attention is the integration of regional stock markets under the name 'Latin American Integrated Market' (MILA), set up in 2010 by Colombia, Peru and Chile, and joined in 2014 by Mexico (Perry 2014). MILA holds potential to attract investors by diversifying the portfolio and types of operations in PA stock markets, which for member states are concentrated

Table 1.2 Tariff reductions under bilateral agreements between Pacific Alliance member states

Exporting →	Chile		Colombia		Mexico		Peru	
Importing ↓	% items	% exports	% items	% exports	% items	% exports	% items	% exports
Chile	–	–	n/a[a]	99	98.3	99	99.6	98.9
Colombia[b]	n/a[c]	99	–	–	n/a[d]	92	100 CAN	100 CAN
Mexico[e]	98.3	99	n/a[f]	92	–	–	n/a	83
Peru[g]	99.6	98.5	100 CAN	100 CAN	n/a	85	–	–

n/a, not available; –, non-applicable relationship; CAN, Andean Community of Nations (Spanish acronym); % items, percentage of items from the total number of tariff lines covered under the bilateral tariff elimination schedules; % exports, percentage of exports of goods entering import country free of tariffs

[a]Estimates by the Ministry of Trade, Industry and Tourism of Colombia suggest that only 41 sub-items or sub-headings are not yet liberalized because they are subject to price bands.

[b]Since 2005 the Andean Community has been a free trade zone when Peru finalized the liberalization schedule. Goods traded intra-regionally are free of duties.

[c]Estimates by the Ministry of Trade, Industry and Tourism of Colombia suggest that 97.6% of the items are liberalized under the pre-existing PTA, while around 182 sub-items or sub-headings are not yet liberalised

[d]Estimates by the Ministry of Trade, Industry and Tourism of Colombia suggest that 95% of the items are liberalized with the pre-existing PTA, while around 373 sub-items or sub-headings are not liberalized.

[e]According to information from the Directorate of International Economic Relations at the Ministry of Foreign Affairs of Chile, 98.3% of the tariff lines imported from Chile to Mexico were liberalized immediately and 99 items were subject to exceptions. The same situation takes place for imports from Mexico to Chile where only 99 items are subject to exceptions and 98.3% of the tariff lines were liberalized

[f]Estimates by the Ministry of Trade, Industry and Tourism of Colombia suggest that 97% of the items are liberalized with the pre-existing PTA, while around 413 sub-items or sub-headings are not yet liberalized

[g]Including items liberalized from the start and items subject to 3, 5, 6, 8, 10 and 15 years. Only three items are excluded from liberalization and 24 more are subject to a liberalization schedule for 18 years

in specific industries.[14] As George (2014) pointed out, in Chile, the securities market is currently concentrated in services and retail trade; for Colombia, concentration is in the energy sector and financial services while mining companies dominate the Peruvian securities market. Additional measures such as the expansion of product range, elimination or reduction of extra charges, dual fees and diverse cross-border

[14]The PA represents the second-largest securities market in the region in terms of capitalization and trading volumes (Cordoba 2015), close behind the Brazilian stock market – Bovespra. However, in terms of the number of listed companies, MILA is the top securities market in Latin America (George 2014), MILA has operated in secondary trading of equities since 2011 and is progressing towards additional types of operations in debt markets and derivatives (Cordoba 2015).

settlement procedures in each member, reduction of barriers to institutional investors, coordination between regulatory authorities, and further regulatory harmonization, are required to realize the potential of this integrated stock market (Perry 2014; Marczak and George 2016; Campa et al. 2015).[15] PA member states have also agreed to share commercial representation offices, starting with a first joint office in Istanbul (Gonzalez et al. 2015), and one in Casablanca.[16] The national trade and investment promotion agencies of PA members are developing a common strategy for coordinating an international presence, including in the Asia-Pacific region.

1.3.1.2 Advances in Non-economic Spheres

The creation of shared diplomatic representations in third countries helps PA member states to make administration more efficient and address budgetary constraints, while showcasing the international presence of the PA as an integrated bloc. Colombia signed general agreements with Mexico and Chile for the shared use of embassies and consulates.[17]

In 2013, member states agreed to eliminate visa requirements for PA nationals travelling to participate in unpaid activities (Cali Declaration 2013). Peru has unilaterally exempted nationals of PA member states from the requirement for business visas for a non-renewable period of 183 calendar days. Colombia has granted reciprocal treatment to Peruvians in relation to business visas. As reported in the XIth Presidential Declaration, with a view to enhancing tourism, the parties have agreed to the free movement of permanent residents of any PA member and exempt them from visa requirements for short stays. PA Member states have also implemented a common platform for the exchange of information on migrants for security purposes (Paracas Declaration 2015).

In addition, the technical group on People Movement and Migratory Facilitation is deliberating on a PA visa for persons from third countries travelling to any of the member states (Cali Declaration 2013), although no significant progress has been reported on this topic recently (Cali Declaration 2017). Furthermore, it is not clear

---

[15] Campa and others reflect on the need to complement market forces for financial integration with policy action providing short-term and long-term recommendations for public policy action.

[16] There were plans reported for sharing commercial representation in Sydney (Australia) and New Delhi (India) but they did not appear to be in operation at the time of writing.

[17] These agreements have resulted in specific accords regulating the sharing of diplomatic offices between Colombia and Chile in Azerbaijan, Ghana, Algeria, Morocco and at the Organisation for Economic Cooperation and Development (OECD). Specific agreements are in place between Mexico and Colombia on the use of diplomatic offices in Azerbaijan, Ghana, and Singapore. And Peru and Colombia have agreed to share embassy facilities in Vietnam and Ghana. These agreements relate primarily to the sharing of the physical infrastructure and buildings, while each member state retains independent diplomatic/consular delegations. The member states also have an inter-institutional agreement between their ministries of foreign affairs to cooperate and provide consular assistance to nationals of other member states when the member state of origin has no consular representation in the host country.

what negotiation efforts are underway to facilitate the movement of business persons conducting paid activities within PA countries. Members have committed to exploring measures to facilitate the movement of business people within the PA, through temporary permits of more than 180 days (Punta Mita Declaration 2014). However, no progress was reported in the XIIth Presidential Declaration (Cali Declaration 2017) on this important issue, which is essential to enhance the free movement of services across member states. This is particularly relevant when services are supplied through the movement of natural persons from one member state into the territory of another.

Cooperation is an important part of the PA and its working plan. Parties are developing a Pacific Cooperation Platform on climate change and the environment; on innovation, science and technology; micro-, small and medium-sized enterprises; and social development. Such platforms are intended to interact with PA member states and third parties.

The PA Platform on Students and Academic Mobility features a scholarship programme for postgraduates, undergraduate studies, and fellowships for researchers and professors. Approximately 1440 people from PA member states have benefited from the scholarship programme to date (Cali Declaration 2017). A preliminary study on opportunities for collaboration on climate change research and the establishment of a Network of Scientific Researchers on Climate Change have resulted from ongoing cooperation efforts.[18]

A good example of the early harvest approach was the Joint Declaration of the Pacific Alliance on Climate Change during the 20th Conference of the Parties of the United Nations Convention on Climate Change and the 10th Conference of the Parties to the Kyoto Protocol held in December 2014. Climate change represents a non-contentious issue for PA members. The Joint Declaration not only sends a message to the international community that PA members share a common view but also increases the visibility of the bloc as a whole. Cooperation initiatives in the areas of innovation, education, science and technology reflect the interest of PA members in producing results by working on other non-contentious issues. Other innovative cooperation projects include the PA's sports diplomacy programme, employing sports activities as a tool for cultural exchange and social inclusion of vulnerable children and adolescents.

PA member states have reached an agreement on cooperation in the tourism sector, and responsible agencies are developing joint activities to promote tourism in the sub-region as a single destination. Such cooperation includes joint tourist guides and packages for travellers, information exchanges and joint participation in tourism fairs and exhibitions with the ultimate goal of increasing the number of tourists visiting the region as well as intra-regional tourism.

The various avenues of PA-wide cooperation depicted above confirm that the parties are committed to the exchange of 'good practices' and experiences in several areas, including migration, consular practices, promotion practices, and regulatory

[18] The Network has been working on a project to be concluded in 2017 to monitor new-generation biodiversity to support adaptation processes and climate change mitigation.

improvement, contributing to future plans for sub-region wide harmonization and a problem-solving approach at the technical level.[19]

It bears recalling that several PA initiatives are based on the successful implementation of policies and programmes carried out by one of the member states at the national level with a view to scaling up these activities in other member states, with one example being the Pacific Alliance Innovation Awards. Thus, many sub-region wide initiatives begin with information exchanges on regulatory practices and experiences with a view to building trust and mutual understanding among officials and relevant agencies that could subsequently underpin deepened region-wide cooperation. A problem-based cooperation approach seems to be emerging at the level of technical groups and in some specialized areas within the PA. This is notably the case among regulatory bodies working on matters of intellectual property and consumer protection. The above dynamic implies a form of integrative cooperation and the use of a cooperative approach to harmonize or "converge" practices among relevant epistemic communities.

1.4 Challenges on the Horizon

1.4.1 Economic Challenges

The economic challenges confronting PA members are both intra- and inter-regional in nature. At the intra-regional level, concerns over exceedingly low levels of economic interdependency make it necessary for PA members to deepen their economic relations through increased two-way trade and investment ties in goods and services alike and promoting the creation or upgrading of regional value chain dynamics linking PA-established firms (Blanco 2015; Greene and Arnson 2016; Marchini 2015; OECD 2015).[20] The United States, the European Union and China remain the main trading partners of PA member states (Blanco 2015; ECLAC 2015).[21] For both Mexico and Chile, exports to MERCOSUR are far more significant than exports to their other two PA partners, which can be readily understood given the size of the Brazilian and Argentine markets (Blanco 2015). A similar situation prevails with regard to foreign direct investment (FDI), where the United States and the European Union remain by far the largest sources of inward FDI flows to the PA (Marchini 2015), with intra-regional FDI accounting for less than a

[19] One example of such cooperation is the technical assistance provided by PA member states whose sanitary authorities have attained National Regulatory Authority Level IV to the authorities of other member states that have not yet attained such certification.

[20] Greene and Arnson (2016) observed that trade has decreased across multiple sectors within the PA since 2013. Moreover, little success is reported in improving intra-industry trade, which decreased between 2014 and 2015. However, in terms of exports to other PA members and intra-industry trade, Peru showed positive results for the period 2013–2014.

[21] The relevance of the trade with China and other Asian counterparts varies significantly from member to member.

tenth of aggregate inflows (Blanco 2015). Though services trade among PA member states is still limited when compared to other major regional groupings, it is higher than for trade in goods (Duran Lima and Cracau 2016). There is evidence of considerable untapped potential for deeper trade ties in services among PA members (Perry 2014) through the removal of regulatory barriers and the attenuation of differences in regulatory frameworks between members.

The Pacific Alliance suffers from its members' geographic dispersion, with Mexico, the regional grouping's largest member, being not only the most distant but also that with the deepest level of integration with higher-income non-PA countries. Such gravity dimensions naturally reduce the scope for intra-regional trade (Bown et al. 2017). Distance and infrastructural shortcomings hampering intra-regional connectivity create additional inefficiencies and trade-inflating costs, both of which discourage trade among PA members (Blanco 2015; George 2014; Marczak and George 2016). The supply of regional public goods in infrastructure, improvements in region-wide logistical performance and more determined steps towards positive integration will all be required to reduce the above gaps (Blanco 2015; SELA 2013). With these limitations in mind, the PA has approved the creation of a regional debt fund for infrastructural investment (FIAP; Cali Declaration 2017).

The Council of Ministers of Finance has been mandated to examine and develop proposals on investment in infrastructure in member states under a model that promotes public–private partnerships (Paracas Declaration 2015). Such investments would focus not only on transport, but also on telecommunications, water, energy (including renewables), public utilities, environment, and tourism. Efforts at improving region-wide infrastructure must be tied closely with efforts at addressing infrastructural bottlenecks within each PA members' hinterland.

At the inter-regional level, the PA requires specific strategies aimed at buttressing the trade (export) performance of Alliance members in the Asia-Pacific region and especially China. Although there has been a steady increase in inter-regional trade in goods since 2010, the pattern shows significantly higher levels of PA imports from across the Pacific.[22] A similar situation prevails with the member states of the Association of Southeast Asian Nations (ASEAN), where PA exports account for less than 30% of the total imports of goods from ASEAN member states.[23] Considering the PA's current balance of trade with countries in the Asia-Pacific region, the regional grouping needs to develop a long-term strategy geared towards better inserting its products and services into Asian value chains and thus diversifying its exports to countries in Asia (Castro Lara and Roldán Pérez 2015). Currently, the PA's actions appear to be limited to various trade promotion activities such as participation in trade shows, exhibitions, business roundtables and related activities. Beyond such efforts, more emphasis will need to be placed on strengthening the

[22] In 2013 the exports of goods from the PA to China were 40% of the total imports of goods from China to the PA.

[23] While exports from the PA member states to ASEAN stood at USD 3,8 billion in 2014, exports of goods from ASEAN to PA member states reached USD 12,8 billion (Observatory Latin America-Asia Pacific 2016).

competitiveness of exporting firms and connecting PA suppliers, especially SMEs, to lead foreign investors. This in turn involves stepped-up efforts at investment promotion targeting Asian sources. Such an overarching strategy is currently lacking.

1.4.2 Political Challenges

At the political level, an important challenge for the PA is to gain recognition as a regional actor speaking on selected issues with a common voice. Ultimately, the PA aims to consolidate inter-regional relations, presenting itself as more than the aggregation of the four countries. This challenge arises from two different sources. A first one is practical in nature and reflects the fact that the PA is a project that is still in its infancy and therefore in learning by doing mode. Additional efforts and time are needed to create heightened international visibility, although things do appear to be working well in this regard.[24] A second, more significant, issue relates to the future ability of PA members to reach agreement on specific topics or issues where they may not all share the same interests or views but would nonetheless benefit from acting as an integrated bloc in the context of international organizations or negotiating fora.

One recent example of such a dilemma arose in the context of (now interrupted) negotiations towards a plurilateral Trade in Services Agreement (TISA), where each PA member negotiated individually.[25]

Each PA member arguably faces particular problems that could slow down the pace of integration within an intergovernmental model of governance. Previous experiences in the region have shown that domestic agendas often relegate the development of integration strategies to second place. As pointed out by George and other researchers, the internal problems that need to be addressed differ in each case in terms of content and magnitude (George 2014; Valencia 2013). George echoes the general concerns for Mexico in regard to drug trafficking and related violence. Mexico also needs legal reforms to strategic service sectors such as education and vocational training in the wake of recent reforms in the country's energy and telecommunications sectors. These reforms have traditionally met with resistance from certain interest groups and strong unions that could determine the success or failure of needed flanking domestic reforms. For Colombia, domestic security concerns relating to ongoing internal armed conflict and the implementation of the peace

[24] Observer status is currently held by the following 52 countries: Uruguay, Paraguay, Ecuador, Panama, El Salvador, Costa Rica, Dominican Republic, Guatemala, Honduras, the United States, Canada, New Zealand, Australia, South Korea, Japan, People's Republic of China, Turkey, France, Spain, Portugal, Trinidad and Tobago, Morocco, India, Israel, Singapore, United Kingdom, Switzerland, Italy, Germany, Finland, Belgium, Netherlands, Austria, Denmark, Georgia, Greece, Haiti, Hungary, Indonesia, Poland, Sweden, Thailand, Argentina, Czech Republic, Norway, Slovakia, Egypt, Slovenia, Lithuania, Croacia, Ukraine, and Romania.

[25] Marczak and George (2016) recommend for instance that PA members negotiate as a bloc with ASEAN and other East Asian countries as a way to leverage its impact.

agreements (George 2014; Nolte and Wehner 2013). Key domestic challenges for Chile are the national agendas for implementation of constitutional and education reforms, while for Peru, concerns relate chiefly to the consolidation of political stability.

1.4.3 Institutional Challenges

The PA faces the challenge of preserving the engagement so far exhibited by its political leaders in ensuring its consolidation and forward progress. As a top-down, intergovernmental model, one of the main strengths of the PA is the strong commitment shared by the presidents of the four member states. However, relying heavily on presidential enthusiasm and preferences could subject the PA to the vagaries of national agendas and the election cycles of member states. This problem has arisen before in other integration schemes within the region (Malamud 2012b). The first years of MERCOSUR for instance recorded positive results of the inter-presidential model, but it proved insufficient to sustain forward movement in more turbulent economic or political times (Malamud 2003, 2016). To avoid the negative impacts of domestic affairs on the regional agenda, the PA needs to anticipate the institutional demands that will come with consolidating its deep integration objectives. The PA requires a review of its institutional design and organizational structure to secure stable and dedicated institutions and human resources, accountable in the long term and freer of the political pressures arising from the domestic agendas of member states.

Although early PA harvests reflect the good intentions of government officials to move forward, a question arises in relation to the accomplishments outlined in the preceding section of this chapter, namely over the adequacy of current efforts towards the freer movement of goods, services and factors of production within the region, in the fostering of deepened ties relations with the Asia-Pacific region, and the reduction of social inequality? While PA achievements to date are impressive in many regards, they arguably do not proceed from an articulated strategy aligned to the fulfilment of basic PA goals. To illustrate this point, initiatives such as the volunteering program for young people, the scholarship program, sports diplomacy, and the work plan for health authorities on equitable access to medicines are all laudable projects with positive outcomes for targeted beneficiaries and for PA societies as a whole. However, a more comprehensive and shared vision embracing the social dimension of the PA is needed if the core aims of durably reducing social inequalities and poverty and promoting more inclusive growth are to be achieved. Experience within the MERCOSUR and CAN has shown that isolated, stand-alone, programs are rarely able to consolidate longer-term results in the realm of social equity or to counteract the inevitable distributional downsides and dislocations flowing from the pursuit of selected liberalization policies.[26] There are positive effects of economic development and growth on social indicators and poverty reduction, but market enhancement alone is by no means sufficient to tackle the issues of poverty and inequality in the PA.

Concerns may thus be voiced that the early harvest approach taken in the PA might target objectives that are easy to achieve with minimal efforts rather than tasks that require more determined longer-term structural efforts, involve potentially difficult policy compromises and generate less visible results in the short run. As Fig. 1.1 illustrates, the first three levels of decision-making within the PA comprise national officials – presidents, ministers, and deputy ministers – that either depend on electoral cycles or are freely appointed and removed. This situation creates a disincentive to work on longer-term strategic plans and their implementation. In addition, the PA's intergovernmental governance model requires that public servants working on the PA share their time and scarce resources between national concerns and the integration agenda, again suggesting an incentive to work on less complex tasks or those that can be achieved more quickly and with fewer resources. Officials may also be averse to addressing on a regional basis issues likely to prove sensitive at the domestic level.

Considering the above incentive structure, PA members need to reflect on the desirability of establishing a permanent body tasked with coordinating and administering region-wide initiatives and staffed with adequate human resources devoted to the planning and execution of the PA's integrated strategies and work programs. As demands by different actors emerge, especially from the business community, new *ad hoc* working groups are routinely created without any clear view of how instrumental they and their agendas will be to the fulfilment of the PA's core underlying objectives.

All PA members share a common view on the relevance of innovation, the internationalization of small and medium-sized enterprises, the need to boost the competitiveness of firms and workforce resilience, and the desirability of heightened insertion into regional and global value chains. Greater clarity on common approaches to achieve such objectives would help guide the problem-based approach taken by the relevant PA technical working groups. However, pursuing such goals at the regional level must be seen as a work in progress. Resistance to developing what some fear might represent costly bureaucracies and the advantage of flexibility are justifications used to avoid engaging in discussions over the establishment of more permanent administrative and technical-based bodies (Wilhelmy 2013).[27]

An additional institutional consideration is important because the PA is not an international organisation endowed with a legal personality (Gardini 2013; Díaz-Cediel 2016). At the moment, it is merely an instrument of inter-state cooperation. The PA's intergovernmental structure makes it difficult to draw a clear distinction

[26] In the case of MERCOSUR, after 9 years of existence members realized that there was a need to develop a social dimension: this was named 'Mercosur Social' and includes various organizational structures such as the Social Institute of the MERCOSUR.

[27] Wilhelmy (2013) points out that in the future a more technical body could be required.

between the exercise of an autonomous will by the PA and that of the individual PA states comprising it. At present, this situation prevents the PA from being considered – or operating – as an independent international organization.[28]

The difference between the representation of collective interests of the members and the autonomous interests or individual will of the PA is obviously a matter of opinion. However, at this early point in the development of the PA, a cursory review of the different factors at play points to the absence of a will of the PA that is distinct from that of its members collectively. More flexible and less formalized institutional arrangements do not mean *per se* the absence of an international organization and international legal personality, but the constitutive agreement and other documents refer to the PA more as a mechanism than a subject under international law.

Nothing prevents the PA from becoming an international organization endowed with an international legal personality. However, this will require adjustments to the constitutive documents as well as to the practices of its internal bodies. More affirmative actions along these lines are likely to prove necessary to distinguish and establish a distinct and autonomous organization capable of expressing its independent will with respect to the fulfilment of its own functions and objectives. This is a desirable path considering regional experiences and the broad scope of the PA's goals, which is unlikely to be achieved in the long term under the current intergovernmental cooperation process. From a functional perspective, there are strong grounds to believe that the PA will require international legal capacity to fulfil its ambitious objectives.

1.5 Concluding Remarks

The objective of deep integration, the use of regional integration as a tool for insertion into the global and regional economies, and the recourse to regional integration as a means to stimulate economic growth are hardly new to Latin America and the Caribbean. Deploying such tools with a view to advancing development and social welfare is not new either.

The PA's problem-based approach may well attain better practical results than previous or ongoing integration schemes if it is anchored in adequate (and more formal) technical support, offers more clarity as to the policy pathway, pursues medium-term objectives, and rests on robust and objective performance evaluation metrics. This chapter's main observation is that the lack of an overarching

[28] Several factors point to a complete and effective control by the members of every single aspect of the PA and its decision-making process in practice (Reparations Advisory Opinion 1949). Moreover, it seems that the limited instances in which the Presidency Pro-tempore could take action relate more to the representation of collective interests of the member than to representation of the interests of the PA (Klabbers 2013). In addition, as stated in the Framework Agreement, every decision taken by the Council of Ministers as well as any other agreement adopted within the PA requires explicit consensus.

development plan or vision stands for the region may ultimately frustrate the achievement of the PA's lofty aims.

Proper institutional design and organizational structures are fundamental to the conception, development and implementation of any such plan. Technical assistance from regional organizations such as the Inter-American Development Bank, the Organization of American States or the World Bank can usefully complement internal efforts but cannot replace or substitute for an endogenous capacity at generating short-, medium- and longer-term visions for the PA. Care is needed however is not loading the PA journey with too many coordination or implementation bodies, as this could prove just as damaging to the integration process as the current undue reliance on top-down presidential impetus. Readjustments to the PA's institutional setting and organizational structure appear necessary in the medium-term to cope with the demands of developing more detailed blueprints for deep integration, social equality and poverty reduction and scaling up ties with partners throughout the Asia-Pacific region.

The PA has been conceptualized and driven as more than the repackaging of pre-existing preferential agreements or initiatives. However, its success will be contingent on the path its members follow in implementing their shared vision. This chapter has argued the need for greater thought to be given to developing an overarching PA plan with corresponding short-, medium- and longer-term milestones as well as to revisit the organizational foundations best able to support the PA's stated aims.

By situating the PA in a broader context, this chapter advances a future policy research agenda on two fronts. A first one concerns the relationship between the PA legal regime and the domestic regimes of each of its members in identifying possible sources of conflict and the means to tackle instances of dysfunctionality. A second front relates to the need for an overarching institutional architecture with four distinct organizational features: (i) decision-making; (ii) dispute settlement and legal oversight; (iii) administrative and technical matters; and (iv) monitoring and evaluation. An examination of the constraints that domestic procedures for incorporation of PA rules into national legislation impose on the long-term consolidation of a PA-wide legal system may also be required to facilitate adjustments to the Alliance's institutional design.

References

Abusada-Salah, R., et al. (2015). *Dimensiones y Efectos Económicos de la Alianza del Pacífico. Konrad Adenauer Stiftung*. http://www.kas.de/wf/doc/kas_40265-1522-4-30.pdf?150218210307. Accessed 26 Jan 2016.

Blanco, E. A. (2015). *La Alianza del Pacífico: Un largo Camino por Recorrer hacia la Integración.* Wilson Center/Latin American Program. https://www.wilsoncenter.org/sites/default/files/La_Alianza_del_Pacifico_Blanco_0.pdf. Accessed 18 Jan 2016.

Bown, C. P., Lederman, D., Pienknagura, S., & Robertson, R. (2017). *Better Neighbors: Toward a Renewal of Economic Integration in Latin America*. Washington, DC: The World Bank. https://openknowledge.worldbank.org/handle/10986/25736. Accessed 3 Apr 2017.

Campa, M., Essl, S., Gundogdu, M., Page, C., Zhang, H., & Zhao, L. (2015). *Regional capital markets integration in Latin America: MILA and beyond*. Inter-American Development Bank and Columbia University. https://sipa.columbia.edu/sites/default/files/IDB%20Capstone%20Report.pdf. Accessed 2 Sept 2016.

Castro Lara, A.-S., & Roldán Pérez, A. (2015). La Alianza del Pacífico y su Vínculo Comercial con el Asia Pacífico. In I. R. Aranda & E. V. Posada (Eds.), *Perspectivas y Oportunidades de la Alianza del Pacífico* (pp. 153–177). Editorial CESA: Bogotá.

CEAP (The Pacific Alliance Business Council). (2012). *Constitución del Concejo Empresarial de la Alianza del Pacífico*. https://alianzapacifico.net/?wpdmdl=2153. Accessed 24 Feb 2015.

CEAP (The Pacific Alliance Business Council). (2014). *Declaración del Concejo empresarial de la Alianza del Pacífico junio de 2014*. https://alianzapacifico.net/?wpdmdl=2164. Accessed 22 May 2015.

Centro de Estudios Internacionales Gilberto Bosque. (2014). *La Alianza del Pacífico; ¿el Futuro de la Integración Latinoamericana*? http://centrogilbertobosques.senado.gob.mx/docs/Doc_Analisis_Jul2014.pdf. Accessed 10 Feb 2015.

Congreso de la República de Perú. (2014). *Comisión Especial de Seguimiento Parlamentario al Acuerdo de la Alianza del Pacífico*. http://www4.congreso.gob.pe/comisiones/2014/ce-seguimientoalianzapacifico/index.html. Accessed 1 Feb 2015.

Cordoba, J. P. (2015). *The Latin American Integrated Market: Introduction to MILA*. https://www.set.or.th/ICMC/files/20151130_Session1_02_Juan_Pablo_Cordoba.pdf. Accessed 20 Jan 2016.

Dade, C., & Meacham, C. (2013). *The Pacific Alliance: An Example of Lessons Learned*. Washington, DC: Center for Strategic & International Studies. https://www.csis.org/analysis/pacific-alliance-example-lessons-learned. Accessed 15 Jan 2016.

Díaz-Cediel, S. (2016). The Pacific alliance: Judicial scrutiny of the content of the law of international organizations. *Anuario Colombiano de Derecho International, 9*, 347–390. http://revistas.urosario.edu.co/index.php/acdi/article/view/4500. Accessed 2 Aug 2017.

Duran Lima, J., & Cracau, D. (2016). *The Pacific Alliance and its economic impact on regional trade and investment*. Santiago: ECLAC. http://repositorio.cepal.org/bitstream/handle/11362/40860/1/S1601207_en.pdf. Accessed 25 May 2017.

ECLAC. (2015). *Databases and statistical publications (CEPALSTAT)*. http://www.cepal.org/comercio/ecdata2/index.html. Accessed 4 Mar 2016.

Gardini, G. L. (2013). The added value of the Pacific Alliance and "modular regionalism" in Latin Americas. *International Affairs at LSE Blog*. http://blogs.lse.ac.uk/ideas/2013/06/the-added-value-of-the-pacific-alliance-and-modular-regionalism-in-latin-america/. Accessed 2 Aug 2017.

George, S. (2014). *Los Pumas del Pacífico/un Modelo Emergente para Mercados Emergentes*. Bertelsmann Foundation. http://www.bfna.org/publication/los-pumas-del-pac%C3%ADfico-un-modelo-emergente-para-mercados-emergentes. Accessed 28 Jan 2016, Accessed 2 Aug 2017.

Gonzalez, P., Alejandra, M., et al. (2015). Pacific Alliance: Bringing back open regionalism to Latin America. *Análisis,* May–August. http://www.scielo.org.mx/pdf/mcp/v4n11/2007-5308-mcp-4-11-00021.pdf. Accessed 2 Aug 2017.

Greene, M., & Arnson, C. J. (2016). *The Pacific Alliance: Ongoing challenges to trade integration*. Wilson Center/Latin American Program 2016. https://www.wilsoncenter.org/sites/default/files/pacific_alliance_ongoing_challenges_trade_integration.pdf. Accessed 25 Aug 2016.

Klabbers. (2013, Janaury). Unity, diversity, accountability: The ambivalent concept of international organization. *Melbourne Journal of International Law 14*, 1–22.

Kotschwar, B. (2013). *Will the Pacific Alliance succeed in Latin America after other trade pacts have failed?* Washington, DC: Peterson Institute for International Economics. http://blogs.piie.com/realtime/?p=3586. Accessed 28 Jan 2016.

Kuwayama, M. (1999). *Open regionalism in Asia Pacific and Latin America: A survey of the literature*. ECLAC, Serie Comercio Internacional N 4. http://www.cepal.org/en/publications/4380-open-regionalism-asia-pacific-and-latin-america-survey-literature. Accessed 9 Sept 2015.

Lawrence, R. Z. (1996). *Regionalism, multilateralism, and deeper integration*. Washington, DC: The Brookings Institution.

Malamud, A. (2003). Presidentialism and MERCOSUR: A hidden cause for a successful experience. In F. Laursen (Ed.), *Comparative regional integration: Theoretical perspectives* (pp. 56–73). Farnham: Ashgate.

Malamud, C. (2012a). *La Alianza del Pacífico: un Revulsivo para la Integración Regional en América Latina*. Real Instituto Elcano. http://www.realinstitutoelcano.org/wps/portal/rielcano/contenido?WCM_GLOBAL_CONTEXT=/elcano/elcano_es/zonas_es/america+latina/ari46-2012. Accessed 28 Jan 2016.

Malamud, C. (2012b). *La Alianza del Pacífico: un revulsivo para la integración regional en America Latina* (27 June 2012) Real Instituto ElCano. http://www.realinstitutoelcano.org/wps/portal/web/rielcano_es/contenido?WCM_GLOBAL_CONTEXT=/elcano/elcano_es/zonas_es/america+latina/ari46-2012.

Malamud, A. (2016). Interdependence, leadership and institutionalization: The triple deficit and fading prospects of MERCOSUR. In S. Dosenrode (Ed.), *Limits to regional integration* (pp. 163–178). New York: Routledge.

Marchini, G. (2015). Flujos de Inversión Directa e Inserción en las Cadenas de Valor Globales: ¿Qué Puede Cambiar la Alianza del Pacífico? In I. R. Aranda & E. V. Posada (Eds.), *Perspectivas y Oportunidades de la Alianza del Pacífico* (pp. 179–225). Bogotá: Editorial CESA.

Marczak, J., & George, S. (2016). *Pacific Alliance 2.0: Next steps in integration*. Washington, DC: Atlantic Council and Bertelsmann Foundation. http://www.atlanticcouncil.org/publications/reports/pacific-alliance-2-0-next-steps-in-integration. Accessed 2 Sept 2016.

Ministerio de Comercio, Industria y Turismo de Colombia/Dirección de Integración Económica. (2013). *Análisis General Alianza del Pacífico*. http://www.tlc.gov.co/publicaciones.php?id=6326. Accessed 2 Nov 2015.

Nolte, D., & Wehner, L. (2013). The Pacific Alliance casts its cloud over Latin America. *GIGA Focus*, 8. https://www.giga-hamburg.de/en/system/files/publications/gf_international_1308.pdf. Accessed 2 Aug 2017.

Observatory Latin America-Asia Pacific. (2015). *Statistical Bulletin Latin America-Asia Pacific*. http://www.observatorioasiapacifico.org/data/OBSERVATORIO.Images/Bulletin/temp/20161011104143Boletn8AsiaPacfico.pdf. Accessed 28 Aug 2017.

Observatory Latin America-Asia Pacific. (2016). *Commercial-economic monitor/bilateral exports/bilateral exports indicator Pacific Alliance-ASEAN*.http://www.observatorioasiapacifico.org/OBSExternalUI/pages/public/monitor.jsf. Accessed 28 Aug 2017.

Organisation for Economic Co-operation and Development (OECD). (2015). *Towards a joint Pacific Alliance Agenda for promoting SME internationalization and integration in global value chains*. http://www.tlc.gov.co/publicaciones.php?id=6326. Accessed 8 Sept 2016.

Pacific Alliance. (2011). *Declaración de Lima*. https://alianzapacifico.net/?wpdmdl=1329. Accessed 21 Sept 2015.

Pacific Alliance. (2013a). *Noticias Oficiales/Países Miembros*. http://www.cancilleria.gov.co/newsroom/news/chile-deposita-instrumento-ratificacion-del-acuerdo-marco-la-alianza-del-pacifico. Accessed 25 May 2015.

Pacific Alliance. (2013b). *Declaración Conjunta/Reunión de los Presidentes de Parlamento de la Alianza del Pacífico*. https://alianzapacifico.net/?wpdmdl=2168. Accessed 28 Jan 2015.

Pacific Alliance. (2014). *Declaración de los Presidentes de la Alianza del Pacífico en Materia de Cambio Climático en la COP 20/CMP10*. https://alianzapacifico.net/?wpdmdl=2092. Accessed 14 Sept 2015.

Pacific Alliance. (2015a). *Declaracion de Paracas*. https://alianzapacifico.net/?wpdmdl=4078. Accessed 21 Sept 2015.

Pacific Alliance. (2015b). *Declaración de Cali*. https://alianzapacifico.net/download/3-6-declaracion-de-cali/. Accessed 21 Sept 2015.

Pacific Alliance. (2016a). *Declaración de Cali*. https://alianzapacifico.net/?wpdmdl=9850. Accessed 27 Aug 2017.

Pacific Alliance. (2016b). *Declaración de Puerto Varas*. https://alianzapacifico.net/?wpdmdl=7888. Accessed 13 Sept 2016.

Perry, G. (2014). *The Pacific alliance: A way forward for Latin American integration?* London: Center for Global Development. https://www.cgdev.org/publication/pacific-alliance-way-forward-latin-american-integration. Accessed 18 Jan 2016.

Primer Protocolo Modificatorio del Protocolo Adicional al Acuerdo Marco de la Alianza del Pacífico, Paracas, 3 de Julio de 2015. https://alianzapacifico.net/documentos/.

Protocolo Adicional al Acuerdo Marco de la Alianza del Pacífico, Cartagena de Indias, 10 de febrero de 2014. Available from https://alianzapacifico.net/documentos/. Accessed 2 Aug 2017.

Seatzu, F. (2015). The alliance of the Pacific: A new instrument of Latin American and Caribbean economic integration? In M. Odello & F. Seatzu (Eds.), *Latin American and Caribbean international institutional law* (pp. 193–218). The Hague: Springer.

Secretaría General de la Comunidad Andina. (2013). *Dimensión Económica Comercial de la Comunidad Andina*. Reporte, Comunidad Andina de Naciones. http://www.comunidadandina.org/Upload/2013422163744Folleto_Dimension.pdf. Accessed 11 Nov 2015.

Secretaría Permanente SELA. (2013). *La Alianza del Pacífico en la Integración Latinoamericana y Caribeña*. http://walk.sela.org/attach/258/EDOCS/SRed/2013/07/T023600005208-0-SP-DI_N%C2%B0_1-13_ALIANZA_PACIFICO_EN_LA_INTEGRACION_LA_Y_CARIBENA.pdf. Accessed 11 Nov 2015.

Tremolada, A. E. (2014). ¿La Alianza del Pacífico Facilita la Inserción de Colombia en la Región de Asia Pacífico? *Papel Político, 19*, 721–752.

Valencia, R. (2013). The Pacific alliance: A promising yardstick of Latin America's prosperity. *Georgetown Journal of International Affairs*. May. http://journal.georgetown.edu/the-pacific-alliance-a-promising-yardstick-of-latin-americas-prosperity-by-robert-valencia/. Accessed 2 Aug 2017.

Vieira, P. E. (2015). La Alianza del Pacífico, Integración Profunda ¿Hasta Qué Grado? In I. R. Aranda & E. V. Posada (Eds.), *Perspectivas y Oportunidades de la Alianza del Pacífico* (pp. 63–103). Bogotá: Editorial CESA.

Vienna Convention on the Law of Treaties, Vienna, 22 May 1969. United Nations Treaty Series, vol. 1155, p 331. https://treaties.un.org/doc/source/docs/A_CONF.39_11_Add.2-E.pdf. 2 August 2017.

Wilhelmy, M. (2013). *Alianza del Pacífico: una Visión desde Chile*. Speech delivered by the executive director of the Chile Pacific foundation to the Andean parliament during its 42nd session. *Estudios Internacionales, 175*, 119–125. http://www.scielo.cl/scielo.php?script=sci_arttext&pid=S0719-37692013000200006.

Legal Documents

Acuerdo de Cooperación en Materia de Turismo, en el Marco del Memorando de Entendimiento entre el Gobierno de la República de Colombia, el Gobierno de la República de Chile, el Gobierno de la República del Perú y el Gobierno de los Estados Unidos Mexicanos, sobre la Plataforma de Cooperación del Pacífico. Ciudad de Mexico. 29 de Agosto de 2012. https://alianzapacifico.net/?wpdmdl=4406. Accessed 2 Aug 2017.

Acuerdo entre el Ministerio de Relaciones Exteriores de la República de Colombia y la Secretaría de Relaciones Exteriores de los Estados Unidos Mexicanos para Permitir el Uso de Instalaciones e Infraestructura de las Embajadas y los Consulados de la Otra Parte Signataria en Terceros Estados. Nueva York. 28 de Septiembre de 2012. https://alianzapacifico.net/?wpdmdl=2134. Accessed 2 Aug 2017.

Acuerdo Interinstitucional de Cooperación que Celebran las Autoridades Sanitarias de los Países de la Alianza del Pacífico. Lima. 20 de Junio de 2013. https://alianzapacifico.net/?wpdmdl=4393. Accessed 2 Aug 2017.

Acuerdo Interinstitucional entre los Ministerios de Relaciones Exteriores de los Estados Parte de la Alianza del Pacífico para el Establecimiento de Medidas de Cooperación en Materia de Asistencia Consular. Cartagena de Indias. 10 de febrero de 2014. *https://alianzapacifico.net/?wpdmdl=4397*. Accessed 2 Aug 2017.

Acuerdo Marco de la Alianza del Pacífico, Paranal, 6 de Junio de 2012. https://alianzapacifico.net/?wpdmdl=4464. Accessed 2 Aug 2017.

Acuerdo para el Establecimiento del Fondo de Cooperacion de la Alianza del Pacífico. 22 Mayo 2013. https://alianzapacifico.net/?wpdmdl=5444. Accessed 2 Aug 2017.

Memorando de Entendimiento entre el Gobierno de los Estados Unidos Mexicanos, el Gobierno de la República de Colombia, el Gobierno de la República de Chile y el Gobierno de la República de Perú sobre la Plataforma de Cooperación del Pacífico. Merida. 4 Diciembre de 2012. https://alianzapacifico.net/?wpdmdl=2131. Accessed 2 Aug 2017.

Memorando de Entendimiento entre el Ministerio de Relaciones Exteriores de la República de Colombia y el Ministerio de Relaciones Exteriores de la República del Perú sobre Exoneración de Visa en Calidad Migratoria de Negocios. 30 de Junio de 2013. https://alianzapacifico.net/?wpdmdl=4399.

Chapter 2
Trade and Investment Relations in the Pacific Alliance: Recent Developments and Future Trends

Daniel Cracau and José E. Durán Lima

2.1 Introduction

This chapter maps existing links regarding trade in merchandise goods and services as well as foreign direct investment (FDI) between the member countries of the Pacific Alliance. The relevance of regional value chains in the bilateral trade relations of Chile, Colombia, Mexico and Peru are examined in order to identify industrial sectors with emerging productive linkages. The main criterion applied in doing so is the existence of a high intensity of trade in intermediate goods. A complementary analysis of the impact of the Additional Protocol to the Framework Agreement of the PA yields insights into the future of economic integration among its four founding members. The chapter also addresses some of the major challenges the PA faces in meeting its goal of becoming a platform for deepened ties with the Asia Pacific region. The latter analysis is somewhat speculative, since the PA project is still in its early stages. Given the uncertain legal and political status of the Trans-Pacific Partnership (TPP) after the withdrawal of the US administration, the future role and influence of the PA might be strengthened. The integration of Costa Rica as a full member of the Alliance, also taken up in Chap. 10 of this volume, is discussed in this regard.

The views expressed in this chapter are those of the authors and do not necessarily reflect the views of the Organization. The present chapter builds on Durán Lima, José and Daniel Cracau. 2016. The PA and its economic impact on regional trade and investment: Evaluation and perspectives. International Trade Series No. 128, Santiago de Chile: ECLAC.

D. Cracau (✉)
HTW Berlin University of Apllied Sciences, Treskowallee 8, 10318, Berlin, Germany
e-mail: daniel.cracau@un.org; cracau@htw-berlin.de

J. E. Durán Lima
United Nations Economic Commission for Latin America and the Caribbean (UN ECLAC), Santiago, Chile
e-mail: jose.duran@un.org

P. Sauvé et al. (eds.), *The Pacific Alliance in a World of Preferential Trade Agreements*, United Nations University Series on Regionalism 16,
https://doi.org/10.1007/978-3-319-78464-9_2

Before analysing PA-wide trade and investment linkages, it is worth reviewing some macroeconomic and social indicators of Alliance members (see Table 2.16 in the Appendix). In 2015, PA members accounted for slightly more than a third of the population of Latin America and the Caribbean (LAC), or 225.1 million inhabitants. The regional grouping's gross domestic product (GDP) amounts to US$ 1.87 trillion, equivalent to 37% of LAC GDP. The above metrics alone suffice to reveal the importance of the four PA countries to the region as a whole. In terms of per capita GDP, the PA as a bloc averaged US$ 8800, a level 10% above the LAC average. Note that this figure reflects the GDP per capita in Chile (US$ 13,341) and Mexico (US$ 9009), while values in Colombia (US$ 6021) and Peru (US$ 6021) remain lower than the LAC average. The same pattern holds if this indicator is adjusted to account of differences in purchasing power parity (PPP). Here, the regional average for the PA countries is US$ 17,169. Looking at average unemployment and inflation rates, the PA as a bloc also shows values below those of LAC. While in 2015 Chile and Peru registered unemployment rates around the regional average of 6.1%, Mexico reported a significantly lower value (4.3%) and Colombia a significantly higher value (8.9%). In contrast, inflation rates in the PA member countries range from 2.7% (Mexico) to 5.0% (Colombia), levels significantly lower than the LAC average of 8.4%. The above macroeconomic indicators provide a first hint of the PA's potential as a driver of LAC growth and development. Somewhat surprisingly, 2014 average poverty rates for the PA (33.2%) were higher than that of the LAC region as a whole (28.2%), mainly reflecting the relatively high poverty rate in Mexico (41.2%). Despite this, Mexico slightly exceeds the LAC average Human Development Index (HDI), achieving a value of 0.756 in 2015 compared to a regional value of 0.748. Together with Chile (0.832) this leads to an average PA HDI of 0.761. The latter trends suggest that PA members have room for improvement that could turn their common economic potential into even more favourable and inclusive growth prospects (Abusada-Salah et al. 2015).

In terms of business environment and trade openness, the four PA members perform better than the LAC region as a whole. Chile, for example, occupies the top position region-wide in both the Global Competitiveness Index of the World Economic Forum and in the World Bank Group's Doing Business Indicators. The other PA countries rank 5–7th among LAC countries in the former index and occupy positions 2–4 in the latter ranking. PA members' open trade policy stance is undoubtedly one of the most salient features of the regional compact. All four countries maintain a trade policy based on the promotion of open trade and deep integration into global markets, indicated by their moderate most-favoured nation (MFN) tariffs, averaging 7.4%, and a significantly lower average applied tariff (2.4%). The low level of tariff bindings relates to the high number of preferential trade agreements entered into by PA members: 25 in the case of Peru and 27 in that of Chile. In total, the PA has concluded PTAs with 79 trading partners. On average, the countries of the PA receive tariff preferences with near-zero tariffs for 65% of their exports, and grant tariff preferences with near- zero tariffs on 55% of their imports. The image that emerges is that all four PA members are relatively homogeneous in their pattern of openness towards global business and their insertion into world trade and international financial markets.

2.2 Trade in Goods and Potential Productive Linkages Between PA Members

In 2015, the PA was the source of 57% of total merchandise exports from LAC. While this figure appears to reveal the overall importance of the PA countries, one has to consider the particular trade pattern of Mexico with its strong orientation towards the North American (mainly US) market. Given its prominent role in the region, Mexico is by far the largest exporter among the four PA members, representing 74% of total PA exports. It is followed by Chile with 12%, and Colombia and Peru with similar shares of about 7% each. As already noted, PA member countries trade very little with each other. Indeed, in 2015, intra-PA trade accounted for only 3.2% of total goods exports of its members (see Table 2.1). This is less than in 2013 when it stood at 3.5%.

This low level of intra-regional trade relates more to the fact that PA members are not natural trading partners than to the presence of high trade barriers. Nearly 90% of trade between the four member countries is already fully liberalized under the various PTAs that link them. Thus, geography matters. The PA is not a contiguous economic area. Mexico, the largest and most diversified member of the group, is geographically remote from its three South American partners. As a result, Mexico sends only 2% of its exports of goods to the other PA members, and less than 1% of its imports originate there. Additionally, the composition of the export basket of the three South American PA members limits the options for expanding trade between them. The export profile of PA countries is shown in Fig. 2.1.

The share of intermediate goods (specifically parts and components) in total trade flows is an indirect indicator of the importance of trade in manufacturing value chains (Durán Lima and Zaclicever 2013). Productive integration among members of the PA is very low according to this measure. Less than 7% of total intra-bloc exports are represented by "parts and components" (Rosales et al. 2015).[1] Compared to the three leading "factories" in the world, this participation in intra-regional trade seems to be particularly low. In the so-called Factory Asia, which comprises East Asia, parts and components account for a third. In the second manufacturing centre, which comprises countries currently connected through the North American Free Trade Agreement (NAFTA) – namely Mexico, the United States and Canada – parts and components account for about 20% of intra-regional trade. The same holds true within the European Union, the third manufacturing powerhouse globally. In LAC as a whole, the percentage approximates 17% (Rosales et al. 2015). Despite these rather low figures, an analysis of this type of trade at the industry and product group level is useful because it can help identify those sectors where further strengthening of productive integration is possible. Durán Lima and Lo Turco (2010) analysed the

[1] The definition of parts and components follows Fung, Garcia-Herrero and Siu (2009). This includes all products classified as "Parts of…" in Revision 2 of the Standard International Trade Classification (SITC), plus other products in the following groups: textiles (chapters 61 and 65), machinery and transport equipment (section 7), manufactures of metals (chapter 69) and miscellaneous manufactured articles (section 8).

Table 2.1 PA: total and intra-block goods exports, 2015 (in US$ million and %)

	Destination						
Origin	Chile	Colombia	Mexico	Peru	Total PA	World	Participation PA (%)
Chile		787	1344	1636	3766	63,362	5.9
Colombia	737		914	1148	2799	35,491	7.9
Mexico	1861	3668		1651	7180	380,772	1.9
Peru	1069	871	545		2484	33,247	7.5
PA	3667	5325	2803	4435	16,231	512,872	3.2

Source: Authors, based on figures from the United Nations Commodity Trade Statistics Database (Comtrade)

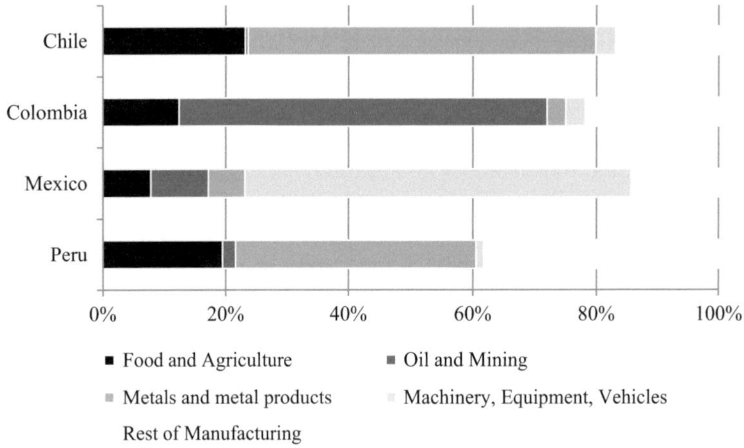

Fig. 2.1 Composition of total goods exports of PA members by sectors, 2013–2015
Source: Authors, based on figures from Comtrade

patterns of specialization in Latin American intra-regional trade looking at the potential gaps in bilateral trade. Their results showed potential for expansion, especially in trade in natural resources and in low and medium technology manufacturing industries. Among the bilateral relations identified are those between the member countries of the PA. As a measure of the intensity of intra-industry trade (IIT, also called two-way trade), the authors calculated the Grubel-Lloyd index (GLI).[2] Their analysis covers the period between 1990 and 2008. They found that in all bilateral trade relationships within the PA, the intra-industry relationships had increased in intensity, indicated by higher GLI values. Back in 1990, almost all bilateral relations were of the inter-industry type with the exception of Colombian–Mexican trade, which had a moderate GLI level of 0.13. In contrast, all bilateral relationships, except for that between Mexico and Peru, showed GLI values higher

[2] The GLI assigns values between 0 (when trade is only inter-industrial) and 1 (when it is only IIT). In order to characterize the depth of the intra-industry relations, Durán Lima et al. (2016) define three levels. Level I includes GLI less than 0.10 (inter-industrial business relationship); level II ranges within values 0.10 < GLI < 0.33 (with potential IIT); and level III includes GLI greater than or equal to 0.33 (intra-industry trade relationship).

Table 2.2 Intra-industry trade among countries of the PA, 1990, 2008 and 2015

Grubel-Lloyd index	1990	2008	2015
Colombia–Chile	0.05	0.18	0.17
Colombia–Mexico	0.13	0.16	0.24
Colombia–Peru	0.08	0.29	0.37
Chile–Mexico	0.06	0.16	0.20
Chile–Peru	0.06	0.20	0.33
Peru–Mexico	0.01	0.06	0.12
Simple average	0.07	0.18	0.24

Source: Authors, based on Durán and Lo Turco (2010) and Comtrade
Note: GLI calculated with information from SITC Rev.2, at the 3-digit level

than 0.15 in 2008. Those relationships were therefore classified as showing potential for IIT. In the special case of trade between Mexico and Peru it should be noted that the GLI value increased from 0.01 to 0.06. Looking at the more recent figures for 2015, it can be seen that this trend has continued and we now find potential for IIT in all bilateral PA relations. Meanwhile, the GLI of the PA as a whole has increased to 0.24 (see Table 2.2).[3]

For the sub-region as a whole, intra-regional IIT represented an annual average of US$ 5611 million during the 2013–15 period. This is equal to a 30.7% share in total intra-regional exports, with Colombia having the highest level (43.3%) and Mexico the lowest (24.9%). Trade statistics from 2015 show that IIT and potential IIT represent 47% in terms of total intra-regional exports and 49% when the number of products is considered. In the following, the analysis of the trade relationships between the individual PA members will be deepened based on the pattern of intra-PA trade.

Table 2.3 lists the top five product groups of intra-regional exports for all four PA member countries according to the Standard International Trade Classification (SITC) at the 3-digit level considering those industries holding IIT potential. It also identifies the share in total intra-regional exports of the country, the predominant type of good (capital, consumption or intermediate) and the share of intermediate goods. This information is complemented by the general composition of intra-regional exports as illustrated in Fig. 2.2.

2.2.1 *Mexico*

In general, the share of exports from Mexico to its PA partners is low (less than 2%). However, there are specific connections to certain manufacturing sectors, for example, chemicals, perfumery and some types of inputs to the plastics industry. There, the share of exports from Mexico to the PA is just over 9%, and Colombia is the

[3] Recalling the impact of geographical location on the intensity of trade relations, it is notable that GLI values of the bilateral relations between the direct neighbours Chile and Peru as well as Colombia and Peru are the highest (0.33 and 0.37, respectively).

Table 2.3 Top five product groups exported to the PA by country, 2013–2015

PA member country	SITC Rev. 2	Description	Share in country total (%)	GLI[a]	Predominant type of good	Share of intermediate goods (%)
Chile	057	Fruits and nuts	7.8	0.15	Consumption	0.1
Chile	641	Paper and paperboard	7.0	0.18	Intermediate	100.0
Chile	562	Manufactured fertilizers	5.2	0.60	Intermediate	100.0
Chile	058	Canned fruits and fruit preparations	3.2	0.32	Consumption	3.4
Chile	048	Cereal preparations and preparations of flour	2.6	0.64	Consumption	19.5
Colombia	781	Vehicles (passenger cars)	8.2	0.30	Consumption	0.0
Colombia	583	Polymerization and copolymerization	5.9	0.86	Intermediate	100.0
Colombia	553	Perfumery, cosmetics and prepared	5.3	0.52	Consumption	28.7
Colombia	061	Sugar and honey	4.0	0.59	Consumption	1.7
Colombia	642	Paper and paperboard, cut certain way	3.1	0.39	Intermediate	100.0
Mexico	781	Passenger cars (vehicles)	11.6	0.26	Consumption/ capital	0.0
Mexico	553	Perfumery, cosmetics and prepared	3.7	0.25	Intermediate	0.0
Mexico	541	Medicinal and pharmaceutical products	2.4	0.29	Consumption	3.5
Mexico	582	Condensation products polycondensation	2.3	0.32	Intermediate	62.5
Mexico	583	Polymerization and copolymerization	2.3	0.65	Intermediate	94.1
Peru	334	Petroleum products, refined	9.0	0.21	Intermediate	100.0
Peru	081	Animal feed (unmilled cereals)	3.6	0.51	Intermediate	100.0
Peru	583	Polymerization and copolymerization	2.8	0.60	Intermediate	100.0
Peru	522	Inorganic chemical elements, oxides and salts	2.7	0.35	Intermediate	100.0
Peru	893	Product of plastics	2.4	0.79	Intermediate	78.0

Source: Authors, based on figures from Comtrade and own calculations
[a] Calculated based on weighted average of each chapter in the bilateral relation with PA partners.
SITC Standard International Trade Classification

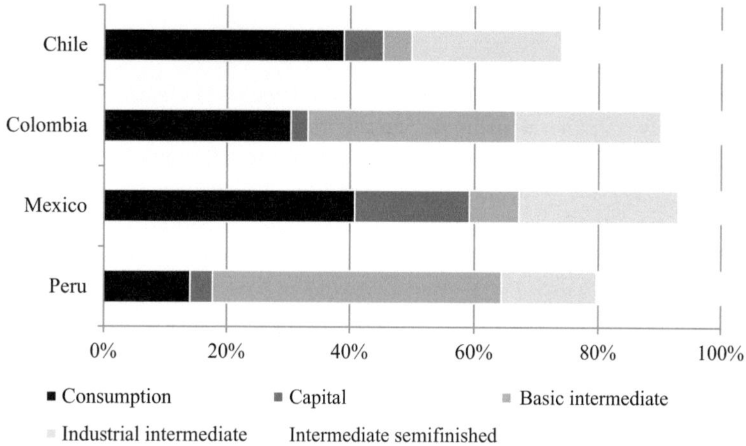

Fig. 2.2 Composition of intra-PA goods exports by broad economic categories, 2013–2015
Source: Authors, based on figures from Comtrade

country with the largest intra-industry linkages. The greater diversification of the export basket of Mexico to the PA in comparison to the other three PA members is also evident when looking at the composition of trade by broad economic categories over the 2013–15 period. A significant proportion of exports fall into the three main groups: intermediate products, capital goods and consumer products (see Fig. 2.2). During period mentioned above, the 20 main commodity groups exported by Mexico to the PA accounted for 38.4% of total shipments. Furthermore, within these 20 groups, intermediate products accounted for 39% of shipments by PA members. The presence of capital goods within the list of exported products is of great importance for Mexico. This stands in marked contrast to the pattern shown by the other countries of the Alliance. Mexico is well known to play a central role in value chains oriented towards the US market. A promising opportunity for other PA countries could be exploited by integrating their firms into some segments of such value chains. This could be achieved either by participation in the supply of components or through the provision of services.[4] Of Mexico's pharmaceutical exports, the most important are: drugs in dosage forms, estrogens and progestogens, penicillins, vaccines and vitamins. These products complement the domestic supplies of pharmaceutical products in the other countries of the PA. Among the 20 major commodity groups exported by Mexico to the PA are also industries that produce medium-technology manufacturing, intensive both in intermediate and capital goods.[5]

[4]The perfumery and cosmetics industry also has a notable presence within Mexico's range of exports. It represents 3.7% of total exports from Mexico to the PA and includes products such as shampoo, hairspray, deodorant and antiperspirant, along with toothpaste and makeup. These products are all complementary to those that Colombia and Peru export.

[5]These include plastics, base metals, machinery and equipment, chemicals and agrochemicals, and telecommunications. The listing is completed by some electrical and electronic products, such as heating and cooling equipment and pumps and compressors.

2.2.2 Colombia

Productive complementarities between Colombia and its PA partners exist in some industries with a high intensity of intermediate goods. Sixty-seven percent of Colombia's exports to PA members are concentrated in intermediate products, especially basic goods and industrial inputs (see Fig. 2.2). Peru is the trading partner with the largest intra-industry linkages to Colombia. This bilateral relationship is most likely to boost the productive relationships that will lead to a deepening of sub-regional value chains. Forty-six percent of the total exports from Colombia to PA members are included in the top 20 export groups. Significant industries include automotive and metalworking, agroindustry, petrochemicals, chemicals, paper and cardboard, textiles and clothing. Between 2013 and 2015, these seven industries accounted for slightly more than 70% of total manufacturing value added of the Colombian economy. As in Mexico, the automotive sector stands out for its contribution to total Colombian exports, primarily directed at Mexico. In addition to oil refining, the petrochemical industry is also important, including groups of polymers and copolymers. These products, in turn, also include products in the domestic value chains of Colombia such as pigments, paints and varnishes, and various plastics. These groups are part of the petrochemical chain of plastics, rubbers, paints, inks and fibres, constituting a well-developed domestic value chain.[6] By 2009, oil refining, rubber and plastics together accounted for 18% of value added in manufacturing in Colombia (Carolina Ramirez et al. 2012). The segments of polymerization and copolymerization (which belong to the category of medium-technology products) are strongly linked to Andean sub-regional value chains in the plastics industry.

Turning to potential IIT in the food industry, six groups of products are traded between Colombia and its PA partners, especially Chile and Peru. These include sugar, honey and animal feed, where the presence of intermediate inputs is greater than 50%. A further set of products in consumer goods where potential IIT is concentrated include coffee, margarine, butter and essential oils.

Cosmetics exported to the PA include facial cosmetics, bath and hair gel, and perfumes. It is noteworthy that these are mainly sold to Peru and Mexico, with sales to Chile representing a lesser share. The Colombian chemical industry accounts for 13.5% of manufacturing value added (Ramirez et al. 2012). When analysing the productive linkages with Mexico and the possible existence of value chains for the Colombian export industry within the PA, the increased presence of intermediate goods in the two-way trade between the two countries is noteworthy.

[6] In the input–output table (IOT) of Colombia, for example, the sectors show a high number of individual links representing the existing relations (on average, between 27 and 37). The manufacturing of rubber and plastic products is a sector with above-average chains (Durán Lima et al. 2014).

2.2.3 Chile

Among the industries with the strongest IIT links in Chile are agriculture and agro-industry, beverages and tobacco, paper and cardboard, plastics, agrochemicals, pharmaceuticals, copper and minerals, and machinery and engineering equipment. Of the country's total exports in 2013–15, the proportion of intermediate goods reached 53%. The high share of semi-finished and industrial intermediate goods is notable (see Fig. 2.2). The five main groups of industries with strong IIT linkages account for 26% of total exports. Extending that picture to the 20 main groups increases the share to 43%. There is also a significant involvement of intermediate products, reaching a mean of 71% in the exports of these sectors. For the 20 main product groups, the weighted Grubel-Lloyd index is 0.37.[7] Among the industries showing high intra-industry content in bilateral trade between Chile and Peru are those with high value added, such as rubber and plastics, paper and cardboard, as well as machinery and equipment and tools for domestic use.

The agricultural and agro-industrial product sector accounts for the largest proportion of Chile's exports to the PA. This sector includes traditional agricultural products, especially fruits, as well as related agro industrials such as wine and sparkling beverages, cereals, oats, pasta and baby food. The sector represents about a quarter of Chile's exports to its PA partners, in particular Mexico and Peru. Because of their strong linkage to the Chilean economy, they generate 20% of direct and 40% of indirect export-related employment (Durán Lima et al. 2014a). The second largest export sector to the PA is paper and cardboard, which account for just over 8% of total exports. The proportion of intermediate goods within this industry is 82%, while the other 18% is consumption goods like paper notebooks and school supplies plus toiletries. Two-way trade is found in all of these product groups. However, a significant comparative advantage in favour of Chile results in a trade surplus in paper and a slight deficit in cardboards.

Copper products, especially cathodes, pipes and wire, represent the third sector in which Chile has a comparative advantage over its partners in the PA and where its trade balance reveals a surplus. This is especially true in the case of trade with Colombia and Mexico. In contrast, Chile imports more base metals than it exports. In this sector, considerable trade potential is indicated by the high share of intermediate goods. Furthermore, the agrochemical industry in Chile has potential in the PA market. This sector includes fertilizers and manures for various industrial crops including flowers, vegetables and legumes, among others. There is a strong IIT relationship with Mexico, and a potential one with Colombia. In the plastics industry, Chile provides its PA partner countries with intermediate inputs (polymers, copolymers such as propylene, ethylene, vinyl, polypropylene monofilament, etc.). It also exports finished products such as boxes, bottles, roof and floor coverings, pipes and office equipment, as well as parts for construction, especially for sanitary

[7]The share of intermediate goods in the trade between Chile and the PA countries increases to 79% if agricultural and agro-industrial products and beverages are excluded. However, it should be noted that the definition used in this section to account for intermediate goods is wider than the sum of the parts and components, because it also includes primary and semi-finished goods.

and kitchen furniture. High GLI values indicate that the intra-PA trade relationships are beneficial from Chile's perspective, because they incorporate trade in intermediate goods among all member countries. Chile's comparative advantage in mining has benefits for the machinery and engineering equipment sector, which is developing strongly. Two of the top 20 product groups exported to the PA belong to this sector (machinery and equipment for industry, and machinery and civil engineering equipment). Medium-technology products, both intermediate and capital goods (boring and drilling equipment, equipment for compaction of land, digging shovels and tongs, bulldozers, excavators, etc.) are also traded. Trade with Mexico and Peru in this sector is two-way. The largest share of Chilean exports of machinery and engineering equipment goes to the members of the PA (45%). Slightly more than 70% of all of Chile's exports in the sector are sold to Peru. Other sectors where Chile has potential IIT with the PA partners are medical and pharmaceutical products, footwear and vehicle parts and accessories. These are also important sectors for other PA members, especially for Colombia and Peru. In particular, these countries have important comparative advantages in the textile and apparel industries as well as in perfumes and cosmetics. Finally, Chile participates in intra-regional automotive value chains and exports a range of products to PA members, especially to Colombia and Peru. Among the products for which Chile reports a trade surplus with these two countries are passenger vehicles, tractor chassis, buses, trucks, parts and pieces of vehicles and motor vehicle transmissions. For the latter case of vehicle transmissions, Chile also reports a surplus with Mexico. This suggests that some Chilean suppliers have successfully managed to integrate into the Mexican automotive value chain despite the distance separating the two countries.

2.2.4 Peru

Analysis of industrial linkages of Peru in intra-AP trade reveals considerable complementarity of the exportable supply with its PA partners, especially Colombia and Chile. Whereas Mexico receives only 5% of Peru's exports, Colombia and Chile receive 95% (61% and 34%, respectively). Exports from Peru to the Alliance countries are mainly intermediate goods (82%), especially basic intermediate goods, in particular mining products (see Fig. 2.2). Most complementarity is observed in agricultural and agro-industrial products, plastics, textiles, apparel and footwear, chemicals and petrochemicals, perfumes and cosmetics, as well as paper and cardboard. Intra-industry relationships are important for all these products. The top 20 selected products with a high intra-industry relationship represent almost a third of total exports from Peru, with a high intensity of intermediate products,[8] especially refined petroleum products such as oils, lubricants and asphalt. Over 90% of the exports in this group are sold to Colombia, whereas Colombia exports crude oil to Peru.

[8] Copper and metal products represent a significant proportion of Peru's exports to the PA countries (26% of the total). However, the low values of GLI calculated indicate that these exchanges are of a purely inter-industry nature.

Further, these trade flows are accompanied by a range of refined products, especially lubricants, although only in small amounts. The second most important groups of goods exported from Peru to the other PA countries are agricultural and agro-industry products. These represent about 15% of the total. Overall, about 64% of these products are intermediate goods, especially in the categories of animal feed (where 100% are intermediate goods), prepared cereal and flour, and coffee and coffee substitutes (49.4%). Reflecting the remarkable recent development of Peruvian cuisine and its dissemination within and beyond the Latin American region, exports of traditional products in this group, like cassava, bananas and tropical fruits, could be strongly increased, in particular to other PA countries. Another significant sector for Peru, of particular relevance for employment and domestic linkages, is exports of textiles, apparel and footwear. This sector represents 6% of shipments to PA members and includes domestic cotton textiles, sheep wool and fine hairs, as well as synthetic and artificial fibres and filament. Consequently, Peru has a trade surplus in textiles, apparel and footwear within the PA. Of Peru's total textile trade flows, 7% are directed to the PA members, and 2% of its imports originate from its PA partners.

Within the PA, Peru's largest intra-industry ties are with its two direct neighbours Colombia and Chile, and Peru's intra-industrial relations with those countries have recently been increasing. Trade relations with Mexico remain inter-industrial. We find a high prevalence of primary exports from Peru to Mexico, while manufacturing products with a higher technological content are imported from Mexico.

To sum up, this section has shown that there are currently rather low levels of trade in goods and productive integration among PA member countries. Trade ties involve a limited number of industries, most notably plastics, food, chemicals, auto parts and agrochemicals. The commitments contained in the Additional Protocol to the Framework Agreement of the PA in force since May 2016 should help boost these flows. Key aspects include: (i) the cumulation of origin; (ii) the harmonization or mutual recognition of technical regulations; and (iii) trade facilitation. While each element is important, the simultaneous interaction of all three will be critical. The absence of any one of them could seriously compromise intra-PA trade dynamics. This holds true even in the presence of full tariff liberalization.

2.3 Trade in Services and Investment Flows Within the PA

Economic relations between PA members are not limited to flows of merchandise trade. Within regional and global value chains, trade in services has become increasingly important in recent decades. Its analysis, together with the study of FDI flows, complements the above analysis of trade in goods and helps identify the extent to which economic linkages between the four PA members can be identified and where future potential exists.

2.3.1 Services Flows in the PA

Acute data limitations complicate attempts at obtaining a complete picture of the magnitude and evolving sectoral composition of trade in services between PA members. Only Colombia and, to a lesser extent, Chile, provide trade data on services broken down by partner country.[9]

Overall, data sources reveal that about 11% of PA members' trade in services could be classified as intra-regional in nature at year-end 2014, the last year for which comparable figures could be assembled. Significant intra-regional flows occur between Chile, Colombia and Peru. For Mexico, as in the case of goods trade, the PA is less important as a trading partner because its exports are orientated towards the United States. Indeed, when only the three Andean members of the PA are considered, the share of intra-regional trade in services increases from 11% to 17% (see Table 2.4). Services trade within the PA is most important in the category 'travel' (22%) and 'other services' (15%). Other services include telecommunications and a range of business services (IT, audit, administration, advertising, management, accounting, legal services and personnel management) (Fig. 2.3).

The value of Colombia's services exports to the PA reached US$ 1219 million in 2014. This represents 17.8% of its global services exports, a figure equivalent to 39% of the value of goods that Colombia exported to the PA in that year. Colombia's services exports are evenly distributed among the PA members: Mexico is the main destination (36%), followed by Peru (34%) and Chile (30%). The value of Colombian imports of services from PA countries reached US$ 1160 million in 2014, accounting for 9.3% of its total services imports whereas, in the same year, 17% of its imports of goods came from the PA. Relative to PA services exports, the pattern of imports of services from PA members is more concentrated. The main source of imports of services is Mexico (53%), followed by Peru (25%) and Chile (22%). Colombia's services imports from PA members have grown more strongly than Colombia's services imports overall from 2008 until 2013 (Rosales et al. 2015). The principal driver is the strong growth of imports from Mexico and Peru. This offsets the relative stagnation of imports from Chile. The pattern of Colombia's services exports with respect to the PA region is relatively stable (see Table 2.5).

When looked at in more detail, trade in services between Colombia and its PA partners shows a significant presence of various categories of business services. These include architectural, engineering, administration and management, agricultural- and mining-related services, as well as IT services. It is notable that many of these services are knowledge-intensive. Similar to IIT in goods, commercial service flows between Colombia and the other PA members can be observed in both direc-

[9]To calculate reliable figures for intra-regional trade in services in the PA, different sources need to be used and certain assumptions made. In the case of Colombia, the National Administrative Department of Statistics (DANE) reports the data in great detail and, for Chile, data accessible from the Central Bank can be used. In contrast, to obtain data for Peru, surveys of exporters of services developed by the Comisión de Promoción del Perú para la Exportación y el Turismo (PROMPERU) were analysed. Finally, mirror statistics from Chile and Colombia were used to estimate export figures for Mexico (see Table 2.4).

Table 2.4 Importance of intra-regional trade in services in the PA (total in millions and shares in total services trade)

	In US$ million	Share in total services	Share in transport	Share in travel	Share in other services
Chile	1105	10.1	10.1	5.2	12.9
Colombia	1219	17.8	14.1	21.0	14.3
Mexico	1645	28.3	23.2	34.4	20.1
Peru	908	4.5	16.7	4.1	3.8
PA	4876	11.1	13.7	10.9	9.8
PA (without Mexico)	3969	16.8	13.4	21.5	14.6

Source: Authors' estimations, based on figures from DANE, Central Bank of Chile, Edery Muñoz (2015) and Balance of Payments of Mexico and other countries

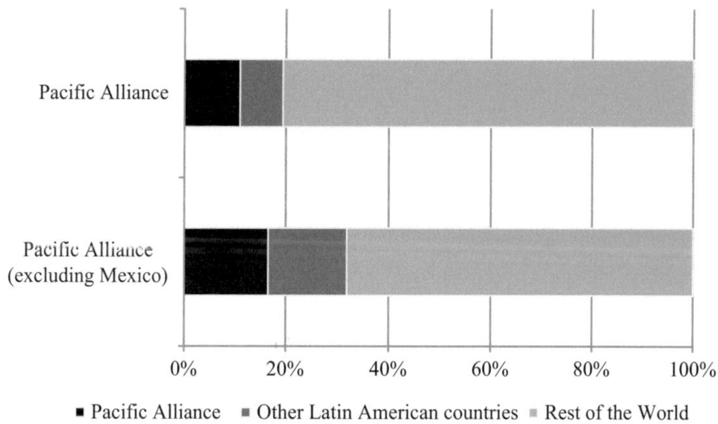

Fig. 2.3 PA trade in services: main destinations, 2014
Source: Authors' estimations, based on figures from DANE, Central Bank of Chile, Edery Muñoz (2015) and Balance of Payment of Mexico

tions, i.e. exports and imports in the same service categories can be identified. In some of these categories, the PA is a market of great importance to Colombia. For instance, the PA absorbed 36% of Colombian exports of architectural, engineering and other technical services, 19% of royalties and licence fees, and 15% of IT services in 2013. The category 'other business services' is also very important in terms of services imports, particularly IT and telecommunication services, as well as 'transportation of cargo', especially by sea. The strongest links at the bilateral level can be observed between Colombia and Peru (see Table 2.6).

For Chile, the value of PA-destined services exports totalled US$ 1105 million in 2013 (see Table 2.7), equivalent to 9% of Chile's total service exports. For Chile, the PA is somewhat more important as a destination for services exports than for goods exports – 9% of Chilean services exports are absorbed by PA members, as opposed to 5% for Chilean goods exports. Of note is the strong performance of business and professional service exports, as well as of IT-related services exports to PA mem-

Table 2.5 Colombia: trade in services with the PA and the world, 2013–2015[a] (in million dollars and percentages)

	Exports			Imports		
	2013	2014	2015[a]	2013	2014	2015[a]
Chile	325	368	258	188	257	217
Mexico	386	434	331	506	614	544
Peru	334	417	297	280	289	245
Total PA	1044	1219	886	974	1160	1006
World (services)[b]	6859	6846	5004	12,774	13,506	8888
Share PA (percentages)	15.2	17.8	17.7	7.6	8.6	11.3

Source: Authors, based on figures from National Administrative Department of Statistics (DANE)
[a]Figures are for January to September
[b]Total exports and imports for 2013 and 2014 coincide with the figures registered in Colombia's Balance of Payments

Table 2.6 Colombia: Main sectors involved in trade in services with PA members in 2013

	Main (%)	Second (%)	Third (%)	Fourth (%)
Exports				
Chile	Air transport of passengers (53)	Other air transport services (10)	Computer and related services (9)	Telecommunications (7)
Mexico	Computer and related services (37)	Telecommunications (11)	Maritime transport of cargo (8)	Commercial and similar franchises (8)
Peru	Air transport of passengers (24)	Architectural and engineering services (15)	Air transport of cargo (14)	Telecommunications (10)
Imports				
Chile	Computer and related services (16)	Maritime transport of cargo (13)	Agricultural, mining and transformational services (13)	Consulting services in administration, management and human resources (10)
Mexico	Computer and related services (22)	Telecommunications (16)	Maritime transport of cargo (13)	Commercial and similar franchises (7)
Peru	Architectural and engineering services (20)	Other air transport services (20)	Commercial and similar franchises (17)	Air transport of passengers (9)

Source: Authors, based on figures from National Administrative Department of Statistics (DANE)

bers. Business services almost doubled their share in total services exports between 2008 and 2013, from 21% to 39%, growing at a rate three times that of total service exports. Likewise, Rosales, Herreros and Durán (2015) reported that exports of Chilean IT services to PA partners also grew significantly more than corresponding global exports – from 31% to 45%.

Recognizing the increasing importance of services in global trade, PA members have all made determined efforts at improving their competitiveness. They have all worked on increasing internet speed and improving their infrastructure to create

Table 2.7 Chile: trade in services with the PA and the world, 2011–2013[a] (in million dollars and percentages)

	Exports			Imports		
	2011	2012	2013	2011	2012	2013
Colombia	113	138	196	144	136	151
Mexico	273	267	267	224	204	187
Peru	668	714	642	295	347	364
Total PA	1054	1119	1105	663	687	702
World (services)[a]	13,105	12,387	12,452	16,158	15,131	15,855
Share PA (percentages)	8.0	9.0	8.9	4.1	4.5	4.4

Source: Authors, based on figures from Central Bank of Chile
[a]Total exports and imports coincide with the figures registered in Chile's Balance of Payments

comparative advantages with respect to Asian countries endowed with cheaper labour, such as India and the Philippines, or at least to close existing gaps, for example in comparison to Japan or Singapore (see Table 2.8). In some cases, however, it may prove more difficult for PA countries to close existing gaps, let alone overtake other leading regions of the world in terms of service sector competitiveness. For example, Chile and Mexico have the highest wages among the four countries of the PA. Although lower than in Japan or Singapore, wages are sufficiently high for other competitors, for example India and the Philippines, to use this to their advantage. However, Chile and Mexico have other key factors in their favour, such as better infrastructure and fast broadband download speeds (almost 15 mbps), well above the Latin American regional average (7.26 mbps). In global rankings of internet speed, Chile and Mexico hold an intermediate position, although still well below that of Japan. Colombia and Peru's internet speeds are still below the LAC average. Thus, Alliance countries need to cooperate on key determinants of service sector competitiveness going well beyond mere tariff reductions.

One drawback of statistics on trade in services derived from countries' balance of payments data is that they do not include sales within the territory of a country because they are provided by service companies of foreign origin with a physical presence in that country. Such sales take place under the so-called "Mode 3 supply of services" (commercial presence) as defined by the General Agreement on Trade in Services (GATS) of 1995. It is estimated that Mode 3 represents about half of world trade in services (Centre for International Economics 2010) and, hence, its lack of coverage in statistics on trade in services results in significant statistical under-reporting. To gain a more complete picture of the true extent of intra-PA services trade, it is necessary to complement the analysis of trade in services statistics with a detailed study of the investment flows within the PA.

2.3.2 *Foreign Direct Investment Activities of PA Members*

FDI flows between Pacific Alliance members represent a high proportion of both inward and outward FDI of all LAC (43% and 96%, respectively). Participation in FDI inflows is more homogeneous than in FDI outflows, where Chile and Mexico

Table 2.8 Competitiveness of PA members in comparison to four selected Asian countries, 2015 or closest year

Key factors	Labour cost	Human Capital	Infrastructure	Logistics	Internet speed
Chile	○	◕	◕	◕	◕
Colombia	◕	◑	◔	◔	◑
Mexico	◑	◕	◕	◕	◕
Peru	◕	◑	◔	◔	◑
India	●	◔	◔	◕	◔
Japan	○	●	●	●	●
Philippines	●	◕	◔	◕	◔
Singapore	○	●	●	●	●

● Most competitive
○ Least competitive
Source: authors, based on various databases including The Conference Board. 2013. International comparisons of hourly compensation costs in manufacturing, 2013. www.conference-board.org/ilcprogram/index.cfm?id=28269. World Economic Forum. 2015. Human capital report 2015. reports.weforum.org/human-capital-report-2015/). Akamai. 2015. State of the Internet. Q3 2015 report. www.akamai.com/us/en/multimedia/documents/report/q3-2015-soti-connectivity-final.pdf and the World Bank's Global ranking of logistic performance index. https://lpi.worldbank.org/

lead the list of investing countries in all of LAC (see Fig. 2.4). Despite limited trade in goods, PA members have growing FDI linkages with each other. Overall, the PA is more important as an export destination for capital than as a source of FDI (which continues to come mainly from the United States and Europe).[10] For example, PA countries accounted for 15% of Chile's accumulated stock of FDI abroad in 2014, equivalent to ten times the participation that the same countries had in the stock of FDI in Chile in the same year. The same phenomenon is observed to varying degrees in Colombia, Peru and Mexico (see Tables 2.9 and 2.10). Among PA members, Mexico is notable for having the minimum share of capital originating from the PA in its FDI stock, with Peru at the other extreme. Chile and Mexico are net exporters of FDI in intra-PA flows. The opposite holds for Colombia and Peru, which receive more FDI flows than they send to the rest of the world (see Tables 2.9 and 2.10). Overall, $1.2 of every ten dollars invested by the country group is destined for the PA. The largest investment flow occurs in South America, where Peru attracts more investment originating from Chile and Colombia.

The importance of PA countries as a destination for capital originating from the regional grouping reflects the growing internationalization of Latin American companies (so-called trans-Latins) that has taken place over the past decade. PA-based multinational firms have played a prominent role in this phenomenon. Of the 50 major trans-Latins in 2012 measured by total sales, 16 were from Mexico, 11 from Chile and 6 from Colombia. Likewise, Mexico, Chile and Colombia ranked first, second and third, respectively, among the top foreign investors in LAC in 2013

[10] It should be noted, however, that in 2015 Chile was the seventh most important source of FDI received by Colombia. Back in 2012 it had been the top source.

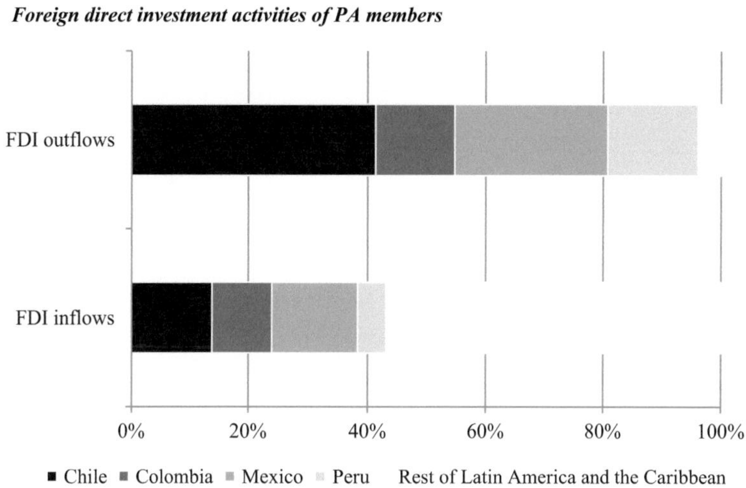

Fig. 2.4 PA FDI activities in Latin America, 2014 (as percentages of total)
Source: Authors, based on figures from ECLAC (2015)

Table 2.9 FDI stock received by PA countries from the PA and the world (2014) (in million dollars and percentages)

Receiving	Origin						
	Chile	Colombia	Mexico	Peru	Total PA	World	Participation PA (percentages)
Chile		2081	1191	163	3435	237,454	1.4
Colombia[a]	5124		4113	808	10,045	139,741	7.2
Mexico[b]	477	486		n.d.[c]	963[d]	360,390	0.3
Peru[e]	1878	1448	629		3956	79,464	5.0
PA	7479	4015	5933	971	18,398	817,049	2.3

Source: Authors, based on figures from Central Bank of Chile, Procolombia (Colombia), National Commission of Foreign Investment (Mexico) and UNCTAD (2014) (Peru), and General Directorate of International Economic Relations, Ministry of Foreign Relations of Chile

[a]The period considered is 1994–2014

[b]The period considered is 2000–2014

[c]FDI originating from Peru represented less than 0.1% of the accumulated stock in Mexico between 2000 and 2013

[d]Corresponds to the sum of FDI originating from Chile and Colombia

[e]Includes only capital contributions (reinvested earnings and net lending with the parent company are excluded). This implies a significant underestimation of the FDI stock from Chile, as several Chilean companies have been present for more than 10 years in Peru

Table 2.10 FDI stock issued by PA countries to the PA and the world (2014) (in million dollars and percentages)

	Destination						
Issuing	Chile	Colombia	Mexico	Peru	Total PA	World	Participation PA (percentages)
Chile		6420	643	10,343	17,406	113,985	15.3
Colombia	2513		2833	3049	8395	43,561	19.3
Mexico	4815	3810		1400	10,025	138,716	7.2
Peru	367	655	n.d.		1 022[a]	6002	17.0
PA	7695	10,885	3476	14,792	36,848	302,264	12.2

Source: Authors, based on figures from Central Bank of Chile, Proexport (Colombia) and UNCTAD (2014) (Mexico and Peru)

[a]Corresponds to the sum of FDI from Chile and Colombia (no data available for Mexico).

(ECLAC 2014a).[11] The expansion of trans-Latins has concentrated heavily in the region itself. In the case of companies in Chile, Colombia and Peru, new investments and the acquisition of existing assets have specifically targeted neighbouring countries, gradually extending to other more distant destinations within LAC. In contrast, Mexico has a more diversified outward FDI profile, with significant investment presence in North America (ECLAC 2014a). Overall, as in the case of trade flows of goods, Mexico appears somewhat disassociated from the dense network of cross-investments among the three other PA members.

As already mentioned, the amounts of intra-PA FDI flows are significant. In fact, the focus on FDI in neighbouring countries has been a strategy widely used by service enterprises in the region (ECLAC 2014a). Unfortunately, very little statistical information is available from PA members on where FDI originates and the sectors to which it is directed. However, there is evidence that much of the FDI flows between PA countries occurs in the service sector. For example, Chile's DIRECON (2014a) estimated that 57.4% of Chilean FDI stock accumulated in all PA countries between 1990 and December 2013 can be attributed to services, with a value of close to US$ 18,886 million.[12] The bulk of such investments went to Colombia and Peru and to a lesser extent Mexico. Also, DIRECON (2014a) estimated that investments in services in the PA partners underpinned 51,000 jobs, of which 84% are direct employees (approximately 127,000 people). More recently, DIRECON (2015) estimated that 52.7% of Chilean FDI stock accumulated in Colombia between 1990 and December 2014 could be attributed to services, reaching an estimated US$ 9239 million dollars, with retail trade (47%), financial intermediation (31%) and transport (16%) accounting for predominant shares (DIRECON 2014b).

[11]Two major mergers and acquisitions in the region took place in 2014 between PA countries: the acquisition of the Chilean company *Tresmontes Luchetti* (operating in the food sector) by *Nutresa* of Colombia, for US$ 758 million, and the acquisition of *Nextel Peru* (operating in telecommunications) by *ENTEL Chile*, for US$ 400 million (ECLAC 2014a).

[12]The methodology and data sources used in the DIRECON reports are different from those employed by the Central Bank of Chile, so the figures produced by the two agencies are not directly comparable.

Table 2.11 Main trans-Latin services enterprises in the PA, 2013

Enterprise	Sector	Chile	Colombia	Mexico	Peru	Sales (in million dollars)
América Móvil	Telecommunications	X	X	PC	X	60,079
CENCOSUD	Retail	PC	X		X	19,743
LATAM	Air transport	PC	X	X	X	11,906
Grupo Falabella	Retail	PC	X		X	11,834
Grupo Aval	Finance		PC	X		9000
Empresas Públicas de Medellín	Electricity and telecom	X	PC	X		6753
Avianca	Air transport		PC		X	4269
Grupo Saba	Retail			PC		3601
Entel Chile	Telecommunications	PC	X		X	3101
Sigdo Koppers	Construction	PC				2953
Ripley	Retail	PC	X		X	2624
Ingenieros Civiles Asociados (ICA)	Construction	X	X	PC	X	2259
Salfacorp	Construction	PC	X		X	2024
Grupo Carvajal	Graphics industry	X	PC	X	X	1813
Sonda	Software	PC	X	X	X	1283
Cruz Blanca SA	Health	PC			X	982
Lipigas Chile	Gas distribution	PC	X		X	440
Grupo Sura	Finance	X	PC	X	X	n.a.
Grupo ACP	Microfinance				PC	n.a.

Source: Authors, based on figures from ECLAC (2014a) and information from international financial press. PC, parent company

Further, DIRECON (2014b, c) estimated that 63.3% of the stock of Chilean FDI in Peru accumulated over the same period was in services, valued at US$ 8820 dollars, with the transport sector (44%) and retail trade (36%) standing out. Although the stock of Chilean FDI in Mexico was worth less than US$1400 million at year-end 2014, investments in services accounted for the largest part (US$ 825 million) of the total. Table 2.11 showcases the strong presence of the leading trans-Latin service enterprises of Chile, Colombia, Mexico and Peru in PA markets. The individual data in Table 2.11 show a predominance of Chilean and Mexican trans-Latins, with a clear specialization by Chilean retail sales companies, together with utilities, such as telecommunications and gas, as well as a strong presence in the air transport, construction and health sectors. Meanwhile, Colombian investors focus on finance, air transport, electricity and communications. Mexico is most active in telecommunications (see Table 2.11).

2.3.3 The Future of the PA's Services and Investment Activity

The strong presence of companies of the four PA countries in each other's markets is a clear demonstration of the importance of market-led integration, which is not confined to services, but applies also to trade in goods. However, this activity is still more vigorous in services and investment. Trade in services is strongly linked to the cross-border mobility of people through GATS Modes 2 and 4 (consumption abroad and the presence of natural persons, respectively). As barriers to such mobility are lowered, greater opportunities will open up for trade in a wide range of services, both through movements of the provider (e.g. a software developer or an architect) and of consumers (e.g. tourists, students, patients).

Given the above considerations, the results of the agreements reached within the PA framework to facilitate the mobility of people are notable. In November 2012, Mexico announced the abolition of visas for nationals of Colombia and Peru (nationals of Chile did not require visas to enter Mexico). Later, in May 2013, Peru announced the abolition of visas for business people from Chile, Colombia and Mexico for up to 183 days, provided that they only perform unpaid activity in the country.[13] These developments complement and reinforce the commitments made on trade in services in the Additional Protocol to the Framework Agreement of the Alliance. A natural next step would be efforts towards the approval or mutual recognition of professional and academic qualifications by PA members. This would allow professionals and technical specialists from any one PA member to provide services in other PA countries. Parallel agreements reached on integrating the stock exchanges in Chile, Colombia and Peru through the Integrated Latin American Market (MILA) may similarly contribute to increasing the amount and variety of trade in financial services among these countries. Such opportunities should expand significantly after the incorporation of the Mexican Stock Exchange into the initiative. Finally, the recommendations on trade in services made by the Business Council of the PA (*Consejo Empresarial de la Alianza del Pacifico*, CEAP) during the Summits of Punta Mita (Mexico) in June 2014 and Paracas (Peru) in July 2015 should be noted. Recognizing the dynamism and potential of trade in services, the CEAP (2014, 2015) called on governments to: (i) detect areas where greater integration and complementarity can be achieved; (ii) fully implement the commitments made in the services chapters in the (bilaterally signed) FTAs in these sectors; (iii) concentrate on measures to facilitate trade in services in the sectors identified, namely (a) regulatory and tax aspects, (b) documentation, and (c) possibilities for harmonization and mutual recognition of professional qualifications; (iv) prepare for negotiations on a possible Additional Protocol on financial inclusion; and (v) promote the use of information technology in existing business programmes.

The CEAP's recommendations are expected to play a prominent role in the PA agenda. To facilitate the collection and use of reliable data, the joint work program should also aim at developing comparable statistics on trade in services by trading

[13] See alianzapacifico.net/temas-de-trabajo/ (accessed 10 November 2016).

partner, sector and mode of supply. This is especially important as the current availability of relevant data remains inadequate for informed policy-making purposes. The PA could benefit from the technical cooperation of specialized international organizations such as the WTO, the World Bank Group or the OECD in this regard.

2.4 The Impact of the Additional Protocol of the PA Framework Agreement

With the aim of deepening their economic relations and increasing two-way trade and FDI in goods and services alike, the founding members of the PA decided to commit to a further common agreement. The so-called Additional Protocol of the Framework Agreement to the Pacific Alliance (the Additional Protocol) which entered into force in May 2016 aims to boost intra-regional ties. It addresses directly the objectives outlined by the four member countries, including: providing the basis for increased trade and investment within the Alliance, achieving economies of scale; developing more integrated supply chains to respond to the new forms of organization of world production; and, promoting greater trade integration in the region to achieve higher levels of competitiveness in third-country markets. To understand the relevance of the agreement and to evaluate its potential impact, this section analyses the tariff schedule negotiated and reviews the aspects treated in the different chapters of the Additional Protocol.

2.4.1 *Agreed Tariff Schedule*

Based on Annex 3 of the Additional Protocol, it is possible to illustrate the direct impact that the PA members can expect with respect to changes in their tariff structure.

Table 2.12 summarizes the main results of selected chapters of the Additional Protocol, taking as a reference imports by each country from other PA members. As a percentage of tariff lines, 96% to 98% are duty free, depending on the country. The remaining tariffs are to be reduced according to an agreed schedule in successive periods of between 2 to 7 years. The biggest changes in the schedule will occur between year 1 and year 3 in the markets of Colombia and Chile, which propose a large proportion of tariff lines with zero tariffs from 1 January 2018 onwards. Another important jump in regional preferences is set to occur in early 2020, when Chile will have just over 99.5% of tariff lines on imports, while other partners have around 97 and 98% at free. In the same year, some sensitive products of Colombia that are of interest to Chile and Mexico (duck meat, goose, dairy products, and sheep and pig meat) will see tariffs eliminated. The calendar between 2020 and

Table 2.12 PA: market access results, tariff schedule

Staging category	Tariff cut period	Year	Number of products[a]				Percentage of total tariff lines			
			Chile	Colombia	Mexico	Peru	Chile	Colombia	Mexico	Peru
A	Immediately	2014	7612	7213	11,840	7429	97.72	95.69	96.12	97.81
B	2 years	2015	34	0	0	4	0.44	0.00	0.00	0.05
C	3 years	2016	61	132	76	3	0.78	1.75	0.62	0.04
D[a]	4 years	2017	0	0	0	1	0.00	0.00	0.00	0.01
E	5 years	2018	0	21	25	29	0.00	0.28	0.20	0.38
F	6 years	2019	0	3	1	0	0.00	0.04	0.01	0.00
G	7 years	2020	56	5	223	12	0.72	0.07	1.81	0.16
H, I, J	8–10 years	2023	0	71	64	24	0.00	0.94	0.52	0.32
K, L M	10–15 years	2026	0	26	20	37	0.00	0.34	0.16	0.49
N, O	16–17 years	2029	0	34	28	19	0.00	0.45	0.23	0.25
P	Seasonality	2030	0	0	7	3	0.00	0.00	0.06	0.04
X	Excluded	–	27	33	34	34	0.35	0.44	0.28	0.45
Total tariff lines			7790	7538	12,318	7595	100.0	100.0	100.0	100.0

Source: Authors' calculation based on Annex 3 of the Additional Protocol of the Framework Agreement to the PA

Note: in the cases of Chile and Mexico, the calculations were performed based on the Harmonized System (HS) 2012 with products at the 8-digit level. For Colombia and Peru, products were at the 10-digit level

[a] Staging only used for Peru to protect its canned animal liver (HS2012, 16022000)

2030 includes annual linear reductions, agreed in advance. Those are of much greater interest to the trade of Colombia and Peru with Mexico than for trade between Colombia and Peru. This is because Colombia and Peru have already fully liberalized their intra-regional trade within the Andean Community (Colombia Ministry of Commerce, 2016), a grouping of which Peru and Colombia are members. By 2030, the PA will have eliminated 99% of all tariff lines of its four member countries (see Table 2.12 and Fig. 2.5).

Peru and Mexico have a special list of products (P List) for which seasonal tariffs are applied to protect their farmers from foreign competition during national crop seasons. Some varieties of onions are examples of products for which the tariffs agreed upon in the schedule to Annex 3 of the Protocol are applied. Only in 2030 will tariffs for all products within this group be completely eliminated.[14]

Measured in terms of import value, the immediate tariff elimination extends to 94.5% of all products, with greater relief in the case of Chile, which grants PA pref-

[14] The last staging category, called X, maintains a list of between 27 and 34 sensitive products that represent between 0.28% and 0.35% of total tariff lines (Colombia and Chile) and about 0.45% in the cases of Mexico and Peru. This list of exclusions covers sugar and related products (fructose, molasses, glucose, lactose, sweeteners, syrups, etc.), all of which were excluded from the preferences. In all of these cases, the countries continue to apply the MFN principle.

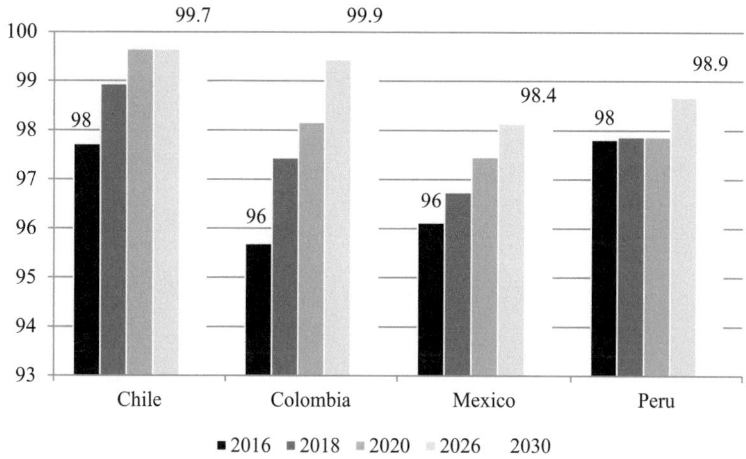

Fig. 2.5 PA: market access results, tariff schedule (in percentage of tariff lines)
Source: Authors' calculation based on Annex 3 of the Additional Protocol of the Framework Agreement to the PA

erence to 97.6% of total imports. In value terms, the greatest impact of market opening occurs in Mexico through the opening of list C products.[15]

In terms of import value, a second milestone in tariff reductions will occur in 2020, when Mexico will reduce tariffs applied in the meat sector (edible offal of bovines, sheep, goats and swine), which have base tariffs of 20%. Tariffs will also be lowered on poultry products, especially meat and edible offal of poultry, for which the average tariff will drop from an average of 200% ad valorem to 26% in 2019 and to 0% in 2020 (see Table 2.13 and Fig. 2.6). Together with the increased opening of the Mexican market, which will reduce tariffs with high base levels, comes an improvement in the relative position of Colombian, Chilean and Peruvian exporters in a large Mexican market of 127 million inhabitants. The same holds true for the removal of tariffs in Colombia and Peru, where, according to DIRECON (2014d), Chile has particular interests in meat products such as beef and pork, plus poultry and dairy products (cheese, butter and whey). Besides the obvious achievement of harmonization in terms of tariff reductions as analysed above, a first recognized benefit resulting from the Protocol is the harmonization of multiple provisions of various existing agreements to establish common standards, specifically in commercial disciplines. This will directly reduce transaction costs for operators in member states.

[15] Here low tariffs for some meat products are noteworthy (e.g. meat and edible offal of poultry, pork) as well as fish (trout, catfish, tilapia and carp), for which the baseline tariff fluctuates between 10% and 20%. This also applies to certain agricultural products (peas, avocados, beans, mushrooms, Brussels sprouts, etc.) that also have base tariffs above 20%.

Table 2.13 PA: market access results based on imports, tariff schedule (millions of dollars and percentages)

		Value of imports from PA members, 2015 (millions of dollars)					Share of total imports (percentage)				
Staging category	Tariff cut period	Chile	Colombia[a]	Mexico	Peru	Pacific Allilance[a]	Chile	Colombia[a]	Mexico	Peru	Pacific Alliance[a]
A	Immediately	4028	7174	2602	4000	17,804	97.6	96.9	84.4	94.5	94.5
B	2 years	0	0	0	0	0	0.0	0.0	0.0	0.0	0.0
C	3 years	7	36	100	0	143	0.2	0.5	3.2	0.0	0.8
D	4 years	–	–	–	0	–	–	–	–	0.0	–
E	5 years	0	18	18	2	38	0.0	0.2	0.6	0.0	0.2
F	6 years	0	0	0	0	0	0.0	0.0	0.0	0.0	0.0
G	7 years	27	0	169	2	199	0.7	0.0	5.5	0.1	1.1
H, I, J	8–10 years	0	19	64	45	127	0.0	0.3	2.1	1.1	0.7
K, L M	10–15 years	0	43	43	10	96	0.0	0.6	1.4	0.2	0.5
N, O	16–17 years	0	24	18	1	43	0.0	0.3	0.6	0.0	0.2
P	Seasonality	0	0	65	0	65	0.0	0.0	2.1	0.0	0.3
X	Excluded	65	92	5	171	334	1.6	1.2	0.2	4.0	1.8
Total imports		4127	7407	3084	4231	18,849	100	100	100	100	100

Source: Authors' calculation based on Comtrade and Annex 3 of the Additional Protocol of the Framework Agreement to the PA

Note: Calculations were based on the Harmonized System 2012 at the 6-digit level. When mapping different products at the 8- and 10-digit level into a common 6-digit group, staging categories were taken into account. Where products mapped into the same 6-digit group showed more than one staging category, the more restrictive staging category (i.e. with a longer period of tariff cuts) was always chosen

[a] Figures for Colombia are from 2014

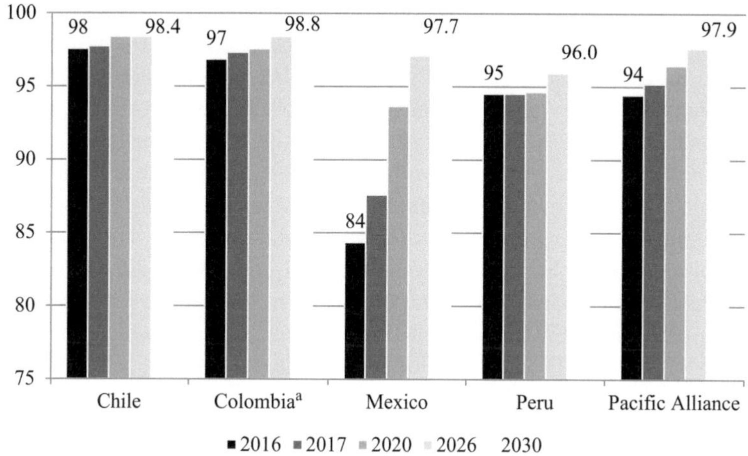

Fig. 2.6 PA: market access results, tariff schedule (in percentage of total imports)
Source: Authors' calculation based on Comtrade and Annex 3 of the Additional Protocol of the Framework Agreement to the PA
Note: Calculations were based on the Harmonized System 2012 at the 6-digit level. When mapping different products at the 8- and 10-digit level into a common 6-digit group, staging categories were taken into account. Where products mapped into the same 6-digit group showed more than one staging category, the more restrictive staging category (i.e. with a longer period of tariff cuts) was always chosen
[a]Trade weights for Colombia are from 2014

2.4.2 A Review of the Chapters of the Additional Protocol

Table 2.17 of the appendix summarizes the core results of a review of the 13 main topics of the Protocol, including the chapter on access to markets. Several of the topics cover new aspects not provided for in the bilaterally signed agreements between the parties in their pre-existing PTAs. Key changes relate to government procurement, telecommunications, e-commerce, financial services and maritime services. These are chapters where a modernization of disciplines is observed, such as the standardization of procedures to be applied in all four PA countries. One example is the procurement chapter, which now includes Peru, whereas the initial PTA between Chile and Peru did not feature such disciplines. Also noteworthy is Colombia's decision to improve its commitments towards Chile. Such regulatory improvements also enabled those Alliance members negotiating the Trans-Pacific Partnership agreement (TPP; all but Colombia) to align their positions more closely and jointly pursue common interests (Castillo 2016). Another noteworthy aspect of the Protocol concerns the cumulation of origin. This refers to a mechanism that opens the possibility for a goods exporter to seek not only domestic intermediate inputs, but also those originating from any other Alliance member, and also possibly of a third country that is not a PA member in determining eligibility for duty-free access to PA markets. This will promote greater regional integration and the development of sub-regional production networks, increasing the ability to leverage the comparative advantages of all producers of intermediate goods within Alliance members. In addition, the Protocol allows producers from Alliance member to import inputs from non-parties and incorporate those into exports to the Alliance as if they were of PA origin.[16] The full entry into force of a scheme allowing for the cumulation of origin provides opportunities for the establishment of sub-regional value chains between member countries in the areas of interest defined in each country, based on their respective comparative advantages.

In terms of disciplines, the Additional Protocol updates the standards of investment protection and updates liberalization schedules for trade in services contained in the earlier bilateral PTAs between PA members, some of which have been in operation for more than a decade.[17] For example, in the case of Chile's relationship with Mexico, the Protocol enshrines the opening of the telecommunications sector to foreign participation in Mexico to 100%, compared with 49% in the bilateral PTA (which reflected the level of market opening prevailing in the late 1990s). Similarly, the Protocol opens up of the Mexican broadcasting sector to foreign participation (up to 49% of capital), whereas, in the bilateral PTA, that sector was reserved for Mexican nationals (DIRECON 2014d). The disciplines agreed in the Protocol on trade facilitation could boost trade in services associated with logistics. The impact could prove significant because the joint strategies mentioned in the chapter on maritime services have been made more concrete, namely the facilitation of regional maritime transport, the development of logistics chains and the facilitation of multimodal transport. These issues are highly complex and their development will be slow, such that significant results will likely materialize over time.[18]

2.5 Between Megaregional and Preferential Trade Agreements: The Future of the PA and the Asia-Pacific Region

One of the core objectives of the PA is to build a bridge between the Latin American and countries in the Asia-Pacific region (Herreros 2016). Of the 49 observer states of the PA, 12 are from the Latin American and Caribbean region and a nearly equal number (11) are from the Asia Pacific region (see Table 2.14). The Alliance has generated considerable interest in the above two regions, which can form the basis of a future strengthening of the economic integration process started by the PA's four founding members.

[16] DIRECON (2014d) cites as examples timber and nitric acid, which are inputs that Chilean processors incorporate into their exports of sawn wood and ammonium nitrate – products that are then exported to other countries of the Alliance.

[17] The Colombia–Mexico FTA was signed in 1994 and the Chile–Mexico FTA in 1998.

[18] For substantial progress to be made in trade facilitation, such as the full interoperability of the Foreign Trade Single Window (FTSW) and the extensive use of information technology in all customs offices of Alliance members, as well as full recognition of Authorized Economic Operators (AEO), it will be necessary to promote flexible and timely cooperation mechanisms to lower the costs associated with the delayed clearance of goods.

Table 2.14 Observer states of the PA (as of May 2017)

Region	Countries	Number of countries
Latin America and the Caribbean	Argentina, Costa Rica,[a] Dominican Republic, Ecuador, El Salvador, Guatemala, Haiti, Honduras, Panama,[a] Paraguay, Trinidad and Tobago, Uruguay	12
North America	Canada, United States	2
Africa	Egypt, Morocco	2
Asia	China, India, Indonesia, Israel, Japan, Republic of Korea, Singapore, Thailand, Turkey	9
Europe	Austria, Belgium, Czech Republic, Denmark, Finland, France, Germany, Georgia, Greece, Hungary, Italy, Netherlands, Norway, Poland, Portugal, Romania, Slovakia, Spain, Switzerland, Sweden, Ukraine, United Kingdom	22
Oceania	Australia, New Zealand	2
Total number of observer states		49

Source: Authors based on PA website (alianzapacifico.net/en/paises/#observer-countries)
[a]Accession candidates

To date, negotiations on accession to the PA have started with only two Latin American countries – Costa Rica and Panama. The accession of Costa Rica is currently frozen as the country's sitting President ponders the pros and cons of joining the Alliance. Such a political review stands in marked contrast to the country's private sector urging the administration to take the necessary steps to join the integration scheme as quickly as possible. Nevertheless, Costa Rica remains the most probable candidate for an expansion of the Alliance.[19] The case of Panama is different. In 2012, a free trade agreement with Colombia was not ratified because of a tariff dispute between the two countries. This is apparently one of the main barriers to the launch of official negotiations between the PA and Panama. For the rest of LAC, concrete measures to foster integration with the Alliance seem most probable in the possible convergence towards the MERCOSUR countries. Among ongoing efforts to increase economic integration levels within the region, the convergence between the PA and MERCOSUR holds considerable potential, as together, these two schemes represent the overwhelming majority of regional trade and investment activity in the region. The two main economies driving trade (Mexico) and production (Brazil) form part of this duo and their joining forces could lead to a significant deepening of economic integration in LAC.[20]

When considering the future relationship of the PA with the Asia Pacific region, it is useful to review the trade pattern of PA countries with their partners across the Pacific (see Fig. 2.7). The importance of trade with the countries of the Asia Pacific region differs markedly between PA members. While Chilean exports to the Asia

[19] See Durán Lima and Cracau (2016) for a detailed discussion of the possible accession of Costa Rica to the PA; and Wong and Palma's chapter in this book.

[20] For a detailed discussion of the possible effects of a gradual convergence between the PA and MERCOSUR, see ECLAC (2014b).

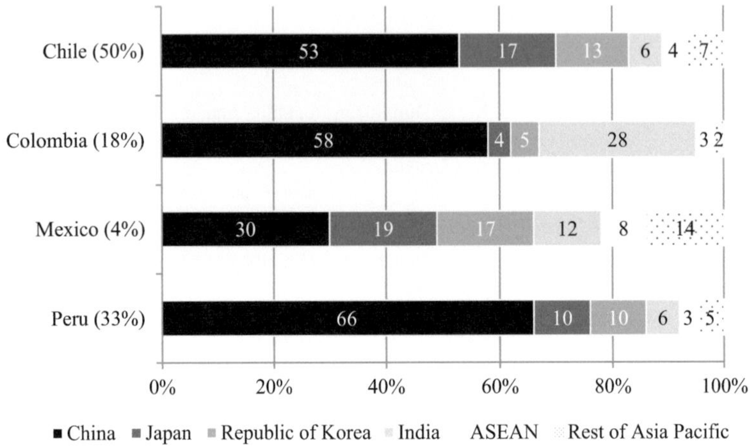

Fig. 2.7 PA: exports to the Asia Pacific region, 2015 (percentages)
Source: Authors, based on COMTRADE database. Note: Figures for Colombia are for 2014

Pacific region represented half of the country's total exports in 2015, for Mexico such exports accounted for only 4% of the total. Peru and Colombia show intermediate values (33% and 18%, respectively). Of the export destinations in the Asia Pacific region, China is the most important for all four PA members (30% of Mexico's exports to the region, and 66% of those from Peru). Exports to China from Chile and Colombia account for more than half of all their exports to the Asia Pacific region. After China, Japan and the Republic of Korea are the next most important export destinations in Asia for Chile, Mexico and Peru. For Colombia, India accounts for 28% of exports to the Asia Pacific region, representing its second most important partner in the Asia-Pacific region. As a bloc, the emerging economies of the Association of Southeast Asian Nations (ASEAN) receive only a minor share of PA goods exports (between 3% in the cases of Colombia and Peru and 8% in the case of Mexico). This is somewhat surprising given the increasing importance of ASEAN member states in global trade, especially their high insertion into global value chains. It is also noteworthy that only three ASEAN countries are PA observer states (see Table 2.14). Against this background, it seems understandable that both trade blocs have recently sought to strengthen their economic relations.

Finally, the future of the PA, particularly with respect to its impact on integration in LAC, will strongly depend on its ability to withstand recent trends in the negotiation of trade agreements worldwide. In this context, two opposite developments come to mind. On the one hand, negotiations of so-called *megaregional* trade agreements have been initiated or completed that cover significant shares of world trade and investment. These include the Transatlantic Trade and Investment Partnership (TTIP) between the European Union and the United States, TPP between the United States and 11 American and Asia Pacific states, and the Regional Comprehensive Economic Partnership (RCEP) between the ASEAN countries and the six Asia Pacific states with which ASEAN has existing PTAs (namely China, India, Japan, Republic of Korea, Australia and New Zealand). Each of these three megaregional agreements either includes the United States or a number of key Asia Pacific countries as negotiating parties, with LAC as a region significantly or fully underrepresented. Only Chile, Mexico and Peru have negotiated the TPP. The uncertain legal and political status of the TPP following the withdrawal of the US administration leaves the LAC region *de facto* outside the significant trade negotiations taking place at the global level (Meacham 2014).

On the other hand, recent political developments, most notably in the United States and the United Kingdom, have led to calls for a return to bilateral trade diplomacy. A prominent example is the ongoing re-negotiation of the NAFTA between Canada, Mexico and the United States proposed by the US administration, and its possible replacement by two bilateral free trade pacts. In general, bilateral trade agreements between individual countries or trade blocs can be a preliminary step towards a more comprehensive agreement between multiple parties. Note, for example, that existing bilateral PTAs with each of the four current members of the PA were a prerequisite to the negotiation of Costa Rica to become the first additional member of the PA, while the freezing of the PTA between Panama and Colombia has been described as one the single largest obstacle to Panama's formal initiation of accession negotiations with PA members.

Table 2.15 summarizes the existing PTAs of each of the PA members within the LAC and the Asia Pacific region. Chile and Peru have already established a complex network of PTAs with Asia Pacific countries, most notably with China, Japan, the Republic of Korea and Thailand. Chile has also deepened its relations with the Asia Pacific region through its so-called P4 FTA with Australia, Brunei, Singapore and New Zealand. The trans-Pacific economic relations of Peru and Mexico, however, mainly depended on the successful ratification of the TPP, which – at the time of writing – remains shrouded in uncertainty. Colombia, for its part, is well connected to the various integration schemes in the region, but has to date successfully negotiated only one PTA with an Asia Pacific country – the Republic of Korea, which entered into force in July 2016.

Summing up, the PA is the only integration scheme in the LAC region that is actively directed towards establishing economic relations outside the region. While the main objective of the PA as a bloc is to create a bridge across the Pacific, its individual members maintain differing economic relations with Asia Pacific countries. While the TPP was likely to strengthen linkages between its Latin American members and participating Asia Pacific countries, its present uncertain status presents opportunities for alternative policy pursuits. The PA could try, at least partially, to fill the current gap and foster deeper economic ties between both regions to promote regional and global value chains. At the same time, RCEP – the leading ongoing Asian integration initiative, can will also likely substitute for the TPP, even as its substantive remit may be less ambitious. Thus, the PA faces three main challenges in deepening economic relations in the LAC region as well as in the Asia Pacific region: (i) managing the accession of Costa Rica and Panama to prove its ability to successfully integrate new members into the regional grouping; (ii) deepening its economic relations with the MERCOSUR countries in order to foster economic integration in the region; and (iii) creating new linkages to the Asia Pacific region to strengthen the insertion of its member countries and firms into regional and global value chains.

Table 2.15 PA: main PTA partners (as of May 2017)

Regions	Countries			
	Chile	Colombia	Mexico	Peru
MERCOSUR	X	X	X[a]	X
Andean Community		X		X
Central American Common Market (CACM)	X	X	X	X
Panama	X	X[c]	X	X
Cuba	X	X		X
Caribbean Community (CARICOM)		X		
Canada	X	X	X	X
United States	X	X	X	X
European Union	X	X	X	X
European Free Trade Association (EFTA)[d]	X		X	X
Turkey	X	X[e]		N[e]
Israel		X	X	
Asia Pacific countries				
Australia	X[b]		X[c]	X[c]
Hong Kong (SAR)	X			
India	X			N[e]
Japan	X		X	X
China	X			X
Republic of Korea	X	X		X
Thailand	X			X
India	X			
Malaysia	X		X[c]	X[c]
New Zealand	X[b]		X[c]	X[c]
Singapore	X[b]		X[c]	X[c]
Brunei	X[b]		X[c]	X[c]
Vietnam	X		X[c]	X[c]
Indonesia	N[e]			
Asia-Pacific Economic Cooperation (APEC)	X		X	X
Trans-Pacific Partnership Agreement (TPP)[f]	X		X	X
Asia Pacific countries	13	1	7	10

Sources: Authors, based on OAS (2017), Foreign Trade Information System and others official sources

[a]Mexico has FTAs with Uruguay and a Partial Complementary Agreement with Brazil; [b]P4 Free Trade Agreement between Chile and Australia, Brunei, Singapore and New Zealand; [c]pending ratification; [d]Iceland, Liechtenstein, Norway and Switzerland; [e]under negotiation; [f]the legal and political status of the TPP is uncertain after the withdrawal of the US administration

Appendix

Table 2.16 Macroeconomic and social indicators of the PA members, 2015

Indicator	Chile	Colombia	Mexico	Peru	PA[a]	Latin America and the Caribbean
GDP (million dollars)	240,222	293,243	1,144,334	192,141	1,869,940	5,052,489
Real growth rate (percentages)[b]	2.1	3.1	2.5	3.3	2.6	−0.1
GDP per capita (dollars)[b]	13,341	6084	9009	6021	8800	7966
GDP per capita PPP (dollars)[c]	23,460	13,847	17,534	12,195	17,169	15,377
Population (million inhabitants)	18.0	48.2	127.0	31.9	225.1	634.3
Unemployment rate (percentage)	6.2	8.9	4.3	6.0	5.4	6.1[c]
Annual inflation (percentage)	4.3	5.0	2.7	3.5	3.4	8.4[d]
Poverty rate, 2014 (percentage of population)	7.8[e]	28.6	41.2	22.7	33.2	28.2
Human Development Index	0.832	0.720	0.756	0.734	0.761	0.748
Rank competitiveness index (out of 144)	34	66	61	65	…	…
Rank competitiveness index (within LAC)	1	7	5	6	…	…
Rank Doing Business (out of 189)	34	42	43	53	…	…
Rank Doing Business (within LAC)	1	2	3	4	…	…
Exports (million dollars)	63,362	35,491	380,772	33,247	512,872	906,548
Imports (million dollars)	59,220	54,058	395,232	38,060	546,569	1,007,032
Number of signed trade agreements	27	18	17	25	22	74
Number of trade partners with agreement	65	64	54	58	79	83
Exports with agreement (percentage of value)	96.0	64.2	92.9	94.3	91.4	…
Imports with agreement (percentage of value)	77.0	63.7	65.1	92.1	68.1	…
Average MFN tariff (percentage)	6.0	8.8	7.8	3.7	7.4	…
Average applied tariff (percentage)	1.4	3.2	2.7	0.3	2.4	…

(continued)

Table 2.16 (continued)

Source: Authors based on ECLAC (2016), International Monetary Fund, World Economic Outlook Database (April 2016), and UNDP

[a]Figures for the Alliance are estimated by summing up or averaging the figures from its members, according to the indicator

[b]Average of each country's index weighted by its GDP share within the joint GDP of the Alliance

[c]Figure for the region from 2013

[d]Figure for the region from 2014

[e]Figure for Chile from 2013

Table 2.17 PA: main outcomes of the Additional Protocol of the framework agreement

Topics	Main outcomes
Market access	17 sets of staging categories for different product baskets were established (from A to X).
	Category A calls for full liberalization of between 7200 and 7600 products according to the Harmonized System 2012. This is between 96% and 98% of total tariff lines at 8-digit level, and 94.5% of import value.
	About 1.8% of products with tariff elimination scheduling between 3 and 7 years (2% of intra-regional imports).
	0.95% of products with high sensitivity are liberalized in between 8 and 17 years (2% of imports).
	Sugar and related products such as fructose, molasses and glucose products were excluded from preferences (0.38% of total tariff lines and 1.8% of total intra-regional imports).
Rules of origin	Unique rules of origin are negotiated for the four members.
	An accumulation of origin mechanism among the four members was established.
	In textiles and clothing a committee was established that may grant waivers to import products from third countries where not possible to obtain supplies from within Alliance members.
Trade facilitation and customs cooperation	The parties agreed to the rapid resolution of difficulties at customs through exchange of information.
	Commitments to expediting shipments of goods were established by using international standards and automation of information.
	Mutual recognition of Authorized Economic Operators (AEO) among member countries was agreed upon.
	The progressive interoperability of the Foreign Trade Single Window (FTSW) was agreed upon, starting the process with health and origin certificates.
Technical barriers to trade	Provisions go beyond WTO rules and include transparency, conformity assessment procedures and regulatory cooperation.
	A Committee on Technical Barriers to Trade was established for the monitoring and implementation of the provisions and issues of the agreement.
Sanitary and phytosanitary measures	Agreed rules considered by the parties tend to increase transparency in implementation of the Sanitary and Phytosanitary Standards (SPS), to strengthen the science-based use in its application.
	A Committee on Sanitary and Phytosanitary Standards was created for the monitoring and implementation of the provisions and issues of the agreement.

(continued)

Table 2.17 (continued)

Topics	Main outcomes
Public procurement	Public procurement provisions of all existing agreements between the countries were certified.
	The chapter applies to all members for purchases of both goods and services (including construction services) required by plants and sectional entities as well as public companies.
	Public procurement between Chile and Peru was integrated and standards in the bilateral relations of the rest of the members were improved.
Trade in services	National treatment to all parties that signed the agreement on the basis of negative lists is available. This involves the application of non-conforming measures, the same as those listed for each country (see Annex I of the Protocol).
	The parties agreed to work together in sharing information, sharing methodologies, as well as the publication of statistics on services based on international standards.
	A Joint Committee on Investment and Services was created with a set of tasks towards implementation, coordination and development of common standards and the identification and analysis of barriers to trade in services with a view to their reduction or elimination, to coordinate the exchange of data and methodologies, and to promote the development of standards and criteria for the Provision of Professional Services,
Financial services	National treatment to all parties that signed the agreement on the basis of negative lists is available. This involves the application of non-conforming measures, the same as those listed for each country (see Annex 1 of the Protocol).
	A Committee on Financial Services with a set of tasks aimed at monitoring and implementation of the Chapter was created.
	A specific commitment of the chapter is that the parties agreed to allow a financial institution, organized outside its territory to provide investment advisory services to a collective investment scheme located in the territory of the party. It requires registering or authorization, as well as the possibility to regulate the service.
Maritime services	The parties are obliged to grant a treatment no less favourable to the vessels of the other party than it grants to its own vessels with regard to free access to, stay in and departure from ports, the use of port facilities and all secured facilities in its trade and navigation, for ships operations, its crew and cargo. This assignment also applies for the allocation of docks and loading and unloading facilities.
	Mutual recognition of the nationality of ships and of the documentation of the travel of crew from all member states of the Alliance is established. If one state recognizes the documents, they will be recognized by the other member states.
	The countries agreed to establish cooperation mechanisms to overcome obstacles that may arise in the development of maritime transport services. Among others are mentioned: sharing information and experiences on laws, best practices, and exchanges of students, management experiences, regulations as well as programmes to encourage greater efficiency of maritime transport services.

(continued)

Table 2.17 (continued)

Topics	Main outcomes
E-commerce	The main objective of this chapter is to promote paperless trade by providing opportunities that open electronic commerce to economic growth.
	Electronic transactions of goods and services are regulated, including digital products.
	The parties commit themselves not to apply customs duties to digital products.
	The countries agreed to establish cooperation mechanisms to facilitate the use of electronic commerce by micro, small and medium enterprises, share information, and promote the development of electronic commerce.
Telecommunications	Telecommunications companies of the four countries are guaranteed to be able to provide telecommunications services in all countries of the PA under conditions of free competition.
	Among others, aspects such as interconnection between telecommunications companies, number portability, access to infrastructure and transparency in promoting transparent tariffs for fixed telephony and mobile services, including international roaming, are secured.
	The independence and impartiality of the Telecommunications Regulatory Bodies is guaranteed.
Dispute Settlement	The parties agreed on a mechanism for settling disputes applicable to disputes in all areas covered by the Protocol, with the exception of investment disputes, for which the settlement mechanism investor-state dispute provisions of the investment chapter applies.

Source: Authors, on the basis of the text of the single chapters of the Additional Protocol of the Framework Agreement. (www.acuerdoscomerciales.gob.pe/index.php?option=com_content&view=category&layout=blog&id=187&Itemid=206)

References

Abusada-Salah, R., Acevedo, C., Aichele, R., Felbermayr, G. J., & Roldán-Pérez, A. (2015). *Dimensiones y efectos económicos de la Alianza del Pacífico*. Berlin: Konrad-Adenauer-Stiftung.

Castillo, J. (2016). *Acuerdo de Asociación Transpacífico – El Nuevo Horizonte Comercial del Perú*. Presentation at the Seminar 'El Acuerdo de Asociación Transpacífico: impactos para América Latina y el Caribe', ECLAC, Santiago, Chile, April 6.

CEAP (Consejo Empresarial de la Alianza del Pacífico). (2014). *Declaración del Consejo Empresarial de la Alianza del Pacífico*. Punta Mita, Mexico, June 19. http://www.acuerdoscomerciales.gob.pe/images/stories/alianza/espanol/declaracion_ceap__junio_2014.pdf. Accessed 15 June 2017.

CEAP (Consejo Empresarial de la Alianza del Pacífico). (2015). Declaración del Consejo Empresarial dela Alianza del Pacífico. Paracas, Peru, July 2. https://alianzapacifico.net/download/declaracion-ceap-paracasjulio-de-2015/. Accessed 3 March 2018.

DIRECON (Dirección General de Relaciones Económicas Internacionales del Ministerio de Relaciones Exteriores de Chile). (2014a). *Presencia de inversión directa de capitales chilenos en los Países miembros de la Alianza del Pacífico 1990-diciembre 2013*. https://www.direcon.gob.cl/2014/11/presencia-de-inversion-directa-de-capitales-chilenos-en-paises-miembros-de-alianza-del-pacifico-1990-diciembre-2013/. Accessed 3 May 2017.

DIRECON (Dirección General de Relaciones Económicas Internacionales del Ministerio de Relaciones Exteriores de Chile). (2014b). *Presencia de inversión directa de capitales chilenos en Colombia 1990-diciembre 2013*. https://www.direcon.gob.cl/2014/10/presencia-de-inversion-directa-de-capitales-chilenos-en-colombia-1990-diciembre-2013/. Accessed 3 May 2017.

DIRECON (Dirección General de Relaciones Económicas Internacionales del Ministerio de Relaciones Exteriores de Chile). (2014c). *Presencia de inversión directa de capitales chilenos en Peru 1990-diciembre 2013*. http://www.direcon.gob.cl/wp-content/uploads/2013/07/004_Presencia-ID-Cl-en-per%C3%BA-1990-junio2013.pdf. Accessed 16 June 2016.

DIRECON (Dirección General de Relaciones Económicas Internacionales del Ministerio de Relaciones Exteriores de Chile). (2014d). *Protocolo Adicional al Acuerdo Marco PA. ¿Qué significa?* February. http://www.direcon.gob.cl/wp-content/uploads/2014/02/Protocolo-de-la-Alianza-delac%C3%ADfico.pdf. Accessed 16 June 2016.

DIRECON (Dirección General de Relaciones Económicas Internacionales del Ministerio de Relaciones Exteriores de Chile). (2015). *Presencia de inversión directa de capitales chilenos en el Mundo 1990-diciembre 2014*. https://www.direcon.gob.cl/wp-content/uploads/2015/05/Presencia-ID-Cl-en-mundo-1990-dic2014.pdf. Accessed 3 May 2017.

Durán Lima, J., & Cracau, D. (2016). *The PA and its economic impact on regional trade and investment: Evaluation and perspectives* (International Trade Series No. 128). Santiago de Chile: ECLAC.

Durán Lima, J., & Lo Turco, A. (2010). El comercio intrarregional en América Latina: Patrón de especialización y potencial exportador. In M. I. Terra & J. Lima Durán (co-ord.), *Los impactos de la crisis internacional en América Latina: ¿Hay margen para el diseño de políticas regionales?* (Serie Red MERCOSUR No 18), Montevideo.

Durán Lima, J., & Zaclicever, D. (2013). *América Latina y el Caribe en las cadenas internacionales de valor* (Serie Comercio Internacional No. 124). Santiago de Chile: ECLAC.

Durán Lima, J., Zaclicever, D., & Castresana, S. (2014a). *Empleo y comercio exterior en América Latina y el Caribe (mimeo)*.

Durán Lima, J., Castresana, S., & Mulder, N. (2014b). Value chains in Colombian exports to the European Union: How inclusive are they? In R. A. Hernández, J. M. Martínez-Piva, & N. Mulder (Eds.), *Global value chains and world trade. Prospects and challenges for Latin America*. Santiago de Chile: Economic Commission for Latin America and the Caribbean (ECLAC) (ECLAC Books No 127).

Durán Lima, J., Mariano, A., & Daniel, C. (2016). *Manual on foreign trade and trade policy: Basics, classifications and indicators of trade patterns and trade dynamics* (Project Document, LC/W.430). Santiago de Chile: ECLAC.

ECLAC (Economic Commission for Latin America and the Caribbean). (2016). *Social Panorama of Latin America 2015* (Briefing Paper, LC/G.2691-P).

ECLAC (Economic Commission for Latin America and the Caribbean). (2014a). *Foreign Direct Investment in Latin America and the Caribbean 2013* (LC/G.2613-P). Santiago, Chile.

ECLAC (Economic Commission for Latin America and the Caribbean). (2014b). *La Alianza del Pacífico y el MERCOSUR: hacia la convergencia en la diversidad* (LC/L.3922). Santiago, Chile.

ECLAC (Economic Commission for Latin America and the Caribbean). (2015). *Foreign Direct Investment in Latin America and the Caribbean 2015* (LC/G.2641-P). Santiago, Chile.

Edery Muñoz, D. (2015). *Avances y desafíos de la promoción de exportaciones peruanas de Servicios*. PERUSERVICE Summit 2015, PROMPERU.

Fung, K. C., García-Herrero, A., & Siu, A. (2009). *Production sharing in Latin America and East Asia* (BBVA Working Papers, No 0901). https://www.bbvaresearch.com/wp-content/uploads/migrados/WP_0901_tcm348-212941.pdf. Accessed 3 May 2017.

Herreros, S. (2016). The PA: A bridge between Latin America and the Asia-Pacific? In S. Basu Das & M. Kawai (Eds.), *Trade Regionalism in the Asia Pacific: Development and Future Challenges*. Singapore: ISEAS-Yusof Ishak Institute.

Meacham, C. (2014). *The PA and New Zealand. Latin American origin, global reach.* Washington, DC: Center for Strategic and International Studies. http://csis.org/publication/pacific-alliance-and-new-zealand.

OAS (Organization of American States). (2017). *Multilateral treaties and bilateral Agreements.* http://www.oas.org/en/sla/dil/treaties_agreements.asp. Accessed 3 May 2017.

Ramírez, A. C., Suárez, J. C., & Lesmes, J. M. (2012). *La Cadena de Valor Siderúrgica y Metalmecánica en Colombia. En la primera década del siglo XXI.* Bogota: ANDI Cámara Fedemetal e ILAFA.

Rosales, O., Herreros, S., & Durán Lima, J. (2015). La Alianza del Pacífico: comercio inversión y desafíos a futuro. In A. Roldán Perez (Ed.), *La Alianza del Pacífico: plataforma de integración regional con proyección al Asia Pacífico.* Medellín: Colección Académica EAFIT.

UNCTAD (United Nations Conference on Trade and Development). (2014). *Bilateral FDI Statistics 2014.* Geneva. http://unctad.org/en/Pages/DIAE/FDI%20Statistics/FDI-Statistics-Bilateral.aspx. Accessed 3 May 2017.

Chapter 3
The Pacific Alliance: WTO+ and WTOx?

Camilo Pérez Restrepo and Alma Sofía Castro Lara

3.1 Introduction

Trade and economic integration processes in Latin America began in the 1960s with the emergence of diverse initiatives intended to promote intraregional trade. The most recent of these initiatives is the Pacific Alliance (PA) established by Chile, Colombia, Mexico and Peru in 2011 with the Declaration of Lima. After a series of high-level meetings to discuss the agreement further, the PA's institutional foundations and objectives were laid down in the *Framework Agreement* signed in Antofagasta, Chile in June 2012, which entered into force in July 2015. The process was further advanced with the negotiation of an *Additional Protocol to the Framework Agreement* signed on 10 February 2014 in Cartagena, Colombia, which entered into force in May 2016. This agreement builds upon previously existing (mainly bilateral) trade agreements between PA members, going beyond basic tariff reduction and the disciplines traditionally covered by earlier agreements.

The PA members have a combined population of 217 million and a gross domestic product (GDP) of US$ 2.2 trillion, equivalent to 40% of regional GDP, and an average per capita GDP (PPA) of US$ 16,759. The four member countries represent 50% of total trade in goods in the region, with a value of exports exceeding US$ 498,667 million and imports worth US$ 521,426 million in 2016. In that year, these four countries received foreign direct investment (FDI) amounting to almost US$ 59,000 million, and were the destination of more than 39 million tourists and business travellers.

The PA represents one of the most promising mechanisms for regional economic integration because of its scope, objectives and the common foreign and economic policy orientation of its members. Moreover, this is the first Latin American regional

C. Pérez Restrepo (✉) · A. S. Castro Lara
Asia Pacific Studies Center-Universidad EAFIT, Medellín, Colombia
e-mail: cperezr1@eafit.edu.co; acastrol@eafit.edu.co

P. Sauvé et al. (eds.), *The Pacific Alliance in a World of Preferential Trade Agreements*, United Nations University Series on Regionalism 16,
https://doi.org/10.1007/978-3-319-78464-9_3

integration initiative to include among its founding objectives, to serve as a platform for its members to approach the Asia-Pacific region, in the areas of trade, investment and cooperation.

In addition to this important objective, the group was created with the goals of attaining deep integration among its members, facilitating the free movement of goods, services and investment, as well as enabling freer movement of people, including business travellers and tourists. The group also introduced for the first time in Latin America, the idea to serve as a common platform to share efforts in the relationship with Asia-Pacific economies (Pacific Alliance 2012). This was a novel element considering the increasing economic importance of the region and the trade agreements being negotiated in the region, included the Trans-Pacific partnership (TPP) and the Regional Comprehensive Economic Partnership (RCEP), and the ASEAN Community, among other regional initiatives.

In order to attain these objectives, PA leaders initially established five priority areas: trade and integration; cooperation; services and investment; and facilitation of business people's mobility and migratory transit (Pacific Alliance 2012). The Declaration of Cali increased the number of priority areas and established working groups on: institutional affairs; regulatory convergence; government procurement; communication strategy; intellectual property; small and medium-sized enterprises (SMEs); external relations; fiscal transparency; and the business council, among others (Pacific Alliance 2013).

The PA has gained momentum due to its dynamism and rapid evolution founded upon the previously negotiated free trade agreements (FTAs) among its member economies. This chapter aims firstly to answer the question of whether the PA is a WTO+ (i.e. it goes beyond what is in the WTO) or a WTOx agreement (i.e. its provisions cover issues for which there are no WTO agreements) on distinct topics. Secondly, it looks at whether the PA's provisions (those included in the PA's *Additional Protocol to the Framework Agreement* hereafter referred as PAAP) represent an improvement compared to those included in previous FTAs among its members.

3.2 Methodology

The existence of diverse trade liberalization instruments has been documented since the 1950s and a series of regional trade liberalization initiatives around the world, such as the Treaty of Rome in Europe and the Economic Complementation Agreements (ACE, from the acronym in Spanish) were signed during the late 1980s among some of the Latin American nations. However, it was in the 1990s that the legal framework for negotiation of FTAs truly took shape. Back then, FTAs were conceived as an exception to the most-favoured nation (MFN) principle and the other principles included in the 1994 General Agreement on Tariffs and Trade (GATT) of the WTO. This related, in particular, to Articles XXIV 4; XXIV 5 and

XXIV 5(b), where the purpose and the conditions for the establishment of a free trade area between two or more of its members were stipulated.

FTA negotiations proliferated in the early 2000s, particularly in regions with high levels of protectionism, such as the Asia-Pacific region and Latin America. Since then, FTAs have played an important role in the foreign trade policies of regional economies and have become one of the tools most frequently used to liberalize trade. The scope of the agreements has also widened, covering more issues related to trade, beyond the elimination of tariffs. Thus, the provisions contained in the FTAs have been classified as either WTO+ or WTOx, depending on the obligations and coverage. WTO+ provisions – although they exist in the WTO agreements – go beyond the established disciplines. WTOx provisions, on the other hand, are those that are outside (do not exist in) the current WTO framework (Baldwin 2011).

There is abundant literature covering the phenomenon of the proliferation of FTAs. In the early studies, academics focused their research on the reasons that motivated the countries to negotiate FTAs and the effects that they could have on the creation or diversion of trade (Frankel 1997). With the emergence of the new-generation issues[1] – including government procurement, e-commerce, intellectual property and competition policies, among others – studies have attempted to evaluate the FTAs' characteristics and areas of negotiation beyond the traditional focus on trade liberalization. Studies such as those of Estevadeordal et al. (2009), Hicks and Kim (2012) and Baier et al. (2014), have demonstrated that provisions related to investment, trade facilitation and intellectual property are as important as tariff reduction in explaining trade flows. Therefore, comprehensive studies must go beyond the analysis of market access provisions, to take into consideration the depth of negotiated provisions in areas such as services, FDI, competition and intellectual property rights (IPRs) (Dür et al. 2014).

As a result, academics such as Wignaraja et al. (2012) interested in conducting this type of analysis have developed instruments to evaluate the depth of the provisions contained in the agreements. This assessment is based on the evaluation of FTA provisions compared to those of the WTO framework. Some of the provisions in the agreements could be classified as WTO+ when they already exist in WTO agreements, but the clauses included in the FTA go beyond WTO commitments. Other provisions can be deemed WTOx when they cover obligations that go beyond the current WTO mandate. Along these lines, the agreements are considered "deep" if they are labelled as WTO+ or WTOx. The baselines for evaluation are further described in Table 3.1.

This chapter compares the FTAs signed among Chile, Colombia, Mexico and Peru prior to establishment of the PA in 2011 to the PAAP signed in 2014. Based on

[1] The new-generation issues include provisions on areas that were not previously included in most FTAs. These issues go beyond tariff reduction or elimination of tariff barriers with the goal of facilitating trade, reducing technical barriers and promoting investment and cooperation. The new-generation areas include: public procurement, e-commerce and intellectual property, among others.

Table 3.1 Standards used to evaluate the depth of free trade agreements

Provision	Evaluation standard	Classification
Tariff reduction	General Agreement on Tariffs and Trade (GATT)	WTO scope
Services	General Agreement on Trade in Services (GATS)	WTO scope
Investment	Most-favoured nation status and national treatment	WTOx
Competition	The existence or non-existence of competition clauses: restrictions to anticompetitive agreements; abuse of dominant position; and anticompetitive mergers and acquisitions	WTOx
Government procurement	Government Procurement Agreement (GPA)	WTO scope
Trade facilitation	Based on the principles: transparency, simplification, harmonization, cooperation and standardization	WTO scope
Intellectual property	Agreement on Trade-Related Aspects of Intellectual Property Rights (TRIPS)	WTO scope

Source: Based on Wignaraja et al. (2012)

Wignaraja et al. (2012), the agreements are classified into three levels depending on the depth of the agreed provisions as follows:

> The overall depth of FTAs … is classified as being high, medium or low. High depth FTAs are those that have relatively fast tariff liberalization schedules; some or comprehensive services coverage; and "new age" deep integration provisions for new issues. Medium depth FTAs are those that have relatively fast tariff liberalization schedules, some or comprehensive services coverage, and moderate or limited deep integration provisions. Low depth FTAs are those that have gradual tariff liberalization schedules, comprehensive, some or limited/excluded services coverage, and limited or shallow integration provisions.

3.3 Market Access

Countries establish tariff barriers with the goals of protecting national industries and enhancing the competitiveness of local products. Therefore, economic liberalization processes and the negotiation of FTAs have traditionally concentrated on the reduction or elimination of tariffs. Trade liberalization in the PA builds upon previous trade agreements among its members. Since the end of the 1980s, the four countries have negotiated Economic Complementation Agreements (ACE, from the acronym in Spanish) within the framework of their common membership to the Latin-American Integration Association (ALADI). The existence of these agreements, including the Andean Community that first emerged as one of the ACE, facilitated the subsequent negotiations of FTAs among them, with wider trade liberalization clauses as well as more comprehensive service and investment provisions (Table 3.2).

The levels of trade liberalization within the FTAs that entered into force before 2013 among the members of the PA are set out in Table 3.3.

Table 3.2 Previous agreements among Pacific Alliance members

Countries	Agreements
Chile and Colombia	In 1993, Chile and Colombia signed an ACE (Number 24), which entered into force in 1994. However, both countries had to wait until 2006 to sign an FTA, which entered into force in 2009 and liberalized 97.5% of trade between them. This agreement also covered areas such as services, investment and government procurement
Chile and Mexico	Mexico and Chile signed an ACE (Number 17) in 1991. This agreement entered into force in 1992 and was deepened with the negotiation of an FTA that entered into force in 1999. This FTA liberalized 98.4% of all trade between the two countries and included provisions regarding services and non-tariff barriers
Chile and Peru	The ACE Number 38 signed between Peru and Chile was later transformed into an FTA that entered into force in 2006 and liberalized 97.1% of the tariff lines. This FTA also included provisions on investment, intellectual property and services
Colombia and Mexico	Colombia and Mexico began their trade liberalization process within the Group of Three Agreement (in Spanish *Grupo de los tres*) (TLC-G3; ACE Number 33), which also included Venezuela among its original members. The G3 Agreement was signed in 1994 and entered into force in 1995. After Venezuela left the G3 in 2006, Mexico and Colombia negotiated an FTA which they signed in 2009. The FTA entered into force in 2011 and offered broader trade liberalization. Colombia liberalized 91.4% of its trade with Mexico, while Mexico liberalized 81%. The agreement also covered areas such as rules of origin
Colombia and Peru	Colombia and Peru commenced their trade liberalization within the Andean Community.[a] In 1997, Peru began the process of joining the Free Trade Area – which liberalized 100% of the trade among its members – and attained this objective in 2005
Mexico and Peru	Mexico and Peru signed the ACE Number 8 in 1987. However, this agreement had an extensive list of exclusions and did not cover areas such as services and investment. Mexico and Peru signed an FTA in 2011 that entered into force in 2012. This FTA included deeper commitments on trade liberalization as well as other areas; Mexico liberalized 98.2% of its trade while Peru liberalized 97.4%

[a]Note that the Andean Community has its roots in the Andean Pact established in 1969 but advanced trade liberalization in 1990s. Peru was the last country to join the Free Trade Area created within its framework

3.4 Market Access Provisions Negotiated Within the Pacific Alliance

The PA members signed the PAAP in February 2014, establishing a trade protocol for tariff liberalization among them. As a result of this agreement, Chile immediately reduced tariffs on 7607 tariff lines, representing 97.7% of trade and Colombia immediately reduced tariffs on 7182 tariff lines (96.4% of trade). Peru was the member that offered the highest proportional tariff reduction, reducing tariffs on 7423 tariff lines representing 98.3% of its commerce. Mexico, on the other hand, was the country that reduced the highest number of tariff lines (11,776), but they represent only 96% of its trade, thus making Mexico the country that made the lowest proportional tariff reduction.

Table 3.3 Tariff reductions in earlier agreements among the Pacific Alliance members

Agreement	Chile–Colombia				Chile–Mexico				Chile–Peru			
	Common liberalization (number of tariff lines)		%		Common liberalization (number of tariff lines)		%		Common liberalization (number of tariff lines)		%	
Immediate	6.456		82.00		5.756		98.30		2.641		43.40	
Scheduled	1.224		15.50		101		1.70		3.250		53.40	
Excluded	194		2.50		91		1.60		177		2.90	
Total	7.874		100		5.855		100		6.088		100	
Percentage reduction	97.5				98.4				97.1			
Agreement	**Colombia–Mexico**				**Colombia–Peru**				**Mexico–Peru**			
	Tariff liberalization Colombia to Mexico (number of tariff lines)	%	Tariff liberalization Mexico to Colombia (number of tariff lines)	%	Tariff liberalization Colombia to Peru (number of tariff lines)	%	Tariff Liberalization Peru to Colombia (number of tariff lines)	%	Tariff Liberalization Mexico to Peru (number of tariff lines)	%	Tariff Liberalization Peru to Mexico (number of tariff lines)	%
Immediate	5.904	72.20	6.741	75.70	6.531	98.90	6.484	91.10	10.042	81.50	5.814	78.90
Scheduled	1.568	19.20	471	5.30	75	1.10	686	9.60	2.067	16.80	1.368	18.60
Excluded	702	8.60	1.694	19.00	0	0.00	0	0.00	220	1.80	189	2.60
Total	8.174	100	8.906	100	6.606	100	7.120	100	12.329	100	7.371	100
	91.4		81.0		100		100		98.2		97.4	

Source: Pacific Alliance (2014) and Intrade (2017)

Table 3.4 Tariff reduction in Pacific Alliance additional protocol

	Chile		Colombia		Mexico		Peru	
	Number of tariff lines	%	Number of tariff lines	%	Number of tariff lines	%	Number of tariff lines	%
Immediate liberalization	7607	97.70	7182	96.40	11,776	96.00	7423	98.30
Liberalization schedule (3–17 years)	150	1.90	239	3.20	454	3.70	97	1.30
Excluded (no tariff reduction)	28	0.30	33	0.40	33	0.30	34	0.50

Source: Pacific Alliance (2014)

The member countries immediately reduced tariffs on an average of 8947 tariff lines and it is expected that in the next 3–17 years, Chile, Colombia, Mexico and Peru will reduce tariffs on 150, 239, 454 and 97 more tariff lines, respectively. An average of 32 tariff lines were excluded by the four countries, which represent 0.4% of tariff lines traded among these countries (see Table 3.4).

The WTO in paragraph 5 (c) of article XXIV of GATT 1994 establishes that a FTA must substantially reduce all tariff barriers to trade among signatories within a reasonable period of time. Based on this principle, Wignaraja et al. (2012) defined "substantially all trade" as 85% of the tariff lines, and a "reasonable period of time" as a maximum of 10 years, making exceptions only in special cases. According to this model, an FTA is referred to as deep and fast if it removes tariffs on 85% or more of the tariff lines within a period of 10 years or less; otherwise the FTA will be deemed gradual.

For the purposes of this chapter, an agreement will be referred to as deep if it immediately liberalizes more than 85% of tariff lines. Accordingly, the earlier FTAs between Chile and Mexico and Colombia and Peru are deep. Moreover, the trade protocol entered into force in May 2016, with which the liberalization is considered deep (see Table 3.5).

The PAAP does not achieve total liberalization of trade as is the case with some other regional agreements (such as the Andean Community). However, the number of tariff lines included in the PA's trade liberalization list suggests that there is slightly deeper trade liberalization than in the earlier agreements among its members, and this is expected to contribute to an expansion of the trade among them in the years following the PAAP's entry into force.

Table 3.5 Depth and scope of trade in goods in the Pacific Alliance agreements[a]

Previous agreements			Pacific Alliance		
Parties[b]	% immediately liberalized	Deep	Country	% immediately liberalized	Deep
Chile–Colombia	82.00	No	Chile	97.70	Yes
Chile–Mexico	98.30	Yes			
Chile–Peru	43.40	No			
Colombia–Chile	82.00	No	Colombia	96.40	Yes
Colombia–Peru	98.90	Yes			
Colombia–Mexico	72.20	No			
Mexico–Chile	98.30	Yes	Mexico	96.00	Yes
Mexico–Colombia	75.70	No			
Mexico–Peru	81.50	No			
Peru–Chile	43.40	No	Peru	98.30	Yes
Peru–Colombia	91.10	Yes			
Peru–Mexico	78.90	No			

Source: Intrade (2017)
[a]Liberalization percentages are estimated based on the tariff reduction lists included in each of the agreement's market access chapters
[b]This is interpreted as the percentage of tariff liberalization offered by Country A to Country B. For example, in the Chile–Colombia agreement, Chile immediately liberalized 82% of the tariff lines traded with Colombia at the moment their FTA entered into force

3.5 Services

The baseline for evaluating the depth of the provisions on services is the WTO General Agreement on Trade in Services (GATS). This agreement defines five key areas for liberalization of services: business and professional, communications, financial, transport and labour mobility, and entry of business persons. Based on Wignaraja et al. (2012) there are three depths for FTAs' services chapters: broad coverage, medium coverage, limited or excluded coverage of services' provisions. Applying these principles, an FTA with "broad coverage" is an agreement that covers the five key areas mentioned above. Agreements that cover between two and four of these areas are classified as "medium coverage" agreements. The last category includes those FTAs that establish only general provisions or cover only one key area, and hence are considered as "limited coverage" agreements.

Liberalization of trade in services between the PA's members has evolved over the years. Most of the agreements initially agreed between these countries – the previously mentioned ACEs with the important exception of the Andean Community – did not include clauses related to trade in services. This situation changed with the negotiation of FTAs that included chapters on services liberalization. Most of these agreements included liberalization of professional services and of temporary entry of business people – with some special restrictions. Moreover,

Table 3.6 Depth and coverage of services liberalization in the agreements between Pacific Alliance members

Countries	Scope and exclusions in the services chapter	Coverage
Chile–Colombia	Chapter 10 of the FTA liberalized trade in services with the exclusion of financial services (banking and insurance), and public utilities. A different agreement regulated air transportation of passengers	Medium coverage
Chile–Mexico	Financial services and public utilities were excluded. Telecommunications, social and construction services were subject to special conditions (Chap. 12). Mexico restricted energy, and air transportation of passengers was regulated through a different agreement	Medium coverage
Chile–Peru	Financial services and security services were excluded from the FTA. Telecommunications and energy services were restricted. A different agreement regulated air transportation of passengers	Medium coverage
Colombia–Mexico	The FTA excluded financial services and air transportation of passengers. In addition it established special conditions for telecommunications	Medium coverage
Colombia–Peru	Trade in services is regulated by the Andean Community Resolutions 439 and 659. Liberalization of financial services and television are excluded for a 20-year period	Broad coverage
Mexico–Peru	Financial services were partially liberalized. Article 12.11 created a Financial Services Committee with the aim of achieving further liberalization. Air transportation of passengers and public utilities were excluded	Medium coverage
Pacific Alliance	**GATS' five key areas are covered**	**Broad coverage**

Source: Pacific Alliance (2014) and Intrade (2017)

all the earlier agreements among member economies excluded financial services liberalization (see Table 3.6).

The terms agreed in the PAAP reflect its members' interest in reaching a deep agreement in terms of liberalization of trade in services. The agreement deepens services liberalization beyond the commitments included in previous FTAs. The PA's services liberalization covers the five key areas of the GATS, including telecommunications and financial services, which were often restricted in previous FTAs. Moreover, the new agreement also expands the liberalization to areas that were absent from previous bilateral agreements such as e-commerce and maritime transportation.[2]

An important step towards the liberalization of trade in financial services is the establishment of the Integrated Latin American Market (*Mercado Integrado Latinoamericano – MILA*), which seeks to integrate the stock markets of the PA's

[2]The relationship between Chile and Mexico offers a case study. The PAAP contemplates the total liberalization (100% foreign ownership) of telecommunication services, while the previous FTA between the two countries allowed a maximum of 49% foreign ownership. Similarly, the PAAP promotes the openness of Mexican radio broadcasting by allowing up to 49% foreign ownership, while the FTA only allowed national participation.

members. The MILA is expected to increase the presence of financial actors from other countries and to consolidate the banks and companies with regional scope.

However, services liberalization within the PA is still a work in progress. The Pacific Alliance Business Council requested regional governments to: "(1) identify sectors where deep integration and further complementarity can be reached; (2) promote deeper commitments than the ones made in the FTAs' services chapters; (3) [take] actions that facilitate trade in services" (CEAP 2014). Furthermore, the cross-border supply of services[3] has become a matter of particular importance owing to the expansion of e-commerce across the region. The fact that all PA members are engaged in the negotiations on the Trade in Services Agreement (TISA) is also likely to influence the future evolution of services liberalization in the group.

3.6 Investment

FTAs aim to provide a competitive and open environment that facilitates investment flows as well as deeper economic integration between the parties. Consequently, more comprehensive FTA investment chapters contain provisions on liberalization (market access) and regulation (protection). Market access provisions are related to national treatment, both in the pre-establishment and post-establishment stages, the MFN clause and the prohibition of performance requirements. The protection provisions include clauses related to the transfer of investment dividends, and the existence of an investment dispute resolution mechanism, among others.

Based on Wignaraja et al. (2012), there are two classifications concerning the depth of the investment provisions: "deeper than standard", if the agreement includes all the provisions on liberalization and regulation; and "standard" if the agreement is limited to the fundamental principles of liberalization and investment protection.

The previous agreements signed among the PA's members are deeper than standard. The PAAP also covers all liberalization and regulation provisions, such as MFN treatment and post-establishment national treatment for the investors in all areas (including banking and telecommunications). The PA also created a Joint Committee on Services and Investment, which is expected to play an instrumental role to improve the regional investment environment. This Committee is the most important enhancement in terms of investment, when compared to previous FTAs as it allows business sector actors to identify and inform to relevant authorities the existence of potential barriers (see Table 3.7).

[3] GATS mode 1 "cross-border supply" of services. Services provided from the territory of one Member into the territory of any other Member. Most e-commerce services are classified as such.

Table 3.7 Depth and coverage of provisions on investment in the Pacific Alliance and in earlier agreements between its members

Countries	Covered areas	Coverage
Chile–Colombia	All liberalization and regulation provisions	Deeper than standard
Chile–Mexico	All liberalization and regulation provisions	Deeper than standard
Chile–Peru	All liberalization and regulation provisions	Deeper than standard
Colombia–Peru	All liberalization and regulation provisions [a]	Deeper than standard
Colombia–Mexico	All liberalization and regulation provisions	Deeper than standard
Mexico–Peru	All liberalization and regulation provisions	Deeper than standard
Pacific Alliance	**All liberalization and regulation provisions**	**Deeper than standard**

Source: Pacific Alliance (2014) and Intrade (2017)
[a]Provisions agreed upon within the framework of the Andean Community

3.7 New-Generation Issues

The most discussed among the so-called Singapore issues,[4] or new-generation issues, include: competition, government procurement, trade facilitation and intellectual property, which are often included in the most forward-looking FTAs. The PA has further progressed to include additional issues such as e-commerce and telecommunications. Furthermore, working groups on education, SMEs, cooperation, mobility of business people and migratory transit have been established. The inclusion of these areas is evidence of the PA leaders' willingness to achieve a more comprehensive relationship among their countries, beyond the liberalization already achieved within the PAAP framework.

Likewise, significant progress has been made among the PA member countries regarding rules of origin, on which they negotiated a harmonized rules system. The most important improvement in comparison to previous agreements is the establishment of a harmonized system of cumulative rules of origin. This mechanism allows the Alliance's members to engage in regional value chains and supplier diversification; the agreement also covers flexible requirements regarding supplies that are not produced within the PA markets.

Furthermore, progress has been made on technical barriers to trade and sanitary and phytosanitary (SPS) measures, where the main achievement was the creation of a Technical Committee on Trade Obstacles (*Comité de Obstáculos Técnicos al*

[4]These are called "the Singapore issues" because it was back in the 1996 Singapore Ministerial Conference that WTO members established the working groups on trade and investment, on competition policy, and on transparency in government procurement, as well, a commitment towards simplifying trade procedures.

Comercio – OTC) a transparency oversight body that aims for regulatory cooperation between its members. The Agreement also established a Committee on SPS Measures, which goes beyond the commitments made in previous FTAs.

3.7.1 Competition

Competition policies comprise an extensive array of measures and instruments implemented by the governments to prevent competitive distortion and anticompetitive behaviours; hence, these measures help to achieve better resource allocation and market liberalization. A market free of anticompetitive practices allows its businesses to take advantage of liberalization and commercial growth. Wignaraja et al. (2012) establish two classifications for these measures. The "deeper than standard" coverage, refers to the clauses contained in regional or bilateral agreements where parties agree on the definition of anticompetitive behaviour, or parties agree to adopt a competition law. The "standard" coverage applies where clauses that have a more limited scope are included in agreements. Such clauses define the general obligations to take measures against anticompetitive behaviour, and to promote competition between businesses and cooperation among regulatory authorities.

Provisions on competition policies as well as antitrust practices were included in some of the previous agreements negotiated among the PA members. The PAAP includes clauses related to the promotion of competitiveness and antitrust practices; however, these measures are classified as standard since they do not go beyond the commitments included in some of the previous FTAs (see Table 3.8).

Table 3.8 Depth and coverage of provisions on competition in the Pacific Alliance and in earlier agreements between its members

Countries	Covered provisions	Coverage
Chile–Colombia	Not included	
Chile–Mexico	Promotes competition and antitrust policies	Standard
Chile–Peru	Chapter 8 establishes a common competition policy	Deeper than standard
Colombia–Peru	Ruled by Andean Community Decision 608 and the Andean Committee on Free Competition	Deeper than standard
Colombia–Mexico	Antitrust policies and competition are promoted	Standard
Mexico–Peru	Not included	
Pacific Alliance	**Antitrust practices are promoted**	**Standard**

Source: Pacific Alliance (2014) and Intrade (2017)

Table 3.9 Depth and coverage of the provisions on government procurement in the Pacific Alliance and in earlier agreements between its members

Countries	Covered principles	Coverage
Chile–Colombia	GPA[a]	Standard
Chile–Mexico	Not included	
Chile–Peru	Not included	
Colombia–Peru	GPA	Standard
Colombia–Mexico	GPA	Standard
Mexico–Peru	Not included	
Pacific Alliance	**GPA+**	**Deeper than standard**

Source: Pacific Alliance (2014) and Intrade (2017)
[a]The agreement is said to be GPA because despite its members not being part of said agreement, the public procurement provisions included in their FTA are equivalent to those in GPA

3.7.2 Government Procurement

The World Trade Organization Government Procurement Agreement (GPA) serves as a baseline for liberalization of public procurement. The GPA is a plurilateral agreement covering 47 WTO members, and has a number of observers, some of them negotiating their accession to it. The minimum commitments within the GPA's framework include the principles of transparency and national treatment. Based on the classification proposed by Wignaraja et al. (2012), an agreement is "deeper than standard" if it includes, besides these two principles, dispositions such as e-government procurement[5] and incentives for SMEs, as well as cooperation and training on public procurement-related matters (if it is GPA+). An FTA is "standard" if it is limited to the basic principles of transparency and national treatment, or government procurement is not regulated within the agreement.

The PA establishes a common regulatory framework on public procurement since not all the earlier agreements among the PA economies had provisions on this matter, nor its member economies are part of the GPA (Chile and Colombia are observers to the agreement but Mexico and Peru do not share this same status). The PAAP updates previous bilateral stipulations regarding transparency, national treatment, non-discrimination and dispute resolution, where they existed. The agreement also includes rules and actions that promote the participation of SMEs in public procurement. Furthermore, the agreement eliminates the existing reserves,[6] thus increasing the number of public entities that are authorized to procure from foreign suppliers (Table 3.9).

[5]E-government refers to the use of information technology tools to explain how government procedures must be performed (by citizens and private organizations), the processes that must be carried out and whether this can be done online. It also refers to online application to public tenders.

[6]Under the public procurement agreements states can restrict public entities from having foreign suppliers – they are "reserved" to national suppliers. For example, in Colombia, the number of public entities (both national and provincial) that can have foreign suppliers (from other PA countries) increased from 95 to 118.

Table 3.10 Depth and coverage of provisions on trade facilitation in the Pacific Alliance and in earlier agreements between its members

Countries	Covered principles	Coverage
Chile–Colombia	All basic principles	Deeper than standard
Chile–Mexico	All basic principles	Deeper than standard
Chile–Peru	Transparency, simplification, harmonization, cooperation	Standard
Colombia–Peru	All basic principles	Deeper than standard
Colombia–Mexico	Transparency, simplification, harmonization, cooperation	Standard
Mexico–Peru	Transparency, harmonization	Standard
Pacific Alliance	**Transparency, simplification, harmonization, cooperation, standardization**	**Deeper than standard**

Source: Pacific Alliance (2014) and Intrade (2017)

3.7.3 Trade Facilitation

The WTO defines trade facilitation as the "simplification and harmonization of commercial procedures, including activities, practices and formalities required in the collection, presentation, and communication processes that are necessary for the movement of goods across borders" (World Trade Organization 2011). This notion includes five basic principles for trade facilitation: transparency, simplification, harmonization, cooperation and standardization. According to these principles, the baseline for classifying agreements as "deeper than standard", is that they have customs procedures and trade facilitation chapters that include these five principles, as well as relevant measures for their implementation. The chapters that cover three or four principles and measures for their implementation are classified as "standard".

The PA's agreements offer substantial advances on trade facilitation and customs cooperation. Commitments include: sharing of information between the customs authorities; expediting customs clearance; the implementation of international norms and information automatization; simplifying customs procedures; mutual recognition of authorized economic operators; and Single Window interoperability (Table 3.10).

3.7.4 Intellectual Property

Intellectual Property Rights are exclusive rights that allow their holders to exclude others from using protected technology or property. IPRs are customarily divided into two main areas: (i) Copyright and rights related to copyright, and (ii) Industrial property. The Agreement on Trade-Related Aspects of Intellectual Property Rights (TRIPS) in force since 1995 is the reference most often used when establishing

Table 3.11 Depth and coverage of provisions on intellectual property in the Pacific Alliance and in earlier agreements between its members

Countries	Covered provisions	Coverage
Chile–Colombia	Not included	
Chile–Mexico	TRIPS	Standard
Chile–Peru	TRIPS	Standard
Colombia–Peru	TRIPS	Standard
Colombia–Mexico	TRIPS	Standard
Mexico–Peru	Not included	
Pacific Alliance	**Copyrights, industrial property rights, and other trade-related aspects of IP**	**Undefined**[a]

Source: Intrade (2017) and Pacific Alliance (2015)
[a]Since the IP provisions are still being negotiated, it is not possible to assess the depth of the provisions agreed between the PA's members

depth and coverage levels of provisions on IPRs in FTAs. The TRIPS defines a series of minimum standards of protection, sets a number of provisions dealing with procedures and remedies for the enforcement of IPRs, and for dispute settlement (WTO 2017). Intellectual property provisions that go beyond those included in TRIPS are known as TRIPS+. If the agreement includes further protection standards, extended scope and duration, or requires more extensive registration and enforcement procedures, it could be labelled as TRIPS+. Consequently, based on Wignaraja et al. (2012) an agreement is "deeper than standard" if it contains one or more TRIPS+ provisions; and it is considered as "standard" when its scope and protection are limited to TRIPS provisions (Table 3.11).

Chapters on intellectual property (IP) are included in some of the agreements previously negotiated among the PA's members. This chapters are not very comprehensive and often times do not go beyond TRIPS provisions. However, there have been limited advances on IPR-related topics within the PA. The first stage was the establishment of an Intellectual Property Working Group in the Cadiz Declaration in 2012.

As reflected in the 2013 Declaration of Cali, PA members agreed to establish a working group responsible for the negotiation of IPR provisions. This group aims to "prepare and implement a work plan with joint and specific cooperative actions between intellectual property offices, in order to share experiences and extend the collaborative and communication links between them, in order to achieve a better use of the IP system for the benefit of its users" (Pacific Alliance 2013).

Member economies' intellectual property offices have been meeting since 2013, and during the Punta Arenas meeting in October 2015, the Chilean National Industrial Property Institute (INAPI), the Peruvian National Institute for the Defence of Competition and the Protection of Intellectual Property (INDECOPI), the Superintendence of Industry and Commerce of Colombia (SIC) and the Mexican Institute of Industrial Property signed the "Joint Declaration of the IP Offices of the Pacific Alliance" where they agreed to find avenues to accelerate patent processes and to collaborate on the three main aspects: (i) the facilitation of fast, accessible and high quality patent examination procedures that would reduce patent office backlogs; (ii) harmonization and simplification of trademark prosecution procedures; (iii) the creation of a platform for information sharing (Pacific Alliance 2015).

One of the most important achievements resulting from the cooperation among the IP offices is the signature of an agreement on the establishment of a Patent Prosecution Highway (PPH). The PPH is a programme for, "harmonizing and simplifying the trademark registration process, and establishing a technological platform that serves as a pilot program for the information dissemination and technology transfer" (del Carmen Vasquez Callo and Pérez-Restrepo 2016). This would imply a reduction of the cost of patent applications, allowing SMEs and educational institutions to become more involved in the process. However, as noted in del Carmen Vasquez Callo and Pérez-Restrepo (2016), the Joint Declaration promotes cooperation only in the areas of patent and trademark protection, and substantial issues such as copyrights, protection of trade secrets and traditional knowledge have yet to be discussed among PA members.

3.8 Findings

The PA is different from previous liberalization processes in Latin America in the sense that it adopts a pragmatic approach and its members pursue similar economic policies. This group's rapid evolution and the fact that it is maintaining its momentum despite changes in the governments of Peru, Mexico and Chile, are evidence of its importance as a long-term national policy for its member economies. This chapter has assessed the depth of the commitments made within the PA compared with the bilateral FTAs previously negotiated among its members. Using the WTO framework and a series of criteria proposed in the literature as baselines, this assessment provides grounds for concluding that the PA is a new-generation agreement with both WTO+ and WTOx provisions.

The agreement is deemed WTO+ in areas such as trade in goods and services liberalization, trade facilitation, IPRs and public procurement, which, although negotiated within the WTO framework, are more thoroughly covered in the PAAP and other PA declarations. This group's achievements in other areas such as competition, investment, movement of capital, and the environment (not covered in this chapter) could be considered WTOx, as they produced a regional framework that goes beyond any commitments made in the framework of the WTO agreements.

The existence of previous trade agreements (both FTAs and RTAs) among the PA's members has contributed to the rapid evolution of the group. However, the PA has done more than bring together these earlier agreements within a common framework. This group's added value lies in its capacity to further liberalize and integrate by enhancing access to markets for goods and services, strengthening FDI provisions, and including a series of disciplines that were not covered in most of the previous agreements.

The PA has achieved immediate trade liberalization in over 90% of tariff lines negotiated among member economies and, as such, it can be considered a "deep" agreement. Most of the liberalization had already been accomplished through previous bilateral agreements among PA members. However, in the mid-term (time periods of more than 10 years) the PA's liberalization will be much more comprehensive than before. As well as tariff barriers, member economies must continue working to remove non-tariff barriers that are still high, in particular in the agricultural sector and other protected industries. This includes the implementation of agreed measures towards the full harmonisation of SPS –still not achieved- and promote regulatory cooperation among member economies.

Regarding services liberalization, the PA commitments can be considered as "deep", as they offer substantial benefits compared to the previous agreements. The PA liberalises all strategic sectors: professional and business services, telecommunications, financial services, transportation and mobility of business people, beyond WTO commitments. These objectives represent important progress compared to previous FTAs, which often had restrictions on areas such as telecommunications and financial services. However, it is important to remember that the PA still limits labour mobility.

Likewise, in terms of FDI, the PA has a "deeper than standard" regulatory framework, since it offers favourable conditions for market access as well as investment protection beyond that in previous agreements, and strengthens them through the creation of a Joint Commission on Services and Investment. This puts the PA on the path to becoming a WTOx-type agreement and is in line with its members' participation in TISA negotiations. As the PA evolves, its members should consider establishing an investment-specific protocol, independent from the mechanisms established within the PAAP.

The PA includes a series of new-generation areas such as trade facilitation, government procurement and competition, among others. Although these areas were to some extent included in the bilateral agreements, the PA is aiming to harmonize commitments between the parties. One of the issues that demands special attention is the establishment of a mechanism that allows the accumulation of rules of origin, which will be instrumental in strengthening regional value chains. Similarly, the PA has established one of the most substantial regional agreements regarding in areas such as government procurement, support for SMEs, and regulatory coherence. The work on IPRs is still limited; however, the introduction of the PPH is a fundamental step towards regional cooperation in this matter, and could bring substantial benefits to its members as it allows for faster, more affordable and region-wide patent recognition, which could potentially benefit SMEs and research institutions across the PA region, and not only multinational companies.

The consolidation of the PA as comprehensive agreement including both WTO+ and WTOx commitments, would profile this group as a leading force in regional economic integration in the Asia-Pacific region. This is likely to be particularly important in light of the uncertainty surrounding the Trans-Pacific Partnership agreement (TPP) since Trump's administration in the United States of America decided to withdraw from said agreement.

Despite all its achievements, the PA is still a work in progress and some of the measures that make it a deep agreement are yet to be implemented. The PA is a living agreement, so as the progress continues, regional leaders will also need to assess the necessity to further institutionalize the PA, and include new disciplines as new needs emerge. As the PA advances towards the implementation of its commitments including the PAAP, it will be necessary to conduct further research that assesses its effectiveness in terms of trade flow creation, investment and the generation of new regional value chains.

References

Baier, S., Bergstrand, J., & Feng, M. (2014). Economic integration agreements and the margins of international trade. *Journal of International Economics, 93*, 339–350.

Baldwin, R. (2011). *21st century regionalism: Filling the gap between 21st century trade and 20th century trade rules. Centre for economic policy and research.* http://www.cepr.org/sites/default/files/policy_insights/PolicyInsight56.pdfEconomic. Accessed 27 Mar 2017.

CEAP (The Pacific Alliance Business Council). (2014). *Declaración del Concejo empresarial de la Alianza del Pacífico junio de 2014.* www.acuerdoscomerciales.gob.pe/images/stories/alianza/espanol/declaracion_ceap__junio_2014.pdf. Accessed 30 Jan 2015.

del Carmen Vasquez Callo, M., & Pérez-Restrepo, C. (2016). Patent cooperation mechanisms in the Pacific Alliance: An initial assessment of the effectiveness of the Patent Prosecution Highway for intra-regional trade integration. *World Trade Institute Working Paper* No 16/2016. https://www.wti.org/media/filer_public/18/ca/18cab13c-a98f-44f1-8361-23c249d12e59/working_paper_no_16_2016_vasquez_and_perez.pdf. Accessed 27 Mar 2017.

Dür, A., Baccini, L., & Elsig, M. (2014). The design of international trade agreements: Introducing a new dataset. *The Review of International Organizations, 9*, 353–375. https://doi.org/10.1007/s11558-013-9179-8.

Estevadeordal, A., Suominen, K., & Teh, R. (2009). *Regional rules in the global trading system.* New York: Cambridge University Press.

Frankel, J. (1997). *Regional trading blocs in the world economic system.* Washington, DC: Institute for International Economics.

Hicks, R., & Kim, S. Y. (2012). Reciprocal trade agreements in Asia: credible commitment to trade liberalization or paper tigers? *Journal of East Asian Studies, 12*, 1–29.

Intrade. (2017). *Indexed FTA test.* https://www.intradebid.org/intrade/app/web/herramientas/indexed-texts Accessed 27 Mar 2017.

Pacific Alliance. (2012). *Acuerdo Marco de la Alianza del Pacífico.* https://alianzapacifico.net/?wpdmdl=4464. Accessed 30 Jan 2015.

Pacific Alliance. (2013). *Declaración de Cali.* https://alianzapacifico.net/download/3-6-declaracion-de-cali/. Accessed 27 Mar 2017.

Pacific Alliance. (2014). *Protocolo Adicional al Acuerdo Marco de la Alianza del Pacífico.* alianzapacifico.net/documents/2014/PROTOCOLO_COMPLETO.pdf. Accessed 30 Jan 2015.

Pacific Alliance. (2015). *Declaración Conjunta de las Oficinas de Propiedad Intelectual de la Alianza del Pacífico.* https://alianzapacifico.net/declaracion-conjunta-de-las-oficinas-de-propiedad-intelectual-de-la-alianza-del-pacifico/. Accessed 27 Mar 2017.

World Trade Organisation. (2017). *Overview: The TRIPS agreement.* https://www.wto.org/english/tratop_e/trips_e/intel2_e.htm. Accessed 27 Mar 2017.

Wignaraja, G, Ramizo, D., & Burmeister, L. (2012). Asia-Latin America free trade agreements: An instrument for inter-regional liberalization and integration? *ADBI Working Paper* 382. Tokyo: Asian Development Bank Institute. http://www.adbi.org/workingpaper/2012/09/24/5238.asia.latin.america.free.trade.agreements/. Accessed 30 Jan 2015.

World Trade Organization. (2011). *World trade report* 2011. *The WTO and preferential trade agreements: From coexistence to coherence.* https://www.wto.org/english/res_e/booksp_e/anrep_e/world_trade_report11_e.pdf. Accessed 30 Jan 2015.

Chapter 4
The Pacific Alliance As an Instrument for Insertion into Global Value Chains: Lessons from a Progressive and Pragmatic Approach

Iza Lejárraga

4.1 The Pacific Alliance in an Evolving Landscape

In a global political economy in which regional integration efforts struggle to consolidate recent advances, the Pacific Alliance (PA or 'the Alliance') stands out as a role model. Paradoxically, this integration initiative, which has received relatively less attention than other trade blocs, may hold constructive lessons for 'twenty-first century' trade governance. Born out of a presidential initiative that Chile, Colombia, Mexico and Peru launched with the Lima Declaration in 2011, followed with a Framework Agreement signed in 2012, the four "Pumas of the Pacific" have come a long way in materialising their objectives. Taken together, the four Pacific Pumas represent the world's eight largest economy and its seventh largest exporter. The economic size of its market does not make the Alliance part of the league of 'mega-regionals' such as the Comprehensive and Progressive Transpacific Partnership (CPTPP) or the Regional Comprehensive Economic Partnership (RCEP). It has attracted over 50 observer governments worldwide with whom it is forging ties, including the United Stated, Japan, Canada, Germany, China, India and others which are entitled to participate in meetings, albeit without a vote. The Alliance envisions the accession of new countries, with Costa Rica and Panama as candidate members. Regardless of its economic clout, however, the significance of the Alliance lies in the lessons that it can bring to ongoing and future initiatives, both at regional and potentially multilateral levels. That this Initiative is among relatively less

The opinions expressed and arguments employed herein are those of the author and do not necessarily reflect the official views of the OECD or of the governments of its member countries.

I. Lejárraga (✉)
Investment Division, Directorate for Financial and Enterprise Affairs, Organisation for Economic Cooperation and Development (OECD), Paris, France
e-mail: Iza.LEJARRAGA@oecd.org

P. Sauvé et al. (eds.), *The Pacific Alliance in a World of Preferential Trade Agreements*, United Nations University Series on Regionalism 16,
https://doi.org/10.1007/978-3-319-78464-9_4

advanced countries is an example of the new preparedness and leadership emerging economies are playing in forging deep integration schemes.

One of the remarkable features of the Pacific Alliance approach to integration is that they did not wait to have a formal, comprehensive agreement in order to start moving towards their objective. In a relatively short period since the Alliance was launched, countries took a pragmatic approach and started to agree on an implement several economic integration objectives, achieving far-reaching advancement in challenging areas such as the visa-free travel, joint embassies abroad, or a common stock exchange (an integrated Latin American Market – "MILA"). These results already started to be harvested before the conclusion of a comprehensive agreement – the Additional Protocol of the Framework Agreement – which was signed in 2014, and entered into force in 2016. In contrast to the regular approach in trade negotiations that nothings is agreed to until everything is agreed to (the so-called single under-taking approach), Alliance countries moved on a piece-meal fashion and agreed to implement specific items before the comprehensive package was agreed to. While the long-term sustainability of a project-oriented focus that is not underpinned by legal and institutional provisions can be questioned, this pragmatic "early harvest" approach allowed countries to implement reforms in an unprecedented timeframe.

Another distinguishing feature of the Pacific Alliance is how it conceived itself as an instrument of insertion Global Value Chains (GVCs), particularly those in Asia. While there is widespread consensus that the expansion of GVCs over the past two decades has changed the paradigm and patterns world trade, there has been very limited discussion as to what this implies for the design and architecture of trade agreements. The NAFTA can be considered the first GVC-inspired agreement in the sense that it introduced new disciplines that were important to sustain the North American value chains, particularly in the automobiles sector. The Transpacific Partnership was perhaps the next effort to translate GVCs into the agreements, although the signed text did not go as far as initially envisaged. This is already clearly framed in its comprehensive approach to integration, namely to "liberalize trade in goods and services, open foreign investment, integrate securities markets, and allow free movement of people." In effect, when not only goods but whole factories cross borders in production fragmentation processes critical factors of production such as labour and capital need to move. Moreover, firms also move knowledge and intangible assets that need to be protected. Although it is clear that this is what the cross-border business operations call for in GVCs, few agreements have articulated such an integrated strategy in their international integration objectives. The Pacific Alliance may be one of the most comprehensive expressions of a GVC-enabling agreement, particularly with regards to the movement of capital and labour.

A landmark of the Alliance comes from the role the private sector has played as an active agent in the integration process, which has contributed to its progressive and pragmatic approach. From the outset, there has been an institutionalized strategy to engage the business community in the process of discussions and negotiations. In particular the Pacific Alliance Business Council (*Consejo Empresarial de la Alianza del Pacífico* –CEAP) has been constructive and instrumental in recommending measures to strengthen the business sector of PA countries. Active private sector engagement has helped nurture a pragmatic and comprehensive approach, and added elements to the agenda which are not generally found in standard trade agreements, but important for business. These include production linkages, utilization of public procurement opportunities, interconnectivity of single windows, improvement of logistics, standards harmonization, financial market integration, tax harmonization, and best practices in education policy and innovation. The private sector has been a key provider of information on key obstacles and costs to business, and this has been channelled to the negotiating agenda thanks to the close coordination and dialogue that exists between private and public entities.

While the trajectory of the Alliance is laudable, an evolving landscape also intensifies potential limitations of its strategic orientation. A core objective of the Alliance has been to become a platform for economic integration with the rest of the world, especially the Asia-Pacific region. In its pursuit of strengthening trade ties with Asia, it has relayed to a second pursuit trade ties among its own members and neighbourhood, partly due to long standing political differences. The uncertainty surrounding TPP and NAFTA, and the important changes in its neighbourhood particularly with regards to Argentina – which became the newest Observer of the PA – may encourage a different direction moving forward. In any case, it opens new opportunities to address its limitation as a regional block. After all, some PA markets are distant from each other have very low levels of pre-existing trade, hovering around 5%. In this sense, the Alliance hardly qualifies as a natural trading bloc, and as such, is one that can generate greater levels of trade diversion than trade creation. Moreover, global value chains hinge on an important intra-regional supply structure, as reflected in the high level of intra-regional trade –particularly in intermediates – in Asia, North America and Europe. Although this has not been feasible due to the political orientation of PA neighbours, particularly the MERCOSUR bloc, recent changes can suggest a much-needed redrawing of the integration map on South America.

Against this backdrop, the rest of the chapter takes stock of key achievements of the Pacific Alliance as a GVC-enabling arrangement. While it is widely recognised that GVCs have changed the paradigm of world trade, there is less understanding of what this implies in terms of updating trade agreements. Lessons from recent novel approaches such as the Pacific Alliance deserve to be harvested to help inform future paths in design and implementation of GVC-guided integration. The next section reviews the evidence on the role that regional integration plays in participation in Global Value Chains. The second section identifies a set of key achievements of the PA which are consistent with the functioning of GVCs, pointing also to potential areas of improvement. The final section offers concluding remarks, highlighting the need for re-balancing intra- and inter-regional objectives to strengthen insertion into GVCs.

4.2 The Relationship Between Regional Integration and Global Value Chains

One of the objectives of the Alliance has been to become a platform for stronger insertion with Asia in particular, and the rest of the world more generally. Yet, the strategy of insertion into Global Value Chains may depend on its effectiveness in strengthening intra-regional trade to build up regional value chains. After all, the notions of "factory North America," "factory Asia," and "factory East Europe" tend to suggest that there is an important regional eco-system that underpins the formation and expansion of GVCs. Some authors argue that 'global' is a misnomer given the strong regional character of GVCs. As Baldwin has put it "[the] supply chain is not global—it is regional" (Baldwin and López-Gonzalez 2013). Supply chains across the world hinge on regional supply networks that provide a hub for procurement and manufacturing operations. In this context, strengthening intra-regional trade, particularly with respect to intermediate goods and services, is an essential part of the GVC insertion equation.

Regional value chains are found to be particularly important for participation in the global fragmentation of manufacturing processes (Baldwin and Lopez-Gonzalez 2013). The level of intra-regional trade of parts and components tends to be higher than the level of inter-regional trade. Intra-industry trade in a particular sector tends to be associated with greater insertion into the value chain. New data on trade in value-added shows that a higher share of foreign value-added comes from countries that are geographically close (Miroudot 2015). In manufacturing, lead time is of critical importance, particularly in just-in-time production methods that do not draw on large inventory stocks. The existence of an extensive and reliable supply infrastructure at the regional level is one of the key factors driving multinational decisions to locate production in a given region. The regional dimension is less important in natural resources, where commodity chains span across distant regions. Services value chains are also inherently more global in character, particularly those that are digitally enabled and where transport costs and sensitivity to distance is less important. Yet, for manufacturing the regional context matters. If the Pacific Alliance wants to be an economic actor in industrial chains, increasing intra-regional trade in parts and components as well as services will be important. At the moment, the integration of the Pacific Alliance into GVCs is determined by the role that Mexico plays with North America, China Japan, and to a less extent, that of Colombia. The Pacific Alliance factory has yet to emerge on a regional scale.

Arguably, there is a two-way relationship between the emergence of regional trade agreements (RTAs) and GVCs, which recent literature has tried to disentangle. An open question is whether trading partners involved in production sharing tend to form deep integration agreements, or whether higher degrees of regional integration lead to participation in GVCs, or whether existing production networks have deepened integration patterns. Although the direction of causality is difficult to discern, a number of studies tend to support the conclusion that RTAs have given rise to supply networks. In the case of North America, there is evidence that before the enactment of the US-Canada free trade agreement, trade in auto-parts was virtually non-existent. Such trade morphed into a growing value chain only after the agreement was signed and barriers to trade and investment were reduced (Hummels et al. 1998). Similarly, after the expansion of the EU in 2004, there is evidence that new members became much more integrated into the supply chains of older members (Curran and Zignago 2012). In an empirical study using firm-level data, Blyde (2014) show that economic integration agreements have a positive and significant impact on the number of vertically-linked subsidiaries hosted by partner countries. The authors conclude that reverse causality in this two-way relationship is unlikely, and that regional integration initiatives are likely driving the expansion of GVCs.

An important insight from the literature is that the inclusion of deep integration commitments in RTAs are critical for the emergence of production sharing models. Lawrence (1996) coined the terms of shallow and deep integration, in order to distinguish between the mere removal of tariffs and other traditional barriers to trade, and deeper forms of integration involving services, investment, intellectual property rights, standards and regulatory co-operation. In effect, establishing production does not just require market access and trade facilitation for sourcing and selling, but also the protection of valuable assets that firms use in the production process transferred abroad. In more knowledge-intensive production processes, more sophisticated rules may be called for to protect proprietary knowledge. The establishment of overseas production bases or the signing of long term contracts with foreign suppliers increases the exposure of multinational firms to the potentially unfavourable legal, political and regulatory treatment of foreign governments. Hence the increasing recognition of the need for sound regulatory and enforcement regimes. The more knowledge-intensive the production process is, the more sophisticated the institutional arrangements will need to be to protect such assets.

Not all RTAs are created equal, and not all of them yield similar effects. Several studies have aimed to unpack RTA heterogeneity and analyse the depth of commitments. Horn et al. (2010) provides a classification of deep commitment in RTAs, covering over 52 types of measures. The depth of agreements is determined based on whether its measures are WTO-plus (stronger commitments than corresponding obligations in WTO) or WTO-beyond (disciplines contained in RTAs that are not covered in existing WTO agreements, such as anti-corruption or competition policy). The 2011 World Trade Report extended this classification and found empirical evidence for the notion that RTAs with higher levels of WTO-plus and –beyond commitments see higher levels of intra-industry trade in parts and components (WTO 2011). Damuri (2012) measured the depth of RTAs in four degrees, whether they include border provisions related to tariff, border and non-tariff measures, behind-the border provisions dealing with protection and behind the border provisions dealing with market access. He finds that RTAs that cover these four dimensions have the strongest participation in Global Value Chains

Building on these classifications, a stream of empirical work has similarly found evidence that 'deep' regional integration is associated with the emergence and evolution of GVCs. Orecife and Rocha (2014) examine the linkages between regional integration commitments and production methods, and find a positive effect between the depth of an RTA and the participation of countries in global production networks. A revealing finding is that the empirical relationship holds in capital-intensive industries, such as automobiles and ICT sectors, and less in other sectors such as textiles (Orecife and Rocha 2014). Their analysis also confirms that deep integration agreements are among advanced economies or between advanced and developing countries, while less developing countries tend to enter into shallower agreements. Blyde (2014) finds customs unions, common markets or economic unions that allow for the free movement of production factors including capital and labour have the highest effects on GVCs. In addition, RTAs with deep integration disciplines are also found to have significant and positive effects. The effects of RTAs have not just been measured by GVC-related trade (notably, trade in intermediates), but also by FDI flows. Both Blyde (2014) and Osnago et al. (2015) find a positive relationship between the depth of RTAs and increases in vertical FDI flows, generally associated with multinationals slicing parts of their production abroad.

While deep integration agreements provide the legal bridges for factories to cross borders, the physical and digital need to also be in place. In effect, de jure integration can only be de facto integration with the infrastructure. In effect, one of the most robust and economically meaningful findings from the literature relates to the importance of infrastructure connectivity as a determinant of the expansion for Global Value Chains (OECD/WTO 2015; Blyde 2014). Gravity models have consistently shown the importance of distance in trade flows, and this appears to hold with more force in GVCs. Geographically dispersed production has increased the importance of rapid, low-cost and predictable connectivity. Delays in transport translate into costly disruptions across the whole supply chain. Lead time is often cited as one of the major factors why firms locate production in a given country or region. Bergstrand and Egger (2010) for instance show that distance influences patterns of trade in intermediates as well as vertically integrated FDI, confirming the relevance of gravity variables for GVC analysis. Recent empirical work shows that GVC-related trade is more sensitive to the quality of transport and ICT infrastructure than overall trade (OECD/WTO 2013). In a similar vein, countries with better infrastructure and logistics have been seen to attract more vertical affiliates, and the magnitude of this effect increases with distance (Blyde 2014). Hence, this is an important factor for the Pacific Alliance bloc which is formed by countries that have large geographic distances.

Although this literature has provided a convincing basis for the benefits of deep integration, there is still a lot of heterogeneity that needs to be unpacked. Not all deep integration measures have the same objectives or importance, and one would not expect that they would have the same effects. Moreover, the coverage of a measure does not suggest whether it leads to a higher degree of liberalisation or more predictable regulatory environment. Finally, the literature focuses on the classification of RTAs based on the depth of commitments, without looking at the linkages and level of coherence across complementary measures. Arguably, given the interdependence of trade, investment, services, competition, and IPRs, one could expect that the level of coordination and coherence across complementary measures may be as important as the depth of commitments. Baldwin (2011) points out these inter-dependencies as a principal feature of twenty-first century trade, where he identifies a strong trade-investment-service-knowledge nexus given the intertwining of international trade, cross-border investment, and intensive use of infrastructure services. In this context, efforts to achieve well-integrated and not just deeper strategies of integration may be called for.

4.3 Stock-Taking of the Pacific Alliance from a Global Value Chain Perspective

While the past years have seen important advances in the measurement and mapping of GVCs, this research has yet to translate into a comprehensive set of implications for the design of trade agreements. To some extent, GVCs follow the same tenets of classical trade theory, and hence many policy implications are likely to be the same (Lejárraga 2017). Yet, some policy measure may acquire greater importance in the context of GVCs, while new policy efforts that were not previously essential in a context of trade in final goods become key conditions for a GVC-enabling environment. From a GVCs perspective, trade agreements should go beyond a narrower market access optic to a focus on market presence for 'factories' or segments of a production fragmentation process. For the Pacific Alliance to become an effective instrument of insertion into the global economy, it should be as much about improved market access as about creating a regional economy for "factories" that bring jobs, technology and trade.

Although there is no recipe for a GVCs-guided agreement, several elements are consistent with our understanding of the drivers and conditions for international production sharing processes: international mobility of production factors and assets, market access for sourcing and selling, and physical and digital connectivity (Fig. 4.1). First, GVCs require the mobility of production factors and firm-specific assets, counter to the standard assumption in classical trade theory that factors move freely within countries, but are immobile across borders.[1] Establishing a production process abroad entails more than the movement of goods across borders. GVCs require that capital and profits, services, knowledge, technology, management and skills spread across geographies. Services are an input into production and make up a significant part of the final value of goods, a process often referred to as "servicification". Knowledge and information-intensive activities, such as research and development and data, are also increasingly transferred abroad as part of a supply chain. These cross-border flows often entail higher risks for the firm that require more sophisticated regulatory frameworks.

Once a 'factory' is established abroad, firms need market access and market connectivity to operate their global supply chain from a regional location. Firms

[1] The implications of international factor mobility have been addressed in some trade models. As a classical reference, Mundell (1957) introduces international factor mobility and considers it a substitute for international trade in goods and services.

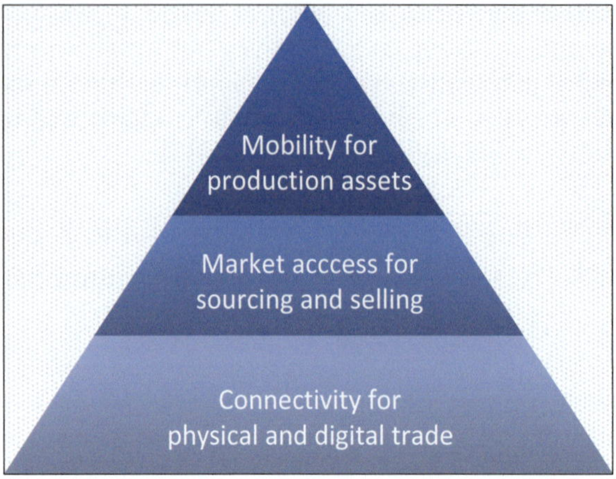

Fig. 4.1 GVCs-Enabling Pyramid for RTAs. (Source: Author illustration)

engaged in GVCs need to be able to undertake global sourcing and selling, regardless of the region in which they establish their production chain. For production to take place firms need to import intermediates and capital goods, and need to re-export semi-processed or processed goods to other producers or consumers in foreign markets. Unlike market-seeking motives for FDI, where investment is a substitute for trade (i.e., tariff-jumping), in GVCs trade and FDI tend to be complementary strategies. Finally, as evidenced in the literature, one of the main determinants of GVCs is the level of physical and digital connectivity, both in terms of hard and soft infrastructure. Improvements in market access are to no avail if there is inadequate market connectivity.

The section below takes stock of these elements of a GVC-enabling pyramid (Fig. 4.1). It looks at the policy initiatives of the Pacific Alliance in these areas and compares their performance with other major regional groupings in Asia, Latin America, Europe, and Africa. Of course, the elements reviewed should not be seen as an exhaustive set of conditions for GVCs. There are obviously other important factors, from technological development to contract enforcement, which are beyond the scope of this analysis. These are however core areas that require international co-operation and are addressed in many regional integration schemes.

4.4 International Mobility of Production Factors in GVCs

If the cross-border movement of production factors is a cornerstone of a GVC-enabling trade agreement, the Pacific Alliance embodies this more than most modern RTAs. Indeed, the comprehensive integration approach of the Alliance is clearly reflected in its objective to "liberalize trade in goods and services, open foreign investment, integrate securities markets, and allow free movement of people." The notion that all of these need to be addressed in tandem is indeed a reflection of the GVCs "nexus", a term coined by Baldwin (2011) to suggest how trade, services, investment and knowledge are inter-twined and need to be addressed in a comprehensive, coordinated, and coherent manner. The nexus highlights that there are inter-dependencies between the movement of factors and therefore should be addressed jointly under a rule-making umbrella. The integration agenda is not about deepening a given discipline, but about addressing complementarities and interactions in cross-border activities in GVCs.

The Pacific Alliance has made remarkable strides in the free circulation of production factors, achieving important outcomes particularly with respect to capital and labour. A major landmark of the PA has been the merger of regional stock exchanges to promote financial integration. In 2011, Chile, Colombia, and Peru integrated their stock exchanges through the formation of the Latin American Integrated Market (MILA); Mexico then became a member and carried out its first operation in 2014. The MILA represents the first private initiative in Latin America to create an integrated financial market, offering a more liquid market to investors, and allowing them to find better risk and yield options within associated markets. Although there is still a complex agenda ahead to achieve full regulatory harmonization, the financial market "coming together" of four of Latin America's best-performing economies can boost competitiveness and international visibility, whilst also offering the attractiveness of a single entry point to four distinct markets. Closely related to the movement of capital and services, PA countries have also been co-operating on a wide network of treaties to avoid double taxation in order to channel their investments more efficiently from a fiscal perspective. Overall, as seen in Fig. 4.2, the Pacific Alliance provides a very open regime for investment, which is being complemented with regional investment promotion efforts that are being undertaken by the four countries, leading to joint representations in several foreign countries.

Another key area where the Alliance has made marked progress relates to movement of business people and the facilitation of migratory transit. Within a short period of time, the Pacific Alliance countries agreed to and implemented the elimination of tourism and business visas within the region for stays of less than 183 days, and significantly simplified procedures. They also facilitated the granting of temporary work permits for specific categories of workers, such as engineers and pilots. In addition, the PA has established a series of intra-regional co-operation programs to facilitate worker training, as well as programs of student exchanges. As an example of these initiatives, the Vacations and Work Agreement allows young citizens from Pacific Alliance countries to visit any other PA country for recreational and tourism purposes for up to 360 days, allowing them to receive partial payment for work during this period. The PA has also created a student and academic movement platform, providing scholarships to promote skills development, research and innovation. In addition, it has engaged in a series of co-operation on educational policies and professional training programs. Skills development and worker mobility are mutually reinforcing and critical components for strengthening the supply chain network

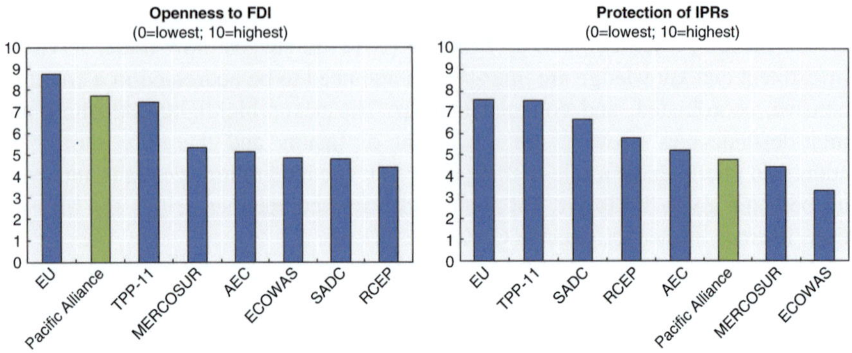

Fig. 4.2 Openness to FDI/Protection of IPRs. (Source: Calculations from Index of Economic Freedom from Heritage Foundation (2016) and Protection of IPR Protection Index from World Economic Forum (2016). Calculations for regional groupings are based on weighed GDP averages of individual country indicators)

within the PA region. Given the limited progress in co-operation in the movement of business persons in many RTAs, the PA is an instructive example.

One area that has received relatively less prominence in PA co-operation relates to the protection of intellectual property rights, which is important for GVCs-related investments in which technology and knowledge are transferred across borders. As Fig. 4.2 shows, this is precisely an area where the Pacific Alliance appears to be lagging behind relative to other regional blocs. Therefore, it is noteworthy that aspects of the protection of intellectual property rights which are typically contained in modern RTAs are not comprehensively addressed in the Additional Protocol of the Framework Agreement. In effect, this is the only element of the so-called 'trade-services-investment-IP' nexus of GVCs that is not further strengthened in the Additional Protocol. That the Additional Protocol does not include obligations on IPR does not mean that Alliance countries are not addressing this matter. In effect, all countries of the Pacific Alliance have signed RTAs that have included far-reaching commitments on intellectual property rights. Moreover, countries have established a working group under the Alliance to discuss co-operation on IPR matters. Nonetheless, this may be an area where the PA may need to intensify efforts in order to become a GVCs platform. This may become more important with the advent of new production methods, which will render differences in wages across countries less important, and other determinants related to the technological needs of future production more critical. The bar will be higher for countries to attract GVCs-related investments, and the level of IPR protection and technological development can become a competitive edge (Fig. 4.2).

4.5 Market Access for Global Sourcing and Selling in GVCs

For RTAs to promote the emergence and expansion of GVCs, they need to facilitate global sourcing and selling strategies of MNEs and their associated suppliers. Investors slicing parts of their production abroad in the Pacific Alliance region will need to be able to source from the most efficient suppliers worldwide, and not just from within countries of the PA region. Moreover, investors are not only considering lower cost sourcing, but also higher quality sourcing which may not be available within PA countries. Many lead firms have well-established sourcing networks globally, and the implication of re-structuring their supply strategies and configurations in each location can be costly, discouraging them to invest in the region. Hence, for supply chain networks to operate efficiently, barriers to global sourcing should be reduced or dismantled, including tariffs, rules of origin, and other non-tariff barriers affecting the formation of GVCs. The negative impact of such policies are higher than for overall trade, because fragmented production processes require that parts, components and partially manufactured sub-assemblies cross borders several times, whereas final goods often just cross borders once. In addition, most of the value-added generated in the country is re-exported in some form within a GVC. This implies that barriers to imports become a direct tax for exporters as well.

The liberalisation of trade barriers has been at the core of the Pacific Alliance. Countries have committed to full tariff elimination, with 92% of merchandise trade to be duty-free immediately, and the remaining 8% to be fully liberalized within a transition period capped at 17 years for sensitive products. The tariffs and tariff peaks that remain are largely on agriculture products, and should be phased out quickly to stimulate the emergence of value chains on primary products and agro-processing, where all PA countries have a comparative advantage. There is also some tariff escalation that could be removed, particularly in food and mining, where countries of the Pacific Alliance can develop regional value chains. Tariffs have been liberalised in the automotive sector, building on previous efforts within the Group of Three and the Andean Community, which are seeing the growth of intra-regional trade in car parts and components among PA countries. Yet, to fully take advantage of the liberalisation of intra-regional trade, perhaps the most important agenda relates to improving customs procedures. As Fig. 4.3 shows, based on the Logistics Performance Index, the Pacific Alliance lags behind other regional groups in the efficiency of customs procedures. The PA's Additional Protocol contains a chapter on trade facilitation and customs co-operation which is aligned with international best practice. It provides for electronic certificates of origin, inter-operability of single windows, and measures for the mutual recognition of authorized economic operators.

A critical GVC-enabling ingredient in RTAs is the treatment of rules of origin, which can give rise to "sourcing diversion" from the most efficient suppliers. There is ample evidence of the negative effects of preferential rules of origin in Latin

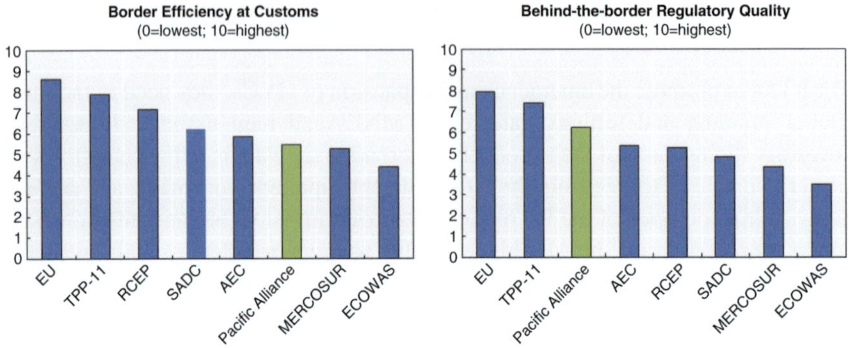

Fig. 4.3 Border Efficiency and Behind the Border Regulatory Quality. (Source: Border efficiency is proxied with the customs efficiency and border control management of the World Bank Logistics Index (2016). Regulatory Quality is obtained from the World Bank Governance Indicators (2016). Calculations for regional groupings are based on weighed GDP averages of individual country indicators)

America (Estevadeordal 2012). The spider's web of overlapping agreements in Latin America has complicated the development of production networks due to "spaghetti bowl effects" and the uncertainty created by overlapping or inconsistent rules governing operations. The Pacific Alliance has improved this spaghetti bowl by harmonizing rules of origin, so that it is the same for all products across the Alliance. In addition, PA members have introduced horizontal cumulation of origin, which will allow firms to add up the materials and inputs for any given good from across the Pacific Alliance. Through this process, the PA countries should be more readily able to share production to jointly comply with region-wide rules of origin. However, these benefits only accrue to the contents sourced from the four countries of the PA, whereas investors will need to source more globally. One direction the Pacific Alliance could take to enhance this effect would be to provide third-party MFN treatment to expand cumulation to countries with which Pacific Alliance members have preferential trade agreements. This would allow firms established in the PA to take advantage of the differences in prices across a broader range of relevant input markets, stimulating more cross-border production sharing across regions and not just within the Pacific Alliance.

In addition to border barriers, the quality of the behind-the-border regulatory regime is an important agenda from a GVCs-enabling perspective. Regulatory divergences, while sometimes necessary to meet different public policy objectives in heterogeneous settings, can create costs for producers and fragment global value chains. Several new agreements that the Pacific Alliance countries are parties to have been at the fore-front of regulatory co-operation efforts. This is the case of the Mexico-Central America Free Trade Agreement, which was one of the first RTAs to include measures on regulatory co-operation. Moreover, the Comprehensive and Progressive Trans-Pacific Partnership Agreement (CPTPP) expanded these commitments into a full-fledged chapter on regulatory coherence. In the Pacific Alliance, a work plan on regulatory co-operation has preceded the signing of the Additional Protocol. A "Regulatory Cooperation Pathway" was established to address regulatory issues in specific sectors, notably pharmaceuticals and cosmetics. The group has adopted international standards and decided methodologies for the measurement of economic impacts. The continued advancement of this agenda is critical given the importance of regulatory compatibility across countries for production fragmentation. As Fig. 4.3 reveals, based on the World Bank Governance Indicators, the Pacific Alliance countries have high levels of regulatory performance in terms of the formulation and implementation of policies and regulations that permit and promote private sector development.

4.6 Market Connectivity for GVCs: Physical and Digital Infrastructure

Co-operation on infrastructure is an area where regional initiatives can be fruitful, given that the nature of infrastructure is inherently regional. The importance of rapid, reliable and low-cost connectivity can be a key challenge for the Pacific Alliance, where countries have vast geographical distances, notoriously high transport costs and infrastructural deficiencies. Addressing the high costs to market connectivity is critical for countries to join distant supply chains in Asia and Europe, and to develop supply chains within their own region, particularly in manufacturing sectors. In GVCs, it is not just the border infrastructure and procedures (e.g., ports and customs) that matter, but also the behind-the-border infrastructure (e.g., ICT, energy) given that firms are establishing abroad. Beyond physical infrastructure, digital infrastructure is becoming increasingly important for new-generation, technologically enhanced, GVCs. In effect, digitally-enabled trade is the most dynamic and fastest growing component of global trade flows. Hence, the level of ICT development is a critical enabler of GVCs.

Although the Pacific Alliance does have an infrastructure development strategy, as other regional groupings in Asia, Europe and Africa do, several pillars of its co-operation can advance this agenda. First, the Pacific Alliance has a chapter on maritime services that provides for national treatment, allows agents and representation from third parties, and the mutual recognition of the documentation on ships. It also recognizes the seaman books of maritime crew, and accords treatment no less favourable than those to its national crews holding such documentation. These measures aimed at easing maritime transport are important achievements. On the other hand, progress in the PA appears to have been slower on air transport. The negotiation of an "open skies" agreement among PA countries would yield important benefits by bringing down the costs of intra-regional mobility of business persons, services provided and goods for production processes. The Pacific Alliance can also be a forum to co-operate on the upgrading of land transport services and infrastructure (trucking and rail especially), and improving regulatory and institutional frameworks to better mobilize long-term public and private investments in the sector. All these areas should receive priority in order to improve the quality of physical connectivity related to trade and transport infrastructure, where the Pacific Alliance behind in comparison to other regional groupings in Asia Pacific.

Beyond physical infrastructure, another strategic area for the Pacific Alliance to attract modern GVCs relates to digital connectivity. The digital economy is the linchpin of modern cross-border businesses. A growing part of business in GVCs is in the form of digital products or intangibles; this requires that countries address forms of digital protectionism and costs. At the same time, it requires a governance to allow for the free flow of data so that businesses and users feel safe and protected and consumer concerns are addressed. The Additional Protocol contains a chapter on telecommunications and a chapter on e-commerce which jointly address important elements of the digital economy. A key WTO-plus element of the telecoms chapter is that countries agree to co-operate on having more reasonable rates for international roaming services. As Fig. 4.4 shows, there is scope for improvement in the PA with respect to digital connectivity measures and the level of ICT development.

Related to digital trade, the PA also includes a package of WTO-plus e-commerce measures, including eliminating customs duties in digital products, promoting paperless trade, and introducing rules on electronic signature and digital certification which enable business. It contains measures protecting personal information of e-commerce users and unsolicited commercial emails. Improving the ease of use of e-commerce can be particularly important for the PA agenda on SMEs, where it has a dedicated Working group, given that it allows small enterprises to plug into distant GVCs networks through electronic trade channels.

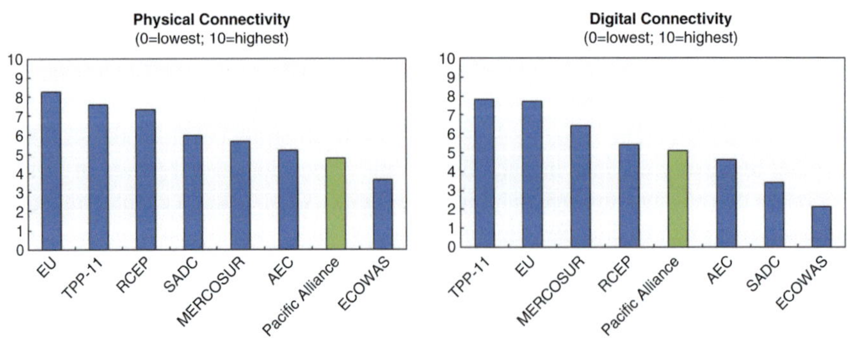

Fig. 4.4 Physical and Digital Connectivity. (Source: Physical connectivity is proxied by the quality of trade and transport infrastructure index of the World Bank Logistics Index (2016). Digital connectivity is proxied by the ICT Development Index of the UN International Telecommunications Union (2016). Calculations for regional groupings are based on weighed GDP averages of individual country indicators)

4.7 Concluding Remarks: Rebalancing Outward and Inward Strategies?

The Pacific Alliance has spear-headed innovate practices for GVC-guided integration. In several key dimensions, the PA is pursuing one of the most comprehensive expressions of 'deep integration' that have emerged in recent RTAs. Several issues may explain its remarkable trajectory. Since its inception, the PA has set out to be an 'agreement of its own,' that does not adhere to any fixed, pre-defined, template and is not held up by complex institutional structures. Unlike other agreements, the PA has not adhered to a single undertaking, favouring a pragmatic and problem-solving approach that has allowed for piece-meal yet rapid progress and continuous experimentation. Because it is composed of a small group of like-minded countries, it has also been able to make progress without the compromises of other larger agreements, including CPTPP, setting a high benchmark in sensitive areas, including movement of people. It has been very effective in galvanizing both political support at the highest levels as well as the institutionalised engagement of the private sector. Importantly, it also sets a precedent in terms of progressive rules being crafted by non-hegemonic countries.

In order to sustain and expand on these achievements, the Pumas of the Pacific may have to refresh their vision and re-calibrate their orientation. Considering the evidence on the importance that intra-regional trade has to support inter-regional trade, the lingering weakness of the intra-PA integration may be an obstacle to its fuller insertion into GVCs. Strengthening and expanding its regional market will allow the emergence of a regional supply infrastructure that can attract factories to locate in the region. Hence, while the Alliance continues to pursue its characteristically outward global integration with Asia Pacific and the rest of the world, it should also forge closer trade ties with its neighbouring market in the Atlantic. Changes in Argentina and its Observer Status in the Alliance since 2016 – joining Uruguay and Paraguay that were the other two PA Alliance Observers from MERCOSUR – may pave the way for a much-needed redrawing of the regional integration map in Latin America. The continued uncertainty surrounding the renegotiation of NAFTA and the implementation of the CPTPP, and the new inward-looking strategy of China, make this a unique opportunity – if not an imperative – for the Pacific Alliance to rebalance its outward and inward integration strategies.

References

Baldwin, R. (2011). *21st century regionalism: Filling the gap between 21st century trade and 20th century trade rules* (WTO Staff Working Paper, No. ERSD-2011-08). World Trade Organization.

Baldwin, R., & Lopez-Gonzalez, J. (2013). *Supply-chain trade: A portrait of global patterns and several testable hypotheses* (NBER Working Papers No. 18957). National Bureau of Economic Research.

Bergstrand, J., & Egger, P. (2010). A general equilibrium theory for estimating gravity equations of bilateral FDI, final goods trade and intermediate goods trade. In S. Brakman & P. Van Bergeijk (Eds.), *The gravity model in international trade: Advances and applications*. New York: Cambridge University Press.

Blyde, J. S. (Ed.). (2014). *Synchronized factories: Latin America and the Caribbean in the era of global value chains*. Washington, DC: Springer. https://doi.org/10.1007/978-3-319-09991-0_2.

Curran, L., & Zignago, S. (2012). EU enlargement and the evolution of European production networks. *Research in International Business and Finance, 26*(2), 240–257.

Damuri, Y. R. (2012). *21st century regionalism and production sharing practice* (CTEI Working Papers); online: http://graduateinstitute.ch/files/live/sites/iheid/files/sites/ctei/shared/CTEI/working_papers/CTEI-2012-04.pdf

Horn, H., Mavroidis, P. C., & Sapir, A. (2010). Beyond the WTO? An anatomy of EU and US preferential trade agreements. *The World Economy, 33*(11), 1565–1588.

Hummels, D., Rapoport, D., & Yi, K.-M. (1998). *Vertical specialization and the changing nature of world trade*. Federal Reserve Bank of New York Economic.

Lawrence, R. Z. (1996). *Regionalism, multilateralism and deeper integration*. Brookings, Washington, D.C.

Lejárraga, I. (2017). Regional trade agreements and international production networks. In J. Velut, L. Dalingwater, V. Boullet, & V. Peyronel (Eds.), *Understanding mega-free trade agreements*. New York: Routledge.

Miroudot, S. (2015). Global production networks in regional trade agreements. In *Trade policy implications of global value chains: Case studies*. Paris: OECD.

Mundell, R. (1957). International trade and factor mobility. *The American Economic Review, 47*(3), 321–335 Retrieved from http://www.jstor.org/stable/1811242.

OECD/WTO. (2013). *Aid for trade and value chains in Transport and logistics*, https://www.oecd.org/dac/aft/AidforTrade_SectorStudy_Transport.pdf

OECD/WTO. (2015). *Aid for Trade at a Glance 2015: Reducing Trade Costs for Inclusive, Sustainable Growth*. Paris: OECD Publishing. https://doi.org/10.1787/aid_glance-2015-en.

Orecife, G., & Rocha, N. (2014). Deep integration and production networks: An empirical analysis. *The World Eocnomy, 37*(1), 106–136.

Osnago, A., Rocha, N., & Ruta, M. (2015). *Deep trade agreements and vertical FDI: The devil is in the details* (Policy Research Working Paper No. WPS 7464). Washington, DC: World Bank Group.

The Heritage Foundation, Index of Economic Freedom, https://www.heritage.org/index/

World Trade Organization (WTO). (2011). World Trade Report 2011. In *The WTO and preferential trade agreements: From co-existence to coherence*. Geneva: WTO.

Chapter 5
Trade, Economic and Political Integration in Latin America: The Cases of the Southern Common Market (Mercosur) and the Pacific Alliance

Nicolas Albertoni and Andrés Rebolledo Smitmans

5.1 Introduction

The main goal of this chapter is to study the different patterns of regional integration throughout Latin America by analysing two leading regional integration initiatives (Mercosur and the Pacific Alliance (PA)). The secondary goal is to highlight the differences and similarities between these two plurilateral initiatives with a specific focus on the analysis of their trade policies.

This study finds that the two regional initiatives share some economic features that should motivate us to think about possible paths to convergence, which may not only strengthen each bloc individually, but could also be important to Latin American trade and economic integration as a whole. This work is not a judgement of whether or not each regional initiative is successful, but rather a look at the extent to which countries from each bloc can benefit from working together.

Why study the PA and Mercosur? First, because these regional initiatives account for more than 80% of Latin American gross domestic product (GDP), total trade and investment. Second, because almost all the documents relating to a comparative analysis of the two initiatives are in Spanish, which limits the ease with which these blocs can be compared with other regional initiatives with similar characteristics in the rest of the world.

N. Albertoni (✉)
University of Southern California, Los Angeles, CA, USA
e-mail: nalberto@usc.edu

A. R. Smitmans
Universidad de Chile, Santiago, Chile

P. Sauvé et al. (eds.), *The Pacific Alliance in a World of Preferential Trade Agreements*, United Nations University Series on Regionalism 16,
https://doi.org/10.1007/978-3-319-78464-9_5

5.2 The Context: Latin American Trade, Economic and Political Integration

One of the first steps towards Latin American integration was taken when Argentina, Brazil, Chile, Mexico, Paraguay, Peru and Uruguay signed the Treaty of Montevideo in 1960 (TM60), which established the Latin American Free Trade Association (LAFTA). Between 1961 and 1967 Colombia, Ecuador, Venezuela, and Bolivia also joined. The main objective of LAFTA was to create a free trade zone among the countries of Latin America over a period of 12 years. Note that during this decade, the economic model of the region was based on import substitution industrialization (ISI).[1] Hence, the main idea behind integration at that time was to encourage the economies of scale needed for industrialization (Tussie 2009; Albertoni 2012).

During the 1980s, its members transformed LAFTA into the Latin American Integration Association (LAIA) through a revised 1980 Treaty of Montevideo (TM80), whose main objective was to create a Latin American Common Market, but over an extended period. In the 1990s, Latin America started a new phase in its economic integration history, defined by a proliferation of regional agreements. As Table 5.1 shows, between the 1970s and the beginning of the twenty-first century, more than ten regional initiatives were developed.

Table 5.1 lists the most important agreements of recent decades. Most of them have trade and economic objectives such as the creation of a free trade zone or a common market. Others focus on political and social issues, for example through the creation of regional intergovernmental organizations (i.e. The Bolivarian Alternative for Latin America and the Caribbean (ALBA) and The Union of the South American Nations (UNASUR). All of them were crucial for regional integration in Latin America.

However, the diversification of regional agreements is not only an issue for Latin America because the regionalization of trade is a global trend. The number of economic integration agreements, based on the mechanisms (customs unions and free trade areas) proposed by the World Trade Organization (WTO) in Article XXIV of the General Agreement on Tariffs and Trade (GATT) in 1994, is significantly increasing.[2] These agreements have become more prevalent since the early 1990s and have inspired numerous regional trade agreements (RTAs) around the world. As of 1 February 2016, some 625 notifications of RTAs (counting goods, services and accessions separately) had been received by the GATT/WTO. Of these, 419 were in force. These WTO figures correspond to 454 RTAs (counting goods, services and

[1]A model which considers that, without adding value to their exports, poorer countries would never earn enough from their exports to pay for their imports. Hence, to protect their national industries most Latin American countries promoted high tariffs, targeted lending, national development banks and development cooperation.

[2]See: Article XXIV General Agreement on Tariffs and Trade 1994 Territorial Application, Frontier Traffic, Customs Unions and Free-trade Areas: http://www.wto.org/english/res_e/booksp_e/analytic_index_e/gatt1994_09_e.htm

Table 5.1 List of the regional agreements in Latin America

Regional bloc	Original treaty	Members and type of agreement
Latin American Free Trade Association, (LAFTA)/Latin American Integration Association (LAIA)	Treaty of Montevideo 1960/1980	Members: 13 members [a]
		Type/objective: FTA (TM60) common market (TM80)
The Caribbean Community and Common Market (CARICOM)	1973, Treaty of Chaguaramas	Members: 15 Caribbean nations and dependencies [b]
		Type/objective: trade and economic integration, common market
The Latin American and Caribbean Economic System (SELA)	1975, SELA, Panama Convention	Members: 28 countries of Latin America and the Caribbean[c]
		Type/objective: creation of a regional intergovernmental organization
Rio Group	1986, Declaration of Rio de Janeiro	Members: signed by Argentina, Brazil, Colombia, Mexico, Panama, Peru, Uruguay and Venezuela
The Central American Integration System (SICA)	1991, succeeded the Central American Common Market (CACM), 1960	Members: created by Costa Rica, El Salvador, Guatemala, Honduras, Nicaragua and Panama. Subsequently, Belize and Dominican Republic joined as a full members.
		Type/objective: creation of an institutional framework for regional integration in Central America
The Southern Common Market (Mercosur)	1991, Treaty of Asuncion	Members: Argentina, Brazil, Paraguay, Uruguay and Venezuela (in 2012)
		Type/objective: trade and economic integration, customs union
The North American Free Trade Agreement (NAFTA)	1994, NAFTA	Members: Canada, the United States and Mexico
		Type/objective: trade and economic integration, FTA
The Andean Community of Nations (CAN)	1994, succeeded the Andean Pact (1969)	Members: Bolivia, Colombia, Ecuador and Peru
		Type/objective: trade and economic integration, customs union. Called the Andean Pact until 1996 and came into existence when the Cartagena Agreement was signed in 1969
The Bolivarian Alternative for Latin America and the Caribbean (ALBA)	2004, ALBA Establishment Agreement	Members: 11 countries [d]
		Type/objective: intergovernmental organization
The Dominican Republic–Central America FTA (CAFTA–DR)	2004, CAFTA	Members: United States, Costa Rica, El Salvador, Guatemala, Honduras, Nicaragua, Dominican Republic
		Type/objective: trade and economic integration, FTA

(continued)

Table 5.1 (continued)

Regional bloc	Original treaty	Members and type of agreement
Petro Caribe	2005, Puerto La Cruz, Venezuela	Members: 18 members [e]
		Type/objective: a regional project to promote energy sector cooperation
The Union of the South American Nations (UNASUR)	2008, succeeded the South American Community of Nations (2004)	Members: 12 South American nations [f]
		Type/objective: political/ intergovernmental organization
The CELAC (Comunidad de Estados Latinoamericanos y Caribeños)	2011, in Venezuela	Members: 33 countries in the Americas excluding Canada and the United States [g]
		Type/objective: political integration with some features of economic integration
Pacific Alliance (PA)	2011, Lima Declaration	Chile, Colombia, Mexico and Peru
		Type/objective: trade and economic integration, FTA

Source: Created by the authors based on the original treaties and the information provided on the webpage of each regional agreement

[a]*LAIA* Argentina, Bolivia, Brazil, Chile, Colombia, Cuba, Ecuador, Mexico, Paraguay, Panama, Peru, Uruguay and Venezuela

[b]*CARICOM* Antigua and Barbuda, The Bahamas, Barbados, Belize, Dominica, Grenada, Guyana, Haiti, Jamaica, Montserrat, Saint Lucia, St. Kitts and Nevis, St. Vincent and the Grenadines, Suriname and Trinidad and Tobago

[c]*SELA* Argentina, Bahamas, Barbados, Belize, Bolivia, Brazil, Chile, Colombia, Costa Rica, Cuba, Dominican Republic, Ecuador, El Salvador, Grenada, Guatemala, Guyana, Haiti, Honduras, Jamaica, Mexico, Nicaragua, Panama, Paraguay, Peru, Suriname, Trinidad and Tobago, Uruguay and Venezuela

[d]*ALBA* Antigua and Barbuda, Bolivia, Cuba, Dominica, Ecuador, Grenada, Nicaragua, Saint Kitts and Nevis, Saint Lucia, Saint Vincent and the Grenadines and Venezuela

[e]*Petro Caribe* CARICOM (excluding, Barbados, Montserrat and Trinidad and Tobago), Venezuela, Cuba and Dominican Republic. Haiti and Nicaragua joined the union at the third summit. Guatemala joined in 2008 but left the organization in November 2013

[f]*UNASUR* Argentina, Bolivia, Brazil, Chile, Colombia, Ecuador, Guyana, Paraguay, Peru, Suriname, Uruguay and Venezuela

[g]*CELAC* MERCOSUR, UNASUR, SELA, ALBA. CELAC is the successor of the Rio Group and the Latin American and Caribbean Summit on Integration and Development (CALC)

accessions together), of which 267 are currently in force.[3] What all the RTAs have in common is that they are reciprocal trade agreements between two or more partners. It is noteworthy, however, that 90% of these agreements are free trade areas (FTAs) and only 10% are customs unions.[4]

Apart from the proliferation of agreements in recent years, Latin American regionalism continues to oscillate between unity and diversity (Gardini 2012). Writing on these regional transformations, Andrew Hurrell points out that diverse human interactions such as a significant level of integration at the societal level,

[3]World Trade Organization. Regional trade agreements. https://www.wto.org/english/tratop_e/region_e/region_e.htm accessed February 2016.

[4]Ibid.

regional awareness or identity and inter-state cooperation on a variety of issues all form part of the broad term 'regionalism' (Hurrell 1995).

On the future of Latin American regionalism, Gardini (2012) suggests that the region is inspired by four driving principles:

1. *Moving on from, or evolving, the neoliberal model in favour of a model that promotes sustainable development as opposed to macroeconomic orthodoxy and mere economic growth.*
2. *Learning constructive lessons from the mistakes of the past, in particular avoiding overly ambitious undertaking in favour of a more realistic and feasible approach proportionate to available resources.*
3. *Building a unique path to regionalism that does not imitate imported models, but instead is based on the real needs of the region together with its culture and tradition.*
4. *Pragmatism and openness towards all potential international partners.*

On the other hand, de la Mora and Rodriguez (2011) argue that "the evolution of Latin American integration has no doubt reflected the region's political and economic realities, as well as the absence of any concrete and viable project [...] For decades Latin America offered a highly unfavourable environment for integration or business development among the region's countries, which is why trade was geared to extra-regional markets and any integrationist ambitions were curtailed, resulting in a *de facto* fragmentation of the region".

Taking into account all the aforementioned points, many questions arise. For example: Are all the regional initiatives necessary and complementary? Does the overabundance of initiatives mean less progress for the integration of the entire region, and is this perhaps a reason why Latin America has not progressed as much as other emerging regions? The following sections try to answer these questions by focusing on two regional initiatives: Mercosur and the PA.

5.3 The Case Studies: Mercosur and the Pacific Alliance

This section compares Mercosur and the PA from two different perspectives. First, it studies the openness to trade of each regional initiative using a trade to GDP ratio. Second, it compares the two blocs from a trade policy perspective by analysing each bloc's members' average applied tariff levels.

As already mentioned, both regional initiatives share some economic features that should motivate us to think about possible paths to convergence. Convergence between these two blocs may not only strengthen the individual blocs, but could be important to Latin American trade and economic integration as a whole.

Mercosur and the PA have particular economic features that are complementary. The aims of this section are to (a) describe each initiative; (b) compare the most important features between one bloc and the other; (c) and identify areas in which both blocs can work together.

5.3.1 The Case of Mercosur

Mercosur was founded in 1991 by Argentina, Brazil, Paraguay and Uruguay, with the signing of the Treaty of Asuncion.[5] Venezuela became a full member in July 2012 and Bolivia has been in the process of becoming a full member since December 2012. Chile, Colombia, Ecuador and Peru have remained associated states. Today, Mercosur is one of the most important blocs in the region, with more than 275 million inhabitants and a GDP of US$ 3.5 trillion (making it the fifth largest economy in the world).

In 1986, after many years of rivalry, Argentina and Brazil decided to enter into a cooperative relationship by creating the Argentine–Brazilian Economic Integration Program (ABEIP, PICAB in Spanish), a programme aimed at economic and political cooperation. The political side of ABEIP aimed to strengthen the nascent democratic regimes, which emerged during the mid-1980s (after periods of military rule). At the same time, from an economic perspective, ABEIP tried to expand and diversify trade between the two countries with a special focus on agribusiness and the automotive sector (Manzetti 1993).

When Carlos Menem in Argentina and Fernando Collor de Mello in Brazil took up office (in 1990 and mid-1989, respectively), the conception of the free market and of integration changed dramatically. As Manzetti (1993) points out, during those years, "both countries re-affirmed their commitment to the integration effort. Indeed, economic integration was a key component of both their foreign policies." In 1990, after several meetings, Collor de Mello and Menem signed the Buenos Aires Act, which established the objective of creating a common market by the end of 1994. When Argentina and Brazil started to formalize this agreement, Paraguay and Uruguay joined the proposal. Finally, on 26 March 1991, the Foreign Ministers of the four countries signed the Treaty of Asunción, which defined the common market as:

> The free movement of goods, services and factors of production between countries through, inter alia, the elimination of customs duties and non-tariff restrictions on the movement of goods, and any other equivalent measures; the establishment of a common external tariff and the adoption of a common trade policy in relation to third States or groups of States, and the co-ordination of positions in regional and international economic and commercial forums; The co-ordination of macroeconomic and sectorial policies between the States Parties in the areas of foreign trade, agriculture, industry, fiscal and monetary matters, foreign exchange and capital, services, customs, transport and communications and any other areas that may be agreed upon, in order to ensure proper competition between the States Parties; the commitment by States Parties to harmonize their legislation in the relevant areas in order to strengthen the integration process.[6]

[5] See Treaty of Asuncion: http://www.sice.oas.org/trade/MRCSR/treatyasun_e.asp, accessed February 2016.

[6] Treaty of Asuncion, http://www.sice.oas.org/trade/MRCSR/treatyasun_e.asp, accessed February 2016.

Based on the conception of the common market, the main objectives of the Treaty of Asunción can be defined as follows (Manzetti 1993):

1. An across-the-board-tariff reduction would replace the sector-by-sector approach used by the ABEIP.
2. The coordination of macroeconomic policies in accordance with the tariff reduction schedule, and the elimination of non-quantitative restrictions.
3. The establishment of a common external tariff for trade partners outside Mercosur, with the objective of increasing the competitiveness of the member countries.
4. The development of accords for specific sectors of the economy in order to optimize the use and mobility of production factors and achieve efficient economies of scale.
5. The implementation of an institutional framework to solve trade litigations.

Mercosur's main goal is to "create a Customs Union in which goods, independently of where they are produced, can circulate free from import tariffs and certificates of origin within the integrated zone. In a complete Customs Union, the requirement of a certificate of origin for trade within the Union is considered to be equivalent of a non-tariff barrier" (Vaillant 2005).

Through Decision 32/00, adopted by the Common Market Council (CMC) in 2000, Mercosur members tried to provide a new impetus to the process of integration. During the summit of Buenos Aires on 29 June 2000 the members "re-launched" the process of integration in order to strengthen the bloc both internally and externally. Known as the "Re-launching Agenda of Mercosur" (CMC decisions 22/00 to 32/00), the strategy sought to identify Mercosur's main problems in order to provide proposals for measures to solve them. These measures were redefined and their deadlines changed during 2001. Even though an institutional reform adopted by the Administrative Secretariat (SAM) was approved, other implementation measures are still in the pipeline. In June 2001, a CMC meeting took place in Asuncion and emphasized the need to make progress in the following key areas (European Commission 2007):

(a) reformulation of the system of dispute settlement (decided in 18 February 2002);
(b) identification and elimination of intra-regional barriers to trade (internal);
(c) elaboration of common trade disciplines to prevent the imposition of trade-distorting measures (internal);
(d) creation of a Free Trade Area of the Americas (external);
(e) creation of an Inter-Regional Association Agreement with the EU (external).

Despite the many challenges Mercosur still faces – most of them derived from asymmetries among the partners – it is nevertheless one of the longest lasting, most sophisticated and deepest regional integration initiatives.

5.3.2 The Case of the Pacific Alliance

The PA is another Latin American trade initiative, with several features of deeper integration.

From the beginning, the main goal of Colombia, Chile, Mexico and Peru was to "achieve the awaited regional integration among like-minded countries that share the idea of trade liberalization and the need to strengthen Latin American links with the Asia-Pacific region."

A study by the World Economic Forum (WEF) shows that intra-bloc exports are no more than 5% and the added value of Pacific Alliance inputs is 12% in Peru, 10% in Colombia and Chile, and 2.5% in Mexico. As a consequence of very important commitments "there is great potential for further integration of their value chains in sectors such as mining, chemical, textile and apparel and agroindustry" (World Economic Forum 2014).

All member countries of the PA are already partners in FTAs between themselves. Therefore, the objective was to go beyond their existing FTAs, contemplating among other benefits:

1. Total trade liberalization (immediate for 92% of trade in goods and the remaining 8% in a tariff reduction schedule until 2030; applicable to less than 10 products which in certain cases had been excluded or had limited access in prior agreements)
2. Practically complete harmonization of rules of origin, being able to cumulate origin in their production processes (one of the most significant contributions)
3. Trade facilitation through connecting each country's single window for trade operations and electronic certificates of origin, among other customs cooperation measures
4. Regulatory cooperation through promoting mutual recognition agreements on technical standards
5. Elimination of visa requirements
6. Cooperation on many fronts (opening of common embassies and trade and investment promotion agencies; environment and climate change; science and technology; tourism; and scholarship programmes for academic exchanges).[7]

[7] These benefits were incorporated in a memorandum of understanding signed in 2011 as well as in the Protocol to the Pacific Alliance Framework Agreement that its members entered into on 10 February 2014. Given its level of ambition, the PA has caught the attention of the international community, and hence the number of countries accepted as observers has grown significantly to include: Costa Rica, Panama, Australia, Canada, New Zealand, Spain, Uruguay, Guatemala, Japan, China, Portugal, Paraguay, France, Turkey, South Korea, Honduras, United States, Ecuador, El Salvador, Dominican Republic, Finland, The Netherlands, India, Israel, Italy, Switzerland, Germany and the United Kingdom.

As shown, the PA agreement is flexible and open enough for participation to be expanded to include not only more Latin American countries, but also countries of other regions that have expressed interest in participating as observers.

As the WEF report points out, "being an integrated region will significantly help Latin America to have greater leverage to negotiate vis-à-vis other regions; successfully integrate into global and regional value chains; and resolve many common economic, social and political challenges" (World Economic Forum 2014).

5.3.3 Comparative Analysis of the Two Initiatives

The elements introduced by Fuentes and Douglas (2014) are used as the basis for this comparative analysis. Although the two trade blocs are similar in size, they "have notably different legal frameworks and trade policies […] At market exchange rates, Mercosur economies recorded a combined GDP of US$3.3 trillion in 2013, while the total GDP of Pacific Alliance countries was US$2.1 trillion." They also note that "Chile, Peru and Colombia have been consistent about pursuing trade to increase development, and all three have signed comprehensive free trade agreements with the U.S. in recent years" (Fuentes and Douglas 2014).

As mentioned above, given its aim of being a common market, the tool that Mercosur uses to prevent re-exportation within the bloc is a common tariff. On the other hand, the PA "has concerned itself less with equalizing tariffs and more with the free movement of goods, capital and labour. The PA also seeks to create a common equity market. The Mercado Integrado Latinoamericano includes the Peruvian, Chilean and Colombian stock exchanges, and Mexico's IPC is in the process of joining" (Fuentes and Douglas 2014).

In terms of investment agreements, the two blocs have important differences. For example, both dealt with investment in separate protocols, but those of Mercosur (Protocols of Colonia in 1993 and Buenos Aires 1994) were never ratified, while that of the PA recently entered into force on 1 May 2016. During the 99th Regular Meeting of the Common Market Group (GMC), which took place in Asunción, Paraguay, Brazil presented a proposal to negotiate an "Intra-MERCOSUR Cooperation and Investment Facilitation Protocol," which is still under discussion by Working Subgroup No. 12 for Investments.[8]

Other variables examined by Fuentes and Douglas (2014) were "autonomy versus collective action". On those variables, they noted that "the two blocs differ markedly in the autonomy that member nations are allowed in negotiating trade agreements. Mercosur requires its members to negotiate as a group. Trade talks are thus often delayed by individual nations' protectionist concerns", which could partly explain the small number of FTAs with other countries, and regional initiatives. In contrast, the PA does not require all trade agreements to be negotiated as a

[8] See: INTAL. 2015. Brazil proposes a MERCOSUR investment agreement. Goo.gl/HLB90v, accessed October 2017.

Table 5.2 Trade openness in Mercosur and the PA

	Year				
Country	2001 (%)	2005 (%)	2010 (%)	2013 (%)	2014 (%)
Argentina	19	38	33	30	31
Brazil	25	26	21	25	25
Paraguay	54	68	87	83	n/d
Uruguay	34	55	50	49	50
Venezuela [a]	41	60	44	75	69
Average Mercosur	**34**	**49**	**47**	**52**	**44**
Chile [b]	61	73	71	67	67
Colombia	31	34	32	36	36
Mexico	49	55	61	64	67
Peru	35	47	50	49	46
Average Pacific Alliance	**44**	**52**	**54**	**54**	**54**

Source: Departamento de Estudios, DIRECON, based on Trademap and IMF
[a]Exports and imports for Venezuela obtained from WTO
[b]Exports and imports for Chile obtained from Central Bank of Chile

bloc. Finally, Fuentes and Wynne consider "trade and economic performance" as another possible explanation for the differences between the two blocs. They point out that "Mexico and Chile are among Latin America's more open economies. Chile was the first in South America to pursue bilateral trade agreements, in an effort to expand its exports beyond copper. Trade liberalization was accompanied by macroeconomic stabilization measures that have lifted growth rates and given Chile the region's highest per-capita GDP by purchasing power. Trade makes up an even larger part of GDP in Mexico than in Chile, thanks largely to the North American Free Trade Agreement signed in 1993."[9]

The current situation of the two regional initiatives is shown in Tables 5.2 and 5.3 and Figs. 5.2 and 5.3 from two different perspectives: (1) openness to trade, using a trade to GDP ratio; and (2) each bloc's members' average applied tariff levels.

As shown in Table 5.2 and Fig. 5.1, for all the years analysed, the PA has a better trade openness performance than Mercosur, and Chile always has a trade openness ratio above 60%. The PA also performs better in terms of simple average tariff measures (Table 5.3 and Fig. 5.2).

5.4 Conclusion: The Importance of Convergence in Diversity

For all the reasons discussed above we could argue that far from all the disparities being weaknesses, they offer enough reasons to conclude that the PA and Mercosur could attempt convergence in the future. There is no better way to put it than "convergence in diversity" (Muñoz 2014).

[9] Ibid.

Table 5.3 Simple average tariffs in Mercosur and the PA

	Year				
Country	1997	2000	2005	2010	2014
Argentina	11.91	15.05	11.19	13.63	13.64
Brazil	16.04	15.55	12.38	13.68	13.53
Paraguay	12.92[a]	13.16	10.51	10.19	10.04
Uruguay	13.7[a]	13.91	10.57[b]	10.54	10.48
Venezuela	12.4	12.41	12.7[c]	12.47	12.85
Chile	10.91	8.98	6.0	5.99	5.98
Colombia	12.19	12.23	12.45	12.50	5.84
Mexico	14.7	17.9	14.38	8.83	7.39
Peru	13.38[a]	13.38	10.19	5.36	3.37

We only consider these years due to missing data for some of the countries of our analysis
Source: Departamento de Estudios, DIRECON, based on WTO
[a]Year 1998, [b]Year 2006, [c]Year 2003

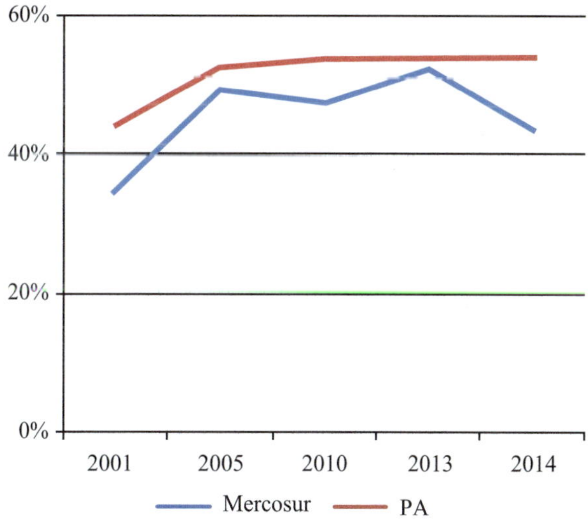

Fig. 5.1 Average trade openness in Mercosur and the PA. (Source: Created by the author based on DIRECON)

Recently, the two blocs have shown several signs pointing to convergence in the coming years. A clear example of this was the first meeting to assess opportunities for accords between the PA and Mercosur, which took place in November 2014 in Santiago de Chile. The meeting's objective was "to establish a road map that could lead to a convergence of the open market Pacific countries, Chile, Peru, Colombia and Mexico with Mercosur Argentina, Brazil, Paraguay, Uruguay and Venezuela, which have a more restrictive approach towards the private

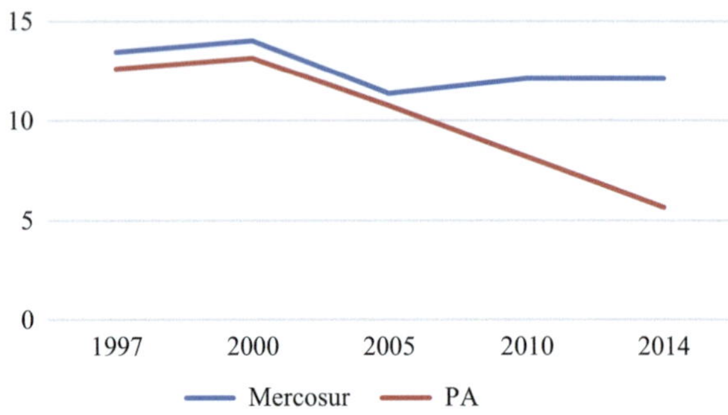

Fig. 5.2 Simple average tariffs in Mercosur and the PA. (Source: Created by the author based on DIRECON)

sector."[10] About this meeting, the Chilean Foreign Minister Heraldo Muñoz, said that "the idea is to discuss different forms for specific accords between the Pacific Alliance and Mercosur, on the understanding that at this stage it is not realistic to think about tariff and regulatory convergence, given the existing differences" (Merco Press 2014).

On the other hand, it is relevant that there are many mega-regional plurilateral agreements currently in the pipeline around the world. Hence, the convergence of two blocs such as Mercosur and the PA makes sense from an economic and trade perspective. Convergence could give the region more negotiating power with the rest of the world. This convergence could focus on a supply-chain trade view. On this, Baldwin (2012) says that while "traditional trade means selling into one nation goods that were made in another nation [...] supply-chain trade arises when high-tech firms combine their know-how with low-wage labour in developing nations; supply-chain production is thus mostly about making things internationally, although international selling is also important."

The first step towards convergence between the two blocs was announced by Chile in June, 2014 during the summit meeting of the PA presidents in Mexico. At that meeting, Chile also conceded that in the event of possible convergence between the two blocs, a 'two speed' approach should not be disregarded (Baldwin 2012). More specifically, Muñoz said that "if some countries can move faster towards integration and are willing to do so, they should be encouraged and facilitated to move in that direction, while the rest can move at a slower pace but with a common horizon. You can argue that the PA will move faster and Mercosur has its own rhythm, in a way it meets its own commitments, but we must be aware that a convergence is needed, almost imperative for a strong regional architecture" (Baldwin 2012).

[10]The November 2014 meeting had been held at foreign minister level together with representatives from regional organizations such as the Inter-American Development Bank, the UN economic office ECLAC, Latin American Integration Association, and academics.

The main conclusion of this chapter is that, considering the divergent patterns of integration of Latin America, the region needs to rethink its trade, economic and political integration to enable it to become a more active and dynamic actor in the global economy. Given the relevance of the PA and Mercosur for the region, convergence between these initiatives could help considerably in pursuing this aim.

Acknowledgements We wish to thank Pierre Sauvé, Rodrigo Polanco, Roberto Pizzaro and Barbara Kotschwar for their helpful comments on this paper. Any errors that remain are our own responsibility.

References

Albertoni, N. (2012). Integración económica para América Latina. *Diálogo Político, 29*(3), 195–215.

Baldwin, R. (2012). *WTO 2.0: Global governance of supply chain trade* (Centre for Economic Policy and Research Policy Insight No. 64).

de la Mora, L., & Rodríguez, D. (2011). *Why is it worth rethinking Latin American integration?* Institute for the Integration of Latin America and the Caribbean IDB-INTAL 15:8,9.

European Commission, (2007). Mercosur regional strategy Paper 2007–2013.

Fuentes, J. P., & Douglas, W. (2014). *Why mercosur lags the Pacific alliance trade liberalization is a key to economic success*. https://www.economy.com/dismal/analysis/free/248931. Accessed 1 Sept 2017.

Gardini, G. L. (2012). *Latin America in the 21st Century: Nations, regionalism, globalization*. London: Zed Books.

Hurrell, A. (1995). Explaining the resurgence of regionalism in world politics. *Review of International Studies, 21*, 331–358.

Manzetti, L. (1993). The political economy of Mercosur. *Journal of Interamerican Studies and World Affairs, 35*(4), 101–141.

Merco Press. (2014). *Pacific alliance and Mercosur will attempt convergence, sponsored by Chile*. http://en.mercopress.com/2014/10/04/pacific-alliance-and-mercosur-will-attempt-convergence-sponsored-by-chile. Accessed 1 Sept 2017.

Muñoz, H. (2014). *Convergencia en la diversidad: la nueva política latinoamericana de Chile*. Diario El País Madrid. http://elpais.com/elpais/2014/03/12/opinion/1394642773_153377.html. Accessed 1 Sept 2017.

Navarez, A. (2015). *Mercosur and Pacific alliance: Latin America divided*. World Press. Org. http://www.worldpress.org/article.cfm/Mercosur-and-Pacific-Alliance-Latin-America-Divided. Accessed 1 Sept 2016.

Tussie, D. (2009). Latin America: Contrasting motivations for regional projects. *Review of International Studies, 35*, 169–188.

Vaillant, M. (2005). *Deepening Integration of MERCOSUR: Dealing with Disparities. Asymmetries and Disparities in the Economic Integration of a South-South Customs Union* (pp. 5–10). Washington (DC): IADB Integration and Regional Programs Department.

World Economic Forum. (2014). *Mega-regional Trade Agreements Game-Changers or Costly Distractions for the World Trading System? Global Agenda Council on Trade & Foreign Direct Investment*. July 2014, full text in: http://www3.weforum.org/docs/GAC/2014/WEF_GAC_TradeFDI_MegaRegionalTradeAgreements_Report_2014.pdf

World Trade Organization. https://www.wto.org/english/tratop_e/region_e/region_e.htm. Accessed Feb 2016.

Nicolas Albertoni is a Fulbright-Laspau Scholar at University of Southern California pursuing a Ph.D. in political science and international relations. Trade Policy Project's Principal Investigator at the Security and Political Economy Lab (SPECLab) at USC. He received a Masters from Georgetown University's School of Foreign Service.

Andrés Rebolledo Smitmans is an economist from the Universidad de Chile and former Minister of Energy and Vice Minister of Foreign Trade of Chile.

Chapter 6
Market Access Challenges for Costa Rica in the Process of Accession to the Pacific Alliance

Susana Wong Chan and Carolina Palma

6.1 Introduction

It has been argued that international institutions or regional integration processes, such as the Pacific Alliance (PA), help to increase governance as well as welfare and form part of the solutions to current democracy problems (Keohane and Nye Joseph 1971; Simmons et al. 2012). Issues related to democracy, political fragmentation and governance (Cottier and Maya 2003) have found ground for discussion in the field of trade partnerships (Risse 2007). Even though the PA is not an organization *per se,* it can be considered as an initiative with its particular institutional arrangement in which decisions are taken at summits and rules are approved by consensus in committees. In this sense, the PA is an institution *à la* Latin America, characterized by institutional flexibility and dynamic movement.

The PA can be seen as a pragmatic way of problem-solving integration challenges, to create market-opening opportunities and enable the group to present itself as a larger trading partner to other leading regions and the world market (about reducing commercial risks: Zürn 2011). Presenting the PA as a platform to trade with the Asia-Pacific region is one of the objectives that exemplify this trend. When

S. Wong Chan (✉)
Customs Administration and Foreign Trade Bachelors Program, University of Costa Rica, San Jose, Costa Rica

Cross-border Research Association, Lausanne, Switzerland
e-mail: Susana.wong@ucr.ac.cr; susana.wong@cross-border.org

C. Palma
Customs Administration and Foreign Trade Bachelors Program, University of Costa Rica, San Jose, Costa Rica

Global Trade and Customs, Trade and Customs Leader for Central America, Panama and the Dominican Republic with EY LAW, San Jose, Costa Rica
e-mail: Carolina.palma@cr.ey.com

P. Sauvé et al. (eds.), *The Pacific Alliance in a World of Preferential Trade Agreements*, United Nations University Series on Regionalism 16,
https://doi.org/10.1007/978-3-319-78464-9_6

analysing the PA, one should not forget the political objectives that lie behind the initiative (such as democracy and like-minded foreign policies as mentioned by Friedman 1999). This chapter outlines the economic grounds for Costa Rica's accession to the PA – specifically in market access terms – but political arguments about its importance as an economic and political platform should not be forgotten.

The PA pursues a wide-ranging regulatory convergence agenda among like-minded countries (like-minded countries are more likely to close agreements as in Nye and Donahue 2000). An important issue is whether this regional integration process will succeed in its convergence aims or alternatively deepen the divergence of norms between the domestic (regional) and international spheres. A crucial question is whether globalization forces countries to become more equal, or at least significantly more alike in their political economy, institutions, culture and social structure.

Important questions that arise in the context of the accession of Costa Rica to the PA, include the following:

- Is there regulatory convergence between the PA and the Central American Common Market?
- Are there diverging norms that will require a process of adaptation?

This chapter does not conduct a legal analysis but focuses instead on market access, the identification of sensitive products and further negotiating opportunities. The chapter covers only the commercial benefits of the PA for Costa Rica. Sensitive products are those that require a measure of protection against trade in identical or similar imported goods. The chapter also explains the cumulation of origin regulation in all the preferential trade agreements (PTAs) that Costa Rica has negotiated with PA Member States and provides figures on trade in goods and services. Rules of origin and cumulation provisions are important in this analysis because they reveal whether it is feasible for Costa Rica to become a full member of the PA and in which areas member countries can benefit from greater market access.

The chapter is divided into five sections. Firstly, general aspects regarding the PA are discussed together with the most important milestones that impact Costa Rica's accession to the PA. The second section describes the most important benefits that Costa Rica would reap from becoming part of the PA. The third section presents a thorough analysis of market access and origin cumulation in each of the PTAs negotiated by Costa Rica with PA member states. The objective of this section is to identify the key sensitive products that the Ministry of Foreign Trade of Costa Rica (COMEX) would need to pay close attention to. In section four, the most important challenges to Costa Rica's accession to the PA are discussed. Finally, the concluding section makes some recommendations for ensuring balanced and strategic outcomes in accession negotiations.

6.2 Accession Process of Costa Rica to the Pacific Alliance and Status of the Negotiations

To become a Member State of the PA, a candidate country must have PTAs in force with all members of the PA (Alianza del pacífico 2013a). That is why, since 2011, Costa Rica has been actively working to complete a PTA with Peru and Colombia.

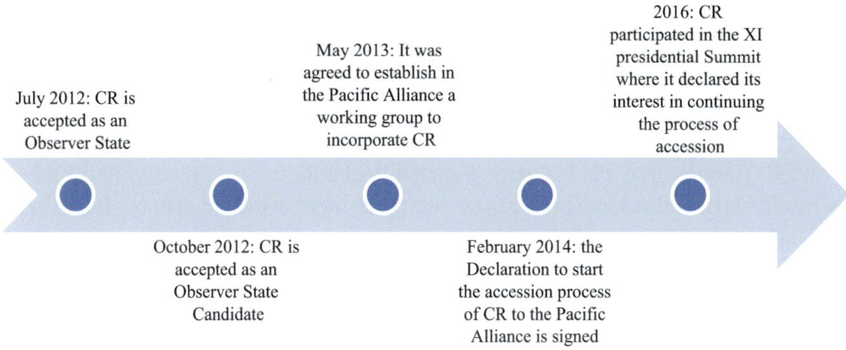

Fig. 6.1 Background to the accession of Costa Rica to the Pacific Alliance. *CR* Costa Rica. (Source: Own elaboration)

In October 2013, Costa Rica was granted Candidate Observer State status. Fig. 6.1 shows the process of accession of Costa Rica to the PA.

On 10 February 2014, at the Summit of Cartagena, Costa Rica signed the Declaration to start the accession process to the PA. This date marked the beginning of the process of analysis and the start of work towards the incorporation of Costa Rica in the PA. Since then, two sectoral consultations have taken place, one in 2014 and another in 2015 (COMEX 2014a, b). In 2016, during the XI Presidential Summit, the current president of Costa Rica, Luis Guillermo Solís, indicated the importance to Costa Rica of joining the initiative (Avendaño 2016).

Although the process of consultation with the interested sectors was completed by December 2015, COMEX had not yet begun to negotiate specific issues of trade in goods. Given that Costa Rica declared its intention to pursue accession in 2014, it was recommended to start negotiations early in 2017 in order to conclude the process in that year. Given the timing of negotiations within the PA, the key to the success is to seize the political momentum and the commercial advantages of the bloc. Costa Rica, as a small economy, should not delay joining the PA, and should quickly launch the process of consultation with sectors, especially in the case of sensitive products.

Furthermore, the country must act cautiously following the 2016 presidential elections in the United States (US). The US is Costa Rica's top trading partner, absorbing more than 40.3% of the country's exports in 2015 (COMEX 2016). Since the new US president was elected, he has pursued a series of policies that could potentially affect the overall trade and economic environment.[1]

[1] As an example: on 23 January 2017, President Trump signed a presidential memorandum to with draw from the Trans-Pacific Partnership following a promise made during the 2016 presidential campaign (Diamond and Bash 2017). Also, in its National Trade Policy Agenda for 2017, the USA states that the trade policy of the USA will be guided by the principle of expanding trade "in a way that is freer and fairer for all Americans". In order to do so, the US Administration will focus "on bilateral negotiations rather than multilateral negotiations – and by renegotiating and revising trade deals when our goals [i.e. those of the USA] are not being met". The USA will also resist "efforts by other countries – or international bodies like the World Trade Organization – to weaken the rights and benefits of, or increase the obligations under, the various trade agreements to which the United States is a party" (USTR 2017).

Developments in US trade policy agenda are a matter of concern for small, export-dependent, countries such as Costa Rica. In March, the president of Costa Rica visited the US to discuss the future of the Dominican Republic–Central America Free Trade Agreement (DR-CAFTA). According to the official declarations of the Government of Costa Rica, the DR-CAFTA will not be renegotiated nor affected (Cambronero 2017). Despite such a declaration, it is a reality that some of the trade barriers that have been raised and other trade restrictions may affect Costa Rica adversely. Therefore, it is important for it to start looking for new opportunities in other markets such as those of the PA and in the Asia-Pacific region.

6.3 Benefits for Costa Rica of Joining the Pacific Alliance

In economic terms, PA members are important trading partners for Costa Rica. In the past 10 years, trade with those countries rose in value from US$ 859 million in 2003 to US$ 2.260 million in 2012. The members of the PA accounted for 21.4% of the foreign direct investment (FDI) during 2012, according to Costa Rica's Ministry of Foreign Trade (COMEX undated-a).

Regarding the negotiation process, the accession of Costa Rica must be negotiated with caution because of its sensitive products. Nonetheless, part of the work has been done because the country has already signed PTAs with all the members of the PA. Currently, Costa Rica has 95% free trade with Chile (COMEX 1999), 98% with Mexico (COMEX 2012), 78% with Peru (COMEX 2011) and 71% with Colombia (COMEX 2013b). However, these PTAs include some products that are excluded from the Costa Rican tariff schedule as discussed in detail below. These include: meat, poultry, milk, yogurt, cheese, tomatoes, onions, potatoes, beans, coffee, rice and sugar, and other products subject to long periods of liberalization – approximately 15 or 20 years. However, a careful process of consultation could direct this challenge towards better negotiation. This process has already started in 2014 and it continued in 2015, but should maintain a steady pace.

From an economic perspective, because Costa Rica is a small economy, it is important to have trade facilitation, investment and the liberalization of trade in both goods and services. These are essential to achieving the aim of integrating the country into global markets, particularly since studies have shown that countries with a higher level of liberalization also achieve economic progress (Hertel et al. 2000). In 2015, the Latin American region experienced the lowest trade exchange. The only comparable situation was the Great Depression, according to the Commission for Latin America and the Caribbean (ECLAC) (2015b). This emphasizes that the diversification of exportable goods, the integration into global value chains and the business opportunity provided by the integration of regional markets, such that offered by the PA, are crucial to address the macroeconomic problems of the region. Moreover, the Konrad Adenauer Stiftung reported that

Costa Rican GDP would increase by 0.8% if it takes advantages of the opportunities offered by the PA (Felbermayr et al. 2015).

Costa Rica has a long history of trade openness and friendly investment. The latter is reflected in the amount of FDI, which has risen rapidly in the last 10 years and has achieved an annual growth of 13% (Organisation for Economic Co-operation and Development (OECD) 2013). FDI is also an example of how trade and investment facilitates development and reduces poverty: the proportion of Costa Rica's population living in poverty fell from 29% to 18.5% in the period between 1987 and 2009. According to the OECD (2013), the relative reduction of extreme poverty from 9% to 4% is most notable, In this sense, becoming a member of the PA is a natural step that will bring benefits to the country from the political, economic, developmental and poverty-reduction point of view (ECLAC 2015b; OECD 2013).

Joining the PA would allow Costa Rica to have access to a wider market. Costa Rica is not attractive for bigger economies because of its small size. Therefore, access to more robust regional integration, as well as having increased growth, development and participation in initiatives for competitiveness and trade facilitation would make the country more visible and more important to other countries.

The PA represents a market with plenty of opportunities for Costa Rican producers. The purchasing power of these countries is high; therefore, it offers a niche for quality products produced in Costa Rica. Between 2011 and 2012, the GDP of the Member States of the PA represented 36% of total GDP in the Latin America and Caribbean area.

Costa Rica's trade with PA countries has been increasing in recent years. According to COMEX, the value of trade between Costa Rica and PA countries reached US$ 2199.3 million in 2014: this figure represents 7.7% of Costa Rica's total trade with the world. In the period 2004–2014, exports grew at an annual average of 7.2%, while imports grew at an annual rate of 8.2%. Although trade between Costa Rica and the PA only represents 8.6% of its total trade with the world in 2015, with the accession of Costa Rica to the PA, this level of trade may increase (COMEX undated-a). Furthermore, according to the Konrad Adenauer Stiftung study, the country's GDP would increase.

A possible increase of trade will be accompanied by trade facilitation and customs cooperation. According to the Additional Protocol of the PA, the members will exchange information on cases related to customs offences, accelerate customs clearance through automatized systems and, in general, customs procedures will be simplified (Alianza del pacífico 2016). This is a crucial aspect inside the PA because, according to Cudmore and Whalley (2005), the border delays can offset the benefits brought about by lower tariffs.

For some time, Costa Rica has also been interested in trade with the Asia-Pacific region, specifically the Asia-Pacific Economic Cooperation (APEC). This is why Costa Rica has signed PTAs with China, Singapore, the United States and Canada and is in the process of negotiating an FTA with South Korea. In this sense, the initiative of the PA facilitates Costa Rica's entry into the Asia-Pacific market, since Mexico, Peru and Chile are part of this bloc and Costa Rica has PTAs with other APEC members. Being part of the Asia-Pacific bloc as well as the focus on other trading partners, such as the PA, is very important for Costa Rica because of dependence on exports to the US and the volatility of the political and economic policies of the US under the current presidency.

Furthermore, the PA is seeking regulatory convergence. In the Additional Protocol of the PA, there are some articles that aim to achieve regulatory convergence or, in some cases regulatory harmonization (the process by which technical guidelines are developed to be uniform across participating authorities) (U.S. Food and Drug Administration (FDA) 2016). The most important areas where the PA is seeking regulatory convergence are:

- *TBT and SPS measures.* According to the Additional Protocol to the Pacific Alliance Framework Agreement, the PA seeks to increase transparency on these two issues, as well as harmonization, mutual recognition and equivalence of the rules (Alianza del pacífico 2013b). A Committee on SPS and TBT has been created for the monitoring and implementation of provisions of the agreement.
- *Trade in services.* The PA is aiming for mutual recognition of professional service providers, especially for architects and engineers.
- *Intellectual property.* The PA aims to harmonize and simplify the procedures related to trademarks.
- *Authorized Economic Operator (AEO).* The AEO is "a party involved in the international movement of goods in whatever function that has been approved by or on behalf of a national customs administration as complying with World Customs Organization (WCO) or equivalent supply chain security standards" (World Customs Organization 2010).
- *Customs cooperation.* This relates to the harmonization of documents needed during trade operations.

6.4 Bilateral Free Trade Agreements with Peru, Colombia, Mexico and Chile

Costa Rica has a trade policy oriented to exports and to attracting FDI. By August 2016, Costa Rica had ratified 14 PTAs.[2]

This study analyses the four PTAs that Costa Rica has in force with the Member States of the PA (Mexico, Chile, Peru and Colombia). The goods excluded within these PTAs are outlined to determining which goods might be sensitive in the negotiation of Costa Rica's accession to the PA. Also, the diagonal cumulation provision and investment and service trends are described.

For easier comparison between exempted goods in the tariff schedule of each of the PA countries, all the products affected are arranged in the order of the chapters established by the Harmonized Commodity Description and Coding (HS system).

[2] These are as follows: Colombia, Central America, Canada, CARICOM, Chile, China, Dominican Republic-Central America-United States (CAFTA-DR), Mexico, Panama, Dominican Republic, Peru, Singapore, European Union and the European Free Trade Association (EFTA).

This allows the reader to see whether or not the countries excluded the same product. The lack of an entry for a specific good means that it was not exempted by the corresponding country. Note that the table of excluded products contains only the overall description of the product; for more detailed information the tariff classification in the final FTA text should be consulted.

6.4.1 *FTA Between Costa Rica and Mexico (and FTA Between Central America and Mexico)*

The FTA between Costa Rica and Mexico was signed in 1994 and entered into force on 1 January 1995. This FTA was primarily aimed at creating a Free Trade Area to promote the process of regional integration between these two Latin American countries (Cetys University Campus Ensenada undated).

A new FTA between Costa Rica and Mexico was negotiated and entered into force on 1 July 2013. The main objective of the new agreement is to converge the PTAs that each Central American country had with Mexico and to adapt those PTAs to modern rules and productive realities in Central America, which has been evolving over the last 15 years.

Since the entry into force of the FTA between Costa Rica and Mexico (1995), trade has increased substantially. Figure 6.2 shows that from 2007 to 2015 trade flows tripled between the two countries, i.e., increased on average by 8% per year.

Among the major exports from Costa Rica to Mexico are: edible preparations, palm kernel oil or babassu oil, refined palm oil, rubber or gaskets, lids, caps and

Fig. 6.2 Costa Rica: Trade flow with Mexico, 2004–2016. (Source: Own elaboration, based on data from COMEX, INEC, PROCOMER and BCCR. Preliminary figures subject to revision for 2016)

other accessories, of metal, tyres; sheets and strips of unalloyed aluminium, articles and prosthetic devices, processors and controllers, and parts and accessories for vehicles. The main imports from Mexico to Costa Rica are: food preparations, avocados, cereal products, television sets, drugs, vehicles, combined refrigerator-freezers, coated paper and board (COMEX undated-b).

As shown by the list of import and export products, there are only a few raw agricultural products, the majority are intermediate products and final products, which means that both countries have an industrialized economy and their exports are highly complementary.

6.4.2 Market Access

An average of 98% of tariff lines classified in the HS system are totally liberalized; the rest were excluded from the FTA (COMEX 2012).

According to COMEX (2012), Mexico excluded from its schedule list 1.3% of tariff lines – the equivalent of 147 tariff lines. As for Costa Rica, it indicated that 2.10% of tariff lines – the equivalent of 164 tariff lines were excluded. The majority of excluded products are agricultural commodities, especially poultry, milk and dairy products, potatoes, onions, coffee, bananas and tobacco, which are also traditionally sensitive goods in Costa Rica. Products excluded from the list by the two countries are quite similar. Although approximately 2% of the tariff lines were excluded during the negotiation process between Mexico and Costa Rica, it is possible to include in the Costa Rican protocol of accession to the PA some products of interest, such as raw materials, cigarettes, custard, yogurt powder, chicken sausages and jams.

6.4.3 Cumulation of Origin

On the issue of cumulation of origin, section 5–08 of the FTA between Mexico and Costa Rica states that “for purposes of determining whether a good is originating, an exporter or producer may accumulate production with one or more producers in the territory of one or both Parties of materials that are incorporated into the good so that the production of the materials is considered as if performed by that exporter or producer, provided that they comply with the provisions of Article 3.5” (COMEX 2013a). This means that the cumulation of origin applies only between Mexico and Costa Rica. However, Article 4.9 of the FTA between Central America and Mexico, allows, in cases where the parties have entered into PTAs with other non-states party to the FTA, goods or materials originating in the Party not incorporated in goods of a Party, to be considered as originating in the territory of that Party, provided they comply with the rules of origin. For this to apply, that provision must be explicit in the other PTAs.

6.4.4 Services and Investment

FDI from Mexico to Costa Rica since the enactment of the FTA in 1995 has a growing trend. According to COMEX (2000), in the report entitled "Free Trade Agreement between Costa Rica and Mexico: an assessment five years of operation" indicates that during the first 5 years in which the FTA was implemented, CR had a substantial increase of Mexican investment, to the extent that during that time the study was considered Mexico was the second in order of importance regarding the source of FDI in Costa Rica, only surpassed by the US which has historically been the main investor in the country.

Table 6.1 shows the latest figures, which show that Mexico's investment has experienced a sustained growth in Costa Rica, except during the period 2008–2009 -attributed to the world's economic crisis.

During the period 2012–2015, Mexican FDI accounted for 7.9% of the total investment received by the country. The amount invested in 2012 stands out, which reached US $ 336.5 million. In the following years, FDI flows were smaller and variable; in 2013 the amount was US $ 171.7, while in 2014 FDI reached US $ 237.2 million. In 2015, this figure stood at US $ 122.7 million, which were mainly due to services and industry sectors. In conclusion, from the point of view of the services sector, the accession of Costa Rica to the PA would strengthen investment flows from Mexico, which are very valuable for a small economy.

6.4.4.1 Current Situation of the FTA Between Costa Rica and Chile

The FTA between Costa Rica and Chile entered into force on 15 February 2002 and was negotiated under a general framework of the agreement between Costa Rica, El Salvador, Guatemala, Honduras, Nicaragua and Chile. Each Central American country negotiated a bilateral protocol with Chile based on its particular market access needs. Since the enactment of the bilateral FTA between Costa Rica and Chile, there has been a steady increase in trade. According to figures from COMEX shown in Fig. 6.3, between 2005 and 2015 there was an annual increase of approximately 7.2% of trade flow.

There are 85 companies registered as exporters to Chile, of which 31.8% had not registered exports in previous years (COMEX undated-c). This reflects the increasing importance of the Chilean market for Costa Rican products.

Table 6.1 Top 10 countries with the largest flow of FDI in Costa Rica (2007–2016) in millions of dollars

Country	2007	2008	2009	2010	2011	2012	2013	2014	2015[a]	2016[a]
US	1154.5	1569.8	1119.5	1253.5	1658.7	1015.1	1042.1	1148.2	1601.0	1298.1
Holland	50.6	24.3	26.6	7.0	30.1	31.6	109.4	−65.5	516.7	371.3
Italy	19.1	18.8	10.2	−1.8	58.6	114.6	106.1	117.9	14.3	186.1
Switzerland	44.2	85.7	−32.3	67.7	4.8	−3.4	25.8	37.8	−50.9	169.1
Spain	56.8	140.8	79.0	28.4	247.4	310.8	246.5	315.5	131.6	154.9
Mexico	70.9	19.8	6.8	40.4	183.4	336.5	171.7	250.2	134.6	120.0
Colombia	30.2	50.0	6.4	98.3	151.6	105.7	78.6	192.8	171.6	92.5
Canada	97.1	64.0	32.6	47.2	42.3	7.2	47.9	85.9	39.0	92.1
Germany	59.4	67.7	17.4	19.8	9.0	−9.8	32.3	91.0	109.7	58.7
Panama	−3.1	19.9	22.0	37.2	−3.1	10.5	332.0	189.5	47.8	30.2

Source: *Grupo Interinstitucional de Inversión Extranjera Directa* (BCCR, CINDE, PROCOMER, COMEX and ICT)
[a]Preliminary data

Fig. 6.3 Costa Rica: trade flow with Chile 2004–2016. (Source: Own elaboration, based on data from COMEX, INEC, PROCOMER and BCCR. Preliminary figures subject to revision for 2016)

6.4.5 Market Access

According to the FTA between Chile and Costa Rica, on 1 January 2015, on average, only 2% of tariff lines classified in the HS system were excluded from the Agreement (COMEX 1999).

Both countries excluded exactly the same type of products. This is because, during the process of negotiations, the parties agreed that any product excluded by one party would also be excluded by the other party. The main types of excluded products can be divided into five main areas: poultry, dairy, agricultural products, oils and wood products. Therefore, these are sensitive products, but they are not necessarily the sensitive products for Costa Rica because of the arrangement described above.

6.4.6 Cumulation of Origin

Article 4.06 of the FTA states that originating materials or goods originating in the territory of a Party incorporated into a good in the territory of another Party shall be considered as originating in the territory of the latter. In addition, in paragraph 2, it stipulates that for determining whether a good complies with the rule of origin, the producer may accumulate its production with that of one or more producers in the territory of one or more Parties of materials that are incorporated into the good, so that the production of the materials is considered as done by that producer, provided that the good satisfies the provisions of Article 4.03 (COMEX 2002).

This provision precludes diagonal cumulation with non-Party members. Even though Article 4.02.5 of the Agreement provides that 2 years after the entry into force of the Agreement, a work programme will be established to examine the possibility of creating diagonal cumulation, this applies only to Central American and Chilean products, it does not apply to other non-member states (COMEX 2002).

Of the four individual PTAs negotiated by Costa Rica, the FTA with Chile is the oldest and therefore it does not contain provisions that are nowadays included in the most recent PTAs. An example of this is the diagonal cumulation provision. Therefore, the accession of Costa Rica to the PA could offer a way to update this FTA and create a new one that will be aligned with the current trade reality. To seek coherence, appropriate legislation could be implemented, for instance the legal form of a suspension of the FTA due to introduction of a newer norm on the same matter could be the legal means to introduce this change. In this sense, the PA is highly beneficial in terms of origin by allowing cumulation with Chile.

6.4.7 *Services and Investment*

In the period 2004–2014, Chilean investment reached a cumulative total of US$ 55.9 million, of which US$ 28.3 million was invested during 2013, mainly in the industrial and real estate sectors. During 2014, Chile registered investments in Costa Rica worth US$ 18 million and in 2015, the Chilean investment was destined mainly to the commerce sector and in less measure to the real estate sector.

6.4.7.1 Current Situation of the FTA Between Costa Rica and Peru

The FTA between Costa Rica and Peru was ratified in 2012, offering Costa Rica a market of more than 30 million people. Trade with Peru has tripled in the last decade. Figure 6.4 shows a substantial increase in trade flow between Costa Rica and Peru between 2005 and 2016: during this period, exports showed an average annual growth of 11.3%.

From the 76 companies that entered Peru in 2015, 27 did not have a presence in in the last 2 years. This indicated that companies are taking advantage of the negotiated agreement and shows the importance of this new market for the Costa Rican producers. The main products exported from Peru to Costa Rica are: plaques, strips and sheets made of plastic; fruits and seeds for planting; preparations for animal feed and fresh grapes.

Fig. 6.4 Costa Rica: trade flow with Peru 2004–2016. (Source: Own elaboration, based on data from COMEX, INEC, PROCOMER and BCCR. Preliminary figures subject to revision for 2016)

6.4.8 Market Access

In accordance with the FTA between Peru and Costa Rica, by 1 January 2027, on average, 98.7% of tariff lines classified in the under the HS system will have free trade access to Costa Rica. The remainder of the products originating from Peru were excluded from the Agreement (approximately 1.3% of the tariff lines) (COMEX 2011).

Many of the product exclusions are virtually the same in both countries. It is also remarkable that, as a more recent agreement, this FTA has a smaller number of excluded goods, which is helpful for the process of accession of Costa Rica to the PA, but the list of exclusions must nevertheless be taken into account during the negotiations.

6.4.9 Cumulation of Origin

Article 3.6 sets out the cumulation provision in the FTA between Peru and Costa Rica. It states that goods or materials originating in the territory of a Party incorporated into a good in the territory of the other Party shall be considered as originating in the territory of that other Party. The FTA between Costa Rica and Peru thus provides for bilateral cumulation (COMEX 2011).

Additionally, paragraph 6 of Article 3.6 states that when each Party has established a PTA with a country or a group of countries not party to the Agreement, the goods or materials of the non-Party incorporated in the territory of one Party may be considered as originating in the territory of that Party. This means that diagonal cumulation is agreed in the FTA; therefore, the origin should not be an obstacle when inserted into the PA. The reasons will be explained further in the recommendations and conclusions section (COMEX 2011).

6.4.10 *Services and Investment*

According to COMEX (undated-d), during the period 2004–2014 investments from Peru reached a cumulative total of US$ 54.6 million. In 2007 and 2008, investment was higher (US$ 14.1 million and US$ 8.9 million, respectively) in the manufacturing sector and real estate. Given that Peru country with a growing economy, with the accession of Costa Rica to the PA it is expected that Peruvian investments in Costa Rica would increase as well as investment in the other direction.

6.4.10.1 Current Situation of the FTA Between Costa Rica and Colombia

The negotiation process of the FTA between Costa Rica and Colombia began in 2012. The aim was to strengthen and enhance trade and investment relations, especially because the two countries are geographically close and they have established transport routes. The negotiation of the treaty ended on 6 March 2013 and it was signed on 22 May of the same year. The FTA has been implemented since 1 August 2016 (COMEX undated-e).

As shown in Fig. 6.5, bilateral trade between Costa Rica and Colombia in 2005 totalled US$ 303.9 million, while in 2015 the figure reached US$ 389.2 million. That is, the trade between Costa Rica and Colombia grew by 28% over that decade. The main export products in 2015 were: raw lead, parts of planes and helicopters, tyres, medicines, articles and prosthetic devices, iron bars or steel, syringes, needles, catheters, cannula and the like. The main imports from Colombia in 2015 were: medicines, polypropylene, fertilizers, fungicides, chemical products, and polystyrene (COMEX undated-e).

6.4.11 *Market Access*

According to the FTA between Colombia and Costa Rica (COMEX 2013b), 15 years after the FTA's entry into force, 95.8% of tariff lines classified in the HS system will have free trade access to Costa Rica. This means that 4.2% of the tariff lines were excluded from Costa Rica's tariff schedule of. In this FTA, the longest period

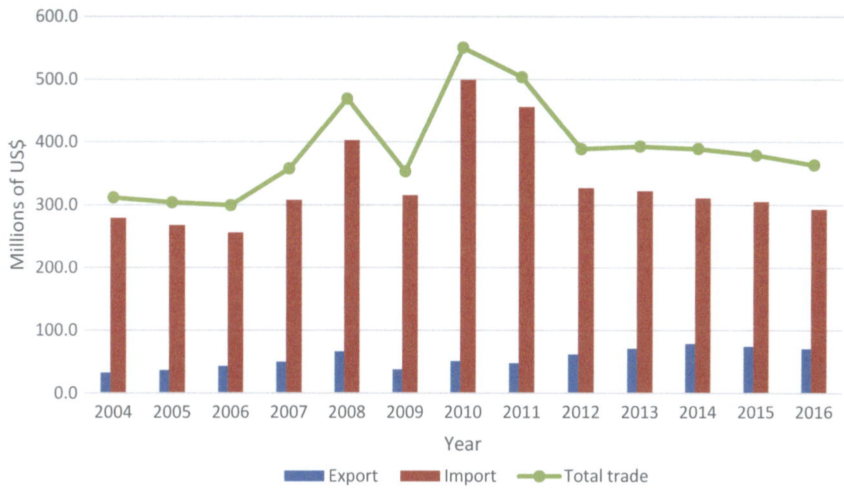

Fig. 6.5 Costa Rica: Trade flows with Colombia 2004–2016. (Source: Own elaboration, based on COMEX, PROCOMER and BCCR. Preliminary figures subject to revision for 2016)

allowed for tariff reduction is 15 years counted from the moment of implementation of the Agreement (COMEX 2013b).

It is notable that the list of excluded products is slightly different between the two Parties. This is not the case in the other agreements where the list of exclusions is virtually equal. This could pose a challenge when negotiating the accession of Costa Rica to the PA.

6.4.12 Cumulation of Origin

The FTA between Colombia and Costa Rica also allows materials originating from a non-Party country to be taken as originating where all Party countries have an FTA with the same non-Party country, i.e. diagonal cumulation is allowed (Article 3.6, paragraph 3 of the Agreement). As in other cases, diagonal cumulation is allowed on the condition that all the countries (parties and non-party countries) have the same rules established in their own FTA.

6.4.13 Services and Investment

COMEX reports that between 2012 and 2015, Colombia contributed an accumulated investment of 4% of the total received by Costa Rica. Investments in this period relate mainly to the financial sector, but also include investments in the industrial and real estate sectors. The strong competitiveness of the Costa Rican economy is postulated as making it a major destination for FDI in many countries. This has been demonstrated over the years and is a reason why the PA will strengthen these opportunities.

6.5 Challenges to Costa Rica's Accession to the Pacific Alliance

The accession of Costa Rica to the PA will bring economic benefits, but there are also challenges to be taken into account. As in any process of regional integration, policy-makers should seek a balanced negotiation taking into account that research supports the need for this regional bloc.

One challenge concerns market goods and sensitive products. As indicated above, Member States of the PA aim to achieve almost 100% free trade in goods originating in them, except for sugar (including mixtures used in the food industry with high sugar content) and ethanol. This poses a challenge, because Costa Rica and its counterparts excluded some products from their PTAs, which should be liberalized in the PA. Not all of them have to be liberalized immediately (some are allowed a 15 year period for liberalization) but, in practical terms, they will all have to reach a 0% tariff rate.

Handling sensitive products is a difficulty for the Costa Rican government that will take some political capital. As stated already, Costa Rica has traditional sensitive products such as rice, coffee, milk, dairy products, poultry, sugar, and vegetables like tomatoes, onions and potatoes etc., which are usually excluded in treaties, but that will nevertheless be liberalized when the DR-CAFTA reaches full liberalization. However, the sensitiveness of products also depends on the other party to an agreement and specific sectors cannot be protected unjustifiably when there are significant gains to be made from trade openness. Moreover, taking a closer look at the excluded products in each of the individual PTAs that Costa Rica has with Mexico, Chile, Peru and Colombia, some products were not included in a specific tariff schedule. For instance, in the FTA between Mexico and Costa Rica and the FTA between Chile and Costa Rica, Costa Rica did not exclude any swine products from its list, but these products are excluded in the PTAs with Peru and Colombia.

It is important to question the treatment of these sensitive products and it is relevant to consider the particular rules of accession. For instance, Costa Rica could evaluate accession terms and adjustment timeframes before full liberalization for a balanced negotiation.

The second challenge concerns rules of origin, specifically on the cumulation issue. The type of cumulation was analysed in this chapter to determine whether or not diagonal cumulation existed in all the individual PTAs that Costa Rica has negotiated with each PA member State. If all PTAs had included a provision on diagonal cumulation in their agreements – in market access terms – Costa Rica would have been considered as part of the PA. This is because the diagonal cumulation provision would have allowed Costa Rica to cumulate origin with Mexico, Peru, Chile and Colombia as all of those countries have a common FTA. As indicated earlier in this chapter, all PTAs Costa Rica has negotiated with the individual PA member States have a diagonal cumulation provision except for the one with Chile. Costa Rica's FTA with Chile is one of the oldest PTAs that Costa Rica has negotiated and the trend of including the diagonal cumulation provision in PTAs is more recent. Diagonal cumulation was created with the aim of reducing the impact of the spaghetti bowl of regional integration, as explained by Gasiorek et al. (2007). The idea is to facilitate the application of an FTA. The first FTA between Costa Rica and Mexico in 1995 did not include this provision; it was incorporated later, in the process of updating of the agreement. Since Costa Rica's agreement with Chile is relatively old, the PA would be a great opportunity to bring the FTA between Chile and Costa Rica up to date.

Other questions arise such as the compatibility of the tariff schedule of the PA with the commitments relating to the Central American Customs Union (CACU). Although a detailed analysis was not carried out in this chapter, Costa Rica has almost 100% free trade in CACU (Costa Rica only excluded coffee and sugar from its tariff schedule) (Foreign Trade Information System undated-b); therefore, liberalization should not be major challenge in economic terms for the country. It would be interesting to know what the impact in other Central American countries that are not part of the PA has been, since market access is not the only element that is included in the agreement. As the research shows, Costa Rica will gain from the PA, but will other Central American countries lose?

Furthermore, this chapter did not analyse in detail the issues of migration and facilitation of the movement of people in the region. Customs and immigration authorities could encounter difficulties in trying to exercise control in a region that is highly vulnerable, but business benefits from greater flexibility. This is an issue that deserves further study. The same applies to the coordination of prevention and containment of organized crime.

Finally, another issue concerns the contribution of the parties through the development of cooperation mechanisms and the promotion of a cooperation platform in the PA. This development would be very positive for Costa Rica, but clear delineation and a practical approach is recommended.

6.6 Conclusions and Recommendations

The four individual PTAs between Costa Rica and the PA member States are relatively similar. However, there is a group of products that are excluded from an FTA that are not excluded from the rest of the PTAs. These products require special attention. One recommendation is to conduct an analysis of all the products that were excluded from the individual agreements taking into account whether such products are already liberalized under other agreements and if protection is justified.

Once this information is available, sectorial meetings should be set up in order to define a position on the PA. Furthermore, Cost Rica should determine the best approach in terms of timeframes for full liberalization taking into account that studies project the achievement of a 0.8% increase in GDP under a full liberalization scenario.

Products included in the individual PTAs should, to some extent, be considered automatically in category A of the tariff schedule (i.e., duty free access) during Costa Rica's accession to the PA, since diagonal cumulation already exists in Costa Rica's agreements with the PA countries – except with Chile – which means that those products already enjoy free trade inside the PA provided that they comply with the rules of origin.

Regulatory discussions on regionalism attained great importance when the European regional integration process started and neo-functionalist thinking emerged, which explains regional integration efforts. Haas (Haas 1964, 1976) argues that the decision in favour of integration is the result of the work of different sectors that support integration and that have effects, essentially pragmatic rather than altruistic (Carlsnaes et al. 2011; Zürn 2011). Furthermore, Haas (Hass 1976) argues that international programmes are beneficial to both welfare and integration (also in Verdier 1994). In other words, they are a way to achieve welfare as part of the regional integration effort. Likewise, the neofunctionalism of Nye (Nye 1971) believes that the establishment of a sense of identity is a powerful force in support of regional integration. Although Nye points out many challenges to these regional organizations, he did not study the case of the PA – a *sui generis* institution. The PA is not comparable with the European Union because its development has been completely different. However, the PA represents a deeply integrated forum, not only because it has a fully integrated economic system, but also because it implemented cooperation mechanisms of joint representation, integration of customs, and others. The PA constitutes a step beyond a customs union with a particular kind of institutionalism, but it cannot be viewed in the same way as European integration. It represents a process of deep integration like no other, but with special regional features based on a strong political will.

Lastly, the accession of Costa Rica to the PA represents a challenge, but is a necessary process in today's world of alliances and trade blocs, which certainly brings added value to the economy. Studies by ECLAC (2015a, b, c), the Konrad Adenauer Stiftung and the World Bank confirm this view. Further research is still needed on the economic advantages to Costa Rica of joining the Trans-Pacific Partnership, an agreement to which some of the PA members are parties and that will open up market access to more than half of the world's trade.

In order to achieve accession and to continue with the discussion of possible membership of the TPP, the Government of Costa Rica should start seeking a balance. For the country to achieve a win–win situation it is necessary to develop an internal informative process, and ensure transparency and consultations with different production sectors and civil society. This process should start as soon as possible in order to finalize accession as soon as possible.

References

Books and Articles

Carlsnaes, W., Risse, T., & Simmons, B. A. (2011). Foreign policy. In *Handbook of international relations*. London: Sage.

Cottier, T., & Maya, H. (2003). The prospects of 21st century constitutionalism. In B. von Armin & R. Wolfrum (Eds.), *Max Planck yearbook of united nations law* (Vol. 7, pp. 261–328). Leiden: Koninklijke Brill N.V.

Felbermayr, G., et al. (2015). *Dimensiones y Efectos Económicos de la Alianza del Pacífico.* Instituto Ifo de Investigación Económica Konrad Adenauer Stiftung. Santiago: RiL editores.

Friedman, T. L. (1999). *The Lexus and the olive tree*. New York: Anchor Books.

Haas, E. B. (1964). *Beyond the Nation-State*. Stanford: Stanford University Press.

Haas, E. B. (1976). Turbulent fields and the theory of regional integration. *International Organization, 30*(2), 173–212. https://doi.org/10.1017/S0020818300018245.

Hertel, T. W., Anderson, K., Francois, J. F., & Martin, W. (2000). *Agriculture and non-agricultural liberalization in the millenium round* (GTAP Working Paper, Paper 8). Purdue University.

Keohane, R. O., & Nye Joseph Jr., S. (1971). Transnational relations and world politics. In *The journal of international organization* (Vol. 88, No. 1 pp. 329–349). Cambridge, MA: MIT Press. https://doi.org/10.2307/2148689

Nye, J. S., Jr. (1971). *Peace in parts: Integration and conflict in regional organization*. Boston: Little Brown.

Nye, J. S., Jr., & Donahue, J. D. (Eds.). (2000). *Governance in a globalizing world*. Washington, DC: Brookings Institution Press.

Risse, T. (2007). Transnational actors and world politics. In *Handbook of International Relations* (pp. 251–286). London: SAGE Publications Ltd. https://doi.org/10.1007/978-3-540-70818-6_19.

Simmons, B. A., Carlsnae, W., & Risse, T. (2012). *Handbook of International Relations*. London: Sage Publications.

Verdier, T. (1994). Models of political economy of growth: A short survey. *European Economic Review, 38*(3–4), 757–563.

Zürn, M. (2011). From interdependence to globalization. In *Handbook of international relations*. London: Sage. https://doi.org/10.4135/9781446247587.n16.

News

Avendaño, M. (2016). Costa Rica será 'transparente' sobre déficit fiscal en Cumbre Alianza del Pacífico. *La Nación,* 29 June. http://www.nacion.com/economia/empresarial/Costa-Rica-Cumbre-Alianza-Pacifico_0_1569643130.html. Accessed Aug 1 2016.

Cambronero, N. (2017). Luis Guillermo Solís concluye, tras gira a EE. UU., que el TLC no se verá afectado. *La Nación,* 20 March. http://www.nacion.com/nacional/politica/Guillermo-Solis-EE-UU-Cafta_0_1622637798.html. Accessed 4 Apr 2017.

Diamond, J., & Bash, D. (2017). Trump signs order withdrawing from TPP, reinstate 'Mexico City policy' on abortion, *CNN,* 24 January. http://edition.cnn.com/2017/01/23/politics/trans-pacific-partnership-trade-deal-withdrawal-trumps-first-executive-action monday sources-say/. Accessed 4 Apr 2016.

Institutional

Alianza del pacífico. (2013a). *Acuerdo Marco de la Alianza del Pacífico.* https://alianzapacifico.net/?wpdmdl=4464f. Accessed 8 Oct 2015.

Alianza del Pacífico. (2013b). *Primer protocolo modificatorio del protocol adicional al Acuerdo Marco de la Alianza del Pacífico.* https://alianzapacifico.net/?wpdmdl=4580. Accessed 1 Aug 2016.

Alianza del Pacífico. (2016). *Representantes de Aduanas de los países de la AP firmaron un Plan de Acción para avanzar hacia un Acuerdo de Reconocimiento Mutuo.* https://alianzapacifico.net/representantes-de-aduanas-de-los-paises-de-la-alianza-del-pacifico-firmaron-un-plan-de-accion-para-avanzar-hacia-un-acuerdo-de-reconocimiento-mutuo/. Accessed 1 Aug 2016.

Cetys Universidad Campus Ensenada. (undated). *TLC México – Costa Rica.* https://sites.google.com/site/tratadosinternacionalesmexico/tlc-mexico---costa-ricahttps://sites.google.com/site/tratadosinternacionalesmexico/tlc-mexico---costa-rica. Accessed 15 July 2015.

COMEX. (1999). *Tratado de Libre Comercio entre la República de Costa Rica y la República de Chile, Documento explicativo.* http://www.comex.go.cr/tratados/vigentes/chile/doc_explicativo_chile.pdf. Accessed 19 July 2015.

COMEX. (2000). *Tratado de Libre Comercio entre Costa Rica, y México: Una evaluación a cinco años de su vigencia.* http://www.sice.oas.org/TPD/CRI_MEX/Studies/Ev5TLC_s.pdf. Accessed 19 July 2015.

COMEX. (2002). *Tratado de Libre Comercio entre Centroamérica y Chile y del Protocolo Bilateral Adjunto Celebrado entre las Repúblicas de Costa Rica y de Chile: Capítulo 4 sobre Reglas de Origen.* http://www.comex.go.cr/tratados/vigentes/chile/texto_tratado/capitulo%204/00_Capitulo%20IV.pdf. Accessed 19 July 2015.

COMEX. (2011). *Tratado de Libre Comercio entre Costa Rica y Peru, Documento explicativo.* http://www.comex.go.cr/tratados/vigentes/peru/documento_explicativo_peru.pdf. Accessed 19 July 2015.

COMEX. (2012). *Tratado de Libre Comercio entre Centroamérica y México, Documento explicativo.* http://www.comex.go.cr/tratados/proceso_legislativo/mexico/Documento%20explicativo%20Mexico.pdf. Accessed 19 July 2015.

COMEX. (2013a). *Tratado de Libre Comercio entre los Estados Unidos Mexicanos y las Repúblicas de Costa Rica, El Salvador, Guatemala, Honduras y Nicaragua: Capítulo IV sobre Reglas de Origen.* http://www.comex.go.cr/tratados/proceso_legislativo/mexico/texto_tratado/capitulo4/00_Capitulo4%20Reglas%20de%20Origen.pdf. Accessed 19 July 2015.

COMEX. (2013b). *Tratado de Libre Comercio entre Costa Rica y Colombia, Documento explicativo.* http://www.comex.go.cr/tratados/proceso_negociacion/colombia/documento%20explicativo/Documento%20Explicativo.pdf. Accessed 19 July 2015.

COMEX. (2014a). *Alianza del Pacífico consulta sectorial sobre acceso a mercado de bienes y servicios.* http://www.comex.go.cr/tratados/proceso_negociacion/alianza%20del%20pacifico/Consulta%20Sectorial%20AP.pdf. Accessed 16 Oct 2015.

COMEX. (2014b). *Consulta Pública.* http://www.comex.go.cr/tratados/proceso_negociacion/alianza%20del%20pacifico/Consulta%20Publica%20AP.pdf. Accessed 16 Oct 2015.

COMEX. (2016). *Exportaciones de bienes cifras globales por destino 2004–2015.* http://www.comex.go.cr/estadisticas/exportaciones.aspx. Accessed 19 Nov 2015.

COMEX. (undated-a). *Alianza del Pacífico.* http://www.comex.go.cr/tratados/proceso_negociacion/alianza%20del%20pacifico/AlianzadelPacifico.aspx. Accessed 28 Oct 2017.

COMEX. (undated-b). *Tratado de Libre Comercio entre los Estados Unidos Mexicanos y las Repúblicas de Costa Rica, El Salvador, Guatemala, Honduras y Nicaragua.* http://www.comex.go.cr/tratados/vigentes/mexico.aspx. Accessed 19 Nov 2015.

COMEX. (undated-c). *Tratado de Libre Comercio entre Centroamérica y Chile y del Protocolo Bilateral Adjunto Celebrado entre las Repúblicas de Costa Rica y de Chile.* http://www.comex.go.cr/tratados/vigentes/chile.aspx. Accessed 28 Oct 2017.

COMEX. (undated-d). *Tratado de Libre Comercio entre el Gobierno de la República de Costa Rica y el Gobierno de la República de Perú*. http://www.comex.go.cr/tratados/vigentes/peru.aspx. Accessed 28 Oct 2017.

COMEX. (undated-e). *Tratado de Libre Comercio entre el Gobierno de la República de Costa Rica y el Gobierno de la República de Colombia'*, http://www.comex.go.cr/tratados/proceso_negociacion/Colombia.aspx. Accessed 3 Aug 2016.

Cudmore, E., & Whalley, J. (2005). *Barriers to prosperity – Developing countries and the need for trade liberalisation*. http://www.nber.org/chapters/c10140.pdf. Accessed 19 July 2016.

Economic Commission for Latin America and the Caribbean (ECLAC). (2015a). *Informe del Estado de las Exportaciones en América Latina*.

Economic Commission for Latin America and the Caribbean (ECLAC). (2015b). *Panorama de la Inserción Internacional de América Latina y el Caribe 2015. La Crisis del comercio regional: diagnóstico y perspectivas*. Santiago, Chile. http://repositorio.cepal.org/bitstream/handle/11362/39010/S1501143_es.pdf. Accessed 15 Oct 2015.

Economic Commission for Latin America and the Caribbean (ECLAC). (2015c). *El Comercio Regional ante una encrucijada: diversificación e integración en un contexto global de bajo crecimiento*. Press Release. http://www.cepal.org/es/comunicados/comercio-regional-encrucijada-diversificacion-integracion-un-contexto-global-crecimiento. Accessed 15 Nov 2015.

Foreign Trade Information System. (undated). *Marco jurídico de la integración centroamericana*. http://www.sice.oas.org/sica/instmt_s.asp. Accessed 19 Nov 2015.

Gasiorek, M., Augier, P., & Lai-Tong, C. (2007). *Multilateralising regionalism: Relaxing rules of origin or can those PECS be flexed?* World Trade Organization. https://www.wto.org/english/tratop_e/region_e/con_sep07_e/gasiorek_augier_lai_tong_e.pdf. Accessed 4 Aug 2016.

Organization for Economic Co-operation and Development (OECD). (2013). *Investment policy reviews: Costa Rica* http://www.keepeek.com/Digital-Asset-Management/oecd/finance-and-investment/oecd-investment-policy-reviews-costa-rica-2013_9789264203952-en#page11. Accessed 3 June 2014.

U.S. Food and Drug Administration (FDA). (2016). *Regulatory harmonization and convergence*. http://www.fda.gov/BiologicsBloodVaccines/InternationalActivities/ucm271079.htm. Accessed 22 July 2016.

USTR. (2017). *The president's 2017 trade policy Agenda*. https://ustr.gov/sites/default/files/files/reports/2017/AnnualReport/Chapter%20I%20-%20The%20President%27s%20Trade%20Policy%20Agenda.pdf. Accessed 4 Apr 2017.

World Customs Organization. (2010). *The authorized economic operator and the small and medium enterprise, FAQ.*. http://www.wcoomd.org/en/topics/facilitation/instrument-and-tools/tools/~/media/93162547322F462A97F8767D0987A901.ashx. Accessed 1 Aug 2016.

Part II
The Pacific Alliance's Substantive Disciplines: Current and Future Challenges

Chapter 7
Services Commitments in the Pacific Alliance

Dorotea López, Felipe Muñoz, and Angélica Corvalán

7.1 Introduction

The Pacific Alliance (PA) is a regional integration initiative formed by Chile, Colombia, Peru and Mexico. First promoted by the former Peruvian President Alan Garcia at the Pacific Rim Forum, it was launched by the Presidential Declaration for the Pacific Alliance (Lima Declaration), in April 2011, and officially established through the Framework Agreement signed in Paranal, Chile, in June 2012. The stated aim of the PA is to deepen the integration process among participants by speeding up measures for the free circulation of goods and financial flows, the delivery of services and the movement of people across borders (Wilhelmy 2013). While the nature of the PA has eluded precise definition, it shares elements of a hard law free trade zone (built on the foundations of bilateral treaties among members) and a soft law construct for greater facilitation, cooperation and partnership (Wilhelmy 2013; López and Muñoz 2012). It is based on the model of "open regionalism", i.e. a process that aims to create economic interdependence between countries through preferential trade agreements (PTAs) that increase their competitiveness (Rojas and Teran 2016). It has shared values regarding respect for the rule of law, democracy and protection of human rights, through a focus on liberalizing and increasing trade and investment (Villarreal 2014).

The PA has drawn attention from within the region and outside it. It has attracted a large number of countries participating as observers of this process, which is something new to integration schemes, and is meant to be open to the participation of new members, with Costa Rica and Panama as the most probable ones. The objective of creating an economic platform out of the PA is interesting as it may become a leading bloc in Latin America, albeit not such an important player globally.

D. López (✉) · F. Muñoz · A. Corvalán
Institute of International Studies, University of Chile, Santiago, Chile
e-mail: dolopez@uchile.cl; fmunozn@uchile.cl; acorvalana@fenuchile.cl

P. Sauvé et al. (eds.), *The Pacific Alliance in a World of Preferential Trade Agreements*, United Nations University Series on Regionalism 16,
https://doi.org/10.1007/978-3-319-78464-9_7

As mentioned by Bhagwati (2013), "…in the face of failure to conclude Doha, the damage to multilateralism has been compounded by a substantial push, led by the United States (for the Trans-Pacific Partnership, or TPP) and the European Union (for the Transatlantic Trade and Investment Partnership, or TTIP), toward discriminatory, preferential 'regional' trade initiatives. The Pacific Alliance of Chile, Colombia, Mexico, and Peru is far less significant than the other two". Despite this, the PA may become an important regional player although "[f]rom a focus more of their political position, this alliance has the risk of creating animosity by those countries that do not belong to it, which could have effects on the parallel blocks where these same countries are involved" (López and Muñoz 2012). The PA is also seen as a reaction to the movement towards left-leaning governments in the region (Mora et al. 2016). "The PA has provoked reactions from regional actors such as Venezuela and the other [Bolivarian Alliance for the Peoples of Our America] ALBA countries, as well as from Brazil and some of its Mercosur partners. The former considers the PA to be an alternative, anti-podal project to its socialist regional model in Latin America and a US tool with which Washington can reassert its hegemony. For Brazil, its concerns lie with losing control of its own sphere of influence as Mexico tries to get a foothold in the region" (Nolte and Wehner 2013).

However, despite the attention received, and its novel features, does the PA go beyond previous integration schemes in the region? The PA has been described as a pragmatic process; therefore, countries will commit in those areas where they can reach agreements and may advance in the near future on the basis of shared interests. Due to this pragmatic approach, some authors have claimed that the PA has produced more rhetoric than concrete achievements, and therefore few new commitments are likely to arise in the near future. Notwithstanding the goodwill regarding the integration of the four countries, the instruments that have emerged to date would not appear to meet the requirements of a deep integration scheme.

The objective of this chapter is to review whether the PA goes beyond previous agreements, particularly for services, and determine whether the instruments developed to date within the PA contribute to the objective of creating an area in which services may flow freely across PA members' borders. To this end, commitments achieved in services within the framework of the Alliance will be analyzed, since there is a general belief that member countries provide better access and treatment conditions to major trading partners (i.e. to the United States (US)) than to the other members. Therefore, this chapter looks at the services dimension of the PA answering the following questions: Have the PA countries committed more deeply than in previous agreements? And, do PA members afford treatment on services liberalization to their developed country partners than to their fellow member countries?

The following section presents an overview of the services sector in the countries of the PA. To provide a benchmark, the third section reviews the commitments under the General Agreement on Trade in Services (GATS) of the World Trade Organization (WTO), previous agreements between the PA countries, and in the trade agreements with the US. The fourth section analyses how services have been included in the PA, paying particular attention to the commitments included in the PA Trade Protocol. Finally, some concluding remarks put forward.

7.2 Trade in Services in the Pacific Alliance

Although the four countries forming the PA have been identified as open to trade, and to some extent have defined development pathways linked to closer international economic relations, an analysis of the data reveals marked differences between the PA members. Chile and Mexico, which had already embarked on an aggressive openness policy, are far more engaged in international trade and investment than are Peru and Colombia, and this is reflected in the contribution of trade to gross domestic product (GDP). As shown in Fig. 7.1, for Chile and Mexico trade represents over 65% of their GDP, whereas for Colombia and Peru it does not account for more than 50%. Another aspect is the continued importance of trade in goods. For all PA countries, more than 85% of total trade is in goods, whereas services only account for around 10%. Although not the focus of this chapter, it is noteworthy that, with the exception of Mexico, much PA merchandise trade is in commodities (petroleum and copper) or low-tech *maquila*, and the PA countries see trade in services as a way to diversify and upgrade their export baskets.

Despite the relatively low contribution of services to the export baskets of the PA countries, trade in services in the region has shown notable progress in recent years. Over the past couple of decades, rapid growth of services exports has occurred in the four PA countries (Fig. 7.2). Chile and Mexico lead this process, which is consistent with their earlier trade policy orientation towards an open economy. Despite having had a relatively stagnant international services sector until the early 2000s, since 2005 PA countries have witnesses a strong, two digit growth of their exports. For Chile and Mexico, although the long-term trend also shows sustained growth, the 2008 financial crisis had a dire impact on their trade in services, which contracted by 21% and 15%, respectively.

The PA is not an important player in world trade in services. With a total value of 45.54 billion dollars in exports in 2015, it represents less than 1% of world services

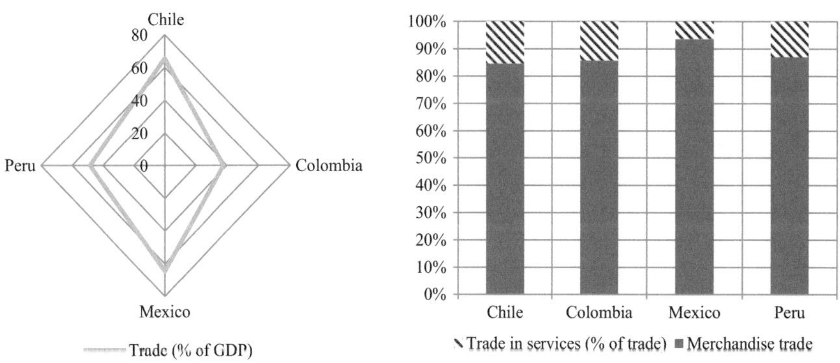

Fig. 7.1 Trade as a percentage of GDP in 2015. (Source: Authors' elaboration based on World Bank (2016))

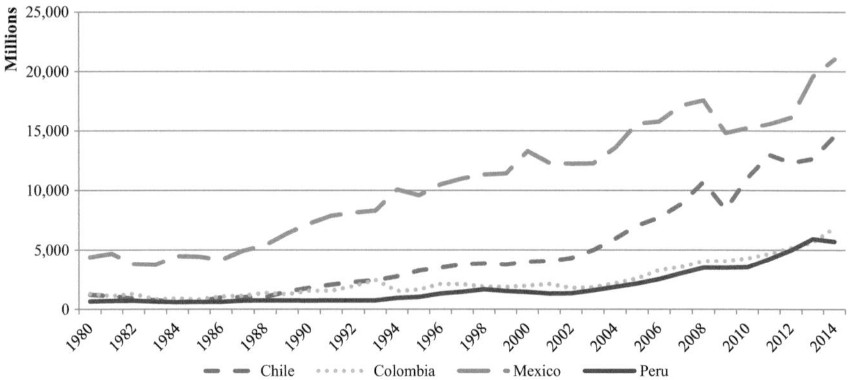

Fig. 7.2 Trade in services in Pacific Alliance countries, 1980–2014. (Source: Authors' elaboration based on WTO (2016))

Fig. 7.3 Pacific Alliance services exports, 2015. (Source: Authors' elaboration based on WTO statistics)

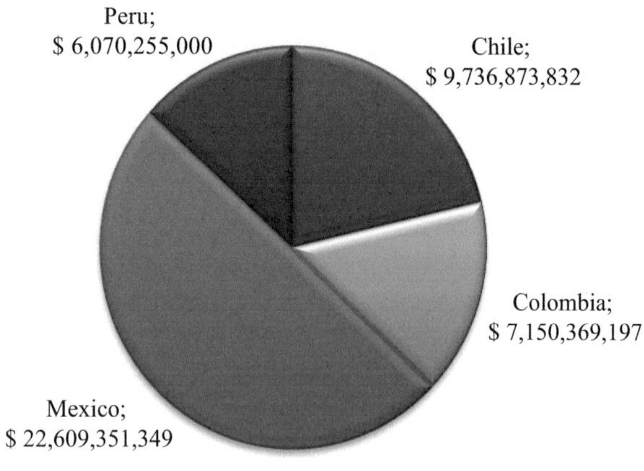

exports. As shown in Fig. 7.3, Mexico is the source of almost half of the Alliance's service exports (49.6%), Chile ranks second with 21.3%, while Colombia (15.6%) and Peru (13.3%) lag behind.

Notable differences become apparent when looking at the sectoral composition of trade in services in the Alliance. While for Mexico, Colombia and Peru, travel is the most important component of services exports, accounting for more than 50% (reaching 77% for Mexico), for Chile, transport is the most important activity, accounting for nearly 45% of total exports. Other commercial services (which include high value added services, such as business or knowledge oriented services) have a secondary importance in the region (Fig. 7.4).

The world rankings of the PA countries' participation in services trade confirm the secondary role these countries currently play (Table 7.1). No PA economy is

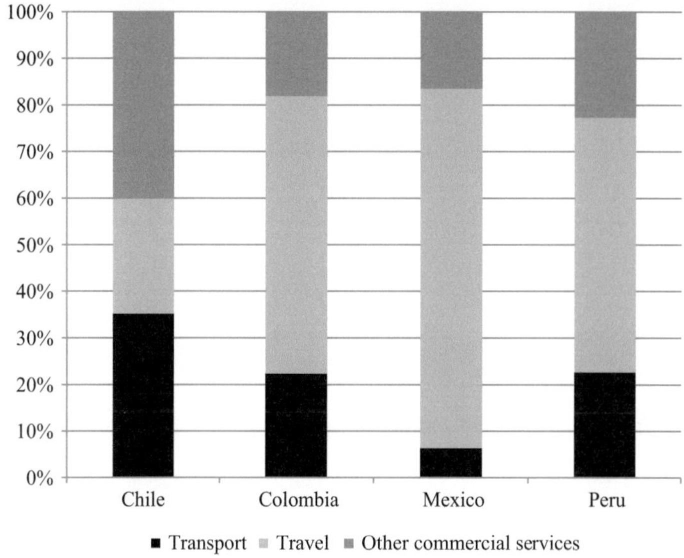

Fig. 7.4 Services export composition in Pacific Alliance countries, 2015. (Source: Authors' elaboration based on WTO statistics)

Table 7.1 Pacific Alliance countries' services exports – world ranking in 2014

	Commercial services		Transport		Travel		Other commercial services	
	Rank	Share (%)	Rank	Share (%)	Rank	Share (%)	Rank	Share (%)
Chile	55	0.23	37	0.53	67	0.18	43	0.15
Colombia	65	0.14	60	0.19	51	0.32	67	0.04
Mexico	40	0.43	75	0.09	22	1.31	44	0.15
Peru	71	0.12	65	0.14	55	0.24	63	0.05

Source: Authors' elaboration based on WTO statistics

among the top 10 exporters in any of the three main categories: transport, travel or other commercial services. PA countries rank in the middle of the global ranking. The best relative position is held by Mexico, which ranks 22nd in travel services with a market participation of nearly 1.3%.

Taking the share of world GDP as a reference, some conclusions about the PA can be drawn. First, regarding trade in merchandise, we see differences between Chile and Mexico on one side, and Colombia and Peru on the other. While the first two have higher relative trade participation than their share of GDP, reflecting the important role of trade in their economic development processes and their rapid internationalization, Colombia and Peru still lag behind. For services trade, all four countries have a relatively lower participation than their share of GDP (Fig. 7.5).

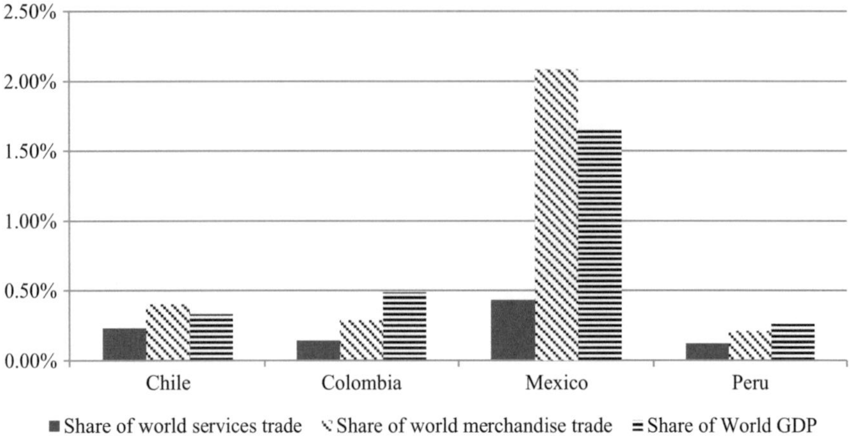

Fig. 7.5 Pacific Alliance countries' share in world GDP, merchandise and services trade, 2015. (Source: Authors' elaboration based on WDI, World Bank)

7.3 Pacific Alliance Countries' Services Commitments

Despite their relatively low participation in world services trade, PA countries have identified this sector as an important driver of growth and development, particularly because their export baskets are anchored in natural resources. To stimulate trade in services, they have initiated various export promotion programmes and are including services in their trade negotiations, with a view to finding new openings for market access. This section reviews the level of commitments in services made by PA countries, taking the WTO's GATS as a baseline.

7.3.1 Specific Commitments in the General Agreement on Trade in Services

The GATS is a result of the Uruguay Round of trade negotiations and part of the Marrakesh Agreement establishing the WTO "based on the non-discrimination principle that governs the multilateral trading system contained in the most favored nation (MFN) clause that ensures non-discrimination in the treatment to which a WTO Member is entitled from other Members" (Sáez 2005). GATS is composed of a framework agreement, which defines the obligations with eight annexes addressing horizontal[1] and sector-specific matters, and schedules of specific commitments. As mentioned by Sauvé (1998), "definition of 'trade in services' was a central issue

[1]Horizontal commitments stipulate limitations that apply to all the sectors included in the schedule.

of the negotiations, the substantive issue being whether the GATS would apply only to cross-border trade in services or would also include transactions requiring the relocation of factors of production". The GATS addresses services in terms of their mode of supply: mode 1: cross-border supply, mode 2: consumption abroad, mode 3: commercial presence, mode 4: presence of natural persons. Due to its negotiation approach, specific commitments became the most important part of the agreement. "Negotiators chose to pursue a hybrid positive-negative list scheduling specific commitments. It is positive in determining the sectorial coverage of market access and national treatment commitments, negative with regard to identifying measures that violate either national treatment or market access disciplines" (Hoekman 1996). To analyze the extent to which countries committed under GATS a review of these schedules was conducted.

The review revealed that the PA countries did not list horizontal commitments for modes 1 and 2. Chile scheduled market access and national treatment limitations only for modes 3 and 4. For commercial presence, market access commitments only apply to those suppliers of services established as a subsidiary and that comply with the rules and legal procedures on foreign direct investment in force in the country. National treatment restrictions relate to transfer of capital abroad, real estate acquisitions and the performance of other legal acts in the frontier zone; and the staff employed by a supplier of services established in Chile must be Chilean. Regarding the presence of natural persons (mode 4), market access is unbound, except for transfers of natural persons within a foreign enterprise established in Chile, national treatment unbound as well, except for the categories of natural persons listed under market access.

Colombia, like Chile, did not schedule any commitments on modes 1 and 2. For commercial presence, the country listed market access limitations regarding investment in activities relating to national defense and the processing and disposal of toxic, hazardous or radioactive waste not produced in Colombia, taxes on remittances; ownership of coastline and border regions; and special provisions for commercial presence in San Andrés and Providencia Archipelago. For mode 4, commitments on both market access and national treatment are unbounded, except for managers, legal representatives and technical specialists, apart from in the professional services subsectors.

Regarding Mexico's commitments, the horizontal section in mode 3 stipulates that foreign investment in activities reserved for Mexicans should be done through neutral stocks previously listed on the Mexican stock exchange (market access) and that foreigners may not acquire direct ownership of lands and waters within a defined band (national treatment). For mode 4, market access is unbounded except for the entry and temporary stay of natural persons in a few categories. For national treatment, the schedule is unbounded except for those categories listed under market access, but it defines a list of activities reserved for Mexican nationals and stipulates that subsidies may only be granted to Mexican citizens.

Finally, Peru remained unbounded in regard to market access for both modes 3 and 4, except for natural persons providing services and employed by

Table 7.2 PA countries' specific commitments in GATS

Sector	Chile	Colombia	Mexico	Peru
Business services	×	×	×	×
Communication services	×	×	×	×
Construction and related engineering services	–	×	×	–
Distribution services	–	–	×	×
Educational services	–	–	×	–
Environmental services	–	×	–	–
Financial services	×	×	×	×
Health and related social services	–	–	×	–
Tourism and travel-related services	×	×	×	×
Recreational, cultural and sporting services	–	–	–	×
Transport services	×	–	×	×
Other services	–	–	×	–

Source: Authors' elaboration based on I-tip data

service-providing companies in the sectors and subsectors included in its schedule, who are nationals of countries that are members of the GATS as listed.

Moving into specific commitments, the first step is to find out in which sectors PA members scheduled them. As shown in Table 7.2, PA members were not active in listing commitments under the GATS. Out of 12 sectors, Chile committed in only five, Peru and Colombia did so in six, and Mexico in seven. Such a finding is based on work by Marchetti and Roy (2008), who calculated the extent of the commitments made by countries in GATS and PTAs. In their study, they scored Chile's GATS commitments at 19.8, Colombia's at 27.8, Mexico's at 40.3, and Peru's at 30.8, in a scale from 0 to 100, being 0 completely close and 100 completely open.

As the multilateral instrument regulating trade in services, the GATS establish most of the baselines and definitions used in subsequent preferential negotiations covering services. As for most countries, including PA members, it was the first approximation to trade in services negotiations. Therefore, specific commitments – the core liberalization value of the agreement – are scarce. Except for Mexico, which had recently negotiated the North American Free Trade Agreement (NAFTA) when the Uruguay round was concluded, the PA countries had never before addressed services in a trade policy petting. Therefore, they faced two main concerns: dealing with a new topic on which they did not have expertise, and committing on a multilateral MFN basis.

7.3.2 *Commitments in Preferential Trade Agreements*

The GATS did not substantially liberalize international trade in services. Most of the liberalization has occurred in PTAs, particularly those signed with the US. The NAFTA approach to services negotiation, using a negative list (where countries

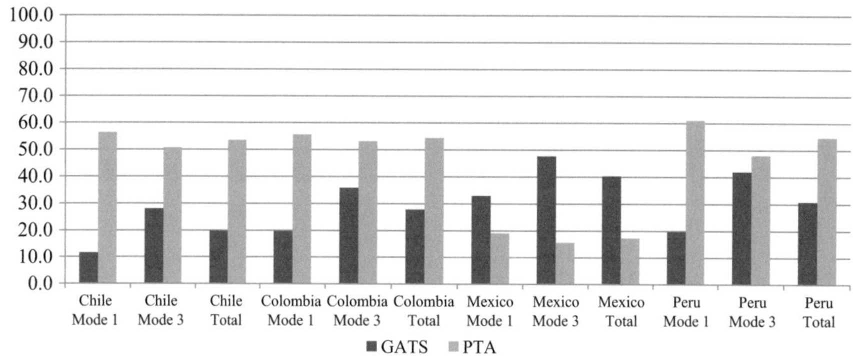

Fig. 7.6 GATS versus PTA commitments of Pacific Alliance countries. (Source: Author's elaboration with data from Marchetti and Roy (2008))

agree to liberalize all sectors, except those "reserved" in lists of non-conforming measures) has generated greater advances as negative lists: "foster greater transparency, as it will be immediately obvious which sectors or activities are excluded from coverage… may generate a greater pro-liberalization dynamic, as governments might be embarrassed by long lists of exceptions… finally, a negative list approach would imply that any new services developed as a result of innovation or technological advancement, or for any other reason, would automatically be subject to established disciplines" (Low and Mattoo 2000).

Comparing the level of commitments included in GATS and in the PTAs of the PA members, we may conclude that, for these countries, most liberalization has been preferential. Fig. 7.6, using data elaborated by Marchetti and Roy (2008), shows how much further the PTAs of PA countries have gone than their commitments in GATS. Except for Mexico (whose main liberalization took place under NAFTA, and which therefore could commit more in GATS), the other PA countries show a significant difference between liberalization undertaken in GATS and in their PTAs.

To understand the extent of this trade openness, this section will review commitments made by the PA members in their bilateral agreements and in agreements with the US, as it would appear that more concessions have been given to developed countries than to the PA partners. First, we note that all agreements have been negotiated following the NAFTA model, i.e. a negative list approach has been used. Therefore, their structures are quite similar. A close review of Annex I and Annex II exceptions was undertaken to identify real barriers to trade in services.

A look at the number of reservations made under each agreement reveals no marked differences between the PTAs (Table 7.3). As reservations included in bilateral agreements reflect domestic legislation, we may expect countries to have more

Table 7.3 Reservations contained in bilateral trade agreements

		Chile	Colombia	Peru	Mexico	United States
Chile	Annex 1	–	22	22	25	24
	Annex 2	–	17		11	16
Colombia	Annex 1	28	–	na	na	26
	Annex 2	13	–	na	na	14
Peru	Annex 1	27	na	–	26	20
	Annex 2		na	–	15	11
Mexico	Annex 1	14	na	49	–	28
	Annex 2	7	na	9	–	10
United States	Annex 1	12	11	12	16	–
	Annex 2	6	6	6	8	–

Source: Authors' elaboration based on the agreements
Due to data availability, and for a correct comparison, the Andean Community Agreement and the Colombia–Mexico–Venezuela Agreement are excluded
na not applicable

or less the same non-conforming measures across agreements.[2] We must also take into consideration that the number of reservations does not necessarily reflect their extent, as some reservations may contain more than one restriction, so sometimes reserves included in one agreement are equivalent to two or more reserves contained in another.

Another way to assess the reservations included in the agreements is to identify which obligations are affected, understanding that a sector may have under more than one obligation. Table 7.4 summarizes the number of reservations included in Annex I regarding national treatment, MFN, local presence, performance requirements, high-ranking executives and directors, and market access in the different bilateral trade agreements between PA members and in agreements with the US. The most reserved obligation is national treatment, which is present in almost every reservations included in the agreements. Local presence is the second most recurred reserve, with a frequency of about 50% of affected obligations.

Regarding Annex II, most of the reservations concern minorities, indigenous communities and cultural activities. Table 7.5 summarizes the obligations affected by these reservations; the most commonly affected obligation is national treatment.

Even though the analysis of the number of reservations, or main obligations affected by them, does not provide a complete picture regarding the level of restrictions imposed by a country, nor whether the restrictions are equivalent, it helps us to understand the degree of openness achieved by the participating countries. We observe similar reservations in PA members' bilateral agreements and in their agreements with the US (which are usually considered as the benchmark for developing countries). In general, PA countries have opened their markets, with few sectors remaining closed to foreign competition or ownership. These sectors are the

[2] Often, in order to open up a sector, and therefore, take out a reservations, domestic regulation has to be amended, a process that is normally done on an MFN basis, so, once a country opens a sector to one trading partner, this sector is open for other partners too.

Table 7.4 Affected obligations in Annex I

		Chile	Colombia	Peru	Mexico	United States
Chile	NT	–	21	21	22	21
	MFN	–	8	8	6	9
	Local presence	–	13	12	9	11
	Performance requirements	–	3	3	3	3
	High-ranking executives and directors	–	5	6	6	6
	Market access	–	0	0	0	0
Colombia	NT	18	–	na	na	17
	MFN	2	–	na	na	2
	Local presence	18	–	na	na	18
	Performance requirements	4	–	na	na	3
	High-ranking executives and directors	1	–	na	na	1
	Market access	11	–	na	na	9
Peru	NT	24	na	–	23	15
	MFN	1	na	–	1	1
	Local presence	9	na	–	9	8
	Performance requirements	2	na	–	2	2
	High-ranking executives and directors	4	na	–	4	3
	Market access	0	na	–	0	4
Mexico	NT	14	na	46	–	24
	MFN	2	na	10	–	1
	Local presence	4	na	18	–	2
	Performance requirements	2	na	1	–	8
	High-ranking executives and directors	1	na	3	–	2
	Market access	0	na	0	–	0
United States	NT	12	11	12	13	–
	MFN	7	7	7	8	–
	Local presence	6	6	6	6	–
	Performance requirements	1	1	1	1	–
	High-ranking executives and directors	3	3	3	2	–
	Market access	0	0	0	0	–

Source: Authors' elaboration based on the agreements
MFN most-favoured nation, *na* not applicable, *NT* national treatment

ones we would expect the PA to tackle in order to construct a real integration zone in services among member countries. The following section reviews the treatment services have reserved in the PA, to find out whether the identified reservations have been lifted.

Table 7.5 Affected obligations in Annex II

		Chile	Colombia	Peru	Mexico	United States
Chile	NT	–	14	na	11	12
	MFN	–	12	na	9	11
	Local presence	–	7	na	7	7
	Performance requirements	–	4	na	4	4
	High-ranking executives and directors	–	5	na	4	5
	Market access	–		na	0	1
Colombia	NT	10	–	na	na	na
	MFN	6	–	na	na	na
	Local presence	3	–	na	na	na
	Performance requirements	6	–	na	na	na
	High-ranking executives and directors	0	–	na	na	na
	Market access	1	–	na	na	na
Peru	NT	na	na	–	11	8
	MFN	na	na	–	8	5
	Local presence	na	na	–	7	6
	Performance requirements	na	na	–	6	4
	High-ranking executives and directors	na	na	–	2	2
	Market access	na	na	–	0	2
Mexico	NT	19	na	9	–	10
	MFN	6	na	4	–	8
	Local presence	6	na	7	–	7
	Performance requirements	6	na	1	–	0
	High-ranking executives and directors	3	na	2	–	4
	Market access	3	na	0	–	0
United States	NT	4	7	na	8	–
	MFN	3	7	na	6	–
	Local presence	3	6	na	5	–
	Performance requirements	3	6	na	2	–
	High-ranking executives and directors	1	6	na	5	–
	Market access	0	2	na	0	–

Source: Authors' elaboration based on the agreements
MFN most-favoured nation, *na* not applicable, *NT* national treatment

7.3.3 Services in the Pacific Alliance

PA countries have identified services as a key element in their growth and development processes, especially as a way to diversify their export baskets, which are currently primarily anchored in natural resources. The Alliance's objective is to "promote the free circulation of services and capital among its members" (Alianza del Pacífico 2016), and it is working to become an attractive destination for trade in services and to increase trade flows between its members and with the rest of the world. For this reason, in December 2011, the Alliance established a joint committee on investment and trade in services and a sub-committee on trade in services with the following objectives:

(a) "Share information and promote cooperation in those matters related to trade in services, in particular professional services;
(b) Hold periodic meetings to discuss mechanisms, instruments, or agreements to facilitate and increase trade in services, in particular professional services;
(c) Look for solutions or elimination of identified barriers to trade in services, in particular in professional services;
(d) Permanently meet in a way agreed by participants;
(e) Make proposals to the Committee for the more effective functioning or the consecution of the objectives of this sub-committee; and
(f) Discus any other aspect related to trade in services" (Alianza del Pacífico 2011).

The initial mandate, as stated in various Presidential Declarations, aimed to converge existing bilateral treaties into a single instrument, and to then add value to it. Therefore, more ambition derived of liberalization was expected within the PA than under previous agreements.

In 2012, the four countries signed the Pacific Alliance Framework Agreement, which stated, in Article 3, an objective to "build, in a participative and agreed way, a deep integration area to progressively advance towards the free circulation of goods, services, capitals and persons" (Alianza del Pacífico 2012). It was also established, in Article 8, that those agreements reached in the context of the Alliance will not replace or modify the previous agreements of which the PA countries are members, allowing their coexistence. As a framework agreement, it laid out an institutional basis for the PA's work, and left to upcoming instruments the realization of the objectives it had established. Following domestic ratification processes, the Pacific Alliance Framework Agreement entered into force on 20 July 2015. A working group on services and capital, which focuses on services trade, including e-commerce, investment negotiations, cross-border trade in services, financial services, telecommunications, air and maritime transport, and professional engineering services was established, the first objective being the inclusion of these topics in the Trade Protocol of the Alliance.

To achieve the trade objectives of the Framework Agreement, the PA signed an Additional Protocol (Trade Protocol) in 2014, in which aspects of trade in services were included in various chapters. These includes chapter 9: cross-border trade in

Table 7.6 Number of affected obligations in Annex I of the Pacific Alliance Trade Protocol and in US bilateral FTAs

	Pacific Alliance	United States
Chile	23	24
Colombia	25	26
Peru	26	20
Mexico	49	28

Source: Authors' elaboration based on the agreements

services; chapter 10: investment (a critical issue for the provision of many services); chapter 11: financial services; chapter 12: maritime services; chapter 13: electronic commerce; and chapter 14: telecommunications. As the Protocol does not include specific provisions for temporary admission, those contained in the bilateral agreements prevail (Observatorios Estratégicos de la Alianza del Pacífico 2017). The structure of the agreement follows a NAFTA approach and is similar in content to previous agreements signed by the PA members. As the PA's objectives include achieving the free movement of services among its members, the ratification of the Trade Protocol, and the incorporation of trade in services, make it worthwhile to analyse the efforts of the Alliance members towards meeting the objective of establishing an area of free movement for services. To this end, we review the reservations and restrictions included in the PA Trade Protocol.

In general, member countries have maintained the restrictions they had incorporated into earlier agreements, for example, their bilateral free trade agreements and agreements with the US. As can be seen in Table 7.6, the number of obligations included in Annex 1 of the Trade Protocol by each of the members of the PA is similar to the number in the FTAs with the US. The notable exception is Mexico, which apparently incorporated a greater number of reservations into the text of the Alliance Trade Protocol. However, this is not necessarily due to a greater number of restrictions, but to the form in which the Mexican government listed the commitments in the agreements.[3]

Taking into account the degree of openness of the four PA countries, and the fact that this has been achieved in a relatively non-discriminatory manner, Table 7.6 suggests that the Alliance's Trade Protocol is consolidating the degrees of openness that the member countries have consented to in their different negotiations and has not necessarily generated significant new levels of market openness.

To illustrate the idea that the Trade Protocol mainly consolidated the openness achieved in previous agreements and did not necessarily promote new liberalization, we reviewed the main reservations PA members have included in the Trade Protocol, and found them to be broadly similar to those included in the previous agreements.

[3]Some reservations included in the earlier agreements are divided into two reservations in later ones. Therefore, the number of reservations does not reflect necessarily the amount of restrictions included in the agreements.

Table 7.7 Main horizontal reservations included in Annex 1 of the Pacific Alliance Trade Protocol

	Reservations
Chile	Ownership of "state land" (borders and coastlines)
	Minimum national labour requirement
Colombia	Portfolio investment
	State trading enterprises
	San Andres and Santa Catalina – local presence restriction
Mexico	Land ownership in "restricted zones" (borders and coastlines)
	Investment evaluation in "restricted activities"
	Evaluation for investment over 49% in non-restricted activities
	Minimum national labour requirement
	Micro industrial classification
Peru	Land ownership (borders and resources)
	Minimum national labour requirement

Source: Authors' elaboration based on the Pacific Alliance Trade Protocol

Table 7.7 lists the main horizontal reservations included in Annex 1 by the PA countries. These reservations affect all sectors, and commonly reflect general restrictions applied by the states, usually including waiver conditions as stipulated by laws or internal procedures. They include the reservations that are likely to be the most difficult to remove from the negotiation agenda of the participating countries, as they usually relate to issues of national security, discriminatory national policies, and special protected zones and activities. Taking this into consideration, the PA negotiations on services led to the inclusion of almost the same clauses as in previous agreements.

Reviewing sector-specific reservations, as shown in Table 7.8, not many clauses are included in the agreement. Their impact should be analysed on a case-by-case basis, as some limitations may affect particular sectors and others may completely close an economic activity to foreign competition. Table 7.8 shows which sectors are affected by the reservations identified. All countries have included provisions on business and professional services, communication, energy and transport services. These sectors have commonly been more protected, partly in response to lobbying by interest groups not wishing to allow international competition in their respective fields. Other sectors are considered strategic or linked to national security, or of cultural value (such as cinema, television, and broadcasting services).

According to a governmental analysis of the Protocol, the main achievement of the PA's cross-border and investment chapters has been the updating of protection standards and liberalization commitments, particularly for old agreements such as Chile–Mexico (Direcon 2016). We may observe changes in the commitments, such as the possibility of 100% participation in the telecommunications sector in Mexico

Table 7.8 Sectoral reservations included in Annex 1[a] of the Pacific Alliance Trade Protocol

	Chile	Colombia	Mexico	Peru
Business and professional services	×	×	×	×
Communication services	×	×	×	×
Construction and related services	–	–	×	–
Distribution services	–	–	×	×
Education services	–	–	×	–
Energy services	×	×	×	×
Environmental services	×	×	–	–
Health and social services		–	–	–
Tourism services	–	–	–	–
Recreational, cultural and sporting services	×	–	–	×
Transport services	×	×	×	×

Source: Authors' elaboration based on the Pacific Alliance Trade Protocol

[a]Besides the cross-border trade in services chapter, the Trade Protocol includes three other relevant sector-specific chapters that should be considered in a full review of the extent of the obligations of the PA members: financial services; a chapter on maritime services, which complements the transport commitments included above, and a chapter on telecommunications

or the elimination of the nationality requirements to become a lawyer in Chile, which reflect how the countries have evolved in recent years. No telecommunications chapter was included in the agreements between Chile and Colombia or Chile and Peru; and electronic commerce and digital trade are new and fast growing area requiring the development of new rules. Moreover, owing to the importance of maritime services for the achievement of the goals of the Alliance, the specific chapter dealing with this issue will guarantee non-discriminatory treatment of ships in PA ports.

7.4 Concluding Remarks

The PA started as a very promising economic integration process. The countries of the PA depend heavily on commodity exports or on one major destination country for their exports. The PA was conceived in part as a means to increase services trade, and as a way to add value and develop more sophisticated regional and global value chains. The economic model implemented over the past 30 years in the four member countries is deeply rooted in their trade policies and their increasing insertion in production networks. For this reason, the deepest level of economic integration achieved represents a foundation for developing more services trade between the PA members and with Asia. Up to now it has not been clear whether there is any strategy in place to reach Asian countries with a joint initiative on services.

After reviewing the commitments made by PA countries in their various services negotiations, the first conclusion is that, in the framework of GATS, PA countries definitely have fewer commitments than they have in other trade negotiations including the text of the PA, which seems to be the most complete in some respects. Chile is the country that shows the biggest differences, because it made very few commitments to services openness in GATS compared with subsequent negotiations. Nevertheless, PA countries have expanded on their bilateral agreements, particularly between themselves, and with the US, which is used as a benchmark because of its importance as a major trading partner for all four PA countries.

A second point, is whether convergence among agreements can be seen to take place. When reading the Protocol, the PA members agreed to a legal text similar to that of their NAFTA-inspired bilateral agreements. Furthermore, the reservations are listed individually but applied on an MFN basis.

The structure suggests that the PA members had more understanding or political will in some sectors. An innovation initiative is also part of the process; all the members need to foster development in this area and it is strongly linked with services. In spite of the progress made, the liberalization of trade in services is far from complete, but mostly locks in the regulatory states across the four PA members.

Even though the PA does not appear to represent a big step towards greater services openness, it is nevertheless important in promoting liberalization in a region that has long found it more difficult to grant preferences to Latin American countries than to developed economies. Although little trade liberalization has so far been achieved by the PA, particularly under its Trade Protocol, we should remember that this instrument has been conceived as a starting point for building a deep integration scheme. Having been consolidated in to a single agreement, the norms and clauses related to trade in services may lay the foundations for the achievement of the free movement zone objective. For this, the upcoming work of the working group and the deepening commitments together with the political will required to do so remain critical.

Acknowledgement Research for this paper was funded by the Swiss State Secretariat for Economic Affairs under the SECO/WTI Academic Cooperation Project, based at the World Trade Institute, University of Bern, Switzerland; and the WTO Chairs Programme.

References

Alianza del Pacífico. (2011). *Memorandum de Entendimiento*. Santiago.
Alianza del Pacífico. (2012). *Acuerdo Marco de la Alianza del Pacífico*. ed. Alianza del Pacífico. Chile.
Alianza del Pacífico. (2016). *Temas de Trabjo*.
Bhagwati, J. (2013). Dawn of a new system. *Finance and Development, 50*(4), 8–13.
Direcon. (2016). *Protocolo Adicional al Acuerdo Marco de la Alianza del Pacífico ¿Qué implica para Chile?* Santiago: Direcon.
Hoekman, B. (1996). Assessing the general agreement on trade in services. The Uruguay round and the developing countries. In W. Martin & A. Winters (Eds.), *The Uruguay round and the developing countries* (pp. 88–124). Cambridge: Cambridge University Press.
López, D., & Muñoz, F. (2012). El inicio formal de la Alianza del Pacífico. *Revista Puentes, 13*(4), 18–22.

Low, P., & Mattoo, A. (2000). Is there a better way? Alternative approaches to liberalization under the GATS. In P. Sauvé & R. Stern (Eds.), *GATS 2000, New directions in services trade liberalization* (p. 449). Washington, DC: The Brookings Institution.

Marchetti, J., & Roy, M. (2008). *Services liberalization in the WTO and in PTAs*. Geneva/Cambridge: WTO/Cambridge University Press.

Mora, B., Nelson, L., & Ferrer, H. (2016). The Pacific Alliance: A geopolitical and economic perspective. *Dimensión Empresarial, 14*(1), 79–94.

Nolte, D., & Wehner, L. (2013). The Pacific alliance casts its cloud over Latin America. *German Institute of Global Area Studies* 8.

Observatorios Estratégicos de la Alianza del Pacífico. (2017). *Estudio sobre comercio de servicos en la Alianza del Pacífico. Normas vigentes para prestar servicios de ingeniería y de tecnologías de información en los países miembros*. Santiago.

Rojas, D., & Teran, J. M. (2016). La Alianza Del Pacifico: Nueva Muestra Del Regionalismo En América Latina. *Oasis, 24*, 69–88.

Sáez, S. (2005). *Trade in services negotiations: A review of the experience of the United States and the European Union in Latin America, Serie Comercio Internacional*. Santiago: CEPAL.

Sauvé, P. (1998). Assessing the general agreement on trade in services – Half-full or half-empty? *The World Trading System, 4*(4), 78.

Villarreal, M. A. (2014). *The Pacific Alliance: A trade integration initiative in Latin America*. Congressional Research Service. United States.

Wilhelmy, M. (2013). *The Pacific Alliance: A Latin American initiative for Asia-Pacific regional integration*. Pacific Economic Cooperation Council, Singapore: 5. https://alianzapacifico.net/?wpdmdl=4391.

World Bank. (2016). *World development indicators*. Washington, DC: World Bank.

WTO. (2016). *International trade statistics*. Geneva: WTO.

Chapter 8
Trade in Services and the Pacific Alliance: Contrasting Ambitions with Reality

Eric H. Leroux

8.1 Introduction

The objective of the Pacific Alliance (PA)[1] with respect to trade in services is to "build in a participatory and consensual way an area of deep integration to move progressively towards the free movement of […] services." The key word in this sentence is "progressively", and the missing, but (at least) equally important, one is "seriously".

If one were to speak of the PA's achievements in the services area in speed terms, one would say that it is still in first gear. Not that this is any different from what is taking place under other trade-liberalizing agreements; to the contrary, the PA is dutifully espousing the existing models reflected in, on the one hand, the North American Free Trade Agreement (NAFTA),[2] and on the other, the General Agreement on Trade in Services (GATS).[3] The PA's services disciplines negotiated thus far draw on both models, using, presumably, what is considered to be the best of each model (López et al. 2015). Under this scheme, the "additional protocol" to liberalize trade—signed by all Pacific Alliance countries and in force since 1 May 2016 – guarantees an eventual 100% elimination of barriers for all goods and

[1] The Pacific Alliance is a regional economic integration initiative between Mexico, Columbia, Peru and Chile, with Costa Rica and Panama being engaged in the process of becoming full members. A large number of countries, including Canada and the United States, presently have observer status (Organization of American States (OAS) 2015).

[2] North American Free Trade Agreement between Canada, the United States and Mexico (NAFTA), entered into force on 1 January 1994.

[3] General Agreement on Trade in Services (GATS), entered into force on 1 January 1995 as part of the World Trade Organization Agreement.

E. H. Leroux (✉)
Faculty of Law, Universidad Panamericana, Mexico City, Mexico
e-mail: eleroux@up.edu.mx

P. Sauvé et al. (eds.), *The Pacific Alliance in a World of Preferential Trade Agreements*, United Nations University Series on Regionalism 16,
https://doi.org/10.1007/978-3-319-78464-9_8

services (Marczak 2016, 10). The problem is that those two models are now flawed: they no longer reflect the reality of the marketplace, nor truly tackle head-on those issues that will be determinative of real, significant, liberalization of services trade in the coming decades.

Darwinism teaches us that if one does not adapt to, nor evolve together with, changing circumstances, the future is bleak. More than 20 years after the NAFTA and the GATS, which were watershed events in their own right, it is now time to re-assess the principles of market access and non-discrimination as the key drivers of future trade liberalization in services, because, to a large extent, they no longer are. To be sure, these principles remain relevant and useful in the context of services supplied through a commercial presence in the host State. To a significant extent, however, the future liberalization of trade in services is intrinsically linked to cross-border trade, more specifically E-commerce, where market access and non-discrimination do not reflect the key barrier that one really is faced with (Meltzer 2015, 17–19).

Indeed, the main obstacle to cross-border trade in many services sectors, for example, financial services, no longer pertains to quantitative restrictions and discrimination so much as to legitimate concerns about qualifications obtained in another country and a State's inability to exercise regulatory oversight outside its borders. The achievement of further, significant, trade liberalization in the coming decades therefore depends more on the recognition and harmonization of regulations than the negotiation of commitments in accordance with standard market access and non-discrimination principles, which do nothing to address the main stumbling block.[4]

It is now time to think outside the confines of existing models and negotiate further trade liberalization in accordance with revamped principles that reflect the new, fast-evolving, reality of the services marketplace. Otherwise, further trade liberalization, and certainly the achievement of a free movement of services objective in the context of the PA, can only remain, for the most part, elusive.

This chapter examines, first, the problem with the existing NAFTA and GATS models, which are too often blindly followed as templates for new agreements (Monardes 2016, 390–392) – including, possibly, the PA – and then delineates the path towards the difficult, yet necessary, long-term solution.

8.2 What Is the Problem?

The problem with the existing NAFTA and GATS models for the liberalization of services trade is, fundamentally, that they were created at a time when the Internet was nascent and E-commerce was, at best, at an embryonic stage (Tinawi and

[4]The concept of "harmonization", as used in this chapter, refers to the harmonization of the *substantive* aspects of laws, regulations, etc. Similar or equivalent requirements, conditions, etc., can naturally be enshrined in legal instruments that will vary in form from one country to another, depending on each country's legal system. What matters for mutual recognition to take place is not the form of the legal instruments being used, but rather the similarity or equivalency of substantive legal norms applied in respect of a given subject-matter.

Berkey 1999). In other words, the NAFTA and GATS models were not created to address, front and centre, the supply of services via electronic means, which scarcely existed at the time but is now becoming the most important means of trading services, and, in all likelihood, we have only seen the beginning of this fast-evolving, irreversible, phenomenon.

This is not to say that NAFTA and GATS-type agreements have not served the objective of trade liberalization well, or that they are no longer appropriate to serve that purpose. The point rather is that those models need to be adapted to the fast-changing reality of the services marketplace, so that the framework put in place to support future trade liberalization provides one with the means to effectively achieve it. The way things are going right now, with countries often following the old or existing models without really asking themselves whether they remain fully apt now and for the years and decades to come, there is increasingly a discrepancy between, on the one hand, the objective being pursued (further trade liberalization), and on the other, the tools being used to achieve that objective (principles used as drivers of future trade liberalization).

This discrepancy becomes even more acute and obvious when, as in the case of the PA, the desired objective is to go beyond free trade and attain the free movement of services. The services disciplines negotiated thus far among the PA members are wholly inadequate to reach that goal; at best, they are a very intermediate step to go beyond existing World Trade Organization (WTO) commitments, and they cannot, by themselves, serve as the bedrock for the progressive attainment of the stated objective of free movement of services.

The key principles upon which the NAFTA and GATS-type services disciplines, including those of the PA, are based are (i) non-discrimination, and (ii) prohibiting quantitative limitations that often take the form of monopolies, restrictions on the amount of capital invested, or licence/permit quotas.[5] These principles are perfectly suitable to address the key obstacles faced in the context of the supply of services through a commercial presence in a host State, which is a good reflection of how things were more than 20 years ago, when the NAFTA and GATS models were created. Trade in services was first and foremost a "mode 3" (commercial presence) issue, and the kinds of barriers that needed to be addressed were mostly of the quantitative or discriminatory type. In a commercial presence context, one achieves free trade of services once quantitative limitations and discrimination are removed (Van den Bossche and Zdouc 2017, 325, 399, 517).

More than two decades later, though, the way services are traded has shifted considerably towards the supply via electronic means, that is, on a cross-border basis, without the need for a commercial presence in a host State. The phrase "E-commerce revolution" is not too strong to describe what has been happening (The Nielsen Company 2014). From financial services to professional services of all kinds, natural barriers that existed not that long ago are fast fading away as technology – for example, the Internet, Skype and smart phones, to name but a few tools – never ceases to make it easier and cheaper for services suppliers and customers all

[5] See GATS Art. XVI and XVII.

around the world to purchase and sell services without moving from their chair or physical location. No need for a crystal ball to figure out that the future of international trade in services lies, first and foremost, in the supply of services on a cross-border basis, without the need for expensive brick-and-mortar facilities in a host country. Other modes of supply will not disappear; what is clear, though, is that the bulk of growth in international services trade will take place in the realm of cross-border trade. Hence the question of whether the pillars of trade liberalization in the existing models remain fit for purpose (Chander 2015).

In our view, they are not. The reason is that the main hurdle to overcome in the context of cross-border trade is not so much the removal of quantitative restrictions and discrimination (yes, this is important and relevant, but…) as the reluctance of national regulators to allow the supply of services from abroad when they do not have the ability to exercise normal regulatory oversight over the (foreign-based) suppliers. This is a major problem in many important sectors where regulation is extensive and, for the most part, designed to protect the public and ensure the competence and integrity of suppliers. One only needs to think of financial services or professional services: while one does need to address any quantitative or discriminatory issue that may exist, this, in itself, cannot lead one to the sought-after grail as national governments and their regulators will generally refuse to authorize cross-border trade so long as they do not feel comfortable from a regulatory standpoint. As long as that issue is not addressed adequately and squarely, there is simply no hope for meaningful cross-border commitments. It is worth reiterating that general exceptions of the GATS Article XIV type, including prudential carve-outs, cannot resolve this issue as they only allow a state to regulate (obviously) within the limits of its jurisdiction – in its own territory.

Existing models in fact reflect perfectly well this situation. If one looks at the framework for financial services in the GATS, one will see that the most developed countries, which have agreed to additional commitments through the Understanding on Commitments in Financial Services, have explicitly and considerably limited the scope of any cross-border commitments to rather marginal types of financial services. The same is true in the case of regional trade agreements, including the PA. The reason is simple: national regulators have few, if any, powers to regulate foreign-based suppliers, and they are seldom willing to rely on the regulation of such suppliers by their foreign-based regulators. In the event of a serious problem, for instance fraudulent activities, and precedents abound in this regard, national regulators will not be able to do much when seeking redress for harm done to the public who they have a duty to protect. The same concern prevents further cross-border trade services liberalization in many other sectors.

If one is to achieve significant international services trade liberalization in the coming years and decades, this issue needs to be addressed head-on. Otherwise, yes, some liberalization is possible, but it will remain rather marginal.

This is the area where the existing models come up short. In addition to the existing two pillars of non-discrimination and quantitative restrictions, discussed above, a third one is needed – revolving around the issue of mutual recognition and harmonization of regulations. True – existing models do not prevent regulators in different countries from recognizing each other's regulations, and this sometimes happens in some areas, usually when countries have very close ties and happen to have fairly similar regulations on a given subject matter.[6] Existing models do not really promote that, though, nor do they prescribe any rules committing countries to a clear path towards the achievement of that goal. This is where the shortcoming is, and it needs to be addressed if one is serious about reaching, for instance in the context of the PA, the goal of free movement of services.

8.3 What Is the Solution?

It follows from the foregoing discussion that the long-term solution to the problem at hand is to flesh out the disciplines on mutual recognition and harmonization so that national regulators of different countries not only have the option, but the obligation, to move in the direction of mutual recognition and harmonization of regulations. The good thing is that there is a helpful, successful, precedent: that of the European Union (EU) with its EU-wide passport, whereby services suppliers established in one member country can operate throughout the EU, yet, for the most part, remain only regulated by their home regulators (Lodder and Murray 2017). The hard truth, though, is that this is no small matter; it requires a strong, long-term, political commitment and a genuine desire to integrate economies with a view to improving (notably) the economic well-being of people. The challenge cannot be underestimated, especially in the short-term, but it is not an impossible one, and, one might say, the question may well be whether anyone really has a choice!

Indeed, in the current context, national regulators are, more often than not, playing catch-up given the fast-paced evolution of technologies and E-commerce (European Commission 2010, sec. 2.2.1). It is not as if they had a choice to address the new realities of services being traded worldwide via electronic means; it is happening, whether they like it or not, hence they have to find a solution unless they wish to end up looking like bystander "dinosaurs". The phenomenon of mutual recognition and harmonization is therefore, although maybe still in an embryonic stage and not always apparent, very much ingrained in, and an integral part of, the globalization process that is taking place across the board, not only with respect to trade in services. The main difference is that services, unlike products, can be traded in an intangible manner, necessitating (often) a much faster response from regulators. Services, such as financial services, can also be much more complex and so central to an economy that they require significant, immediate, regulatory attention in order to prevent havoc.

It follows that if cross-border E-commerce is happening no matter what, national regulators have no choice but to adapt. In most cases, and realistically, this means being able to increasingly rely on home-State regulation. This, in turn, can only take place in an orderly fashion to the extent that national regulators are equally

[6] *Cf.* GATS Art. VII.

competent, regulations are substantively fairly similar, and there is close cooperation and monitoring of international services suppliers. As exemplified by the EU, this requires more than goodwill; it necessitates binding international and supranational instruments that countries need to implement domestically, sometimes with some flexibility. This is not unlike the WTO agreements and other international trade/investment agreements, which, once agreed to, need to be implemented locally. It is also not too far removed from the "recommendations" of organizations such as the Bank for International Settlements (BIS) concerning core standards for the supervision of banks – a peer-pressure system that one would often wish would have a more binding nature (Basel Committee on Banking Supervision 2015). It is, yes, a big step up in terms of the internationalization of regulations, but, again, this goes hand-in-hand with the globalization phenomenon (including as regards trade; not limited to it), which is gradual, incremental and irreversible. Darwinism, one is bound to find, can be transposed to other areas of life, such as the evolution (or not) of regulatory organizations and their normative activities in tandem with what justifies their existence – the increasingly globalized nature of the marketplace and its stakeholders. Either one adapts and evolves, or else what?

In sum, trade in services via E-commerce is happening, and it is happening fast. National regulators need to respond to this new reality, and the only sensible way to do so is to increase mutual recognition and the harmonization of regulations. For that to happen, international instruments, with possibly, if not likely, international organizations are needed. In the trade area, international organizations such as the WTO present a solid basis to work from and build upon. One will of course face many dubious looks from sceptics who do not see that happening any time soon; well, they are probably right. In the same vein, many are certain to point out that the large membership of the WTO is unlikely to serve such an objective adequately; well, again, they are probably right. But this is beside the point. There is no question that this is a long-term issue and that one needs a convergence of strong political will, acknowledgement of a stark reality, and the setting of gradual, incremental, objectives to get there. But then, was that not needed for the creation of the United Nations, the International Monetary Fund (IMF), and, more recently, the WTO itself, to name but a few major international organizations? These organizations mirror what was or is happening "out there", in the real world; in other words, they are the result of a needed adaptation to new world realities. The question is not *if*; it is *when*.

To be clear, there is no suggestion here that the WTO, with its 160-plus Members, would presently be able to act as the needed international forum where mutual recognition and harmonization of national regulations can be properly addressed. Much less ambitious objectives remain to be addressed adequately. The point is, though, that this issue is not going away. Hence, it will need to be addressed. First, in the context of smaller regional integration arrangements, such as the PA or ASEAN (United Nations Conference on Trade and Development (UNCTAD) 2013), where the objective of free movement of services stands no chance of being achieved unless the supra-national institutions are able to develop and enforce rules on mutual recognition and the harmonization of regulations. Second, and at a broader level, there may be an opportunity, if not a need, for willing WTO Members to agree on additional, possibly sectoral, rules governing future liberalization of trade in services in accordance not only with the existing two pillars of quantitative restrictions and discrimination, but also along the lines of mutual recognition and harmonization of regulations. Consensus on such matters within the WTO clearly is presently elusive; hence, as with many, if not most, significant issues, agreements need to be sought among willing Members. Either that, or needed developments will, in any event, take place in the context of regional trade agreements, the reality of which has already been hitting the WTO rather hard in recent years.

8.4 Conclusion

Adapt to survive and move onwards, or get left behind. Such a little phrase, yet so much content in it. Such an easy truth, yet so often forgotten. Darwinism, or an adaptation of it, applies to all areas of life. This is not new, nor is it original to say it. It is simply surprising that one seemingly needs to remind people (and organizations) of it.

There is presently a reality that is obvious to everyone – who does not increasingly use E-commerce? – yet regulators, governments and international organizations, among others, have difficulties latching on to it. On the one hand, one easily understands that this typically reflects the standard, slow, reaction of established, entrenched organizations to watershed events. On the other, one can also easily mark that as a turning point that will determine whether the organizations concerned will adapt, hence survive and move onwards.

In the long term, nothing is ever set in stone. Whether one is talking about civilizations, States, economies or international organizations, "le passé n'est pas garant de l'avenir" [the past does not predict the future]. Nothing can be taken for granted.

Getting back to the more specific issue of international services trade, this means that espousing old or existing templates in the hope that – as this was the case more than 20 years ago – they will map out the way towards further, progressively significant, trade liberalization is akin to driving towards a wall. This is not the result of a lack of foresight on the part of past governments and negotiators; rather, it is due to fairly sudden, unforeseeable, fast developments in technology leading to drastic changes in the way services (intangible property) are traded around the world. It follows that in order to maintain the same target – further, progressively significant trade liberalization – adjustments have to be made.

In the present case, those adjustments mean that one needs to modify, revamp or complement the existing drivers of services trade liberalization in the current NAFTA and GATS models so that the key barrier to future trade liberalization is addressed, that is, the hurdle to future cross-border trade liberalization. More specifically, the required adjustments are that international trade agreements have to evolve towards a model where, in the case of cross-border trade, obligations are imposed with a view to gradually achieving the harmonization and mutual recognition of different countries' regulations. This is a big step, but it is one that national regulators will increasingly need to take in any event. If international trade agreements touching upon trade in services are to remain fully relevant in the long term, this is the critical area where creativity, innovation and "thinking outside the box" are needed. One can certainly be inspired by the EU system. PA countries need to make progress in the integration of trade in services (Abusada-Salah et al. 2015, 66), but it is a certainty that unless governments can think outside the confines of the existing NAFTA and GATS models, the objectives of the regional integration initiative, insofar as services are concerned, stand no chance of being attained.

References

Abusada-Salah, R., Acevedo, C., Aichele, R., Felbermayr, G., & Roldán-Pérez, A. (2015). *Dimensions and economic effects of the Pacific alliance*. Santiago: Konrad Adenauer Stiftung.

Basel Committee on Banking Supervision. (2015). *Corporate governance principles for banks*. Basel: Guidelines.

Chander, A. (2015). *Robots, the internet of things, and the future of trade* (SSRN Scholarly Paper ID 2679028). Rochester: Social Science Research Network.

European Commission. (2010). *A Digital Agenda for Europe*. Text/html; charset=UTF-8. August 26.

Lodder, A. R., & Murray, A. D. (2017). *EU regulation of E-commerce: A commentary*. Cheltenham: Edward Elgar Publishing.

López, D., Muñoz, F., & Corvalán, A. (2015). *Services dimension in the pacific alliance*. (SSRN Scholarly Paper SECO/WTI Academic Cooperation Project Working Paper Series 2015/04). Rochester: Social Science Research Network.

Marczak, J. (2016). *Pacific alliance 2.0: Next steps in integration*. Edited by Atlantic Council of the United States, Adrienne Arsht Latin America Center, and Bertelsmann Stiftung.

Meltzer, J. P. (2015). The internet, cross-border data flows and international trade. *Asia & The Pacific Policy Studies, 2*, 90–102.

Monardes, R. (2016). Challenges for countries in trade in services' negotiations with the Nafta approach: The experience of Chile in the free trade agreement with the United States. *British Journal of American Legal Studies, 5*, 371–394. https://doi.org/10.1515/bjals-2016-0013.

Organization of American States (OAS). (2015). *Trans Pacific partnership agreement*. SICE – Foreign Trade Information System. March.

The Nielsen Company. (2014). *Ecommerce: Evolution or revolution in the fast-moving consumer goods world?*

Tinawi, E., & Berkey, J. O. (1999). *E-services and the WTO: The adequacy of the GATS classification framework*. www.oecd.org/dsti/sti/it/ec/act/paris_ec/pdf/gatsfin.pdf. 24 May 2001.

United Nations Conference on Trade and Development (UNCTAD). (2013). *Review of E-commerce legislation harmonization in the Association of Southeast Asian Nations* (Vol. UNCTAD/DTL/STICT/2013/1). New York/Geneva.

Van den Bossche, P., & Zdouc, W. (2017). *The law and policy of the world trade organization: Text, cases and materials* (4th ed.). Cambridge: Cambridge University Press.

Chapter 9
The International Investment Agreements of the Pacific Alliance Members and Their Relationship of "Coexistence" with Chapter 10 of the Pacific Alliance Additional Protocol

Victor Saco

9.1 Introduction

This chapter[1] discusses the relationship between the international investment agreements (IIAs) of the Pacific Alliance (PA) members (Chile, Colombia, Mexico and Peru[2]) following the entry into force of the PA Additional Protocol, announced for the first half of 2016 after ratification by Mexico (La Tercera 2016), and the decision of the Constitutional Tribunal of Colombia.

The PA is a regional integration zone established pursuant to Article 1 of its Framework Agreement,[3] and the Article 1.1 of the PA Additional Protocol expressly

[1] This article is based partially on a previous research conducted with Alejandro Matsuno and presented at the conference The Pacific Alliance in a World of Preferential Trade Agreements. Lessons in Comparative Regionalism, held in Bogotá in November 2015 under the title of "MFN clauses in the IIAs of the members of the Pacific Alliance: Does the MFN clause of Chapter 10 of the Pacific Alliance Additional Protocol change the members' scope of obligations on investment protection issues". The author wish to thank Pierre Sauvé, Rodrigo Polanco and the audience of the conference; for their very thoughtful comments that help to redirect the research to the work is now presented.

[2] The PA has two prospective members (Costa Rica and Panama) and 42 countries have the status of observers.

[3] Its main objectives set out in Article 3 of the Framework Agreement are: (i) To build a deep integration zone, to progressively advance towards the free movement of goods, services, capital and persons, in a participative and consensual manner. (ii) To foster mayor growth, development and competitiveness in the economies of the State parties in order to achieve higher levels of welfare and social inclusion; and to eradicate social and economic inequalities. (iii) To become a platform for political articulation and economic and commercial integration; a platform to project the State parties to the world, but with a special emphasis in the Asia-Pacific area. (Free translation and adaptation).

V. Saco (✉)
International Economic Law Professor, Pontificia Universidad Católica del Perú, Lima, Peru

World Trade Institute, Bern, Switzerland
e-mail: victor.saco@pucp.edu.pe

P. Sauvé et al. (eds.), *The Pacific Alliance in a World of Preferential Trade Agreements*, United Nations University Series on Regionalism 16,
https://doi.org/10.1007/978-3-319-78464-9_9

declares that the PA is a free-trade area pursuant to Article XXIV of the General Agreement on Tariffs and Trade (GATT). The PA Additional Protocol has 19 chapters and annexes covering topics ranging from market access, rules of origin, technical barriers to trade (TBT) and sanitary and phytosanitary (SPS) measures, to trade in services (financial services, maritime services, telecommunications and digital trade), public procurement, dispute settlement and investment.

The PA Additional Protocol was adopted in February 2014 and develops the objectives of the Framework Agreement.[4] The latter treaty created the PA, setting out its objectives and structure, formalizing the Declaration of Lima of 28 April 2011, issued by the first summit of the members of this group.

The object of the PA is to create a more attractive market among the members in order to achieve higher levels of competitiveness in the global market. This idea was at the heart of the creation of the PA. According to some Peruvian diplomats[5] the idea came after the government of China offered the former Peruvian president, Alan García, access to the Chinese market for Peruvian Red Globe grapes, a product that is in great demand for the Chinese New Year. Peruvian producers accepted the offer, but could only supply approximately 5% of the quantity of grapes allowed to enter China. This experience led to President Garcia's idea to unite the markets of some Latin American countries in order to export to Asia.

An important component of an attractive market for investors is a coherent regulatory framework for that market. The relationship between IIAs and attractiveness to investors has been debated by various authors,[6] but it is possible to conclude that IIAs are taken into account by investors in their decisions on whether to invest in a country.[7]

In this sense, the IIAs between its members, as well as the PA Additional Protocol, could be taken into account, not only in order to create a "more attractive market", even if the PA is not a fully unified one, but a coordinated one. Also, the study of these agreements, and the relationships between them, can help determine if investors can find in the PA a coherent or, at least, a coordinated framework of investors' rights.

The PA members all have IIAs with each other – a total of six treaties among the four members. All these agreements have similarities, but also differences. According to Article 1.2 of the PA Additional Protocol, all six agreements will *coexist* with the Additional Protocol. In the case of incompatibility, a consultation

[4] Adopted on 6 June 2012, entered into force on 20 July 2015.

[5] Personal communication.

[6] The conclusion of most studies is that there is no direct relationship between IIAs and foreign direct investment (FDI): signing an IIA is not a guarantee that the country will receive more FDI (even though IIAs are considered by the investors). See, for instance Guzman (1998).

[7] IIAs are still an important instrument, either because they are the first step towards deeper economic integration i.e. a preferential trade agreement (in line with Tobin and Busch (2010)) or because they meet some of the demands of investors in the so-called developed countries if they are to invest in developing countries (Franck 2012, p. 502).

process should be initiated, with the aim of achieving an amicable solution.[8] This solution will be assessed in this chapter as a way to generate coherence among the existing international investment obligations between the PA members. Coherence is understood in this document as the possibility to achieve a coordinated framework between the PA members, avoiding treaty shopping and other undesirable situations for the host states.

The first part of this chapter examines the six IIAs among the PA members and the caveats to be taken into the account in their overlapping application. The second part considers why coexistence, as adopted in Article 1.2 of the PA Additional Protocol, cannot provide the best level of coherence, but can signify an open window to treaty shopping. Finally, in the third part of this chapter, an assessment of the coexistence solution from the perspective of public international law will be made.

The main idea behind this work is that a coherent system of regulation set out in a single treaty could be useful to attract value chains of foreign investors that are interested in exporting to the Asia-Pacific countries.

9.2 The International Investment Agreements Between the PA Members

As previously stated, Chile, Colombia, Mexico and Peru have six IIAs bilaterally linking each of the members with one of the other three. Taking these agreements in alphabetical order, **Chile** has a free trade agreement (FTA) with Mexico, which has been in force since 31 July 1999; this treaty represents an extension of the previous Economic Complementation Agreement (ACE) between the two countries (*Acuerdo de Complementación Económica* – ACE No 17) of 1991.[9] The history of the importance of the ACE in Latin American integration will be briefly explained in the concluding paragraphs of this section. This treaty was the second bilateral trade agreement that Chile ratified, and the first of its kind to be ratified by Mexico.[10] Chapter 9 of this FTA regulates investment.

Chile has an IIA with each of the other two members of the PA, Colombia and Peru; both agreements date back to 2009. The agreement with Peru entered into force on 22 August 2009 (having been signed on 22 August, 2006). This agreement complemented the ACE No 38 of 1998.[11] Chapter 11 regulates investment and replaces

[8] Article 1.2 and 1.3 of the PA Additional Protocol.

[9] Dirección General de Relaciones Económicas Internacionales (DIRECON). 2016. Tratado de Libre Comercio Chile – México. http://www.direcon.gob.cl/detalle-de-acuerdos/?idacuerdo=6208. Accessed 12 January 2016.

[10] Ibid.

[11] DIRECON, Acuerdo de Libre Comercio Chile – Perú. 2016. http://www.direcon.gob.cl/detalle-de-acuerdos/?idacuerdo=6255. Accessed 12 January 2016.

the previous BIT of 2002 between the two countries, which terminated upon the entry into force of the FTA.[12]

In the FTA between Chile and Colombia, in force since 8 May 2009,[13] regulations on investment are contained in Chapter 9. This FTA is an additional protocol to the ACE No 24 of 1994. ACE No 24 only regulates investment promotion and contains a kind of MFN clause in Chapter X.[14,15]

Turning to **Colombia**, in addition to the FTA with Chile previously mentioned, it has an FTA with Mexico. This FTA is a modification of the previous ACE No. 33, known as the FTA of *the Group of the Three* (including Venezuela, which withdrew from the treaty in 2006). The new ACE No. 33 entered into force on 2 August 2011[16] and includes regulations on investment in Chapter XVII.

The third agreement between Colombia and Peru is the Agreement on Reciprocal Investment Promotion and Protection, and it entered into force on 30 December 2010 (Organization of American States (SICE) 2016). This is a bilateral investment agreement, but is not a typical bilateral investment treaty (BIT), following the so-called European model; the clauses are similar to the investment chapter of an FTA. It is important to take into account that Colombia and Peru are members of the Andean Community, which has other treaties regulating international trade among its members, but does not regulate investment in general.

In the case of **Mexico**, it has treaties with Colombia and Chile, which have already been mentioned and it also has an FTA with Peru. This FTA has been in force since 1 February 2012.[17] Previously both countries were bound by ACE No. 8 of 1987,[18] which only covered investment promotion or "stimulation".[19] Investment is regulated in Chapter XI of the FTA.

The agreements between **Peru** and the other members of the PA have already been described.

Almost all the above-mentioned agreements are based on the previous integration process in the framework of ALADI. ALADI stands for *Asociación Latinoamericana de Integración* or Latin American Integration Association. It is an

[12] Annex 11-E of the FTA.

[13] DIRECON, Acuerdo de Libre Comercio Chile – Perú. 2016. http://www.direcon.gob.cl/detalle-de-acuerdos/?idacuerdo=6271. Accessed 12 January 2016.

[14] "Artículo 22. Los países signatarios, dentro de sus respectivas legislaciones sobre inversión extranjera otorgarán los mejores tratamientos a los capitales del otro país signatario, ya sea este el correspondiente al capital nacional o extranjero".

[15] MINCOMERCIO INDUSTRIA Y TURISMO. ACE NO: 24. 2016. http://www.mincit.gov.co/tlc/publicaciones.php?id=1426. Accessed 12 January 2016.

[16] MINCOMERCIO INDUSTRIA Y TURISMO. ACE NO: 24. 2016. http://www.mincit.gov.co/tlc/publicaciones.php?id=11963. Accessed 12 January 2016.

[17] MINCETUR. Acuerdos Comerciales del Perú. 2016. http://www.acuerdoscomerciales.gob.pe/index.php?option=com_content&view=category&layout=blog&id=75&Itemid=98. Accessed 12 January 2016.

[18] See: MINCETUR, Acuerdo de Complementación Económica No. 8. Perú-México. 2016. http://www.mincetur.gob.pe/comercio/Legal/ACE8_completo.html. Accessed 12 January 2016.

[19] In Spanish "*estimular las inversiones*" (Article 29 of the ACE No. 8).

intergovernmental organization created in 1980 by the Treaty of Montevideo (which replaces a previous association established in 1960). ALADI's goal is the "expansion of the integration in the region, in order to secure its social and economic development; and its final aim is to establish a Latin-American common market".[20]

The PA members are among the 11 founder members of ALADI, and they have commercial treaties ratified within the framework of ALADI. This is an example showing that the PA member countries have been participating in integration processes for more than 30 years. ALADI set out the framework for the negotiation and ratification of the above-mentioned ACEs, but so far has been unable to achieve the goal of a common market; this could be one of the reasons why the PA is not based on a formal international organization, but on treaties.

At this point, it is possible to draw some preliminary conclusions: first, all the IIAs between the PA members are chapters of an FTA. In the case of the agreement between Colombia and Peru, even if it is not strictly speaking an FTA, the wording of the text is the same as that of a chapter of an FTA. In other words, new-generation investment treaties, following the so-called North American Free Trade Agreement (NAFTA) model or US model, regulate the investment protection that the PA members offer to their foreign investors.

It is important to recall what Alvarez (2011) said about the object and purpose of the 2004 US model, namely that it was a "new generation investment treaty", whose focus is "[…] less about the investor and more about the rule of law itself". In other words, such treaties try to generate a balance between investor and state rights in response to the vague texts of BITs that led to broad interpretations by arbitral tribunals.

The second conclusion is that the PA Additional Protocol's wording of its investment provisions is very similar to those of the six IIAs between the PA members. Not taking into account the annexes, there is in general no substantive differences in the wording of the regulation of the standards and norms in the texts of these agreements. This raises the question: why were the six pre-existing treaties not terminated in view of the entry into force of the PA Additional Protocol (especially given that the wording of the Protocol is similar to that of the previous agreements)? This question will be analysed later in this chapter.

There are some "improvements" in the PA Additional Protocol relating the wording of the agreement and the relation of investment and other matters. In terms of wording, the improvements where made to give more "policy space" to host states, for instance in the wording of the Denial of Benefits clause (Article 10.13). As regards the relation of investment and other matters, Articles 10.30, 10.31 relate to Corporate Social Responsibility-CSR and Health, Environment and "other Regulatory objectives", even if these norms cannot being referred to an arbitral tribunal, nor used as an allegation before these tribunals (Article 10.28), and despite the fact that the wording is programmatic and the verbs used do not imply specific commitments in the case of CSR, is a big step forward to the interrelation of this topics and investment.

[20] Free translation. ALADI. ¿Qué es la ALADI? 2016. http://www.aladi.org/nsfaladi/preguntasfrecuentes.nsf/fd7fc5dc8b0352c1032567bb004f8e78/fe139cfd067aec28032574be0043f17e?OpenDocument. Accessed 03 March 2016.

Thirdly, and related to the previous point, the decision of the PA members not to terminate the six existing IIAs upon the entry into force of the PA Additional Protocol, but instead to opt for the coexistence of the previous agreements with the latest one, creates a situation of overlapping agreements. In some cases the overlap could be composed of three layers, as in the case of Peru and Chile which are linked by an FTA, the PA Additional Protocol and have also signed the Trans-Pacific Partnership (now CPTPP).

An example of this last statement is the announcement by the PA of its intention to negotiate agreements as a block with associated and observer countries. The first country to show interest is New Zealand, which negotiated the TPP, so it is possible that the text of the CPTPP could be the base for the drafting of a New Zealand–PA members' FTA. In parallel, Peru is negotiating an FTA with Australia, another negotiating country of the CPTPP, and has and FTA with Singapore and Japan, which also negotiated the CPTPP Agreement (Andina 2017).

International law has been dealing with overlapping treaties for a long time. But in the special case of international investment law (IIL), the overlapping of treaties could mean that an investor located in one of the member countries can choose "the best/more convenient norm" among the treaties. Treaty shopping can cause instability of the state if investors use it in an abusive manner and it may mean more protection for investors. Treaty shoppers can also make use of the most-favoured nation (MFN) clause.

9.3 The Problem of the Coexistence of the Previous IIA Treaties of the PA Members with the PA Additional Protocol: Effects on Coherence and Limitations of the MFN Clause

International law is based on the agglomeration of multiple treaties which are not necessarily coordinated. In IIL this agglomeration is more evident with more than 3500 treaties; the treaties concerned were created to generate benefits to the nationals of the Parties of the agreement in a bilateral way, without the intention to coordinate with other non-party States (moreover, some States negotiate treaties with the idea to have an advantage – to be more atractive to foreign investment-, and this advantage could consist in having a treaty with a partnen State partner before a third State). There are few multilateral agreements that include investment provisions, but NAFTA, the PA Additional Protocol and the CPTPP are examples of those that do. This can be considered as a new trend that favours multilateral investment agreements, following the failure of the Multilateral Agreement on Investment in the late 1990s. It is possible to conclude that multilateral investment agreements are feasible, but their negotiation can be difficult (Lester 2013). An example of such difficulties was the rejection by some European groups of the investor–state arbitration clauses in the proposed Transatlantic Trade and Investment Partnership (TTIP), which also involved a pronouncement of the European Commission and Parliament.

An argument in favour of multilateral investment treaties is the need to generate coherence by replacing numerous similar treaties with a single treaty. In the special case of the PA members, this would entail replacing six treaties with just one. An endeavour to generate coherence was made by the members of the European Union: In Article 207 of the Lisbon Treaty, complemented by new internal European Union regulations in 2012, the European Commission received the competence on investment matters, to reduce the number of investment treaties of the members. To centralize one unique treaty can make that the European Union can replace around 1200 IIAs (European Commission 2016). So far, there are no indications that this task will be completed any time soon, but a good start has been done with the CETA Agreement.

CETA stands for Comprehensive Economic and Trade Agreement, the name that Canada usually gives to its Free Trade Agreements. In the case of the CETA between the European Union and Canada, according to its Article 30.8 and Annex 30-A, BITs between Canada and 8 European countries (Croatia, Czech Republic, Hungary, Latvia, Malta, Poland, Romania and Slovakia) will be replaced and superseded by the CETA Investment Chapter.[21]

The reduction of treaties is proposed because having numerous treaties regulating the same topic can generate problems such as conflicts of norms and treaty shopping as mentioned above (see Pauwelyn 2009; International Law Commission (ILC) 2006). In the case of investment treaties, problems already exist in the form of treaty shopping by investors using the MFN clause. i.e. the situation where a national of a country can benefit from rights that were not intended to protect him/her according to his or her nationality.[22] Most of the controversy on the application of MFN is related to procedural rights, i.e. the terms to access to an international tribunal, recalling the Maffezini case.[23] In this sense, the MFN clause can represent a threat to coherence when used in an abusive way.

The likelihood of treaty shopping increases with the coexistence of treaties, with an option of choosing from treaties such as the PA Additional Protocol or the CPTPP. As an example, in the case of Chile and Peru, both are members of the PA and signatories of the CPTPP; there could therefore be three treaties applicable to their investors.

The above example shows how coexistence can generate incoherence. According to Joseph Raz, coherence requires a unity of principle, the legal system emanating from a single principle, or at least from the mutual independence of justificatory principles and policies (Balkin 1993). In the case of IIAs, this principle is the protection of investor rights (balanced witwh the protection of social interests of the state), and the unity of the system will imply the reduction of overlapping treaties. This

[21] European Commission. CETA Chapter by Chapter. 2016. http://ec.europa.eu/trade/policy/in-focus/ceta/ceta-chapter-by-chapter. Accessed 22 June 2017.

[22] For instance if person "c", a national of the state C, wants to benefit from the rights established in the treaty between states A and B, using an MFN clause in the treaty between states A and C.

[23] ICSID. Emilio Agustín Maffezini v. The Kingdom of Spain, ICSID Case No. ARB/97/7. http://www.italaw.com/cases/641#sthash.9oCSSeru.dpuf. Accessed 14 February 2016.

also aligns with the definition of coherence suggested by Trachtman: "efficiency in horizontal allocation of authority among international legal rules or organization" (Trachtman 2011). For the same states the coexistence of agreements seems not to be efficient, at least theoretically.

In theory, coherence and termination of previous treaties could represent a coherent solution. The reality could explain the different approach taken. For instance, it could be important to maintain certain concessions to investors made in previous treaties at a bilateral level that would not be offered at the multilateral one. This could reflect the power of investors, interests of the state in certain sectors or the state's economic and political strategy; and might explain the use of the coexistence approach as a political answer and a negotiation strategy.

Relating to this last idea, the remaining question is whether bilateral concessions cannot be multilateralized to the PA members via the MFN clause in the treaties between them. Here it is important to remember that the goal of the MFN clause is to ensure that the parties treat each other in a manner at least as favourable as they treat third parties; in a BIT, this clause has a as a normal effect to widen the rights of the investor (Dolzer and Schreuer 2012). And that "[t]he clause may not have any practical significance if the state concerned fails to grant any relevant benefit to a third party [...] in relation to all matters that fall within the scope of the treaty containing the MFN rule" (Dolzer and Schreuer 2012).

The response of the PA members to this issue, i.e. measures to avoid the use of MFN to extend benefits allocated to investors on the basis of the IIAs in force before the PA Additional Protocol, can be found in the Annex of the PA Additional Protocol. These complement the non-conforming measures in Article 10.10. In this Article, for instance, Peru has the right not to extend via MFN a preferential measure if it is based on a previous agreement (signed or in force).[24] In this sense PA members have used these clauses to allow the states to maintain previous commitments and do not extend them to the other PA members via MFN, thus avoiding one the caveats of coexistence.

Can the PA members use MFN to achieve coherence? The answer to this question lies in the use of MFN by the states and not by investors. Clearly, as stated before, MFN is a right for investors, so the states can use MFN only in assessing the effects of the application of the clause, for instance by considering all its previous treaties (impact assessment). Let us propose the following idea: the role of MFN is to allow the investors to have the best right that the network of treaties of the host state can offer. If the state wants to know what is being granted to foreign investors, it has to identify the "best right" offered by one of its IIAs.

But this "best scenario" can also be advanced by the state and, in order to generate coherence, it can adapt its regulation to this "best scenario". In the case of the four members of the PA, they could also adapt PA norms and the PA Additional

[24] The original text in Spanish reads: "*Perú se reserva el derecho de adoptar o mantener cualquier medida que otorgue trato diferente a países de conformidad con cualquier tratado internacional bilateral o multilateral en vigor o suscrito con anterioridad a la fecha de entrada en vigor del presente Protocolo Adicional*".

Protocol to this scenario. This would also benefit the PA members if they wanted to become more attractive to foreign investment. The above-mentioned adaptation would consist of allocating each investor the "best right" the state grants to its foreign investors, independent of nationality. This solution has some elements in common with the regulatory coherence governed by the PA Additional Protocol. As discussed by Polanco Lazo and Sauvé (2017).

Until this point, the problems of coexistence of treaties can be approached, legally, by "closing" the MFN clause to the investors that want to use a benefit based on a previous treaty. Dispute prevention can also generate "internal coherence"; to prevent investors' claims, a State can enact an internal regulatory framework coherent with the most beneficial provisions on investors' rights regulated in all the IIAs of the PA members (and other IIAs with third parties). In any case, these alternatives do not address all the problems of treaty shopping.

9.4 Reducing the Risks of Coexistence of IIAs of the PA Members

The first alternative to achieve coherent regulation among the PA members would have been a clause in the PA Additional Protocol that regulated the termination of the previous IIAs between the members upon its entry into force following the example opted for in the FTA between Chile and Peru in relation to their previous BIT.

As previously stated, the PA Additional Protocol opted for a different approach: coexistence of treaties even though, in the framework of ALADI, the PA members have agreed to promote common regulation. With regard to investment in the ALADI framework, representatives of Chile, Colombia, Mexico and Peru discussed the convergence of treaties. They agreed to promote common regulation on investment protection for the region, not only for ALADI, but also in relation to the Andean Community and MERCOSUR. This new regulation could complement the work of the Andean Community (Decisions 292 and 292) and MERCOSUR (Protocol of Colonia) (ALADI undated, pp. 24–25). The United Nations Economic Commission for Latin America and the Caribbean (ECLAC) was not very optimistic about the achievement of this goal as it considered that the ALADI members have different approaches towards the aim of its investment treaties and the vast network of bilateral treaties in existence could hinder the achievement of convergence (CEPAL 2010).

The goal of this convergence is to limit the variety of treaties and replace them with a new regulatory framework that encompasses various agreements. Most of the work of ALADI in this sense was focused on trade rather than investment (for instance rules of origin) (Cornejo and Harris 2007; International Business Publications 2013).

Another option that could be explored by the parties is to include a hierarchy or prevalence clause in the PA Additional Protocol, giving this agreement priority over the previous IIAs of the PA members. But, in the meanwhile, given the coexistence option, it is useful to advance some juridical perspectives on facing possible treaty conflicts or treaty shopping. These are followed by some other political and economic perspectives that will be advanced in order to complement the normative option.

9.4.1 Juridical Perspectives

In the case of conflict of norms, as IIAs and the PA Additional Protocol are treaties subject to the Vienna Convention on the Law of Treaties (VCLT). Two norms of the VCLT could be useful for the case under study: the rules on successive treaties and those on treaty interpretation.

Successive treaties relating to the same subject-matter come under Article 30 of the VCLT.

Article 30

Application of successive treaties relating to the same subject-matter

1. Subject to Article 103 of the Charter of the United Nations, the rights and obligations of States parties to successive treaties relating to the same subject-matter shall be determined in accordance with the following paragraphs.
2. When a treaty specifies that it is subject to, or that it is not to be considered as incompatible with, an earlier or later treaty, the provisions of that other treaty prevail.
3. When all the parties to the earlier treaty are parties also to the later treaty but the earlier treaty is not terminated or suspended in operation under Article 59, the earlier treaty applies only to the extent that its provisions are compatible with those of the latter treaty.
4. When the parties to the later treaty do not include all the parties to the earlier one:
   (a) as between States parties to both treaties the same rule applies as in paragraph 3; (b) as between a State party to both treaties and a State party to only one of the treaties, the treaty to which both States are parties governs their mutual rights and obligations.
5. Paragraph 4 is without prejudice to Article 41, or to any question of the termination or suspension of the operation of a treaty under Article 60 or to any question of responsibility which may arise for a State from the conclusion or application of a treaty, the provisions of which are incompatible with its obligations towards another State under another treaty.[25]

As the first rule of this Article advocates the prevalence of the UN Charter, and numbers 4 and 5 do not apply, they will not be taken into account for the purposes of this chapter. Taking into account that IIAs among the PA members and the PA Additional Protocol cover the same subject-matter, it is not possible to assume that the coexistence of treaties, regulated in Article 1.2 of the PA Additional Protocol, is

[25] The original text is available at: https://treaties.un.org/doc/Publication/UNTS/Volume%201155/volume-1155-I-18232-English.pdf

a "conflict clause" in the sense of paragraph 2 of Article 30 of the VCLT as it does not set a prevalence of one or the other treaty (Villiger 2009, pp. 405–6).

But in the case of Article 1.2 of the PA Additional Protocol, a specific provision giving priority to one treaty over another is not necessary as it can be read from its text (first footnote):

> For the purposes of application of this Additional Protocol, the Parties agree that the fact that an agreement provides more favourable treatment of goods, services, investments or persons than that provided for under this Additional Protocol does not mean that there is an inconsistency within the meaning of paragraph 2.[26]

Also, taking into account the above quote and paragraphs 2 and 3 of Article 30 of the VCLT, there are strong arguments for the prevalence of previous IIAs. First, in cases such as the Peruvian non-conforming measures in the Annex of the PA Additional Protocol, addressing the non-extension of the MFN clause, the prevalence of the previous agreement is clear.

Secondly, even in the case of a PA member that does not have a clause like the Peruvian one listed in its Annex, the investor still has Footnote 1 to Article 1.2, which recognizes that "better rights" are not considered as an inconsistency for the PA Additional Protocol. Here it is important to take into account that the investors will look for "better rights" and not for less beneficial norms. Furthermore, the coexistence of treaties with the clauses described above does not generate a conflict of norms but rather a conflict in the application of norms (Pauwelyn 2009).

The second VCLT Article that is pertinent here is Article 31.3.c:

Article 31

> General rule of interpretation
>
> 1. A treaty shall be interpreted in good faith in accordance with the ordinary meaning to be given to the terms of the treaty in their context and in the light of its object and purpose. […]
> 3. There shall be taken into account together with the context:
>   (a) any subsequent agreement between the parties regarding the interpretation of the treaty or the application of its provisions;
>   (b) any subsequent practice in the application of the treaty which establishes the agreement of the parties regarding its interpretation;
>   (c) any relevant rules of international law applicable in the relations between the parties. […]

This norm reaffirms the solution explained above, as the interpretation should look at the ordinary meaning of the terms of the treaties and any relevant rule or norm in the previous treaties. As the language is clear, the option in favour of the previous agreements or the most favourable one is confirmed by the VCLT.

---

[26] Free translation from the Spanish text, that is very similar to the TPP one, reads: "*Para los efectos de la aplicación del presente Protocolo Adicional, las Partes reconocen que el hecho de que un acuerdo otorgue un trato más favorable a las mercancías, servicios, inversiones o personas que el otorgado de conformidad con el presente Protocolo Adicional, no constituye un caso de incompatibilidad en el sentido del párrafo 2.*"

9.4.2 *Economic and Political Reasons Behind the Coexistence Solution*

The coexistence solution was possibly chosen in order to preserve the *status quo* for existing investors and to retain the possibility to allocate certain benefits to partners in bilateral investment relationships. Because the negotiators of the PA Additional Protocol knew about the compatibility of their treaties among the members, they negotiated its text knowing that it would coexist with the previous treaties; in theory the negotiators prevent possible conflicts among the texts of the IIAs.

Also, economically, the four PA economies are not the main investment destination for their investors, although there are strong links between some member countries, for instance between Chile and Peru, the latter being the recipient of 16,000 million US dollars of Chilean investment in 2015. Peruvian investment in Chile amounted to 10,000 million US dollars (Gestion 2015). This indicates that the negligible degree of economic interdependence among the PA members could be an indicator of lower possibilities of treaty shopping among the investors of these countries.

The economic effect of coexistence and the desire to maintain previous benefits and even new ones based on the previous agreements, could also be explained by the fact that the PA members are rivals in attracting foreign investment, as in the case of Colombia and Peru for petroleum (El Comercio 2016). Most of them are also keen to become "exporting hubs" by attracting investors that want to use their FTA networks.

The four PA members are also keen to enter the markets of the Asia-Pacific countries, especially China. For instance, Colombia is very interested in an FTA with China to complement its BIT. Meanwhile Colombian investors can settle in Peru, which already has an FTA with China.

Despite the possible economic reasons to opt for coexistence of treaties, there is still an important opportunity to develop Latin American industries, taking advantage of the value chains that can be generated in the region. To achieve this aim, a coherent framework and perhaps a single treaty could be very useful. Moreover, the text of the treaty could be aligned with that of the CPTPP, which paradoxically has the same coexistence clause as the PA Additional Protocol, or with any subsequent agreement with a CPTPP negotiating partner that uses its text as a basis for a new treaty.

9.5 Final Remarks

The PA members have chosen to allow their IIAs to coexist with the PA Additional Protocol. This decision was made for political and economic reasons but can present a risk for the states as they face the possibility of treaty shopping by the investors.

The architecture of the PA Additional Protocol is such that the previous treaty tends to prevail. This can be concluded from the interpretation of Article 30 of the

VCLT, Article 1.2 of the PA Additional Protocol, Article 10.10 on non-conforming measures and the Annex of the PA Additional Protocol.

As previously stated, with or without rules of prevalence of treaties, the option of coexistence is still not the best theoretical solution, but it is understandable. This solution that reflects the reality of investment treaties coexisting and overlapping in international law. In any case, the desire to increase their commerce with Asia and Oceania may push the PA members to base their production on value chains, and without a CPTPP framework, deeper integration as a bloc will may motivate the PA members to go a step further towards treaty convergence.

References

ALADI (Secretaría General), Comunidad Andina (Secretaría General) and MERCOSUR (Secretaría del Mercosur), Convergencia de los Acuerdos de Integración Económica en Sudamérica. http://www.aladi.org/biblioteca/Publicaciones/ALADI/Secretaria_General/Documentos_Sin_Codigos/Caja_059_012.pdf at 24–25. Accessed 2 Mar 2016.

Alvarez, J. E. (2011). The public international law regime governing international investment. In *Pocket books of the Hague academy of international law: A collection of law lectures in pocketbook form* (p. 164). Maubeuge: AP All-Pocket

Andina. (2017). *Alianza del Pacífico negociaría como bloque los TLC con países asociados*. http://www.andina.com.pe/agencia/noticia-alianza-del-pacifico-negociaria-como-bloque-los-tlc-paises-asociados-664780.aspx. Accessed 28 Apr 2017.

Balkin, J. M. (1993). *Understanding legal understanding: The legal subject and the problem of legal coherence* (Faculty Scholarship Series Paper 273). http://digitalcommons.law.yale.edu/cgi/viewcontent.cgi?article=1272&context=fss_papers, 12; quoting Jospeh Raz, The relevance of coherence, 2 B.U.L.REV. 273, 292 (1992), 286. Accessed 18 Jan 2016.

CEPAL. (2010). *Espacios de Convergencia y de cooperación regional*. Santiago de Chile: United Nations. http://www.cepal.org/es/publicaciones/2938-espacios-convergencia-cooperacion-regional-cumbre-la-unidad-america-latina-caribe at 44. Accessed 28 Apr 2017.

Cornejo, R., & Harris, J. (2007). *Propuesta metodológica para la convergencia del Spaghetti Bowl de las reglas de origen (INTAL-INT, Documento de Trabajo 34)* (p. 12). New York: Banco Interamericano de Desarrollo – Instituto para la Integración de América Latina y el Caribe – Sector de Integración y Comercio.

Dolzer, R., & Schreuer, C. (2012). *Principles of international investment law* (2nd ed.p. 206). Oxford: Oxford University Press.

El Comercio. (2016). http://elcomercio.pe/economia/peru/peru-compite-colombia-atraer-inversionistas-petroleros-noticia-1877968. Accessed 14 Feb 2016.

European Commission. (2016). *EU takes key step to provide legal certainty for investors outside Europe (press release)*. http://europa.eu/rapid/press-release_IP-12-1362_en.htm. Accessed 14 Feb 2016.

Franck, S. (2012). *Book review: The public international law regime governing international investment* (p. 502), by Jose E. Alvarez. 2011. The Hague: Hague Academy of International Law. SSRN Scholarly Paper ID 2156965. Rochester: Social Science Research Network.

Gestion. (2015). *Inversiones chilenas en el Perú suman US$ 16,000 millones*. http://gestion.pe/economia/inversiones-chilenas-peru-suman-us-16000-millones-2126181. Accessed 2 Mar 2016.

Guzman, A. T. (1998). Why LDCs sign treaties that hurt them: Explaining the popularity of bilateral investment treaties. *Virginia Journal of International Law, 38*, 639–688.

International Business Publications. (2013). *Latin America: Economic integration and cooperation handbook, Volume 1, strategic information, organizations and programs* (pp. 44–45). Washington, DC.

International Law Commission (ILC). (2006). *ILC study group on the fragmentation of international law. Fragmentation of international law: difficulties arising from the diversification and expansion of international law.* Report of the Study Group of the International Law Commission. Finalized by Martti Koskenniemi. UN Doc A/CN.4/L.682 and Add.1 and Corr. 1. New York: International Law Commission.

La Tercera. (2016). *Negocios. Senado ratifica protocolo que liberaliza comercio entre países de Alianza del Pacífico.* http://www.latercera.com/noticia/negocios/2016/01/655-662845-9-senado-ratifica-protocolo-que-liberaliza-comercio-entre-paises-de-alianza-del.shtml. Accessed 5 Jan 2016.

Lester, S. (2013). A multilateral investment agreement. *International Economic Law and Policy Blog*. http://worldtradelaw.typepad.com/ielpblog/2013/01/a-multilateral-investment-agreement.html. Accessed 14 Feb 2016.

Organization of American States, Foreign Trade Information System. SICE. Information on Colombia. (2016). http://www.sice.oas.org/ctyindex/COL/COLBits_e.asp. Accessed 12 Jan 2016.

Pauwelyn, J. (2009). *Conflict of norms in public international law how WTO law relates to other rules of international law*. Cambridge Studies in International and Comparative Law. Cambridge: Cambridge University Press.

Tobin, J. L., & Busch, M. L. (2010). A BIT is better than a lot. Bilateral investment treaties and preferential trade agreements. *World Politics, 62*, 1–42.

Trachtman, J. P. (2011). *Fragmentation and coherence in international law*. http://papers.ssrn.com/sol3/papers.cfm?abstract_id=1908862. Accessed 18 Jan 2016.

Villiger, M. E. (2009). *Commentary on the 1969 Vienna convention on the law of the treaties* (pp. 405–406). The Hague: Martinus Nijhoff.

Chapter 10
Situating the Pacific Alliance in Global Electronic Commerce Regulation

María del Carmen Vásquez Callo-Müller

10.1 Introduction

The 'borderless' structure of the internet makes it theoretically possible for a consumer to acquire goods or services from all over the world, and for any business to reach customers worldwide.[1] This phenomenon is referred to as electronic commerce (e-commerce) and is an important driver of economic growth (OECD 2013a).

However, 'even for the most revolutionary global telecommunications technologies (such as the internet), geography and governmental coercion retain fundamental importance' (Goldsmith and Wu 2006). Indeed, there are barriers, including trade barriers, which hold back the internet and e-commerce from reaching its full potential. These barriers are currently addressed at different levels and have been subject to intense debate (Malcom and Sutton 2015).

At the multilateral level, the World Trade Organization (WTO) started a Work Programme on e-commerce in 1998 that included a provision calling on WTO members to 'continue their current practice of not imposing customs duties on electronic transmissions'.[2] This practice, known as the moratorium on customs duties, is generally accepted as positive and it was extended at the 9th WTO Ministerial Conference in Bali, Indonesia in December 2013.

A study of the electronic commerce chapter of the Pacific Alliance Additional Protocol in the context of current preferential trade agreements.

[1] This term is used deliberately in this paper. See Goldsmith and Wu (2006), OECD (2013b).

[2] World Trade Organization (WTO) Ministerial Declaration on Global E-Commerce 1998, WT/MIN(98)/DEC/2.

M. d. C. Vásquez Callo-Müller (✉)
World Trade Institute, Bern, Switzerland
e-mail: Maria.Vasquez@wti.org

P. Sauvé et al. (eds.), *The Pacific Alliance in a World of Preferential Trade Agreements*, United Nations University Series on Regionalism 16,
https://doi.org/10.1007/978-3-319-78464-9_10

Nonetheless, multilateral efforts to tackle other trade-related barriers to e-commerce have been subject to criticism given the slow progress of the negotiations and the difficulty in reaching a decision. Meanwhile, several countries recognized a necessity to address those barriers through preferential trade agreements (PTAs). In 2011, an ambitious PTA was initiated in Latin America. This undertaking, the Pacific Alliance (PA), called for the cooperation of four like-minded countries, Chile, Colombia, Mexico and Peru, to enable free circulation of goods, services, capital and people among their territories. The formal agreement regulating the PA is the Pacific Alliance Additional Protocol (PAAP). The PAAP is similar in structure to a free trade agreement (FTA) and contains an evolving[3] chapter on e-commerce.

At the time the preliminary version of this chapter was written and presented (2015), the PAAP had been recently concluded. Accordingly, the objective of that paper was to analyse where the PAAP chapter on e-commerce stood in relation to other PTAs and to determine which model of regulation it followed, namely the United States (US) or the European Union (EU) model.[4] More importantly, the paper also aimed to briefly touch upon on whether e-commerce regulation in the PAAP was designed to address new trends in the field arising out of the constant development of digital technologies.[5]

Since then, the PA has evolved and other initiatives regarding digital market integration in Latin America have gained increased prominence (ECLAC 2015). Indeed, while the PAAP is still the main legal text governing the PA, the sub-working group on the PA digital agenda has developed a roadmap for the creation of a 'digital single market" based on the potential that the telecommunications and e-commerce chapter of the PAAP offer.[6] While this is a very important development, it is only briefly described in this chapter. The core analysis presented herein is focused on the PAAP.

Therefore, the structure of this chapter will proceed in three parts. The first part will provide the background by explaining the current state of e-commerce in the four PA member countries. This will be followed by an outline of the different approaches to e-commerce regulation being taken around the world, emphasizing the US and EU models, the stalled Trans-Pacific Partnership Agreement (TPP) and the Trade in Services Agreement (TiSA). By means of this overview, the main aspects of contemporary e-commerce regulation will be highlighted. This section will also provide an analysis of the provisions contained in the e-commerce chapter of the PAAP. The chapter will conclude with an assessment of the approach to e-commerce regulation taken in the PAAP. It will consider briefly whether adequate

[3] During the latest Pacific Alliance Summit, held in Paracas, Peru in July 2015, it was decided that the chapter on electronic commerce and telecommunications of the current PAAP would be modified. See Declaración de Paracas (2015), Alianza del Pacifico, https://alianzapacifico.net/?wpdmdl=4078. Accessed 25 October 2015.

[4] In the ambit of e-commerce regulation, the literature has emphasized the predominance of two models: the US and EU model. See Wunsch-Vincent and Hold (2012), pp. 202–204.

[5] It is beyond the scope of this chapter to focus deeply on this issue. However, given its importance, some ideas are put forward to give food for thought for future discussions.

[6] Hoja de Ruta del Subgrupo Agenda Digital (2016), Alianza del Pacifico, https://alianzapacifico.net/download/hoja-de-ruta-subgrupo-agenda-digital/. Accessed 2 May 2017.

and sufficiently progressive policies are incorporated in the current text of the agreement and, secondly, will present an overview of the new features of the PA roadmap for a digital single market.

10.2 General Background

10.2.1 Framing the Phenomenon: What Is E-commerce?

E-commerce is defined by the Organisation for Economic Co-operation and Development (OECD) as 'any transaction for the sale or purchase of goods and services conducted over computer networks by methods specifically designed for the purpose of receiving or placing of orders' (OECD 2013a). This definition is also used by the WTO (2013) and the United Nations Conference on Trade and Development (UNCTAD 2015). Other FTAs and PTAs also contain similar language.[7]

There is a vast literature explaining the benefits of e-commerce. Examples include enhanced participation in international value chains, wider market access, improved internal and market efficiency and lower transaction costs (UNCTAD 2015, xi). Furthermore, e-commerce may spur job creation in the information and technology (ICT) sector (UNCTAD 2015 xi–xii). It also provides new possibilities for small- and medium-sized enterprises (SMEs), which benefit from the adoption and use of online tools, especially in terms of revenue growth and integration into their national and global economies (Zwillenberg et al. 2014, 19).

On the other hand, while much e-commerce happens domestically, a vast amount depends on cross-border transactions.[8] Therefore, e-commerce is conditioned, to a large extent, on cross-jurisdictional coordination. For instance, SMEs' main concerns regarding e-commerce are the protection of consumer data online and the existence of regulations affecting online sales (Zwillenberg et al. 2014). When these issues become cross-border, as they often do, international coordination is vital.[9]

Finally, while rules regulating traditional e-commerce have existed for some time, there is still a need for simple, consistent, transparent, non-discriminatory and

---

[7] The definition included in Article 13.1 of the PAAP refers to '*trade undertaken by electronic*' and means '*commerce conducted through telecommunications, alone or in conjunction with other information and communication technologies*'.

[8] While thinking about trans-border transactions, one should also bear in mind that there are different types of e-commerce transactions. These include transactions between enterprises, individuals, governments, and other public or private organizations: depending on the seller and buyer. In this context, the most common transactions are business to business (B2B), and business to consumer (B2C), business to government (B2G) and, more recently, consumer to consumer (C2C). See OECD (2013a).

[9] On 6 October 2015, the European Court of Justice ruled that the EU-US Safe Harbor arrangement was invalid. This is just one example of how different the approaches to data protection are between the two biggest economies involved in making the rules that regulate e-commerce. See Maximillian Schrems v Data Protection Commissioner (2015) ECJ Case C-362/14.

enforceable rules (UNCTAD 2015, p. 88), especially in light of new trends in e-commerce. These new trends are supported by the extensive use of mobile phones and portable devices and are directed more towards the provision of services than goods.[10]

10.2.2 E-commerce Landscape in Latin America

To understand the development of e-commerce in Latin America, it should be noted that according to the Boston Consulting Group (BCG) e-friction index,[11] Chile ranks 41st in the internet economy while Mexico is 51st, Colombia 56th and Peru 60th. In the cases of Colombia and Peru, in particular, these positions reflect low levels of connectivity (Messano 2013, p. 39). Therefore, Latin America needs to speed up basic reforms related to access to reliable networks. Nonetheless, Latin America is part of the global exchange of data flows and is increasingly benefitting from it,[12] as is evident from a report published by eBay (2012).

According to eBay, more than 2 million Chileans shop online and spend over USD 400 million every year. Moreover, all commercial Chilean sellers using eBay export their products and reach, on average, 28 different markets (eBay 2012, p. 20). Peru's exports over digital services networks reach many more markets than traditional exporters. Peruvian sellers using eBay, reach 25 different foreign markets (eBay 2012, p. 23). Colombia's government has established Vive Digital,[13] a programme aimed at increasing the level of connectivity for micro-enterprises and SMEs (World Economic Forum (WEF) and INSEAD 2013, p. 111). In Mexico, e-commerce development is at an early stage, still behind Brazil and Chile. However, given the density of the market and the rapid penetration of smartphones, the situation is expected to improve very quickly (Parish 2015).

Yet, connectivity *per se* does not create value, but content does. According to Katz, Latin America is still at a very early stage in the creation of content, services and/or applications. Furthermore, around 63% of data traffic in the region is mainly focused

---

[10] Think, for example, of the development of the app economy and the rapid evolution of the internet of things.

[11] The BCG e-Friction Index assesses 55 indicators of friction that inhibit internet use and group them into four components: (i) *infrastructure-related friction,* associated with basic access, speed, price, traffic and architecture of the internet; (ii) *industry-related friction*, affected by the availability of physical infrastructure, labour supply, dynamic capital markets, intellectual property and customs regulation, and the level of technology; (iii) *individual-related friction*, related to ICT literacy, availability of online and secure payment systems, and consumer confidence in how personal data will be used on the internet; and (iv) *information-related friction*, measured by the content creation, commitment to open data, filtering and press freedom indexes. See Zwillenberg et al. (2014) pp. 10–15.

[12] See Servicio Nacional del Consumidor de Chile (SERNAC) 2014, *Estudio Descriptivo de E-Commerce en Chile y Análisis de Reclamos ante SERNAC,* http://www.sernac.cl/wp-content/uploads/2014/08/Reporte_E_Commerce_Reclamos-2013-2014.pdf. Accessed 2 October 2015.

[13] See Ministerio de Tecnologías de la Información y las Comunicaciones de Colombia (MINTIC) 2011, *Vive Digital Colombia, Documento Vivo Del Plan, Version 1.0.* http://www.mintic.gov.co/images/MS_VIVE_DIGITAL/archivos/Vivo_Vive_Digital.pdf. Accessed 25 October 2015.

towards the US (Katz 2015). The 2015 UNCTAD Information Economy Report reveals that about 50% of the digital buyers in Chile, Colombia, Mexico and Peru prefer international websites (UNCTAD 2015, p. 29). While it is still difficult to measure how much e-commerce is online content crossing borders, as opposed to e-commerce based on trade in goods, the huge amounts of data traffic serve as an indicator that this is a factor to take into account when designing modern e-commerce policies.

This raises the question of the extent to which legal harmonization through PTAs can improve this situation. In other words, how can PTAs help to create a thriving market at a regional level for e-commerce transactions among PA members? This question should also be analysed in the light of studies suggesting that 'while cross-country legal differences may create barriers to e-commerce, their relative importance is lower when compared to other barriers, such as consumer related issues' (OECD 2013a, p. 31). Notwithstanding the relevance of those studies, it is necessary first to examine the current legal framework regulating e-commerce at a national level. Therefore, the next subsection provides a brief overview of the relevant regulations in Chile, Colombia, Mexico and Peru.

10.2.3 Legal Framework Regulating E-commerce in Chile, Colombia, Mexico and Peru

The main national regulations applicable to e-commerce transactions[14] relate to electronic signatures and authentication,[15] cross-border data flows and data protection,[16] online consumer protection,[17] intellectual property (IP) rights,[18] domain

[14] The lack of regulations on some of those aspects (e.g. e-transactions, consumer protection, privacy and data protection) has been identified by UNCTAD as a barrier affecting the development of e-commerce. See UNCTAD (2015, p. 63).

[15] In the online environment and in e-commerce, it is essential to provide assurance regarding the identity of the parties. Thus electronic authentication and signatures play a key role. A law granting the same legal value to digital signatures as to handwritten signatures is required in order to enable online transactions. The UNCITRAL Model Law on Electronic Signatures 2001 confirms the necessity of having these types of laws, and provides a model regulation that has been adopted by many countries. Furthermore, inconsistencies in the national approaches to electronic signatures work against any proposal to facilitate the free movement of goods and services. Therefore, cross-border commitments to the mutual recognition of certificates are essential to any RTA willing to foster e-commerce.

[16] Data has been declared as the new currency of the digital economy. Since digital technologies make it relatively easy to collect large amounts of data, governments should work to reach a balance between the rights of citizens to privacy and the ability of companies to use data for the purposes of their business.

[17] According to the OECD, the main aspects to consider in consumer protection policies are: (i) information disclosure; (ii) fraud and misleading commercial practices; (iii) privacy issues; (iv) dispute resolution; and (v) redress. See OECD (2013a, p. 29).

[18] Content is a vital part of the digital economy and e-commerce. Content online (e.g. music, multimedia, podcasts, etc.), can be easily copied and distributed illegally; therefore copyright laws play an important role in ensuring the rights of the authors of these materials. See Fitzgerald (2011, pp. 233–41).

names,[19] cybercrime[20] and intermediary liability of internet service providers (ISPs).[21]

In this regard, **Chile** has the following laws:

- Law 19,799 of 2002 regulates electronic documents, electronic signatures and certification of signatures. This law is based on the UNCITRAL Model Law on Electronic Signatures of 2001;
- Law 19,496 of 1997 regulates consumer protection and applies to electronic transactions and to unsolicited commercial electronic communications;
- Law 19,628 of 1999 concerns the protection of personal data;
- Law 17,336 of 1970 (as amended) provides copyright protection for computer programs and establishes a safe harbour for internet intermediaries[22];
- Law 19,233 of 1993 provides protection against cybercrime. This law has been criticized for providing limited protection given its narrow scope (Lara et al. 2014, p. 101).
- Although there are no laws regarding domain names, Chile has a domain name system registry that follows the RFC 1591 (Domain Name System Structure and Delegation).[23]

---

[19] Ibid., pp. 618, 735–7. Domain names are important business identifiers since they are linked to the source of a good or a service. Since the number of domain names has increased, the number of disputes regarding domain names has also increased. Consequently, adequate regulation at a national level regarding domain name registration, renewal and transfer, registry, resellers, dispute resolution, and new second-level domains is essential.

[20] Ibid., pp. 963–1001. The increased use of the 'borderless' internet for everyday transactions should lead to a re-evaluation of traditional off-line criminal laws. Several jurisdictions have recently enacted cyber-crime laws in brand new statutes or have reformed their criminal codes in order to fight technology-enabled crime. Ideally, a RTA project should aim to harmonize the type of offences in cyberspace and to provide for effective enforcement mechanisms. This will help to avoid the creation of cybercrime safe heavens and also protect critical infrastructures as the number of digital attacks has increased over the years.

[21] Intermediary liability refers to situations where platforms (e.g. Twitter and Facebook) are liable for their users' online activities. Since the platforms are easier to find than individual users, they can be subject to legal obligations in order to regulate online activities. Globally, regulation of intermediary liability varies, especially between the US and Europe. Nonetheless, the most common types of intermediary liability include copyright infringement, defamatory and pornographic content, or activities that are illegal in certain jurisdictions, such as online gambling.

[22] The liability protections for internet intermediaries provided in Law 20,430 resemble the language of the 2004 US–Chile FTA and section 512 of the US Digital Millennium Copyright Act (DMCA). On the other hand, a remarkable difference from the DMCA is the lack of a provision establishing a private notice-and-takedown system. Thus, in Chile, a court order is required to compel blocking or removal of copyright-infringing content.

[23] RFC stands for Request for Comments. These are documents created and adopted, initially, through the Internet Engineering Task Force (IETF) and now also through the Internet Society (ISOC). RFCs can be informational or create a standard. In the case of RFC 1591, it did not specify a standard of any kind. RFC 1591 only provided information on the structure of the names in the Domain Name System, specifically the top-level domain names; and on the administration of domains.

In **Colombia**, the following laws are in place:

- Law 527 of 1999, complemented by Decree 1747 of 2000, regulates e-commerce and electronic signatures.
- Law 1480 of 2011 contains a whole chapter regulating consumer protection in e-commerce transactions;
- Law 1581 of 2012, implemented by Decree 1377, contains comprehensive and broad regulations on personal data protection. In particular, this law prohibits the transfer of data across borders to countries that do not have an adequate level of protection, unless the data subject grants prior express consent;
- Andean Community Decision 351 of 1991 establishes the common provisions on copyright and neighbouring rights. The Decision protects computer programs but does not specifically establish provisions regarding intermediary liability on the internet.[24] On the other hand, the US–Colombia FTA contains a provision regarding the liability of internet intermediaries but the law implementing this provision (Law 1520 of 2012) was struck down by the Constitutional Court in 2013 (Karisma Foundation and Herrera 2015);
- Law 1065 of 2006 regulates the domain .co;
- Law 1273 of 2009 provides comprehensive protection against cybercrime (Ojeda-Pérez et al. 2010, p. 41).

By contrast, **Mexico** does not have a comprehensive legislative framework regulating e-commerce. Instead, it has codes and statutes that have been reformed in order to make them applicable to e-commerce transactions:

- The Federal Civil Code allows electronic signatures, and the Code of Commerce has a special chapter dedicated to e-commerce;
- The Federal Law on Consumer Protection contains an entire chapter on the protection of consumers in electronic transactions. Furthermore, it recognizes the utilization of codes of ethics and self-regulation mechanisms. This has allowed the development of TrustMark schemes, such as the one established in the Asia Pacific Economic Cooperation (APEC) Privacy Framework;
- The Federal Law on Protection of Personal Data held by Private Parties incorporates international standards, especially those developed in the APEC Privacy Framework. The law deviates from EU standards on data protection in the sense that it provides more flexibility in international data transfers[25];
- The Federal Law on Copyright of 1996 grants protection to computer programs. It is pertinent that Mexico has not yet adopted regulations addressing the liability of internet service providers for copyright infringement (Camarena 2015);

[24] While the Andean Community Decision 351 does not contain a specific provision on intermediary liability, Article 54 could be applicable to intermediary liability regarding copyright infringements since it states that 'No authority or person, whether natural person or legal entity, may authorize the use of a work, performance, phonographic production or broadcast, or endorse his support to such use, if the user does not have the express prior authorization of the owner of the rights or his representative. In the event of non-compliance, that entity or person shall be jointly liable'.

[25] For a deeper analysis of Mexican data privacy regulation, see: Gutierrez and Korn (2013) p. 38.

- Mexico has no law on domain names. The organization in charge of them is private and has mechanisms for dispute resolution according to ICANN guidelines;
- The Federal Penal Code contains provisions related to cybercrime.

Finally, in **Peru**, the following laws are in place:

- Law 27269 of 2000 regulates digital signatures and certificates. Additionally, there are sectoral regulations applicable to government procurement, customs and tax administration concerning the use of electronic signatures, and that implement the commitments undertaken in the US–Peru FTA and APEC with regard to paperless trade;
- Law 29571 of 2010 regulates consumer protection in electronic transactions;
- Law 29733 of 2011 guarantees the fundamental right to the protection of personal data as established in the Peruvian Constitution. The law mostly follows EU standards of data protection (Gutierrez and Korn 2013, p. 45);
- Legislative Decree 822 protects computer programs and databases. Nonetheless, as in the case of Colombia, no national legislation regarding the liability of internet service providers was passed after the commitments undertaken in the US–Peru FTA (Morachimo 2014);
- Law 30171 of 2014 includes provisions regarding cybercrime;
- On the other hand, there is no law regulating domain names, but similar to Mexico, a private organization is responsible for administration of domain names and for providing dispute resolution mechanisms.

Table 10.1 summarizes the differences between the legal frameworks of the PA members to enable a better understanding of e-commerce regulations in the region.

10.2.3.1 Is There Any Room for Harmonization?

Looking at their national legislation, the four members of the PA already have regulations on many of the legal aspects relevant to e-commerce (i.e. electronic transactions and signatures, data protection,[26] copyright protection and cybercrime), albeit with different levels of protection (e.g. data protection). On the other hand, currently, the liability of internet service providers is not uniformly regulated in the four PA countries, although this issue has formed a substantial part of the IP chapters in the FTAs with the US.[27] Hence, there is still room for harmonization. It should also be taken into account that only the 2009 Chile–Colombia FTA has an

[26] The level of data protection varies across jurisdictions. While Colombia has had a very comprehensive law since 2012, Chile is still waiting for the approval of a new data protection law that aims to be more comprehensive. Peru's data protection law is inspired by European standards whereas Mexico follows a more flexible approach.

[27] US–Chile FTA, Article 17.11 para. 23; US–Colombia FTA, Article 16.11 para. 29; and US–Peru FTA, Article 16.11 para. 29.

Table 10.1 E-commerce regulations in the Pacific Alliance countries

	Chile	Colombia	Mexico	Peru
Laws on electronic transactions and signatures	Yes	Yes	Yes	Yes
Consumer protection laws	Yes	Yes	Yes	Yes
Data protection laws	Yes (low level of protection)	Yes (comprehensive)	Yes (flexible, APEC standards)	Yes (mostly based on the 1995 EU data protection directive)
Copyright laws	Yes	Yes	Yes	Yes
Intermediary liability laws	Yes (provides for a safe harbour); no private notice and take down system)	No (although the US–Colombia FTA has a provision on this aspect)	No	No (although the US–Peru FTA has a provision on this aspect)
Cybercrime laws	Yes	Yes	Yes	Yes
Domain names laws/regulations	Yes	Yes	Yes	Yes

e-commerce chapter.[28] The rest of the FTAs among the PA members do not regulate e-commerce. Even the fairly recently concluded Mexico–Peru FTA of 2012 does not have an e-commerce chapter.[29]

The next section will take a closer look at how the above-mentioned aspects (and other new topics) are being regulated in current PTAs. This is important given that all PA members are also part of other PTAs that have already been concluded or are under negotiation and this may have influenced the current text of the PAAP.

10.3 E-commerce Regulation in Selected PTAs and the Case of the PA

10.3.1 E-commerce Regulation in Selected PTAs

10.3.1.1 TPP

Negotiations for the TPP were concluded on 6 October 2015 and the final agreement was signed on 4 February 2016. However, the TPP as is can no longer enter into force since the US withdrew from the trade deal in January 2017. It has subsequently been replaced by the CPTPP among 11 of the original 12 signatories.

[28] See Chile–Colombia FTA.

[29] See Mexico–Peru FTA. Although fairly recent, this agreement has no electronic commerce chapter.

While the remaining TPP members are evaluating mechanisms to negotiate a similar trade deal in the future there is no clear indication about the future of the agreement. Yet, if negotiations for a similar agreement eventually take place, the work already done regarding the negotiation of digital trade issues could be of benefit. This is important considering that three out of the four members of the PA were parties to the TPP (and now CPTPP) negotiations, namely Chile, Mexico and Peru. For this reason, it is still important to examine the CPTPP's e-commerce chapter in order to get a better understanding of the state of play of international negotiations regarding e-commerce.

The CPTPP contains the following rules[30]:

- prohibition of the imposition of customs duties on electronic transmissions;
- non-discriminatory treatment for digital products;
- duty to allow free cross-border transfer of information by electronic means, when this activity is for the conduct of the business of a covered person;
- duty not to impose localization requirements on computing facilities[31];
- duty not to require the disclosure of source codes as a condition for the import, distribution, sale or use of mass-market software;
- duty not to impose transfer of technology obligations;
- obligation not to deny validity to electronic signatures and not to hinder electronic authentication systems;
- obligation to maintain laws related to fraudulent and deceptive commercial activities online;
- obligation to maintain a legal framework that provides for the protection of the personal information of the users of e-commerce and to encourage the development of mechanisms to promote compatibility between these different national regimes;
- obligation to maintain measures to stop unsolicited commercial electronic messages;
- obligation to promote paperless trading;
- rules on internet interconnection charge sharing;
- principles on access to and use of the internet for e-commerce;
- cooperation to help SMEs to take advantage of e-commerce, and cooperation on policies regarding personal information protection, online consumer protection, cybersecurity threats and other cybersecurity matters.

Stephenson remarked that the TPP 'was slated to become the nucleus of a possible APEC-wide future FTA of the Asia Pacific' Stephenson and Robert (2014, p. 106). Therefore, the importance of this agreement must be highlighted.

---

[30] See Trans-Pacific Partnership Agreement (TPP) 2016, *Chapter 14: Electronic Commerce*, https://ustr.gov/sites/default/files/TPP-Final-Text-Electronic-Commerce.pdf. Accessed 5 February 2016.

[31] The free flow of information rules are designed to subvert data localization laws such as rules that require data on citizens to be stored and processed on servers located in their own country. Thus, they are aimed at preventing countries from distorting internet traffic flows and imposing unnecessary costs on platform operators.

10.3.1.2 TiSA

All members of the PA, as well as its prospective members (Costa Rica and Panama), were part of the TiSA negotiations. TiSA is a plurilateral agreement on trade in services, negotiations on which began in 2011 at the initiative of the US and Australia.[32] Although the wording of the agreement is not public and negotiations are currently suspended, a leaked text provided an overview of the provisions meant to be included[33]:

- regulation of (free) cross-border information flows;
- obligation to maintain consumer protection laws;
- obligation to maintain laws on protection of personal data;
- obligation to maintain laws regulating unsolicited commercial electronic messages;
- duty not to require transfer or access to source code;
- interoperability obligations;
- net neutrality and network management obligations;
- prohibition of local presence requirements;
- obligation to maintain electronic authentication and electronic signatures;
- prohibition of the imposition of customs duties on electronic deliveries; and
- cooperation commitments.

As Weber points out, 'for the time being (…) it can hardly be said whether and to what extent the TISA negotiations will be successful' (Weber 2015, p. 10). Nonetheless, if TiSA were ever revived and successful, it is possible that obligations regarding cross-border data flows would apply to the entire agreement, not solely to the e-commerce annex (Fefer 2016, p. 24).

10.3.1.3 US FTAs[34]

US FTAs tend to have an organized structure and consistently follow the same (liberalizing) approach (Weber and Burri 2012, p. 10). US FTAs contain rules on:

- recognition of the applicability of WTO trade rules regarding measures affecting e- commerce;

[32] TiSA is a trade agreement currently being negotiated by 24 members of the WTO, including the EU. Together, the participating countries account for 70% of world trade in services. TiSA is based on the WTO's General Agreement on Trade in Services (GATS), which involves all WTO members. The key provisions of the GATS – scope, definitions, market access, national treatment and exemptions – are also found in TiSA. TiSA aims at opening up markets and improving rules in areas such as licensing, financial services, telecoms, e-commerce, maritime transport, and on professionals moving abroad temporarily to provide services.

[33] Trade in Services Agreement (TiSA) Annex on Electronic Commerce 2013, http://www.bilaterals.org/IMG/pdf/tisa-annex-on-electronic-commerce.pdf. Accessed 25 October 2015.

[34] This section is based on the common provisions of three of the latest US FTAs: US–Korea FTA (KORUS) (in force since 2012), US–Colombia Trade Promotion Agreement (US–Colombia FTA) (in force since 2012) and US–Peru Trade Promotion Agreement (US–Peru FTA) (in force since 2009).

- definition of digital products and electronic transmissions;
- non-discriminatory treatment obligation for digital products;
- prohibition of the imposition of customs duties on digital products;
- duty to maintain electronic authentication and electronic signature laws;
- duty to maintain consumer protection laws;
- promotion of paperless trading;
- dropping of local presence requirements;
- transparency.

These commitments are contingent on the provisions of the services chapter, which are liberal in most cases (Burri 2015, pp. 53–55). The US FTAs, however, do not contain binding rules on free cross-border data flows, except in the case of the US–Korea FTA (KORUS),[35] which also contains a provision on 'Principles on access and use of internet for electronic commerce'.[36]

10.3.1.4 EU FTAs[37]

In contrast to the US FTAs, the structure of EU FTAs tends to vary. However, they usually incorporate an e-commerce section and an understanding on computer services. Substantive aspects to be noted in the e-commerce section are as follows (Wunsch-Vincent and Hold 2012):

- recognition of the applicability of WTO trade rules regarding measures affecting e- commerce;
- duty to maintain laws regarding protection of personal information, in some cases according to international standards[38];
- cooperative commitments to work and enter into a dialogue on electronic signatures, consumer protection, paperless trading and, more recently, use of ICT technologies by SMEs;
- prohibition of the imposition of customs duties on electronically supplied services;
- increased focus on some areas such as electronic signatures and IP rights; and

[35] KORUS, Article 15.8: '*Cross Border Information Flows*: Recognizing the importance of the free flow of information in facilitating trade, and acknowledging the importance of protecting personal information, the Parties shall endeavor to refrain from imposing or maintaining unnecessary barriers to electronic information flows across borders'.

[36] KORUS, Article. 15.7.

[37] This section is based on the common provisions of two of the latest EU FTAs: the EU–Korea FTA and the EU–Colombia Peru FTA.

[38] See Comprehensive Economic and Trade Agreement (CETA) between Canada and the EU (signed in 2014, but not in force yet), 'Article X-03: *Trust and Confidence in Electronic Commerce* Each Party should adopt or maintain laws, regulations or administrative measures for the protection of personal information of users engaged in electronic commerce and, when doing so, shall take into due consideration international standards for data protection of relevant international organisations of which both Parties are a member'.

The following subsections will introduce the e-commerce chapter of the PAAP and will provide a comparative analysis of the e-commerce provisions in the PAAP in relation to other PTAs.

10.3.2 E-commerce Regulation in the PAAP

Chapter 13 of the PAAP regulates e-commerce. According to the outcome of the 2015 Paracas Summit, amendments will be made to the original version of the e-commerce chapter as well as to the telecommunications chapter.[39] It should be noted that the PAAP does not contain a chapter dedicated to IP protection.

Table 10.2a, 10.2b, 10.2c outlines how the most important aspects of e-commerce are regulated in the PAAP. For the full text of each provision please refer to the corresponding footnotes. Comparisons with other PTAs will be made in order to clarify the origin of the provisions in the PAAP.

10.3.3 Comparative Analysis of the E-commerce Provisions in the PAAP and the Most Relevant Aspects

10.3.3.1 Comparative Analysis

A comparative approach as shown in Table 10.3a, 10.3b is useful in order to understand the differences between the PTAs reviewed.

10.3.3.2 Important Aspects of E-commerce Regulation in the PAAP

Two aspects should be highlighted before undertaking a deeper analysis of some relevant provisions found in the PAAP e-commerce chapter. First, unlike the US and the EU FTAs, the e-commerce chapter of the PAAP does not mention the applicability of WTO rules to measures affecting e-commerce. Secondly, there is no provision in the PAAP regarding non-discriminatory treatment for digital products, even though the Chile–Colombia FTA[40] already includes an article on this aspect and the US approach is also to regulate this issue.

With regard to the provisions found in the agreement, three aspects are noteworthy. First, the consumer protection provision states the aim of the Parties to create a supranational dispute resolution mechanism for the protection of consumers in cross-border electronic transactions. Secondly, the data protection provision

[39] See Declaración de Paracas (2015) Alianza del Pacifico, https://alianzapacifico.net/?wpdmdl=4078. Accessed 25 October 2015.

[40] Article 12.4 of the Chile–Colombia FTA.

Table 10.2a Main aspects of the PAAP provisions regarding e-commerce (Part I)

Rules	PTAs and other sources with similar language
Definitions[a]	
Trade undertaken by electronic means	Identical to the definition of e-commerce in the comprehensive economic and trade agreement (CETA) between the EU and Canada (not in force)
'*means commerce conducted through telecommunications, alone or in conjunction with other information and communication technologies*'	
Personal data	
'*means any information relating to an identified or identifiable natural person*'	Identical to the definition of personal data in the EU data protection directive 95/46/EC[b]
Digital products	
'*means computer programs, text, video, images, sound recordings, and other products that are digitally encoded*'	Similar to the definition of digital product in the US–Peru FTA
Scope[c]	
'*The present chapter applies to measures affecting electronic transactions of goods and services, including digital products, notwithstanding the regulations on services and investment.*'	Similar wording to article 15.2 of the US–Peru FTA

[a]Article 13.1 of the PAAP:
Definitions

trade undertaken by electronic means refers to commerce conducted through telecommunications, alone or in conjunction with other information and communication technologies;

trade administration documents means forms that a Party issues or controls that must be completed by or for an importer or exporter in connection with the import or export of goods;

personal data means any information relating to an identified or identifiable natural person;

interoperability is the ability of two or more systems or components to exchange information and to use the information that has been exchanged;

unsolicited electronic commercial communications means an electronic message which is sent for commercial or marketing purposes without the consent of the recipient, or despite explicit rejection by the recipient, using an internet carriage service, to the extent provided for under the domestic laws and regulations of each Party, other telecommunications services;

digital products means computer programs, text, video, images, sound recordings, and other products that are digitally encoded.

[b]Directive 95/46/EC of the European Parliament and of the Council of 24 October 1995 on the protection of individuals with regard to the processing of personal data and on the free movement of such data, OJ L 281, 23.11.1995, pp. 31–50

[c]Article 13.2 of the PAAP:
Scope

The present chapter applies to measures affecting electronic transactions of goods and services, including digital products, notwithstanding the regulations on services and investment that are applicable by virtue of the current Additional Protocol

Table 10.2b Main aspects of the PAAP provisions regarding e-commerce (Part II)

Rules	PTAs and other sources with similar language
General provisions[a]	Similar to article 1502 of the Canada–Peru FTA (the PAAP also notes the importance of facilitating the use of e-commerce by SMEs and guaranteeing security on e-commerce activities by considering international standards on data protection)
'the Parties recognise the importance of:	
(…)	
(v) facilitating the use of electronic commerce by SMEs (…);	
(vi) guaranteeing security of the users of e-commerce, taking into consideration the international standards on data protection.	
(…).'	
Custom duties[b]	Similar to corresponding articles in the US–Peru FTA and US–Colombia FTA
Transparency[c]	Similar to US and EU FTAs (the PAAP states that the transparency obligations are subject to the national legislation)
'Each Party, ***according to its national legislation****, shall publish (…) its laws, regulations, and administrative ruling of general application that pertain to electronic commerce.'*	
Consumer protection[d]	
'1. The Parties recognise the importance of maintaining and adopting transparent and effective measures to protect consumers from fraudulent and misleading commercial practices (…).	Para. 1 identical to article 166 of the EU–Colombia, Peru FTA
2. (…) the parties should exchange information and experiences about the national systems relating to the protection of consumers that are part of electronic commerce transactions.	Provisions contained in paras. 2 and 3 are new
3. The Parties will evaluate alternative mechanisms of cross-border dispute resolution that are executed through electronic means and related to the protection of consumers of cross-border electronic transactions.'	
Management of paperless trading[e]	Similar to US and EU FTAs (nonetheless, the PAAP highlights that this obligation is subject to national legislation)
'(…)	
2. Each Party shall endeavour to accept trade administration documents submitted electronically ***according to its legislation,*** *as the legal equivalent of the paper version of such documents.'*	

[a]Article 13.4 of the PAAP
General Provisions
1. The Parties recognise the economic growth and opportunity that electronic commerce provides;
2. Considering the potential of electronic commerce as an instrument for social and economic development, the Parties recognise the importance of:

(continued)

Table 10.2b (continued)

(a) clarity, transparency and predictability in their domestic regulatory frameworks in facilitating, to the maximum extent possible, the development of electronic commerce;

(b) encouraging self-regulation by the private sector to promote trust and confidence in electronic commerce, having regard to the interests of users, through initiatives such as industry guidelines, model contracts, codes of conduct and trust-marks;

(c) interoperability, innovation and competition in facilitating electronic commerce;

(d) ensuring that global and domestic electronic commerce policy takes into account the interest of all stakeholders, including business, consumers, non-government organisations, and relevant public institutions;

(e) facilitating the use of electronic commerce by small and medium sized enterprises;

(f) guaranteeing the security of the users of electronic commerce, taking into consideration the international standards on data protection

3. Each Party shall endeavour to adopt measures to facilitate trade conducted by electronic means by addressing issues relevant to the electronic environment

4. The Parties recognise the importance of avoiding unnecessary barriers to trade conducted by electronic means. Having regard to national policy objectives, each Party shall endeavour to prevent measures that:

(a) unduly hinder trade conducted by electronic means; or

(b) have the effect of treating trade conducted by electronic means more restrictively than trade conducted by other means

[b]Article 13.4 of the PAAP

Custom duties

1. Neither Party may apply customs duties, fees, or charges on or in connection with the importation or exportation of digital products by electronic means;

2. For greater clarity, this chapter does not prevent a Party from imposing internal taxes or other internal charges on digital products transmitted electronically, provided that such taxes or charges are imposed in a manner consistent with the present Additional Protocol

[c]Article 13.5 of the PAAP

Transparency

Each Party, according to its national legislation, shall publish promptly or otherwise shall make available to the public its laws, regulations, and administrative ruling of general application, that pertain to electronic commerce

[d]Article 13.6 of the PAAP

Consumer protection

1. The Parties recognise the importance of maintaining and adopting transparent and effective measures to protect consumers from fraudulent and misleading commercial practices when consumers engage in electronic commerce transactions

2. For the purposes of paragraph 1, the Parties should exchange information and experiences about the national systems relating to the protection of consumers that are part of electronic commerce transactions

3. The Parties will evaluate alternative mechanisms of cross-border dispute resolution that are executed through electronic means and related to the protection of consumers of cross-border electronic transactions

[e]Article 13.7 of the PAAP

Management of Paperless Trading

1. Each Party shall endeavour to make trade management documents available to the public in electronic form

2. Each Party shall endeavour to accept trade administration documents submitted electronically according to its legislation, as the legal equivalent of the paper version of such documents

Table 10.2c Main aspects of the PAAP provisions regarding e-commerce (Part III)

Rules	PTAs and other sources with similar language
Protection of personal data[a]	
'1. The Parties should adopt, develop or maintain regulations and administrative measures for the protection of the personal data of the users that take part in electronic commerce transactions. The Parties will take into account the existing international standards on the subject matter.	Para 1. Is similar to article X-03: '*Trust and Confidence in Electronic Commerce*' of CETA agreement between the EU and Canada
2. The Parties will exchange information and experiences with regard to their personal data protection laws.'	
Unsolicited commercial electronic messages[b]	None
'The Parties will adopt or maintain measures to protect users from unsolicited commercial electronic messages.'	
Authentication and digital Certificates[c]	Identical to article 15.6 of the US–Peru FTA
Cross-border information flows[d]	None
'With the objective to deepen the relations regarding e-commerce, the Parties will consider in the future the negotiation of agreements related to cross border information flows.'	
Cooperation[e]	Identical to article 15.5 of the US–Chile FTA (2004)
Relation to other chapters[f]	Identical to article 12.7 of the Colombia–Korea FTA

[a]Article 13.8 of the PAAP
Protection of Personal Data

1. The Parties shall adopt, develop or maintain regulations and administrative measures for the protection of the personal data of the users that take part in electronic commerce transactions. The Parties will take into account the existing international standards on the subject matter

The Parties will exchange information and experiences with regard to their personal data protection laws

[b]Article 13.9 of the PAAP

Unsolicited commercial electronic messages

The Parties will adopt or maintain measures to protect users from unsolicited commercial electronic messages

[c]Article 13.10 of the PAAP
Authentication and Digital Certificates

1. No Party may adopt or maintain legislation for electronic authentication that would prevent parties to a transaction undertaken by electronic means from having the opportunity to establish before judicial or administrative authorities that their electronic transaction complies with the legal requirements provided by law. (Same as US-Peru FTA, electronic commerce);

2. The Parties will establish homologation criteria and mechanisms that foster electronic authentication interoperability among them according to international standards. With this aim, the Parties can consider the recognition of certificates of advanced electronic signatures or digital signatures, issued by certification service providers operating in the territory of another Party according with the procedure established in its legislation, with the purpose of safeguarding security and integrity standards

[d]Article 13.11 of the PAAP

Cross border information flows

(continued)

Table 10.2c (continued)

With the objective to deepen the relations regarding e-commerce, the Parties will consider in the future the negotiation of agreements related to cross border information flows

[e]Article 13.12 of the PAAP

Cooperation

Recognising the global nature of electronic commerce, the Parties affirm the importance of:

(a) working together to facilitate the use of electronic commerce by small- and medium-sized enterprises;

(b) sharing information and experiences on laws, regulations, and programs pertaining to electronic commerce, including those related data privacy, consumer confidence, security in electronic communications, electronic authentication, intellectual property rights, and electronic government;

(c) working to maintain cross-border flows of information as an essential element in fostering a vibrant environment for electronic commerce;

(d) fostering electronic commerce by encouraging the private sector to adopt codes of conduct, model contracts, guidelines, and enforcement mechanisms; and

(e) actively participating in regional and multilateral fora to promote the development of electronic commerce

[f]Article 13.14 of the PAAP

Relation to other chapters

In the event of any inconsistency between this Chapter and another Chapter in this Agreement, the other Chapter shall prevail to the extent of the inconsistency

includes a reference to international standards that should be used while adapting, developing or maintaining regulations or administrative measures for the protection of personal data. Thirdly, the PAAP includes a provision regarding cross-border data flows, which is drafted in a non-binding way and is only intended to show the willingness of the PA members to hold a dialogue on this point in the future. It is clear that this is not a substantive provision, such as in KORUS or the TPP.

Finally, in terms of length and degree of liberalization, the PAAP contains more provisions on e-commerce than the current US FTAs with PA members, and even more provisions than EU FTAs. Nonetheless, the PAAP does not contain TPP or TiSA style provisions, such as dropping of local presence requirements, prohibitions on requesting access to source codes, and interoperability obligations. Thus, the PAAP e-commerce chapter does not go as far as TPP and TiSA towards greater liberalization, but goes further than the current FTAs between the PA members and the US and the EU.

10.4 Analysis

10.4.1 Which Model of E-commerce Regulation Does the PAAP Follow?

E-commerce regulation goes hand in hand with the global governance models for internet regulation, where the US and the EU play an important role. Therefore, it was originally assumed that the PAAP replicates one of those imported models.

Table 10.3a Comparative analysis of the e-commerce provisions in the US and EU FTAs, TPP, TiSA and PAAP (Part I)

	US (latest) FTAs	EU (latest) FTAs	TPP	TiSA	PAAP
Applicability of WTO agreements	Yes	Yes	No	Yes	No
Unrestricted cross-border data flows	Only in KORUS	No	Yes	Yes	No
Online consumer protection (fraud, deceptive commercial practices)	Yes	Yes (cooperative language)	Yes	Yes (two different articles for online consumer protection and data protection)	Yes
Personal information protection	Yes	Yes (according to international standards)	Yes	Yes	Yes
Unsolicited commercial electronic communications	No	Yes – only cooperation	Yes	Yes	Yes
Prohibition on transferring or accessing source code	No	No	Yes	Yes	No
Access to networks	No (however KORUS has a provision on principles for access to/use of internet for e-commerce	No	No	Yes	No
Prohibition of localization requirements	No	No	Yes	Yes	No

However, given the provisions found in the e-commerce chapter of the PAAP, it is not clear which model the PAAP resembles most closely.

On the one hand, data protection provisions in the PAAP are similar to those in the EU model. Moreover, the PAAP includes the same definition of personal data as contained in the EU Data Protection Directive of 1995, in contrast to the US approach.[41]

[41] Neither the Peru–US FTA nor the Colombia–US FTA mentions personal data. In the US–Chile FTA there is a reference to data privacy in Article 15.5 but in non-enforceable language:

'Article 15.5: Cooperation

Having in mind the global nature of electronic commerce, the Parties recognize the importance of:

(…)

(b) sharing information and experiences on regulations, laws, and programs in the sphere of electronic commerce, including those related to data privacy, consumer confidence, cyber-security, electronic signatures, intellectual property rights, and electronic government.'

Table 10.3b Comparative analysis of the e-commerce provisions in the US and EU FTAs, TPP, TiSA and PAAP (Part II)

	US (latest) FTAs	EU (latest) FTAs	TPP	TiSA	PAAP
Authentication of electronic signatures	Yes	No	Yes	Yes	Yes
Paperless trading	Yes	Yes	Yes	No	Yes
Prohibition of customs duties on digital products	Yes	Yes	Yes	Yes (electronic deliveries)	Yes
Non-discriminatory treatment of digital products	Yes	Not specifically for digital products, but for the services subject to commitments	Yes	No	No
Cyber-security commitments	No	No	No (only cooperation)	No	No
International cooperation	Yes (in SMEs, data privacy, consumer protection and cross-border data flow)	Yes (in electronic authentication, liability of ISPS, treatment of SPAM, consumer protection, paperless trading)	Yes	Yes (in digital literacy)	Yes
Transparency	Yes	No	No	No	Yes

On the other hand, the PAAP includes binding commitments on electronic authentication and transparency that are more similar to the US style. Besides, the mere fact that the PAAP contains a chapter on e-commerce is a sign that the agreement was influenced by previous FTAs signed with the US. Likewise, the PAAP contains a provision (albeit declaratory) of the intention of the Parties to engage in discussions on cross-border data flows, which to some extent is a characteristic of the US FTAs.

With this background in mind, the e-commerce chapter of the PAAP can be described as a hybrid product of the US and EU models. It is clear from the current version of the text that the aim of the four PA members is to strike a balance between a business-friendly framework for e-commerce and maintaining sufficient safeguards regarding data privacy and consumer protection.

Finally, the e-commerce chapter of the PAAP can be said to fall between two levels of e-commerce liberalization. The first corresponds to 'FTA e-commerce regulation', where the US and the EU model are increasingly converging in some respects. The second level corresponds to 'regional PTA e-commerce regulation', where TTP and TiSA are predominant and include very progressive provisions on e-commerce.

10.4.2 Do the Current Provisions Take into Account New Barriers to E-commerce?

E-commerce is currently undergoing important and rapid developments as a result of innovative and disruptive technologies. This subsection will analyse how the future of e-commerce is addressed in the PAAP. We will base the discussion on the findings of the Kommerskollegium (2015) report on barriers affecting new trends in e-commerce in the EU.[42] These new trends are influenced by diverse phenomena arising in the digital economy for example, the rapidly developing app economy, co-sharing activities and the internet of things, among others. Notably, these new trends are mainly focused on the services market. Thus, it no longer concerns only goods traded through eBay, but is relevant to very common services, such as those provided by Airbnb, Uber and other platforms, as shown in Table 10.4.[43]

Table 10.4 stresses the importance of the regulation of two issues in the context of the new trends in e-commerce (deliberately excluding the obvious problem of IP protection in the digital age which is beyond the scope of this chapter). They are: *consumer protection* and *data protection*.

As stated at the beginning of this chapter, legal inconsistencies between jurisdictions might create barriers to e-commerce. However, their relative importance is less than that of other barriers, such as consumer-related issues.[44] Thus, considering also Table 10.4, the PAAP consumer protection clause is right in not only protecting consumers against fraudulent and misleading commercial practices, but also in proposing the creation of a cross-border dispute resolution mechanism.

Further, the first part of this chapter also mentioned that all four members of the PA have data protection laws at the national level, albeit providing different degrees of protection. The challenges posed by the new trends in e-commerce emphasize the need for comprehensive and adequate data protection rules. In this regard, the text of the PAAP should aim to go one step further and propose the discussion of harmonization of data protection laws across the four countries, in addition to the exchange of information and experiences.

Moreover, since the PA has no IP chapter, the lack of norms on internet service provider liability within the PA framework gives cause for concern. This is a feature that was incorporated in the IP chapter of the TPP for copyright infringement[45] but is found neither in the PAAP nor in the PA digital agenda roadmap. This shortcom-

---

[42] Kommerskollegium (2015) (The Kommerskollegium reports analyse obstacles to e-commerce and are a good source of thoughtful analysis on the topic.)

[43] In this regard, many authors agree that 'the exponential growth of online social networking in parallel with electronic commerce not only embeds the internet and digital applications as an all-pervasive general purpose technology within society, but means that the line between social and commercial use becomes blurred, especially around fundamental public policy issues like privacy, fraud and identity theft'. See Fitzgerald (2011) vii.

[44] Ibid., 31.

[45] Article 18.82

Table 10.4 PAAP provisions in light of barriers to new trends in e-commerce

	Barrier	Possible applicable PAAP provision
Online marketplaces	Rules on intermediate liability	Not included
	Rules on product information[a]	Consumer protection
Search engines	Data protection rules (e.g. right to be forgotten)	Data protection
Digital distribution	Intellectual property/licensing procedures[b]	Not included
The app economy	Consumer information requirements[c]	Consumer protection
Cloud computing	Location requirements for data	Not included
	Data protection rules/transfer of data	Data protection
Internet of things and big data	Data protection rules	Data protection
3D printing	Rules on product conformity	Consumer protection
New payment forms	Possible restrictions on virtual currencies	Not included

The OECD has pointed out that adequate payment mechanisms are essential for the successful development of e-commerce. The barriers that would prevent setting up such a payment system include: (i) lack of acceptance of electronic invoicing; (ii) lack of a digital identification and authentication regime; (iii) inadequate mobile ecosystem to deliver both commercial and public services to citizens; and iv) insufficient payment security, data protection and the fear of online fraud. See OECD (2013b)

[a]This refers to requirements that have to be displayed on the seller's website and might be difficult to fulfil on webpages where thousands of products are displayed. See Kommerskollegium (2015) 26

[b]ibid 28. There are many aspects that affect digital distribution. Some are related to an inconsistent intellectual property framework. For instance, the Kommerskollegium notes that in the EU there are problems with licensing procedures for platforms and service providers wishing to cover the whole of the EU. This situation could also arise in the case of the PA since the agreement does not contain an intellectual property chapter

[c]ibid 30. E-commerce transactions are increasing as a result of the rapid development of mobile devices. These devices are characterized by smaller screens than laptops and computers. Rules regarding information that e-traders should provide to consumers were designed with the bigger screens of laptops and computers in mind. Therefore, the switch to smaller devices might translate into information overflow for consumers that could become problematic for mobile transactions

Source: Adapted from Table 10.3, 'Types of trade barriers' Kommerskollegium (2015), p. 41

ing could damage both well-known internet services providers (e.g. Google and eBay) but also small platforms based in the PA countries.

In this context, it may be concluded that the PAAP does make the best efforts to include provisions regarding e-commerce. Nonetheless, the current text of the agreement can also provide the starting point for future discussions aiming for deeper regulation on consumer protection, data protection and ISPs' liability aspects.

10.4.3 The PA Digital Agenda Roadmap

The 2016 PA digital agenda roadmap proposes the development of four core axes:

(i) digital economy,
(ii) digital connectivity,
(iii) digital government; and
(iv) digital ecosystem.

The digital economy axis aims to implement a digital single market and foster the internationalization of the ICT sector. The second axis tackles digital connectivity and is mainly aimed at creating the technological infrastructure. Therefore, efforts will be focused on transitioning to Internet Protocol Version 6 (IPv6) standards, reduction of roaming rates and interconnection costs, and the development of new traffic distribution networks as well as access to high-speed networks. The third axis relates to digital government, and, importantly, puts on the table an initiative to use open data schemes for government services, as well as e-government and cloud solutions services for the public sector. Finally, the digital ecosystem axis focuses on net neutrality, cybersecurity and data protection.

While all these activities lay the hard and soft foundations for a digital single market, there are still features being discussed not only in FTAs, but also at the level of digital regional integration schemes (i.e. the EU and the digital single market), which at some point should be incorporated into the agenda. One such issue is ISP liability for e-commerce companies, which is an aspect usually included in the IP chapter of an FTA. As discussed previously, ISP liability is not harmonized among PA members. Yet, together with other IP issues, such as copyrights, it plays an important role in the success of online platforms, making it essential for e-commerce companies.

10.5 Conclusion

In 2003, Maclay and Coppock found that policies regulating e-commerce at a regional level largely reflected the attributes of the implementing institution. This finding can be applied to the PA, which is characterized as an ambitious and pragmatic institution. Therefore, it would be expected that consensus on rules regarding many deep and innovative aspects of e-commerce regulation will be easily reached.

Although none of the PA members is a world leader in the export of digital goods or services, all of them have at least one FTA with the leading economies shaping global e-commerce (and internet) rules, namely the US and the EU.[46] Previous studies have described the US blueprint regarding e-commerce regulation as fairly

[46] The US has comprehensive bilateral FTAs that include a chapter on e-commerce with all four members of the PA and has significant trade and foreign policy ties with them.

uniform and taking a mostly liberal approach (Burri 2015, pp. 53–57). The EU approach is less uniform; however it frequently includes cooperative language and stresses the adoption of data protection policies (Burri 2015, pp. 58–60). Additionally, the four members of the PA have been involved in either the TPP or TiSA negotiations. Currently, the TPP can no longer enter into force and the TiSA is still under negotiation. According to the final text of the TPP and the available information on TiSA, liberal and far-reaching provisions were included in the e-commerce chapter of both agreements. In this context, the question that this chapter aimed to answer was: *Where does the e-commerce chapter of the PAAP stand against this background?*

The comparative analysis of the provisions contained in the e-commerce chapter of the PAAP in relation to the above-mentioned PTAs (and FTAs) leads to the conclusion that the PAAP e-commerce chapter is a hybrid product that aims to balance the creation of a business-friendly environment (US style) with the need to safeguard consumer and data protection (EU style). On the other hand, the PAAP e-commerce chapter also falls between two levels of liberalization. The first level comprises the increasingly convergent set of FTAs and the second (more comprehensive level) comprises the e-commerce regulation found in the TPP and TiSA.

Finally, new trends in e-commerce emphasize the need for increased coordination and harmonization of rules regarding consumer and data protection. Hence, the proposals included in the PA digital agenda roadmap are to be welcomed. However, at some point they need to translate into tangible commitments that safeguard two often conflicting aims: promoting a thriving digital and e-commerce community and protecting consumers. These two aspects have been covered by the current text of the PAAP, reflecting to some extent the European influence. In this context, the PA digital agenda roadmap is a good starting point from which to map and bring to the table other important aspects relevant to accelerating e-commerce and digital trade within the PA. However, in light of the intrinsic characteristics of the PA as an ambitious trade and integration institution there is scope for further development.

References

Burri, M. (2015). The international economic law framework for digital trade. *Zeitschrift für schweizerisches Recht ZSR, 134*, 10–72.

Camarena, J. (2015). *WILMAP: Mexico. Stanford Law School: The Center for Internet and Society*. http://cyberlaw.stanford.edu/page/wilmap-mexico. Accessed 5 July 2017.

Declaración de Paracas. (2015). *Alianza del Pacifico*, https://alianzapacifico.net/?wpdmdl=4078. Accessed 25 Oct 2015.

eBay. (2012). *Towards commerce 3.0: Roadmap for building sustainable growth in commerce*. www.ebaymainstreet.com/sites/default/files/eBay_Towards-Commerce-3.0-Policy-Roadmap.pdf. Accessed 25 Oct 2015.

Economic Commission for Latin America (ECLAC). (2015). *La nueva revolución digital: De la Internet del consumo a la Internet de la producción*. United Nations: Santiago.

Fefer, R. (2016). *U.S. Trade in services: Trends and policy issues* (Report Number: R43291). US Congressional Research Service. https://fas.org/sgp/crs/misc/R43291.pdf. Accessed 1 June 2017.

Fitzgerald, B. (2011). *Internet and e-commerce law: Technology, law and policy* (2nd ed.). Pyrmont: Thomson Reuters.
Goldsmith, J., & Wu, T. (2006). *Who controls the internet? Illusions of a borderless world* (1st ed.). Oxford: Oxford University Press.
Gutierrez, H., & Korn, D. (2013). Facilitando the cloud: Data protection regulation as a driver of national competitiveness in Latin America. *University of Miami Inter-American Law Review, 45*, 33–61.
Karisma Foundation, & Herrera, J. (2015). *WILMAP: Colombia. Stanford Law School: The Center for Internet and Society*. http://cyberlaw.stanford.edu/page/wilmap-colombia. Accessed 5 July 2017.
Katz, R. (2015). *El Ecosistema de La Economía Digital En América Latina*. Madrid: Ariel and Fundación Telefónica.
Kommerskollegium. (2015). *Online trade, offline rules – A review of barriers to e-commerce in the EU*. http://www.kommers.se/In-English/Publications/2015/Online-Trade-Offline-Rules/. Accessed 23 Apr 2017.
Lara, J., Martínez, M., & Viollier, P. (2014). Hacia una regulación de los delitos informáticos basada en la evidencia. *Revista Chilena de Derecho y Tecnología, 3*, 101–137.
Maclay, C., & Coppock, K. (2003). Electronic commerce: A regional approach. *Info, 5*, 17–23.
Malcom, J., & Sutton, M. (2015). *Big tech does not speak for the internet*. Electronic Frontier Foundation. https://www.eff.org/deeplinks/2015/07/big-tech-does-not-speak-internet. Accessed 25 Oct 2015.
Messano, O. (2013). *Study on international internet connectivity. Focus on internet connectivity in Latin America and the Caribbean*. Geneva: International Telecommunications Union.
Morachimo, M. (2014). *WILMAP: Peru. Stanford Law School: The Center for Internet and Society*. http://cyberlaw.stanford.edu/page/wilmap-peru. Accessed 8 July 2017.
OECD. (2013a). *A borderless world: Realizing the potential of the global electronic commerce*. Paris: France.
OECD. (2013b). *Electronic and mobile commerce* (OECD Digital Economy Papers No. 228). Paris: France.
Ojeda-Pérez, J., Rincón-Rodríguez, F., & Arias-Flórez, M. (2010). Delitos informáticos y entorno jurídico vigente en Colombia. *Cuadernos de Contabilidad, 11*, 41–66.
Parish, N. (2015). Will Mexico become the most important E-commerce market in Latin America? *Forbes*. https://www.forbes.com/sites/nathanielparishflannery/2015/04/27/will-mexico-become-the-most-important-e-commerce-market-in-latin-america/#3ef69d42775f. Accessed 5 July 2017
Stephenson, S., & Robert, M. (2014). Innovating regionalism: The Americas. In P. Sauvé & A. Shingal (Eds.), *The preferential liberalization of trade in services: Comparative regionalism* (pp. 101–159). Cheltenham: Edward Elgar.
United Nations Conference on Trade and Development (UNCTAD). (2015). *Information economy report: Unlocking the potential of e-commerce for developing countries*. Geneva: United Nations.
Weber, R. (2015). Digital trade and e-commerce: Challenges and opportunities of the Asia-Pacific regionalism. *Asian Journal of WTO & International Health Law and Policy, 10*, 321–347.
Weber, R., & Burri, M. (2012). *Classification of services in the digital economy*. Zurich: Schulthess.
World Economic Forum (WEF) and INSEAD. (2013). *The global information technology report: Growth and jobs in a Hyperconnected world*. Geneva: WEF/INSEAD.
World Trade Organization (WTO). (1998). *Ministerial declaration on global E-commerce 1998* (WT/MIN(98)/DEC/2).
World Trade Organization (WTO). (2013). *E-commerce in developing countries: Opportunities and challenges for small and medium-sized enterprises*. Geneva: WTO.
Wunsch-Vincent, S., & Hold, A. (2012). Trade rules for the digital age. In M. Burri & T. Cottier (Eds.), *Trade governance in the digital age: World trade forum* (pp. 179–221). Cambridge: Cambridge University Press.
Zwillenberg, P., Field, D., & Dean, D. (2014). *The connected world: Greasing the wheels of the internet economy*. Boston: The Boston Consulting Group.

Chapter 11
The Pacific Alliance: Adding Value to the Global Intellectual Property Rights Regime?

Rodrigo Corredor

11.1 Background

Countries of the Pacific Alliance (PA) stand out for their good performance in terms of compliance with international standards on the protection of intellectual property rights (IPRs), shaped essentially by the World Trade Organization (WTO) Agreement on Trade-Related Aspects of Intellectual Property Rights (TRIPS Agreement), and IPR provisions included in preferential trade agreements (PTAs) that goes beyond what is in the TRIPS Agreement (TRIPS-plus)

However, the low level of innovation and technical sophistication of PA countries' productive sectors suggest that their attempts to defend these standards as enabling conditions for a virtuous cycle of technological-driven growth have been unsuccessful. PA national administrations have taken advantage of the regulatory space offered by so-called "flexibilities", in many cases mitigating the effects of the extended rights of protection pursued by some stakeholders. For instance, most of these countries import drugs or have drug sectors operating on the basis of the pro-competitive nature of TRIPS flexibilities, like the protection of test data and the "Bolar exception", that have been mechanisms to mitigate the effects of the strict interpretation of IPRs in the protection of pharmaceuticals and agrochemicals.[1]

Yet, the economic logic under which the TRIPS Agreement was designed does not seem to take into account the current trends towards global value chains, digital economy, mobility of scientists and the ubiquity of services or the prevalence of foreign direct investment. In this regard, the ongoing discussion on intangible assets

[1] The Bolar or regulatory exception, allow companies seeking to develop a generic product (therefore needing marketing approval) to use, produce or copy patented materials for this purpose during the patent term (Castro Bernieri 2006, p. 555).

R. Corredor (✉)
Department of Economic Law, Externado University of Colombia, Bogotá, Colombia
e-mail: rodrigo.corredor@uexternado.edu.co

P. Sauvé et al. (eds.), *The Pacific Alliance in a World of Preferential Trade Agreements*, United Nations University Series on Regionalism 16,
https://doi.org/10.1007/978-3-319-78464-9_11

included as protected matter in investment treaties as well as the risks arising from the particularities surrounding international investor–state dispute settlement (ISDS) raises new issues of concern for the PA countries. PA members should therefore define clear positions that allow them to act as an economic bloc with respect to IP issues and by doing so would reduce or mitigate the impact of such disputes. Underlying this complex scenario is one critical fact: the current deadlock in negotiations within the WTO makes a redesign of the TRIPS Agreement unlikely.

As the PA defines itself as a strategic platform, one of its main challenges is the identification of a common strategy that may allow its members to take part in the current wave of industrialization (Rojas and Terán 2016, p. 70). Achieving this endeavour depends on the ability to improve the incorporation of local resources and capacities into global and regional value chains. Based on this understanding, all countries participating in this regional agreement have taken measures to direct their industrial policies towards more knowledge-oriented activity.[2] Intellectual property (IP) standards play a central role in designing these new strategies.

This new reality brings to the fore the question of whether the demand for stronger IP protection as part of the international trade agenda is compatible with the productive transformation programmes undertaken by most PA countries. This is particularly relevant to the emergence of new global issues such as clean energy technologies, strengthening of food security and consolidation of the digital economy, where disruptive innovation demands clear and sound regulations.

This chapter aims to assess the extent to which regionalism as a trend, and particularly the PA with its pragmatic approach, promotes continuity in the implementation of the TRIPS obligations consistent with a *status quo* point of view; or, alternatively, if there are elements that suggest that PA countries have the will to support the design of a new institutional architecture for the protection and enforcement of IPRs.

Looking at the rationale of the regional integration process framed by the PA, one might suggest that after two decades of multilateral trade negotiations, the benefits and drawbacks of trade liberalization have become clear for the majority of its participants. In this regard, the promoted regional integration emerges as a tool to foster differentiation from other political and economic blocs reluctant to engage in trade liberalization and a way to encourage the creation of an integrated market for new products and services.[3]

From a developed countries' perspective, the rationale seems to be quite different. According to Krueger (1999, p. 118):

[2] For example, in the case of Colombia, this policy is found in the Productive Development Policy (Colombia 2014). A detailed analysis of the industrial policy of Chile can be found in Agosin et al. (2010), of Mexico in Calderón and Sánchez (2012), and of Perú in Tavara, J (2010).

[3] In this respect Tokatlian (2012, p. 486) refers to Sanahuja (2007, p. 88) to affirm "Recent regionalism in the region has had a number of precise characteristics: it has been light (rejecting the creation of strong institutions); selective (strongly oriented towards market's liberalization); elitist (does not have support of significant segment of the population); and dispersed (diluted in diverse external commitments)". This reference evidences the pragmatic character of the PA compared to other regional agreements like the Andean Community (CAN) or the Bolivarian Alliance for the Peoples of Our America (ALBA).

> When negotiations on further multilateral liberalization are blocked, countries can use preferential trade agreements to go further and provide a demonstration of the benefits, which may in turn induce other countries to soften their resistance to multilateral liberalization.

Following this reasoning, one might assert that faced with the impasse of the Doha Round of the WTO, developed economies have decided to move forward a new set of rules that are supposedly better adapted to the requirements of their multinational corporations (MNCs).[4] These new rules reflect the belief that the disruptive innovations required for sustained economic growth deserve more adapted – and consequently more stringent – IP standards to ensure a return on their massive investments.[5]

This background of reasons justifying the proliferation of so-called mega-regional agreements made the US administration's withdrawal from the negotiations on the Trans-Pacific Partnership (TPP, now CPTPP) and the stalling negotiations of the Transatlantic Trade and Investment Partnership (TTIP) even more surprising. In this new scenario, bilateral free trade agreements (FTAs) and the proliferation of bilateral investment treaties (BITs) could become the new battleground for advancing more stringent IP standards. The PA could therefore become a legitimate political platform for proposing changes to the IP regime. The withdrawal of the US from the TPP opens the possibility to new approaches to negotiate between countries that agree on free trade as a means to achieve economic development.

In this respect two main questions are relevant:

(i) Is the introduction of higher standards through revision of FTA or BIT obligations likely to significantly impact the coverage of current IP commitments?
(ii) Can we foresee increased weakening of the so-called flexibilities established in the TRIPS Agreement?

As the answers to these questions are likely to be affirmative, the proposed solutions would depend on the ability of PA countries to conceive and implement strategies based on the relevance of IPRs as a fundamental driver for technological transformation. By so doing, they could facilitate industrial policies that are more focused on encouraging and supporting research and development (R&D) among PA countries.

---

[4] In this regard Davis (2009, p. 4) points out: "Whether overlapping institutions will have a positive or negative impact on negotiations for the core multilateral framework depend on the relative economic stakes for the most powerful actors and perceived stability of the rules. Uruguay Round negotiations presented the prospect for new gains for American and European business in the areas of services and Intellectual Property, and the out-dated provisional GATT system was seen to be at risk of collapse. Under these conditions, the rise of competing regional agreements generated renewed political commitment to achieve success in the multilateral forum. In contrast, industries in both, developed and developing countries have seen the Doha Round as offering few gains, while the strength of the WTO system makes the status quo appear to be a safe fall-back option. As attention shifts to other arenas, the unravelling of interests group support reduces the prospects for substantial multilateral liberalization".

[5] Correa (2015, p.11) points out: "R&D intensive sectors are likely to demand broad and strong IPRs protection. However, in countries where technologically mature sectors predominate, factors other than innovation (such as labour and inputs costs) may more decisive in determining output and productivity levels. While, under such circumstances, IPRs may not play a significant role in promoting innovation, they may affect the prices of industrial inputs and, more generally, consumers' options and expenditures".

11.2 What Do We Have?

PA member countries share an interesting link with the international IP regime: Colombia and Peru are signatories of the Andean Community, another regional agreement that achieved a recognized degree of institutionalization notably regarding interpretation of IP standards as defined in Andean Decision 486 of 2000.[6] Chile and Mexico, for their part, have played a role in the proliferation of trade liberalization in the region. As medium-sized economies, both countries are widely recognized for the seriousness of their industrial policies and consistency of their economic development strategies. These included the pro-competitive negotiation of IP rules in previous FTAs with the main IP-demanding countries.

PA countries are therefore not beginners in the field of negotiating IP standards. Indeed, throughout the TTP and TTIP negotiations, trade authorities from PA counties actively monitored the effects of such mega-regionals on IP-sensitive sectors. This fact highlights the nature of this "Alliance", demonstrating the intention to design common strategies to counteract the negative effects of the extreme liberalization fostered by IP-demanding countries.

In a similar vein, it is clear that PA countries are now more conscious about the need to define power allocation levels that allow improved cooperation with their "like-minded" trading partners. This seems to be crucial to avoiding the usual race to the bottom among countries with very similar economic structures and endowments.[7] Furthermore, developing countries now have something they did not have before: access to their own previous trade negotiation records that can provide evidence of the strategies followed as well as the functioning of lobbies that influence the outcomes of negotiations at the national and regional levels.

Academia also plays a role. The increasing awareness of the effects of including IP as part of trade negotiations is reflected in a wide range of scientific research. Outcomes of these studies have also become a tool for trade negotiators willing to move discussions in a more evidence-based direction. For example, the Max Planck Institute has developed a set of principles for IP provisions in bilateral and regional agreements (Grosse Ruse-Khan et al. 2013). Rooted in the analysis of attitudes and performance of past negotiations, these principles represent an important contribution by allowing the proposed advantages to be compared to the actual outcomes for

[6] Complementary information regarding the outstanding role of the Andean Tribunal of Justice, can be found in Helfer et al. (2009).

[7] Jackson (2003, p. 791) notes that "Many reasons could be given for preferring an international-level power allocation, inlcuding what economists call 'coordination benefits', sometimes analyzed in game theory as the prisoners dilema. In this situation, if governments each act in their own interest without any coordination, the results will be damaging to everyone; whereas matters would improve if states assumed certain, presumably minimal, constraints so as to avoid dangers of separate action. Likewise, much has been said about the 'race to the bottom' in relation to necessary government regulation and the worry that competition between nation-states could lead to a degradation of socially important economic regulation".

developing countries. In this sense, public dissemination of such academic research is a useful tool for trade officers, entrepreneurs and civil society as a whole.

There is also the possibility of introducing the useful insights developed by academics and independent experts at the multilateral level. In fact, the increased availability and quality of scientific work in areas such as economics, statistics, law and political sciences provides valuable input for international IP norm setting. For example, in the framework of the World Intellectual Property Organization (WIPO)'s Standing Committee on the Law of Patents, the Group of Latin American and Caribbean Countries (GRULAC) has recently submitted a proposal titled, "Revision of 1979 WIPO Model Law for Developing Countries on Inventions" (SCP/22/5). This proposal aims to integrate new concepts and evidence from economic and legal research into the changing regulatory landscape of international IP regulation.[8]

However, transforming scientific evidence into solid industrial policies is not an easy task. It requires supplementary efforts by both state agencies and entrepreneurs, which often consider this mission to be an "unnecessary burden". In this regard, the PA has pragmatically and appropriately integrated private sector participation into its approach. This could well become relevant in developing new ideas that strengthen regional integration.

11.3 What Should We Do?

In keeping with the challenges acknowledged by PA countries in the context of an integration process, the internal mandate contained in a Declaration of the Presidents (May 2013) recommends the establishment of a working group on intellectual property, with a focus on:

> Preparing and implementing a working plan with specific actions including cooperation between Intellectual Property Administrations, in order to share experiences and increase collaboration and communication links between them, to make better use of the IP system for the benefit of its users.

Although there is no clarity as to the PA's policy goal on IP, and the Additional Protocol does not contain specific provisions on IPRs, the collaborative nature of this mandate is coherent with the principles proposed by the Max Planck Institute, which recommends a serious assessment of the implications of including IP as part of trade negotiations (namely BITs and FTAs). Hence, in the context of PA regional integration, such assessment should also focus on the impacts on public interest, including the effects on the ability to implement industrial policies, something that is at the core of member countries' attempts to break their dependence on the extractive sectors.

[8] Despite its stated purpose, this proposal can also be interpreted as a means for pointing out the lack of transparency attributed to these negotiations and to challenge it through the wide dissemination of results of public and private funded research relevant in some areas of public concern. More information about this proposal can be found at: http://keionline.org.

A first step would be to increase efforts to ease and facilitate the negotiation of better access to new technologies and ensure, as far as possible, the participation of national scientific institutions (and their scientists) in ongoing regional R&D programmes.[9] A second important step is to create a framework to start discussions on the broader issue of how and how much the member countries and the Alliance as an international actor should pay for the fixed costs that R&D incurs.

In this regard, it is important to point out that the relevance of IP in the context of cross-border production systems tends to stem from a regulatory dimension. This is linked more to the broader idea of protecting consumers than to the fulfilment of its traditional function of protecting local industries. It also presupposes a shift in the understanding of technology transfer, allowing a more market-based approach according to which countries with abundant natural resources are not only *demandeurs* of new technologies, but also active players proposing strategies and synergies for the better use of their endowments in global R&D activity.

The shift in the assessment of the relevance of IP becomes crucial in the context of regional norm setting, which to date has been crafted mostly as a tool to fulfil the requirements of MNCs, leading to many criticisms of the so-called "regulatory race to the bottom" in which the use of IP standards or related regulations has deviated from the idea that they should be serving as drivers for sustained economic growth.

11.4 What Do We Expect from This Alliance?

The panorama depicted shows a coherent move towards industrial transformation and insertion in the services economy.[10] However, creating a business environment in which services can flourish requires recognition that PA members are at very different stages of economic development, and their domestic firms are far less advanced and competitive than those from more developed economies.

In the same vein, strong dependence on extractive sectors, which is also common among PA countries, represents a major barrier to achieving so-called "creative destruction". Thus, the prospects for a shift towards a services-based economy seem to depend not only on awareness of the importance of creativity and innovation as engines of sustained economic growth, but also on the right combination of public policies in areas such as education, health, communications and infrastructure. All this requires an ability to analyse the magnitude of trade-offs involving

[9] This is one of the *aquis* of recent US-COL (Article 16.2 FTA US-COL) negotiations. However the possibility that such clauses could be implemented on a regional scale remains uncertain.

[10] Services activities include so-called freedom to operate (FTO) or patent landscaping. Reports (PLRs) which according to WIPO (2015), 'provide a snapshot of the patent situation of a specific technology, either within a given country or region, or globally. They can inform policy discussions, strategic research planning or technology transfer. They may also be used to analyse the validity of patents based on data about their legal status'.

IPRs at the multilateral level. In this sense, Frankel (2013, p. 914) correctly points out:

> A new era of trade-offs has arisen. These trade-offs are different from the TRIPS Agreement trade-offs because they are often more extreme, not only because they involve extensive TRIPS-plus provisions, but also because the nature of a bilateral arrangement often has a power imbalance. Trade-offs of this nature are problematic because they result in countries adopting intellectual property laws that are not correlative to their stage of development and may even inhibit development where those laws prevent follow-on uses of existing intellectual property, including uses which could themselves be new and innovative.

This brings us to the discussion of the PA as an opportunity to challenge the current IP status quo, which, as mentioned above, is frequently associated with some of the difficulties in the implementation of new industrial policies. This issue is crucial as it questions the *raison d'être* of the PA as a driver for economic development and could even justify implementation of contested multilateralism strategies to challenge those institutionalized practices that appear not to be compatible with spurring innovation and industrial development.

In this respect it is worth recalling that, according to Morse and Kehoane (2014), a situation can be framed as contested multilateralism when three relevant criteria are met:

1. A multilateral institution exists within a defined issue-area and with a mission and a set of established rules and institutionalized practices.
2. Dissatisfied with the *status quo* institution, a coalition of actors – whether members of the existing institution or not – shifts the focus of its activity to a challenging institution with different rules and practices. This challenging institution can be either pre-existing or new.
3. The rules and institutionalized practices of the challenging institution conflict with or significantly modify the rules and institutionalized practices of the *status quo* institution.

A review of these three criteria in the light of the needs and expectations of the PA member countries' industrial sectors allows for some quite straightforward reasoning about the deployment of a contested multilateralism strategy linked to IP rule-setting in the PA regional programme. First, the global IP regime is governed by a multilateral set of rules – the TRIPS Agreement – which as mentioned previously, does not seem to take into account current trends such as global value chains (GVCs), the digital economy, mobility of scientists and ubiquity of services or the prevalence of direct foreign investment.[11] Second, to tackle current imbalances in the global IP system, most of the PA members agree on including IP regulatory

[11] Regarding this fact, Gervais (2014. p. 7) rightly points out that "Efforts by the World Intellectual Property Organization (WIPO) to produce economic studies of intellectual property impacts will no doubt help in developing adequate policy options in this regard, as previous efforts by the World Bank and others have done in the past. Put differently, the variegated picture of IP as part of a broader landscape of innovation policies should help calibrate TRIPS implementations and national policies in countries that strive to join the club of innovators. It will also allow all of us better to comprehend the social costs of certain forms of IP and allow mitigation where necessary."

coherence as a means not just to provide more clarity to investors,[12] but also to ensure that funds and efforts deployed through implementation of strategic public policies will not be duplicated, diverted or wasted.[13] Finally, regarding the extent of the institutionalized practices proposed in the frame of the PA, there are some doubts with respect to the political will to transform the current problems of industrial sectors into a declared statement of dissatisfaction vis-à-vis current trends of global IP rule-setting. However, it should be noted that recent declarations from PA member country authorities are indicative of an intention to strengthen the current system rather than reform it.[14]

Despite this situation, the dynamic nature of the dialogues inside the PA –specifically regarding the importance of advancing industrial policies and state support as a condition for competing in world markets – may lead to new institutionalized practices challenging the orthodox understanding of sensitive IP topics, that have not previously been taken into account in the relevant agreements, like the protection of traditional knowledge. These possibilities should not be underestimated with regard to implementation of obligations agreed to in upcoming bilateral FTAs or the possible revival of mega-regionals, which paradoxically might trigger renewed discussions about certain issues relegated for years in the multilateral agenda.[15]

---

[12] This is the idea of the Patent Prosecution Highway for intra-regional trade integration (del Carmen Vásquez Callo-Muller and Pérez Restrepo 2016)

[13] So-called National Systems of Science, Technology and Innovation conceived and often implemented in a mirrored manner in all the PA countries, share common features such as a focus on the creation of innovation-driven ecosystems with strong links with natural resources and manufacturing sectors. However, the fact that claims appear to be focused mostly on technology transfer issues weakens the premise of an existing dissatisfaction with the entire IP system.

[14] In the frame of the Assembly of the Member States of the World Intellectual Property Organization (WIPO) held from October 5 to 14, 2015, PA countries issued a declaration regarding the following IP cooperation activities:

- Expediting patent prosecution through the signature of an agreement regarding a Patent Prosecution Highway (PPH) Program between the patent authorities of the Pacific Alliance members.
- Harmonizing and simplifying the trademark registration process in order to save time and cost. The signatory offices are considering the implementation of unified forms for trademark registration in the four countries.
- Establishing a technological platform pilot programme for information dissemination and technology transfer.

[15] For example, TRIPS has not a standard for the protection of traditional knowledge. In contrast, Article 18.16 of the TPP includes cooperation in the area of traditional knowledge opening the door to a more adapted implementation regarding issues until now underestimated by local and regional authorities. Particularly interesting are the provisions on improvement of quality patent examination, included in paragraph 3:

3. The Parties shall endeavour to pursue quality patent examination, which may include:

(a) that in determining prior art, relevant publicly available documented information related to traditional knowledge associated with genetic resources may be taken into account;

11.5 Past Mistakes That Should Be Avoided

The new global trade agenda is a demanding field for regional integration. In this respect the PA, as a process, appears to have learned from its members' past mistakes in previous regional agreements. The flexible and goal-oriented architecture is one of the innovations that allow an optimistic scenario for economic integration. In this regard, previous mistakes that should be avoided include those related to the idea of building regional integration based on institutional and legal transplants from developed economies.[16] Instead, the PA should continue focusing on increasing the participation of local producers, manufacturing sectors and services providers in GVCs. To make this happen, efforts should concentrate on interpreting IPRs as drivers of economic development.

This issue becomes especially sensitive when considering the inclusion of IPRs in investment treaties. Here, we can imagine two likely scenarios: a proliferation of IP-related disputes resolved through application of all the defective features we recognize in this system today; or, the creation of spaces for coordination and coherence regarding IPRs norm setting at the regional level. The latter certainly supposes a different approach to issues such as technology transfer or working requirements, as well as a political willingness to challenge the current status quo.

Accordingly, in the current global trade agenda, recognition of IP as a driver for innovation, economic development and diffusion of technology requires a different understanding of concepts such as market-creating innovation. This type of innovation requires the identification of emerging, high-potential technologies to tackle critical and unresolved problems.[17] For example, such innovative technologies could help to correct, adapt or mitigate the dreadful, inherited effects of the boom of extractive industries in some PA counties.

(b) an opportunity for third parties to cite, in writing, to the competent examining authority prior art disclosures that may have a bearing on patentability, including prior art disclosures related to traditional knowledge associated with genetic resources;

(c) if applicable and appropriate, the use of databases or digital libraries containing traditional knowledge associated with genetic resources; and

(d) cooperation in the training of patent examiners in the examination of patent applications related to traditional knowledge associated with genetic resources.

[16] In this sense Gervais (2014, p. 5) points out that "The TRIPS Agreement was seen as the poster child for the so-called Development Theory, according to which developing economies should import the normative, judicial and administrative infrastructure of more industrialized nations to achieve a similar level of economic development. According to that theory, copying the infrastructure should lead to increased foreign investment, availability of capital and economic growth. One might naturally question those foundational assumptions."

[17] This trend is discussed by (Mezue et al. 2015) who observe that: "In Chile, government reform and the booming copper industry have received significant acclaim, but market-creating innovations seem to have been the true engine of growth. For example, the blossoming of Chile's agriculture sector was based on market creation—before Chile's innovations, nonconsumption of fresh fruits and vegetables was pervasive during most of the year in nontropical advanced countries. Chile's agricultural exporters leveraged the improving science of cultivation and modern logistics to transform the availability of produce and provide fresh goods all year round."

Such an approach may lead to the configuration of niche markets characterized by strong differentiation of qualitative factors such as sustainability, respect for children's and labour rights, and also origin, where existing IP standards could eventually play an important role, if further precision and adaptation is added.[18] In a similar vein, R&D of new products and services can be figured out through joint action among countries with common resources. For example, Chile and Peru share important sea resources, and Colombia and Peru share one of the world's most incredible areas of biodiversity, recognized as a potential source of solutions in a wide range of economic sectors.

Last but not least, is promoting the development of new sectors linked to the 'digital economy' where market-creating innovations could induce significant social and economic changes. In this regard, development of digital encryption mechanisms to ensure the privacy of users is a thriving field for coordinated regulation and joint research among countries that could provide specific solutions adapted to the region's needs.

11.6 Conclusions

The PA offers an enormous opportunity for challenging institutionalized practices in global norm setting with respect to IP. The new scenario opened by increasing participation in GVCs demands deeper involvement of local industrial sectors interested in achieving effective industrial transformation.

However, the prospects of such a challenge remain slim as demonstrated by the examination of criteria to determine the probabilities of a contested multilateralism strategy being implemented by the PA countries. Rather, the current attitudes of member countries suggest little commitment to proposing new rules. In this scenario changes could eventually be driven by the success of policies promoted to incentivize science, technology and innovation.

Crystallizing this opportunity also requires the integration of new perspectives based on market-creating innovations as well as the strengthening of complementarities among the manufacturing and R&D sectors of PA countries. From this perspective, it is crucial for IPRs to go beyond their traditional function of promoting FDI to provide a real basis for consolidating innovation ecosystems.

Finally, challenging the IP status quo in a context of dynamic negotiation of stringent rules in the bilateral and regional trade agreements may appear unnecessary, ambitious or even impossible. Nevertheless, this option provides a valuable opportunity to profit from the accumulated experiences of 20 years of negotiating and implementing IP rules, producing concrete actions aimed at achieving the

[18] New approaches to established IP categories such as geographical indications, certification and collective marks could help to give additional information to consumers regarding the content and procedures involved in a product's manufacturing process.

objectives and principles of a system to promote creativity and spur innovation as the drivers of economic transformation and improved livelihoods around the world.

References

Agosin, M. R., Larraín, C., & Grau, N. (2010). *Industrial policy in Chile* (IDB Working Paper Series, No. IBD-WP-170). Online: https://papers.ssrn.com/sol3/papers.cfm?abstract_id=1817286

Calderón, C., & Sánchez, I. (2012). Crecimiento económico y política industrial en México. *Revista Problemas del Desarrollo, 170*, 125–154. Online: http://revistas.unam.mx/index.php/pde/article/viewFile/32138/29589

Castro Bernieri, R. (2006). Intellectual property rights in bilateral investment treaties and access to medicines: The case of Latin America. *The Journal of World Intellectual Property, 9*, 548–572.

Colombia. (2014). *Politica de Desarrollo Productivo* (Documento Conpes 3.866). https://compite.com.co/wp-content/uploads/2016/06/Pol%C3%ADtica-de-Desarrollo-Productivo-1.pdf

Correa, C. M. (2015). *Intellectual property: How much room is left for industrial policy?* (UNCTAD Discussion Papers 223).

Davis, C. (2009). Overlapping institutions in trade policy. *Perspectives on Politics, 7*(1), 25–31. https://doi.org/10.1017/S1537592709090045.

del Carmen Vásquez-Callo Müller, M., & Pérez Restrepo, C. (2016). *Patent cooperation mechanisms in the Pacific Alliance: An initial assessment of the effectiveness of the Patent Prosecution Highway for intra-regional trade integration* (SECO/WTI Academic Cooperation Project Working Paper Series 2016/16).

Frankel, S. (2013). Trade-offs and transparency. *International Review of Intellectual Property and Competition Law, 44*, 913–919. Max Planck Institute for Intellectual Property and Competition Law. https://doi.org/10.1007/s40319-013-0124-4.

Gervais, D. (2014). Current issues in international intellectual property norm-making. In J. Drexl et al. (Eds.), *EU bilateral trade agreements and intellectual property: For better or worse? MPI Studies on Intellectual Property and Competition Law*. Berlin/Heidelberg: Springer. https://doi.org/10.1007/978-3-642-39097-5_1.

Grosse Ruse-Khan, H., Drexl, J., Hilty, R. M., et al. (2013). Principles for intellectual property provisions in bilateral and regional agreements. *International Review of Intellectual Property and Competition Law, 44*, 878–883. Max Planck Institute for Intellectual Property and Competition Law. https://doi.org/10.1007/s40319-013-0119-1.

Helfer, L., Alter, K., & Guerzovich, M. (2009). Islands of effective international adjudication: Constructing an intellectual property rule of law in the Andean Community. *The American Journal of International Law, 103*(1), 1–47. https://doi.org/10.2307/20456720.

Revision of 1979 WIPO Model Law for Developing Countries on Inventions (SCP/22/5) http://www.wipo.int/edocs/mdocs/scp/en/scp_22/scp_22_5.pdf. Accessed 24 Oct 2015.

Jackson, J. (2003). Sovereignty-modern: A new approach to an outdated concept. *American Journal of International Law, 97*(4), 782–802. https://doi.org/10.2307/3133680.

Krueger, A. O. (1999). Are preferential trading arrangements trade-liberalizing or protectionist? *Journal of Economic Perspectives, 13*(4), 105–124. https://doi.org/10.1257/jep.13.4.105.

Mezue, B., Christensen, C., & Bever, D. (2015). *The power of market creation: How innovation can spur development*. https://www.foreignaffairs.com/articles/africa/2014-12-15/power-market-creation. Accessed 15 Nov 2015.

Morse, J., & Kehoane, R. (2014). Counter multilateralism and regime complexes. *The Review of International Organizations, 9*, 385–412. https://doi.org/10.1007/s11558-014-9188-2.

Rojas, D., & Terán, J. M. (2016). La Alianza del Pacífico: nueva muestra del regionalismo en América Latina. *OASIS, 24*, 69–88. https://doi.org/10.18601/16577558.n24.05.

Sanahuja, J. A. (2007). Regionalismo e integración en América Latina: balance y perspectivas. *Pensamiento Iberoamericano* (pp. 75–106). ISSN:0212-0208. http://eprints.ucm.es/42577/
Távara, J. (2010). Política industrial y desarrollo en el Perú. In J. Rodríguez & M. D. Tello (Eds.), *Opciones de política económica en el Perú: 2011–2015* (pp. 15–44). Lima: Fondo Editorial de la Pontificia Universidad Católica del Perú.
Tokatlian, J. (2012). Latinoamerica y el complejo integracionista: un concepto a debate. *Revista Desarrollo Economico, Instituto de Desarrollo Economico y Social, 51*(204), 475–492.
World Intellectual Property Organization (WIPO). (2015). *Guidelines for preparing patent landscape reports.*

Chapter 12
Competition Law and Policy in the Regional Context: European Union Experiences for the Pacific Alliance

Ulf Thoene and Loly Aylú Gaitán-Guerrero

12.1 Introduction

The increase in the number of regional trade agreements (RTAs), and the participation of almost all countries in at least one RTA, signifies progress in terms of deepening international relations (Schiff and Winters 2003). Regional integration and competition policy form an inseparable duo in the quest for trade and investment liberalization. This is linked with an efficient allocation of resources, which facilitates the generation of wellbeing among consumers and greater competitiveness in a regional single market. However, the formulation of political tenets adjusted to the economic, political and cultural conditions of the parties to a RTA remains challenging (Bakhoum 2012).

This chapter aims to build a new perspective on competition policy within the framework of an emerging regional integration agreement with political, economic and social objectives, such as increased competition between companies and the protection of consumers' interests in a region.

We start with the activities of companies originating in the diverse member states and their subsequent regulation and incorporation into competition policy. Such policy must be derived from this new regional integration initiative – the PA – which is currently moving towards integration in areas such as tariffs, free mobility of individuals, cooperation for development in educational subjects, and the formalization of meetings between member states' ministers.

This chapter explores the scope for competition policy to help achieve a single market within the PA. To that end, regional integration theory is used to examine the competition policy model used in the European Union (EU). Analysis of competition policy in regional integration settings is presented from a multilevel policy

U. Thoene (✉) · L. A. Gaitán-Guerrero
Universidad de La Sabana, Chía, Colombia
e-mail: ulf.thoene@unisabana.edu.co; loly.gaitan@unisabana.edu.co

P. Sauvé et al. (eds.), *The Pacific Alliance in a World of Preferential Trade Agreements*, United Nations University Series on Regionalism 16,
https://doi.org/10.1007/978-3-319-78464-9_12

approach together with its subsequent plurality of actors. This system is key to the development of the economic policy and market integration that are the expected outcomes of regional integration efforts.

This chapter comprises six sections including this introduction. The second section presents a review of regionalism theory. The third section shortly describes the legal and institutional structure of EU competition policy. The fourth section focuses on the possible future challenges that the PA will have to face if it is to achieve a market with efficient allocation of resources through a competition policy system adjusted to the characteristics and needs of its member countries. The fifth section elaborates on the characteristics of competition policy in the four-member states of the PA. Finally, a set of conclusions are drawn as to the state of competition law and policy in the PA.

12.2 Theories of Regionalism

Within the normative framework of RTAs, a growing number of countries have elaborated competition laws and policies both at the national and regional levels. Analysts agree that this trend reflects the importance of the regionalization of competition policies in developing countries to improve the application and enforcement of these public policies, strengthen institutional regimes and enable greater control to be exercised over conditions of competition in free-trade areas (Bakhoum 2012). Few studies have however linked regionalism and competition policy, especially in developing or emerging markets.

The concept of regional integration has been evolving and there are as many conceptualizations as there are academics looking at it from multiple perspectives. On the one hand, regional integration is a synonym for political integration, explained by Lindberg (1963) as the process through which nations waive the desire and ability to independently design and implement a domestic and foreign policy and, instead, opt 'to make *joint decisions* or to *delegate* the decision-making process to new central organs' (italics in original). It is likely that this regional dynamic impacts political decision-making in areas that were formerly exclusive to the nation-state and are now affected by the growing levels of economic exchange at a regional level.

On the other hand, regionalism theory can also be defined as 'the creation and maintenance of intense and diversified patterns of interaction among previously autonomous units. These patterns may be partly economic in character, partly social, partly political: definitions of *political* integration all imply accompanying high levels of economic and social interaction' (Wallace 1990, italics in original). Companies, civil society organizations and governments constitute this group of patterns. Similarly, regional integration involves the transfer of sovereignty from the nation-state level to the supranational level (Rittberger and Schimmelfennig 2005). In the European case, these processes have involved expansion and deepening of the supranational institutionalization (Rittberger and Schimmelfennig 2005), while with respect to the future of the PA, these processes are yet to be defined.

Likewise, regionalism can be defined as a 'body of *ideas* promoting an identified geographical or social space as the regional project [being] usually associated with a policy program [...] and strategy [that] normally leads to institution building. Regionalism ties agents to one specific regional project that is clearly limited spatially or socially, but not limited in time' (Hveem 2006, italics in original).

For his part, Hettne (2006) identifies trade, development and security as dimensions of regionalism. Another definition considers regionalism as a 'states-led project designed to reorganize a particular regional space along defined political and economic lines [...] that is being constructed [...] by collective human action' (Gamble and Payne 1996). Regionalism also refers to the political decisions designed to drive the creation of trans-border markets as an 'international response to external and domestic challenges' (Mols 1993). This implies that considerations of competition policy play a key role in the evolution of regional integration since the private sector's interests and consumers' interests are transferred to the regional level over time.

Alternatively, the study of regional integration can be separated into a first and second wave (Soderbaum 2003). The first wave of regionalism refers to the regional schemes at the end of the Second World War, which had a protectionist character and hence were considered closed regionalism. The second wave was characterized by more open schemes that sought to integrate a certain regional group into the global political economy (Spindler 2002). Consequently, the motivations behind the first and second waves of regionalism differ in historical terms, as well as in terms of political and economic factors, both exogenous and endogenous. As such, the second wave, or the new regionalism, is not merely the re-establishment of a set of old assumptions; rather, it must be seen in the light of the globalization phenomenon (Hurrell 1995). In fact, theorists were faced with what Caporaso (1998) called 'the single case issue' presented by the EU in the absence of any other successful regional project. The recent RTAs signed worldwide, especially those that involve developing countries, show evidence of an increase in the incorporation of chapters on regional competition policies.

12.2.1 Intergovernmentalism and Supranationalism

The study of regional integration has led to diverse theories that seek to explain the nature and conditions of integration growth. Rittberger and Schimmelfennig (2005) assert that the two theoretical lines, intergovernmentalism and supranationalism, have dominated the integration debate. Neofunctionalism, which was the prototype of supranationalism, was dominant during the early stages of the regional integration theory, while intergovernmentalism emerged in the mid-1960s. These two theoretical lines are discussed in more detail below.

Academics, such as Haas (1958), Lindberg (1963) and Schmitter (1969), were advocates of neofunctionalism, whereas Hoffman (1966) was an advocate of intergovernmentalism. In the mid-1980s, based on the dominant theories, diverse theoretical branches emerged, such as that described by Sandholtz and Stone Sweet (1998), and the liberal intergovernmentalism posited by Moravcsik (1998).

The nature of the integration process is the main point of controversy between the supranational and intergovernmental perspectives. Supranationalists consider the process as 'transformative' and 'self-perpetuating', while the intergovernmentalists emphasize the nation-state's control over integration (Rittberger and Schimmelfennig 2005). Neofunctionalists had asserted that the international system does not remain anarchic and that it can be transformed through institutionalization (Rittberger and Schimmelfennig 2005), emphasizing the importance of supranational institutions in managing, shaping, and ensuring integration processes (Spindler 2005).

Neofunctionalism was very influential in the 'development of theories on European integration' (Hurrell 1995); however, its popularity waned in the mid-1970s before experiencing a revival in the mid-1980s (Spindler 2005). Nevertheless, the neofunctionalists' school of thought has been more powerful at explaining 'the ongoing role of institutions than about the factors' that give the impetus for starting a regional project (Hurrell 1995). Thus, from this perspective, the idea of political order 'beyond the nation-state' is central (Haas 1964), and the state is considered more 'complex than realists [suggest]' (Bache et al. 2006).

Neofunctionalism is pluralist, which implies that transnational interest groups, and not the states, are the key actors in the integration process (Rittberger and Schimmelfennig 2005). This is because it is thought that cooperation on international topics leads to political integration (Hurrell 1995) and, therefore, that it would 'become self-sustaining' (George 1996). Consequently, cooperation in one area extends to another; thus, integration is deepened and expanded. In fact, the creation of a regional common market is highlighted as 'the most conducive to rapid regional integration and the maximization of a spillover' (Haas 1970). Neofunctionalism's 'overly deterministic' nature is criticized for leading to false predictions about the direction of European integration and for '[underestimating] the resilience of the nation-states', particularly in the areas 'of high politics' (Hurrell 1995).

In opposition to the foregoing theory, stands intergovernmentalism, which asserts that 'European integration is driven by the interests and actions of nation-states' (Hix 2005), where political relationships take the form of negotiations between national governments. Therefore, the EU is 'best seen as an international regime for political coordination' (Moravcsik 1993) and regional integration can only proceed 'as far as the governments [are] prepared to allow it to go' (Bache et al. 2006). For supporters of inter-governmental relation, integration mainly focuses on issues of low politics, such as political economy, while high politics areas, such as international relations and security, are kept outside the integration process (Rittberger and Schimmelfennig 2005). According to Moravcsik (1998), 'European integration exemplifies a distinctly modern form of power politics [being] peacefully pursued by democratic states for largely economic reasons'.

Regarding the loss of state autonomy, it can be argued that the integration process has resulted in greater losses for the largest member states than for the smallest ones (Rittberger and Schimmelfennig 2005). However, intergovernmentalists have not come up with additional reasons for the greater development of integration (Malamud 2003).

With respect to the successful implementation of competition policy, it is worth highlighting that the conflict between the theoretical concepts of intergovernmentalists and supranationalists has a pronounced effect on the design of the rules of the game that govern companies' activities and the protection of consumers' interests in economic integration processes. In other words, a regional integration project always and unavoidably fluctuates between the power of the governments of member states and forms of regional governance, which is to say, governmental institutions at a supranational level.

Finally, constructivist frameworks have recently been developed to explain regional integration (Christiansen et al. 2001). Constructivists 'stress the extent to which *regional cohesion* depends on a sustained and durable sense of community based on mutual responsiveness, trust, and high levels of what might be labelled "cognitive interdependence"' (Hurrell 1995, italics in original). Constructivism emphasizes that the interests of the diverse actors participating in regional projects do not arise exogenously, nor are they static; they emerge and change together with regionalism. Constructivism also highlights the impact of certain political cultures and discourses, among others, on the social construction of interests (Wunderlich 2013). Both in the EU and in the PA, one of the main topics of cohesion has centred on political-democratic principles and the commitment to a free market and a capitalist system as a form of social organization.

12.3 Competition Policy in the European Union

The effort to achieve the objective of regional integration poses diverse institutional and legal challenges for the countries that are parties to RTAs. The regulations and specifications developed by each member state of an RTA pose a great challenge during harmonization or, at least, standardization of the diverse normative provisions in the integration process. In the case of the EU, this used to be the main concern when a country expressed its interest in adhering to the agreement. However, with the purpose of serving the objective of a common market through the competition policy in the regional integration process, the European Commission and the Court of Justice of the European Union undertook the task of analysing and settling disputes resulting from the diversity of rules of the member states. Thus, competition law in the EU is practically the only instance of organized and developed central policies on free trade (Lowenfeld 2008). In the case of the PA, the controversy regarding supranational governance systems has been minimal as a consequence of a lesser need for concerted action, the small number of member states, and the emphasis on autonomy in governments' decision-making.

12.3.1 Legal Level

Considering the background to the legal framework relating to competition in the EU, it is worth highlighting that, '[s]ince the Treaty of Rome [1957], competition policy has been seen as an essential element of European integration' (Martin 2001a). The process of integration of the European market that led to the creation of the internal market has been accompanied by competition policy decisions taken at a regional level in the EU. Such decisions have proven to go beyond the borders of the individual nation-state, and also affect the member states' internal policy.

Subsequently, the Single European Act of 1986 gave special emphasis to the European Commission's role, which was to exercise effective political leadership between the nation-state members (Sandholtz and Zysman 1989); additionally, it introduced the design of what would become the European single market, to be completed in 1992. Eliminating obstacles to economic exchanges beyond member states' borders 'was expected to simultaneously increase rivalry and boost economic growth while promoting economic integration' (Martin 2001b). Moreover, the 'pressure for the single market came from the largest industrial concerns in Europe, which were not only European but global players' (George 1996). This suggests that the companies' role in the PA could involve similar pressures towards deeper integration in the future.

The legislative acts that are part of the Treaty on European Union make up the main core of the competition policy in the region Another supranational institution with authority over the competition policy, is the Court of Justice of the European Union (ECJ), which acts as the 'ultimate arbiter of the various rules' (Sauter and Langer 2007). However, the Commission has the most power in investigating, deciding and enforcing the legal regulations and policies relating to competition. It constitutes the best example of how European integration has been carried out through a dynamic process of autonomous bureaucratic regulation, and with total power using the supranational legal order (Wallace and Wallace 2000). So far, this type of political entity does not exist in the PA.

Regarding the regulations governing competition policy in the EU, Article 101 of the Treaty on the Functioning of the European Union (TFEU) constitutes the main mechanism for the control of anticompetitive agreements. It restricts practices that prevent, restrict, or distort free competition, unless the Commission grants an exception (Craig and De Búrca 2003). With respect to the PA, in the absence of a common competition policy, companies could assume a leading role and fill this void, taking advantage of the lack of institutional and normative coordination. It is also important to think about a future association of companies with headquarters in the countries of the PA, which could function as pressure groups (Schneider 2004) or as actors, part of the future agenda of the regional competition policy.

The second set of policies directed at competition regulation is defined in Article 102 of the TFEU. It focuses on the phenomenon of the dominant position that mainly depends on the participation of individual firms in the market and the abusive practices susceptible to being penalized, which are derived from this position.

On the other hand, the 1989 Merger Regulation, which was subsequently reformulated at the beginning of 2004, includes the guidelines necessary to evaluate horizontal mergers; thus, improving the investigations conducted by courts and by the national authorities that make up the European Competition Network.

Integration into a single European market was the objective of overcoming the obstacles presented by 'small, national, segmented markets liable to be dominated by a few national producers, possibly operating at the subnational scale and exploiting considerable monopoly power' (Venables and Winters 2004). Thus, market integration policy has been oriented so that companies can effectively compete in other national markets and to allow the expansion of those that are relatively efficient (Venables and Winters 2004). This coordination and integration has consolidated the EU as the largest regional market and bloc in the world.

The common legal framework in the EU had to be established due to the diversity and, sometimes lack of, national legal traditions and approaches for the formulation of economic policies – merger and antimonopoly – of the member states of the EU. This community legal framework is characterized by the direct application of its provisions and coexistence with the national legislations (Motta 2004). The potential for conflicts between national jurisdictions with respect to competition policy necessitates a common policy (Pelkmans 2001) capable of being reformulated. In the PA, conflict resolution takes place at an intergovernmental level during periodic meetings between member states' governments.

12.3.2 Political Level

Tsoukalis (1997) argues that competition policy has developed as one of the most important community policies and as a relevant source of power for the Commission vis-à-vis private companies and national governments. On the other hand, it is important to highlight that in the EU's constitutional structure, the Commission assumes the role of 'guardian and champion of the European ideal' (Venables and Winters 2004), which in the context of competition policy essentially means greater market integration.

At the public policy design level in the EU, competition law can be identified and classified according to three main policy objectives. The first and most theoretical concerns the basic objectives of competition law that consist of: economic freedom, market integration and efficiency, directed towards maximizing consumers' wellbeing and achieving optimal allocation of resources. The second objective relates to other policies of the community regime, such as employment, industrial policy, environmental policy and consumer protection. The third objective of competition law is to facilitate the creation of a single European market and prevent all actions that hinder the achievement of this objective (Craig and De Búrca 2003).

Achievement of the expected balance between the public policy factors at the national level and their integration in a common market has encountered difficulties in the EU. Hence, the construction of the aforementioned categories can contribute to improving the hierarchical structure in decision-making on competition policy within the diverse EU institutions.

Over time, an important part of the EU's economic integration process has been the incorporation of national competition policies that are consistent with the treaty's approach. However, the significant increase in the number of the EU member states after 2004 generated one of the largest economic market liberalization processes worldwide (Martin 2001a).

It seems inevitable that the decision-making and the power of execution of the competition policy would be delegated to a lower level within the multilevel structure, for example to the nation-state level. This transition in the competition regulation structure requires, however, 'that enforcement at the Member State level is uniformly vigorous and consistent' (Martin 2001a).

A review of the basic principles of the EU's current competition policy system reveals that they are directed to the fight against collusion, antimonopoly, merger control, and state aid. In the analysis of the EU's practices, the desire of some policy actors at a national and supranational level to advance towards greater integration and interconnection, in which the economy is naturally part of the process, is evident. Therefore, the competition policy in the EU is not only motivated by a desire for economic efficiency, but also by the implications of a political and legal order.

In conclusion, the EU today is an entity whose political and economic method of management can be described as multilevel; that is to say, governance is exercised by both supranational (European Commission, Court of Justice of the European Union, European Parliament) and intergovernmental institutions (Council of the European Union) that have proven to be the dominant players contributing to the elaboration and enforcement of the decisions, as well as to the establishment of the legal regulations relevant to the competition policy in the EU as a whole.

12.4 The Pacific Alliance

Regional integration schemes in Latin America pursue different depths of integration and divergent models of regional cooperation. This diversity can be characterized as 'modular regionalism' or 'variable geometry' (Gardini 2013), which implies that member states have the option of cooperating with different partners to achieve common objectives, and at the same time, they maintain the option of leaving the project. The advantage of this type of regional integration model is that each country can choose to join the regional organizations that best meets their interests (Nolte and Wehner 2013).

The PA coexists with and differs from other regional groups, such as the Union of South American Nations (UNASUR, from its Spanish acronym), Bolivarian Alliance for the Peoples of Our America-People's Trade Agreement (ALBA-TCP, from its Spanish acronym), Community of Latin American and Caribbean States (CELAC, from its Spanish acronym), Common Market of the Southern Cone (MERCOSUR, from its Spanish acronym). While UNASUR, ALBA, CELAC and

MERCOSUR tend to view regionalism and integration as tools to fight globalization, the PA views them as critical links to global flows (Ramírez 2013). In fact, MERCOSUR pursues a more protectionist integration initiative in favour of regional industrial interests. The speed with which the PA has advanced in comparison to other initiatives is also remarkable (García 2013).

Additionally, three types of regional projects in Latin America can be identified. A first grouping focuses on trade- and investment-driven integration (the PA and the North American Free Trade Agreement (NAFTA)). A second type consists of hybrid projects that combine trade and political objectives (UNASUR, Central American Integration System (SICA, from its Spanish acronym), MERCOSUR, Andean Community (CAN, from its Spanish acronym)). Lastly are projects that emphasize the social and political aspects of integration, driven by ideas based on leftist doctrines and are therefore characterized by strong state intervention in the economy (ALBA-TCP) (Nolte and Wehner 2013).

12.4.1 Future Challenges in Competition Policy

Trade liberalization tends to intensify the competitive environment within and between countries. Consequently, the main objective of competition rules is to prevent anticompetitive behaviour affecting consumer welfare, combatting collusion, competition-impairing mergers and abuses of dominant positions (Bilal and Olarreaga 1998). This raises the question of what implications this coexistence and the differences in models and rules will have at a legal level. The PA will have to prepare for the issues that are sure to emerge regarding how FTAs and the WTO interact, such as overlaps between the WTO and FTAs versus overlaps between different PA-brokered FTAs. For example, how will the FTAs between the United States and Chile and the EU and Chile interact (Baldwin and Thornton 2010)?

The Alliance has, by design, a limited institutional structure. The Macro Agreement established the Council of Ministers made up of the foreign affairs ministers of the member states as the bloc's main body. This Council meets once a year and its decisions are adopted by consensus. The activities at a technical level take place through the High-Level Group and technical work groups. A Business Council was created to foster dialogue between the governments and the business sector, as well as the Parliamentary Monitoring Committee of the PA, whose function is to monitor the Alliance's work and the development of the pertinent legislation. It is noteworthy that the PA is negotiating a system for conflict resolution in relation to the decisions of the Council of Ministers (Tvevad 2014).

Regarding competition, one of the PA's main challenges over time will be how best to successfully design an authority of an independent nature together with reliable institutions that can conduct a judicial review of the provisions on competition in each of the member states (Fox 2012). The monitoring and enforcement of the provisions on competition must be centralized and be legitimated in this supranational entity, which has to be independent and completely unbiased.

According to Ibarra (1993), '[w]ithin the framework of integration schemes, competition policies must be subordinated to the attainment of the common objectives of the countries that are part of the agreement'. A related challenge is the degree to which the PA forms a relevant market justifying a pooled approach to competition policy enforcement.

The Alliance shows potential; however, its success will depend on both the member countries' commitment and their ability to adapt and learn from other regional experiences. Despite the diversity of PA economic realities, the members' integration ideal can still be consolidated on the basis of a minimum common denominator of sufficient characteristics in order to successfully complete the legal and institutional adjustment that an RTA requires.

12.5 Competition Policy in the Four Pacific Alliance Member States

12.5.1 Competition Policy in Chile

The substantive rules of Chile's competition law tend to be general but nonetheless sufficient to underpin effective policy and enforcement measures. The content of Chilean competition policy is based on experience. The simplicity of Chile's Competition Act can be seen as an invitation to apply economic analysis so as to elaborate how competition policy operates and applies.

A single, general Article of the Competition Act sets out the entire substantive principle. Three subsections with examples of anticompetitive, prohibited conduct speak to the usual aspects of competition law: restrictive agreements and concerted actions, unilateral abusive dominance and predatory exclusion. Merger control is not part of the list, but statutory support for merger control decisions can be inferred from the prohibition of any conduct that is likely to result in anticompetitive effects. Increased accuracy and structure on merger processes and rules could be seen as useful (OECD 2011).

Enforcement efforts are now paying far more attention to the issue of cartels. High-profile action has attracted considerable attention from the private sector. In 2008, the biggest fine thus far imposed was backed by the Supreme Court (in the 'Flat-Panel TV price war' case). The *Tribunal de Defensa de la Libre Competencia* (TDLC) reached its most far-reaching decision going against a merger in the Falabella case. Moreover, the *Fiscalia Nacional Económica* (FNE) issued charges relating to price coordination by retail pharmacies. Yet, abusive dominance remains the most crucial field of antitrust enforcement.

The TDLC has demonstrated what the law covers as abusive dominance, adopting an economic approach that enquires whether abusive conduct is exclusionary or exploitative in an objective way. The TDLC does not tend to interpret as abusive behaviour aimed at improving economic efficiency. Thus far, the distribution of enforcement responsibilities between two separate and independent investigative and decision-making entities has functioned adequately. The TDLC has been efficient and productive, issuing about 20 decisions per year, most of them in adversarial proceedings (OECD 2011). Economic analysis underlies the process of decision-making in a growing body of case law, which might – in more detail – give an account of the scope of doctrines that are meant to be referred to in the actual text of the original statute.

However, flexibility comes at a price that often tends to be rather unpredictable. The Falabella case illustrates how economic creativity functions as a building block of legal instability. Attempting to find a relevant market of 'integrated retail' incorporating department stores, malls and similar consumer credit, the TDLC decision takes into account the importance of economies of scope in the retail sector. Yet it 'departed from the traditional, rather more limited, market definition approach of previous decisions and also from the methodology of the FNE's guidelines' (OECD 2011).

The uncertainty about how the TDLC is likely to proceed is exacerbated by the inconsistency of the directions provided by the Supreme Court. The Supreme Court lacks the capacity to confront complex economic issues on its own and its disagreements with the TDLC demonstrate a lingering judicial preference for decisions in terms of legal categories as well as rules. Uncertainty remains about the methods used to specify what markets are, the legal standard applicable to mergers, and the 'evidentiary standard applied to hard-core cartels' (OECD 2011). The standards for dealing with cases of predatory exclusion are also rather unclear. It is noteworthy that a 'Supreme Court decision implies that pricing could be found to be predatory in the absence of market power, treating it as a nearly per se offence' (OECD 2011).

Enforcement guidelines are meant to specify the breadth and trajectory of policy-making. Guidelines might take into account criticism that standards could not be applied in a transparent or comprehensible fashion. The FNE instructions on mergers do not necessarily have to be taken up by the TDLC, which is an independent entity. 'To be most useful to help businesses in Chile comply with the law, guides about interpretation and analysis should follow the decision practices of the TDLC, as well as rely on models and learning from the international competition community' (OECD 2011).

12.5.2 Competition Policy in Colombia

Free economic competition is a constitutional right expressly referred to in Articles 88 and 333 of the Political Constitution of Colombia of 1991. In addition, this right is considered as a principle regulating the economy, as indicated by Decision C-535/97 of the Constitutional Court of Colombia.

The legal framework for protection of competition is defined by Law 1340, dated 24 July 2009, which updates the regulation to meet the conditions of the current market. There are additional applicable regulations, such as Law 155 (1959), Decree 2153 (1992) and other regulations that may amend it or complete it. These regulations apply to all sectors and all economic activities. However, specific provisions for some sectors or activities will prevail.

Colombia's national competition authority is the *Superintendencia de Industria y Comercio* (the SIC). Within the SIC, the competent entity for the protection of competition is the Office of the Delegate Superintendent for the Promotion of Competition (the DO). This governmental entity is in charge of the administrative investigations and can impose fines for infringements of the regulations. The SIC must detect the competition concerns by monitoring the functioning of each market and, for this reason, the SIC must have a unit of economic studies. The SIC does not have powers to impose trade remedies (e.g. antidumping or countervailing measures) and must operate within the National Development Plan.

In order to fulfil its functions, the SIC has the right to require information from public or private agents. Nonetheless, such agents are not bound to provide information to the SIC, and neither is the SIC empowered to impose sanctions if the agents refuse to provide information. All information gathered by the SIC is subject to the provisions of the Code of Administrative Procedures and Administrative Disputes contained in Law 1437 (2011), and the Personal Data Protection Law (i.e. Law 1581 (2012)).

To comply with its objective, the DO carries out market studies in any sector or economic activity. The purpose of such studies, according to the SIC is to: (i) assess the level of competition in a market or sector; (ii) understand how markets operate; (iii) assess the impact of government policies or regulation in a market; and (iv) increase the general knowledge of the sector.

The SIC can independently decide where it will perform market studies. This choice is based on several factors such as the importance of a market, its structure and barriers to entry. The SIC has also indicated that it uses a de minimis rule and a statute of limitation to prioritize its work. Public entities and business associations can also request the SIC to perform market studies in a specific sector or industry. However, as indicated previously, the SIC is not obliged to comply with such a request.

No specific legal or regulatory requirements are stipulated in any regulation with respect to the period of time within which a market study must be concluded. However, in practice, they should not take longer than one year. Also, the SIC has developed internal manuals and guidelines applicable to market studies, but no external guidelines have been drawn up.

Market studies performed by the SIC are publicly available. The recommendations they contain are not binding on the central government or public bodies, but usually they are taken into account when defining public policy. The regulators, however, must state the reasons why they did not include the SIC's recommendations. Market studies also serve to raise awareness of the functioning of the market.

12.5.3 Competition Policy in Mexico

Mexico implemented its competition policy through an economic reform that sought to help the country transition towards a market-based economy. In line with best practices in worldwide competition policy, the country adopted the Federal Law of Economic Competition in 1993. In order to enforce this law, the government established the Federal Competition Commission (CFC, from its Spanish acronym). Mexico's competition law is based on the principles of competition and efficiency.

It is noteworthy that Mexico's increased interest in competition policy came at a time when the country was opening up the economy to foreign investment and trade and had privatized numerous previously state-owned enterprises. Hence, the adoption of this competition policy paved the way for the adoption of numerous FTAs, starting with NAFTA in 1994.

However, the competition law was not without opposition, especially at a political level. On the one hand, the 1994 financial crisis due to devaluation of the Mexican peso led many to believe that it was a policy imposed on Mexico by the United States and Canada. Hence, some felt that it was not in the country's best interests and the government was seemingly under pressure from those countries as a result of the FTA.

On the other hand, the Competition Commission has been widely criticized for its ineffectiveness and inability to provide real results in practice. In particular, it has encountered strong resistance at a judicial level, being subject to bureaucratic procedural delays and sanctions for unlawful conduct. Likewise, the competition law remained unchanged for many years. The only significant legislation to be enacted since its adoption was the Federal Law of Transparency and Public Access to Governmental Information, which did not really become effective until 2003 (OECD 2004).

The competition policy's legal framework is set out in the Mexican Constitution, specifically in Article 28, which establishes Mexico's antimonopoly stance, lists its strategic areas, discusses the central's bank functions of coinage and currency production, and addresses copyright and patent privileges, as well as the position of labour and trade associations. In terms of the competition policy's content, it banned monopolies pursuant to the Constitution by prohibiting and penalizing the acquisition or strengthening of monopoly power and classified practices as absolute (cartel conduct) or relative (single-firm conduct). The regulatory framework of the 1993 competition law was developed in 1998.

The first time the law was amended was in 2006. The changes addressed the CFC's lack of effectiveness in fighting key cartels, appointed a federal tax authority to collect fines, and allowed the commission to require divestitures in monopoly cases. The 2006 law adopted several changes relating to mergers but the 2006 amendments did not include budget adjustments nor did they give the CFC the power to stop anticompetitive trade decisions. However, the new law did establish the CFC's power to make non-binding recommendations in regulatory processes. This new law supported the cooperation agreement the CFC subscribed to with the Regulatory Reform Commission and the one entered into with the federal consumer protection agency (PROFECO, from its Spanish acronym) to foster public support for competition policy in 2005.

In 2007, Mexico signed an agreement to implement the OECD's Competition Assessment Toolkit aimed at analysing restrictions to competition and recommending modifications to laws and regulations. The next legal reform to the competition policy was in 2011. This amendment gave the CFC the power to conduct unannounced searches and conduct market studies. It also provided the CFC with tools to investigate and sanction violations, and set out the settlement mechanisms.

Mexico underwent a constitutional reform in 2013, which had a direct impact on the country's competition policy since it amended Article 28. Thus, a new competition law was enacted in 2014. These reforms led to the creation of a new competition commission, which replaced the CFC. The new Federal Commission on Economic Competition (Cofece, from its Spanish acronym) is responsible for monitoring, promoting, and guaranteeing competition and access to markets, as well as preventing, investigating and fighting activities that hinder competition in all sectors except telecommunications and broadcasting. The responsibility for the last two falls on the newly created Federal Telecommunications Institute (Spanish acronym, IFT).

Both the Cofece and IFT have the power to conduct market studies relating to competition and barriers hindering it. The new competition law also allows them to request information from other public entities and to sanction those that do not comply. Finally, even though neither entity can take direct measures based on their investigations, these studies promote competition and assist in identifying problems and regulatory gaps as well as educating consumers and companies, among others.

12.5.4 Competition Policy in Peru

Under the Peruvian legal framework, there are two competent entities in the field of competition. The main body is the *Instituto Nacional de Defensa de la Competencia y de la Protección de la Propiedad Intelectual* (INDECOPI), the other is the *Organismo Supervisor de Inversion Privada en Telecomunicaciones* (OSIPTEL). The main regulations in this field are Legislative Decrees No. 1033 and No. 1034.

INDECOPI's primary purpose is to promote free and fair competition and to safeguard intellectual property rights. As part of its advocacy activity, INDECOPI has made recommendations to other public authorities to adopt pro-competition measures, including recommendations to the Congress with respect to the effects in a certain sector of a specific law or regulation.

However, through the Elimination of Bureaucratic Barriers Commission, INDECOPI can enforce pro-competitive regulatory reforms; therefore, its functions are not restricted to advocacy. INDECOPI does not participate in the elimination or reduction of tariff or non-tariff measures, but it does participate in antidumping investigations.

Article 15 of Legislative Decree No. 1034 grants to INDECOPI the right to prepare and publish reports, and entitles it to request information from both private and public entities. Likewise, Article 14 establishes the right to perform market studies for advocacy purposes. Refusal by a private party to provide information entitles INDECOPI to impose fines on such parties. No sanctions can be imposed on public parties if they do not disclose any information.

Specific objectives of the market studies are to: (i) increase the general knowledge about the sector; (ii) assess the level of competition in the market or sector; (iii) define the market for the purposes of applying the competition law; (iv) investigate any alleged market failure that cannot be attributed to the conduct of market players; and (v) prepare to implement legislative reforms. Priority is assigned based on: (a) the nature of the good or service; and (b) the harmful effects of the practice on the market.

Both private and public entities can suggest to INDECOPI which studies it should undertake. However, the final decision remains solely that of INDECOPI. Although no specific provisions regulate the procedure, normally INDECOPI states the reasons for choosing the market and the study scope. Information received by INDECOPI may be considered as confidential pursuant to law, and a breach of confidence can result in criminal sanctions. Results of the studies must be made public according to the Law on Transparency and Access to Public Information. Recommendations issued by INDECOPI are not binding.

On the other hand, OSIPTEL is entitled by law to enforce the Competition Act in the telecommunications sector. OSIPTEL can adopt rules addressed to telecommunication companies. It also has the right to request information from private parties, who are obliged to answer in a truthful, accurate and complete manner. Any refusal to provide the requested information can result in sanctions according to the Resolution of the Board of Directors No. 087-2013-CD-OSIPTEL.

The main objectives of market studies conducted by OSPITEL are to: (i) understand how markets operate in order to decide which measures to take; (ii) assess the level of competition in the market or sector; (iii) increase general knowledge about the sector; (iv) define a relevant market; and, (v) evaluate the impact of government policies and regulation on the market. Some of the criteria for prioritizing the work include the importance of markets, level of market concentration and entry barriers.

Information provided by the companies to OSIPTEL can be treated as confidential upon request by the private party concerned, in accordance with the provisions of the Organised Single Text of OSPITEL's Regulation of Confidential Information, and the List of Public and Restricted Information, both approved by the Board of Directors of OSPITEL. The publication of the market studies depends on the information contained in the reports. OSPITEL can issue non-binding recommendations to public entities, including the legislative branch.

12.6 Conclusions

There can be no doubt about the importance of consolidating a consistent and coherent competition policy framework within the PA to help member countries meet their ambitious integration aims. The internal market requires an effective framework of competition law and policy to set the rules for an efficient allocation of resources and the protection of consumer welfare. However, in the medium term, it will not be surprising to find multiple political and economic interests that coincide both with entities at the nation-state level and with possible future supranational institutions, which in turn will push the demand for deeper integration. Accordingly, the strengthening of competition law and policy will depend to a great extent on the resolution of policy tensions and divergences arising among PA members.

Over time, the governance structure of competition policy in the PA can be expected to become multilayered in character, as in the EU. However, in light of the EU's experience, it is necessary to pay attention to developments such as the undesired duplication of efforts between the supranational governance system and member states' competition regimes. Therefore, it will prove essential to clearly define the functions, activities, and limits of each actor that forms part of the competition policy network within the PA. Consequently, the PA could follow the EU's model without this being the only possible future direction for the PA.

The member states of the PA can take as a baseline the integration experience of the EU and enrich it by transforming and adjusting some of the elements related to specific topics. The PA does not have to depend solely on this model for an institutional and community law structure. Other competition models that might contribute to the construction of a more *sui generis* system for regulating competition in the PA require greater scrutiny.

The challenge of regulating competition at a regional level in the PA will be even greater for those member countries which currently face anti-competitive challenges inside their own domestic markets. For example, conflicts can already be foreseen between the different levels of governance of the actors that will form part of the competition policy system. These include the nation-states, future institutions and meetings of ministers that will regulate this topic, and consumers represented in interest groups. Even though the Alliance has a more liberal and economic purpose, and is also more limited than the EU, the member states have to face the indirect effects of integration, especially with respect to the political initiatives adjusted to the economic, political, and cultural situation of the member states.

The agenda and debate around competition policy in the PA must include the private sector, and union representatives should be invited to be part of the construction of the evolving regulatory framework. By playing a more active role in the definition of competition policy, private enterprises are likely to be more willing to get involved in other matters that indirectly affect the development of their activities. The biggest challenges will be those related to poverty and inequality, where the role of the private sector can be aligned to social responsibility and business sustainability.

Hence, this chapter is intended to encourage the debate on competition law and policy, and to invite researchers to work on theories and gather empirical data for a new dialogue that is opened up by the PA and the turn towards the Asian region. In this effort, the EU model, evolving regionalism theories, and the development of the Pacific Rim area between Latin America and Asia will all be central topics of discussion.

References

Alianza del Pacífico. (2013). *Alianza del Pacífico*. http://alianzapacifico.net. Accessed 20 Aug 2014.

Amat, Y. (2014). *Canciller explica el alcance del acuerdo comercial de Alianza del Pacífico*. http://www.eltiempo.com/archivo/documento/CMS-13473735. Accessed 10 Sept 2014.

Bache, I., Stephen, G., & Bulmer, S. (2006). *Politics in the European Union*. Oxford: Oxford University Press.

Bakhoum, M. (2012). Introduction. In *Competition policy and regional integration in developing countries*. London: Edward Elgar Publishing.

Baldwin, R., & Thornton, P. (2010). *Multilateralising regionalism: Ideas for a WTO action plan on regionalism*. Geneva: Graduate Institute of International and Development Studies.

Bilal, S., & Olarreaga, M. (1998). Regionalism, competition policy and abuse of dominant position. *European Institute of Public Administration Working Paper, 98*(01), 1–22.

Caporaso, J. (1998). Regional integration theory: Understanding our past and anticipating our future. In *European integration and supranational governance*. Oxford: Oxford University Press.

Christiansen, T., Jørgensen, K. E., & Wiener, A. (2001). *The social construction of Europe*. London: SAGE.

Craig, P., & de Búrca, G. (2003). *EU law: Text, cases and materials*. Oxford: Oxford University Press.

Fox, E. M. (2012). Competition, development and regional integration: In search of a competition law fit for developing countries. *NYU Law and Economics Research Paper Series, 11*(04), 1–24.

Gamble, A., & Payne, A. (1996). Introduction: The political economy of regionalism and world order. In *Regionalism and world order*. Basingstoke: Macmillan Press.

García, P. (2013). *Acotación a la Alianza del Pacífico*. http://blog.uexternado.edu.co/acotacion-a-la-alianza-del-pacifico/. Accessed 2 Feb 2015.

Gardini, G. L. (2013). *The added value of the Pacific Alliance and 'modular regionalism' in Latin America*. http://blogs.lse.ac.uk/ideas/2013/06/the-added-value-of-the-pacific-alliance-and-modular-regionalism-in-latin-america/. Accessed 2 Feb 2015.

George, S. (1996). The European Union, 1992 and the fear of 'Fortress Europe'. In *Regionalism and world order*. Basingstoke: Macmillan Press.

Haas, E. B. (1958). *The uniting of Europe: Political, social and economic forces*. Stanford: Stanford University Press.

Haas, E. B. (1964). *Beyond the nation-state: Functionalism and international organization*. Stanford: Stanford University Press.

Haas, E. B. (1970). The study of regional integration: Reflections on the joy and anguish of pretheorizing. *International Organization, 24*(4), 607–646.

Hettne, B. (2006). Beyond the 'new' regionalism. In *Key debates in new political economy*. Abingdon, Routledge.

Hix, S. (2005). *The political system of the European Union*. Basingstoke: Palgrave Macmillan.

Hurrell, A. (1995). Regionalism in theoretical perspective. In *Regionalism in world politics*. Oxford: Oxford University Press.
Hveem, H. (2006). Explaining the regional phenomenon in an era of globalization. In *Political economy and the changing global order*. Oxford: Oxford University Press.
Ibarra Pardo, G. (1993). *Políticas de competencia en la integración en América Latina* (pp. 45–51). Buenos Aires: Integración Latinoamericana.
Lindberg, L. (1963). *The political dynamics of European economic integration*. Stanford: Stanford University Press.
Lowenfeld, A. (2008). *International economic law*. Oxford: Oxford University Press.
Malamud, A. (2003). Presidentialism and Mercosur: A hidden cause for a successful experience. In *Comparative regional integration: Theoretical perspectives*. London: Ashgate.
Martin, S. (2001a). Competition policy. In *The economics of the European Union: Policy and analysis*. Oxford: Oxford University Press.
Martin, S. (2001b). *Industrial organization – A European perspective*. Oxford: Oxford University Press.
Mejía López, R. (2014). *Alianza Pacífico: mal negocio para el agro colombiano*. http://www.portafolio.co/opinion/alianza-pacifico-mal-negocio-el-agro-colombiano. Accessed 20 Sept 2014.
Mols, M. (1993). *Regionalismus und Kooperation in Lateinamerika und Suedostasien. Ein politikwissenschaftlicher Vergleich*. Berlin: LIT Verlag.
Moravcsik, A. (1993). Preferences and power in the European Community: A liberal intergovernmentalist approach. *Journal of Common Market Studies, 31*(4), 473–524.
Moravcsik, A. (1998). *The choice for Europe, social purpose and state power from Messina to Maastricht*. Ithaca: Cornell University Press.
Motta, M. (2004). *Competition policy: Theory and practice*. Cambridge: Cambridge University Press.
Nolte, D., & Wehner, L. (2013). The Pacific alliance casts its cloud over Latin America. *GIGA Focus, 8*, 1–8.
OECD. (2004). *Competition law and policy in Mexico: A peer review (2004)*. http://www.oecd.org/daf/competition/prosecutionandlawenforcement/31430869.pdf. Accessed 10 Nov 2015.
OECD. (2007). *Peer reviews of competition law and policy in Latin America: A follow-up*. http://www.oecd.org/daf/competition/2007Follow-up-LA-peer-reviews_EN.pdf. Accessed 10 Nov 2015.
OECD. (2011). *Chile – Accession report on competition law and policy*. Paris: OECD. http://www.oecd.org/daf/competition/47950954.pdf. Accessed 10 Nov 2015.
OECD. (2015a). *Competition and market studies in Latin America. The Case of Chile*, Colombia, Costa Rica, Mexico, Panamá and Perú. http://www.oecd.org/daf/competition/competition-and-market-studies-in-latin-america2015.pdf. Accessed 10 Nov 2015.
OECD. (2015b). *Competition and market studies in Latin America 2015: The case of Chile*, Colombia, Costa Rica, Mexico, Panama and Peru. http://www.oecd.org/daf/competition/competition-and-market-studies-in-latin-america2015.pdf. Accessed 10 Nov 2015.
OECD & IDB. (2012). *Follow up to the nine peer reviews of competition law and policy of Latin American countries*. http://www.oecd.org/daf/competition/2012Follow-upNinePeer%20Review_en.pdf. Accessed 10 Nov 2015.
Pelkmans, J. (2001). *European integration: Methods and economic analysis*. Harlow: Pearson.
Ramírez, S. (2013). *Regionalism: The Pacific Alliance*. http://www.americasquarterly.org/content/regionalism-pacific-alliance.
Rittberger, B., & Schimmelfennig, F. (2005). Integrationstheorien: Entstehung und Entwicklung der EU. In *Die Europaeische Union: Theorien und Analysekonzepte*. Paderborn: Schoeningh.
Sandholtz, W., & Stone Sweet, A. (1998). *European integration and supranational governance*. Oxford: Oxford University Press.
Sandholtz, W., & Zysman, J. (1989). 1992: Recasting the European bargain. *World Politics, 42*(1), 95–128.

Sauter, W., & Langer, J. (2007). Competition policy. In *The European Union: Economics and policies*. Cambridge: Cambridge University Press.
Schiff, M., & Winters, L. A. (2003). *Regional integration and development*. Oxford: Oxford University Press.
Schmitter, P. (1969). Three neo-functional hypotheses about international integration. *International Organization, 1*(23), 161–166.
Schneider, B. R. (2004). *Business politics and the state in twentieth-century Latin America*. Cambridge: Cambridge University Press.
Soderbaum, F. (2003). Introduction. In *Theories of new regionalism*. Basingstoke: Palgrave Macmillan.
Spindler, M. (2002). New regionalism and the construction of global order. *CSGR Working Paper, 93*(2), 1–31.
Spindler, M. (2005). *Regionalismus im Wandel: Die neue Logik der Region in einer globalen Oekonomie*. Wiesbaden: VS Verlag.
Tsoukalis, L. (1997). *The new European economy revisited*. Oxford: Oxford University Press.
Tvevad, J. (2014). *The Pacific Alliance: Regional integration or fragmentation?* Policy Department, Directorate-General for External Policies. http://www.europarl.europa.eu/RegData/etudes/briefing_note/join/2014/522318/EXPO-AFET_SP(2014)522318_EN.pdf. Accessed 15 Jan 2015.
Venables, A., & Winters, L. A. (2004). Economic integration in the Americas: European perspectives. In *Integrating the Americas: FTAA and beyond*. Cambridge, MA: Harvard University Press.
Wallace, W. (1990). Introduction. In *The dynamics of European integration*. London: Pinter for the Royal Institute of International Affairs.
Wallace, H., & Wallace, W. (2000). *Policy-making in the European Union*. Oxford: Oxford University Press.
Wunderlich, J. U. (2013). Regionalism, globalization and international order. In *Europe and Southeast Asia*. London: Ashgate.

Chapter 13
The Pacific Alliance Dispute Settlement Mechanism: One More for the Heap

José Manuel Álvarez Zárate and Diana María Beltrán Vargas

13.1 Introduction

The proliferation of FTAs gained momentum as part of the global economic liberalization process that began in the 1980s. Their negotiation impetus began immediately after the WTO Agreement was signed in 1994. The mandate to seek progressive liberalization at the end of the Uruguay Round through negotiations on a multilateral scenario proved difficult, and the consolidation of economic blocs through free trade agreements (FTAs) started to increase in order to achieve deeper economic liberalization, albeit fragmented (Bown 2016, p. 5; Guzman 2002, p. 320; Jovanovic and Damnajovic 2015, p. 38).

Nowadays, considering the variety of issues that can be negotiated as part of international trade (World Trade Report 2011, p. 109; Crawford and Fiorentino 2005, p. 5), as well as the deadlock of the Doha Round (Lester et al. 2012, p. 333), FTAs are a means to enable liberalization on matters that affect international trade where the WTO law does not provide any guidance. This phenomenon is known by scholars as "deep integration" (Trebilcock et al. 2013, p. 95), and it has affected the scope of the commercial treaties that are currently being negotiated: for instance, the FTAs signed separately by Chile, Colombia, Mexico and Peru with the United States,[1] and the Additional Protocol to the Pacific Alliance Framework Agreement

[1] Chile-US Free Trade Agreement (entry into force 1 June 2004), Colombia–United States Trade Promotion Agreement (entry into force 15 May 2012); North American Free Trade Agreement (entry into force 1 January 1994), Peru–United States Trade Promotion Agreement (entry into force 1 February 1 2009).

J. M. Álvarez Zárate (✉) · D. M. Beltrán Vargas
Universidad Externado, Bogotá, Colombia

P. Sauvé et al. (eds.), *The Pacific Alliance in a World of Preferential Trade Agreements*, United Nations University Series on Regionalism 16,
https://doi.org/10.1007/978-3-319-78464-9_13

(the Additional Protocol)[2] comprise not only the usual trade chapters, but also special provisions regarding public procurement, investment and e-commerce, among others, which are key topics that are either regulated superficially or not at all by the WTO.[3] Those agreements are considered 'beyond borders' (Barbee and Lester 2014, p. 213; Chauffour and Maur 2010, p. 2), and the development of this WTO-plus trend has led to talks about an *open regionalism* (Bertola and Ocampo José 2013, p. 220; O'Keefe 2008 (n 10), 2).

While north–south FTAs were being negotiated, several southern countries considered to open their markets to other countries with similar economic structures through new FTAs negotiations. For instance, diverse FTAs were pursued between countries such as Colombia–Chile, Peru–Mexico or Mexico–Colombia, among others. As a result, there was a consolidation of regional trade agreements (RTAs) between these nations, and this provided the background to create an economic and political bloc (Bhagwati 2008 p. 32, 41–43). Some scholars think that the trade groups that have arisen as a consequence of treaties of this nature have gained relevance and negotiating power in the global economy (Vazquez López 2011, p. 113; Whalley 1998, p. 72). This assertion has yet to be proven in the case of the PA.

Also, despite the proliferation of FTAs, where it is difficult to identify which are the preferred trade partners, the theory goes as far as to claim that this kind of integration implies that the now-partners not only regulated the liberalization of trade through a preferential treatment, but also that their relationship would involve a higher level of economic and political commitment considering that they have relinquished some of their sovereign power in order to fulfil their specific needs at a regional level (Crawford and Fiorentino 2005, p. 2).

Additionally, it is important to highlight that the legal tools that are created under FTAs, such as the PA, have governance structures that would enable the harmonization of trade measures and economic regulation. According to some scholars, such institutional structures would guarantee the welfare of the group (Barbee and Lester 2014, pp. 210–211; Bertola and Ocampo José 2013, p. 220; Baldwin 2012, p. 649).

As a result, there are typical trade and legal chapters incorporated into these kinds of treaties, the dispute settlement mechanisms (DSMs) being one of them. These have been consistently included in all FTAs that have been signed, using the same language and limitations. Indeed, all of them have used identical language, which was provided by the US through the blueprint of the North American Free Trade Agreement (NAFTA)'s (Baldwin and Freund 2011 p.224), and later in the FTAs signed between the US and each of the PA members. Regarding the particular issue of the DSMs, it seems that the purpose was to establish an entity that adapts to the intrinsic needs of that particular agreement (Hayter and Edenhoffer 2014, p. 636; Jo and Namgung 2012, p. 1043). In other words, even though an FTA's DSM is

[2] "Protocolo Adicional al Acuerdo Máximo de la Alianza del Pacífico" (entry into force 1 May 2016)

[3] In the case of the FTA between developed and LDC, the issues subject to negotiation where those that were of interest of the developed one that were left unaccounted for by the WTO, or where their aims were not achieved completely after the Uruguay Round negotiations, which at the end of the bilateral negotiations were achieved.

going to operate concurrently with the WTO's Dispute Settlement Body (DSB), and for similar matters, if the parties are members of the latter, it also coexists with other DSMs that have been agreed in other FTAs signed among them. Although the existence of so many DSMs can be questioned, in theory, it seems that the reason for considering and even creating yet another one in the PA is because the scope of the obligations created by this new treaty is going to need a particular approach on certain issues, even though the topics are the same and follow a previous models (Davey 2006, p. 349). This does not seem accurate because the DSM template used in Latin American FTAs is the one that the US has included in its FTAs with Latin American countries since the implementation of NAFTA, which, in comparison to the WTO's Dispute Settlement Understanding (DSU), is less effective, as it does not have intimidating powers to guarantee the FTAs' commitments (Álvarez 2005, p. 147).

The situation described above is replicated in the case of the PA: all of its members (Colombia, Chile, Mexico and Peru) have previously signed FTAs with the US and thereafter with each other. They are also WTO Members. Therefore, the question that arises and that we intend to contribute to as part of the discussion, is whether it is useful to have a DSM in the PA under the same basis as previous DSMs, despite the fact that most of their provisions do not provide enforceability powers and/or a consolidated institutional nature to make commitments credible. This is in contrast to the DSB, and the Andean Community's Court of Justice DSMs, which are institutionalized and do have enforcement powers to make countries comply with their international obligations (Jo and Namgung 2012, p. 1045).

To answer this question, firstly this chapter will focus on the DSM setting provided in the Additional Protocol to the PA and its principal features, contained in Chapter 17 (1). Subsequently it will analyse and detail the relationship between the WTO's DSU and FTA-style DSMs such as that of the PA (2), and it will enquire whether it is useful to have them both for the same purpose i.e. to guarantee the fulfilment of trade commitments among its members, or whether it would be better to have a single institution to consolidate and harmonize the international trade and legal concepts that are duplicated on in the WTO system and the FTAs (3). Finally, it will conclude that the system that international trade requires for a DSM that is effective regarding the enforcement of its decisions gives more certainty to the trade system, because provides for certainty about the enforcement of the decisions that potentially could be adopted by the DSM.

13.2 The Additional Protocol's Chapter 17: A DSM for the Special Needs of the Pacific Alliance

The PA is a development of trade relations which pursues the establishment of a deep integration system between its members. Its purpose is to consolidate an economic bloc that will enhance not only the relationship between its members, but will also take advantage of this relationship to establish trade links with the South-East Asian market.

According to Article 12 of the Framework Agreement, one of the mechanisms to implement the common market should be the DSM, as it allows PA members to institute the obligations and the concepts on which the whole system is based, considering the solutions to any controversy that might arise among its members regarding its implementation or its interpretation (Pacific Alliance Framework Agreement, Article 12.1). It is important to note that the wording of the Article provides that the solution of any dispute shall be *satisfactory* to guarantee and enhance the operation of the PA system.

In addition, it is relevant to consider that disputes may arise regarding the implementation or interpretation of the Framework Agreement, the Additional Protocol and any future complementary regulations that help to develop the economic bloc, as detailed in Article 17.3 of the Additional Protocol. Therefore, the Members of the PA have to comply with the obligations entailed in the treaty, not only by adopting regulations in accordance with its provisions, but also by determining whether the current measures or projects awaiting approval could be in breach of the rules of the PA, thus triggering the DSM.

As a result of such commitments, the PA members developed Article 12.1 of the Framework Agreement in chapter 17 of the Additional Protocol. The chapter sets out the procedure that members have to follow when a dispute that affects the implementation and enforcement of the system occurs. The purpose of Chapter 17 is to establish a DSM that enhances the application of the concepts on which the PA system is based. This is clearly stated in Article 17.2 (1). It is understood that the members' main obligation is to reach a "*mutual satisfactory solution about any issue that might affect its* (the PA's) *operation*", such as restrictive measures that might affect any of the members in the terms set out in Annex 17.3, or that are clearly discriminatory and that do not enhance the integration of the bloc.

Following the same disposition, the PA's DSM's aim is to provide a process which is not only effective and efficient, but also transparent[4]; such characteristics are ideal under any legal procedural system, and they should be interpreted not only in a general sense, but also in accordance with the purpose of the Agreement.

13.2.1 Considerations on an Effective and Efficient DSM

On the one hand, as the DSM has to be efficient and effective, these features should be understood as contributing to guaranteeing the fulfilment of the obligations provided in the agreement, which in turn help to pursue the economic goal of liberalizing trade among the members. Also, it is not clear how the DSM will guarantee that the implementation of a DSM decisions will actually have the same effect. In the first place, Article 17.3 describes three different situations under which a dispute among members might emerge: (i) a current measure or a project that is against the obligations established in the Additional Protocol; (ii) the breach of any of the

[4] Additional Protocol to the Pacific Alliance Framework Agreement, Article 17.2 (2).

obligations in the Protocol; and (iii) a current measure or a project that might cause nullification or impairment or affect any benefit expected from the Additional Protocol's enforcement, particularly the ones established under Annex 17.3.[5] The situations clearly illustrate the circumstances under which the liberalization of trade is affected; hence, whenever a member witnesses any of those it is entitled to activate the DSM. One of the functions of the latter is to verify whether the behaviour of the respondent member falls within the scope of Article 17.3. In the case of an affirmative answer, the DSM must review the situation and compel the respondent to adopt a measure in line with its obligations.

Secondly, regarding the implementation of a Panel decision, Article 17.19 (1) establishes that on the decision awarded by the Arbitral Tribunal, the members involved in the dispute must reach an agreement on the outcome's enforcement. However, when the parties do not reach such an agreement, Article 17.20 foresees that the members will first have to negotiate provisional compensation until they reach a solution. Furthermore, when is not possible to reach agreement, the claiming member is entitled to suspend benefits and obligations from the Additional Protocol in a proportionate and temporary way. Regarding such measures, Article 17.22 entitles both parties to have them reviewed by the same tribunal that awarded the decision.

Also, it is important to note that Article 17.19 (2) establishes that when a tribunal finds that a situation considered under Article 17.3 has arisen, the member has to remove the measure in question from its legal order "*whenever possible*". Although Article 17.19 establishes that the award will be implemented, once the parties to the dispute have agreed on the terms established by the tribunal – Article 17.19(1) – and that by imposing on the breaching party the duty to remove the measure, the wording of the provision does not inspire confidence in the enforceability of the PA obligations that have been breached. The main problem of this approach is that by leaving the implementation of the decision to the parties in the dispute, the negotiation process will leave it up to the party with the strongest economic and political power to determine not only the conditions of the implementation, but also whether the award will have an effect or not, which implies a breach of the whole equilibrium of the undertakings reached in the PA System (Álvarez 2005, p. 145).

Another problem concerns the lack of clarity regarding whether the analysis of the possibility to remove a restrictive measure has to be the object of assessment in the negotiation to enforce the award, or, furthermore, the review. It is logical to conclude that it must be the object in both instances, as the question of its existence implies an effect on the functioning of the PA system, and by extension on the members' relationship.

---

[5] Additional Protocol to the Pacific Alliance Framework Agreement, Annex 17.3 nullification or impairment, allows to understand better the consideration (iii) of Article 17.3. According with this provision a Member is entitled to resort to the DSM when the measure, although does not contravene other provisions of the Protocol, it nullifies or impairs the legitimate expectations regarding the chapters on Market Access, Rules of origin, Sanitary and phytosanitary measures, Technical obstacles on trade, Public Procurement, Cross border Trade on services.

It is interesting that the provision might entail a consideration that there are certain situations which imply a breach of the Additional Protocol or the General Agreement, and which can persist until the breaching member is able – or wants - to remove and amend them. In other words, it seems that the rule states that, even though the members have to make their best efforts to facilitate trade, there are certain restrictive measures that can be maintained by the states. Hence the system has to anticipate how to work despite them.

Although Chapter 17 establishes provisions such as the ones mentioned in the previous paragraphs, it can be concluded that the system lacks effectiveness and efficiency in the enforcement of awards when a country is reluctant to fulfil its commitments. Article 17.16 (2) clearly establishes that the award rendered is binding on the parties, as the whole enforcement is based on the agreement they reach, but the consequence can be that temporary measures, such as compensation and suspension, extend indefinitely. This would have implications for the functioning of the economic bloc. Consequently, the trade system is vulnerable to a deadlock situation, and this would mean that the goal of trade liberalization cannot be met. In this regard, the effectiveness of the award that is intended through its binding power can be easily blocked because of the negotiations the parties have to go through in order to comply.

(i) Moreover, Chapter 17 follows the same model as the previous FTAs signed by the PA partners, including the implementation of a DSM and the enforcement of its decisions. Given that the main objective of a FTA is to liberate trade, this goal should have been a premise upon which the DSM was based. Limiting the analysis to the treaties signed between the PA members, for instance, in Chapter 16 of the Colombia–Chile FTA it is stipulated that its DSM can be activated whenever there is a risk of dispute about the interpretation and implementation of the agreement;
(ii) there is a breach of any of its obligations; or
(iii) one of the parties adopts a measure that affects any of the benefits that arise from Annex 16.2 (1).

Similar considerations are found under Article 19-02 (1) of the FTA between Colombia, Mexico and Venezuela,[6] under Article 18-02 of the FTA between Chile and Mexico,[7] under Article 16.2 of the FTA between Chile and Peru,[8] and under Article 18-02 of the FTA between Peru and Mexico.[9]

On the matter of the trade relationship between Peru and Colombia, both countries belong to the Andean Community, which is why a footnote to Article 17.3 establishes that the application of the DSM chapter has been excluded because

[6] Economic Complementation Agreement N°33 (Colombia, Mexico and Venezuela Free Trade Agreement) Article 19-02.

[7] Economic Complementation Agreement N°41 (Mexico and Chile Free Trade Agreement) Article 18-02.

[8] Free Trade Agreement between Chile and Peru. Article 16.2.

[9] Trade Integration Agreement between Mexico and Peru. Article 15.2.

Andean rules prevail between these two countries. Nonetheless, it is important to highlight that Article 4 of the Treaty Creating the Court of Justice of the Cartagena Agreement binds the Andean Community members to adopt all the measures required to enhance the Andean Community trade system, and also to restrain from making difficult the application of Andean norms and eliminate any and all measures that affect it.[10] In this matter, the Court of Justice is entitled to solve any dispute regarding the implementation of the legal system. However, unlike the FTAs, the Andean Community is based on specific procedural actions with different functions, and the decision awarded by the Court implies immediate enforcement by the legal system of each member,[11] which means that it does not require any agreement between the parties to a dispute to actually take effect. This characteristic avoids the potential deadlock that arises under systems where the enforcement and effect of the DSM decision rely on the parties' agreement.

So far, it can be concluded that the DSM provided in Chapter 17 suffers from the same weakness that other DSMs provided in FTAs also suffer from. If the purpose was to guarantee that the DSM could actually enhance the trade system by resolving implementation and interpretation issues, then it should have a stronger body that was allowed to intervene not only when there was a restrictive trade situation, but that also had the power to make the members comply with their obligations.

Moreover, if the scope of the FTA, and by extension the DSM, is not sufficient to resolve the dispute, these treaties establish the possibility for the parties to choose the most convenient forum for their needs.[12] Considering that the issue under dispute can also be an obligation included in several FTAs, then choosing a forum can be a convenient solution where there is a substantial difference between the DSMs. However, as reiterated previously, most of these mechanisms follow the same formula and raise the same concerns. As a result, there is no reason why a PA member would opt for a DSM apart from the one set out in Chapter 17 that does not offer any additional advantage in terms of effectiveness and efficiency.

[10] Treaty Creating the Court of Justice of the Cartagena Agreement Article 4- "Member Countries are under the obligation to take the necessary steps to enforce the rules comprising the legal system of the Cartagena Agreement. They are also hereby committed to refrain from adopting or employing any measure that opposes these rules or that in any way restricts their application."

[11] Treaty Creating the Court of Justice of the Cartagena Agreement Article 41.- In order to comply with the Court's verdicts, no official approval or exequatur will be required in any Member Countries.

[12] Additional Protocol to the Economic Complementation Agreement N°24, article 16.3; Economic Complementation Agreement N°33, article 19-03; Economic Complementation Agreement N°41. Article 18-03; Free Trade Agreement between Chile and Peru, article 16.03; Trade Integration Agreement between Mexico and Peru. Article 15.3.

13.2.2 The Transparency Feature of the Pacific Alliance DSM

The second characteristic that the DSM must have is transparency. This requirement has the purpose of creating predictability about the system's functionality and has two different dimensions: in a broader sense, transparency refers to making available to public the information on the operation of the trading organization. In the WTO, this element has been highly valued: citizens are entitled to know the rules that guide international trade and the decisions adopted in this regard (Matsushita et al. 2015, p. 927; Caichiolo 2016, p. 8).

Accordingly, it is interesting that under the PA provision – Chapter 17, Article 17.14 (3) (d) – there is a possibility for hearings to be open to the public, unless the information subject to debate is confidential or there is another justification. The parties must agree to secrecy. Although the publicity of the hearings depends on the disposition of the parties, the Additional Protocol incorporates an important element that the other FTAs of the members do not. On this point, the question that arises is whether such an element implies that the PA citizen has been granted a degree of participation in the decision-making process. The fact that there is public access to the hearings implies that the mechanism of the PA is making a matter of public knowledge the state of the debates that will eventually influence and affect trade policies, as well as allowing politicians and academia to support or criticize the path that is being followed in the implementation of the economic bloc.

On the other hand, the DSM's requirement of transparency refers to the procedure established to solve the differences that might arise regarding the interpretation and implementation of the PA's legal system. Its purpose is to guarantee to its members that the implementation of the whole system will be based on the rules that have been agreed, and that the decisions adopted will be enforced in accordance with the rules settled (Jo and Namgung 2012, p. 1045).

The trend among FTAs, regardless of their natural power structure, has been to move towards a DSM with a more legally based decision-making process (Brewster 2006, pp. 255–257; Keohane 2000, pp. 460–462). Even though diverse FTAs incorporate consultations as a mechanism to solve disputes regarding certain measures, they also include adjudicatory mechanisms that follow a legal procedure, as the decision is based on the rules of law within their own systems. Disputes resulting from a trade agreement are solved in accordance with a legal procedure, rather than a diplomatic one - such as consultations-, – and the outcome is based on the trading rules previously agreed and not on the political or economic power that the parties, which has been the case of the mechanisms of more political and diplomatic nature (Holbein and Carpentier 1993, p. 570).

In this respect, FTAs generally state that the mechanisms to solve disputes are arbitration, conciliation, mediation and good offices. Chapter 17 is no exception to this rule, as it incorporates the previously mentioned instruments.

Considering the procedures under which the whole proceedings are set, it does enhance the right to a fair process and a decision based on the PA rules. Furthermore, as the Additional Protocol sets out the steps of the procedure and the elements that should be the object of assessment, the members involved in a dispute can count on a level of predictability of the proceedings (Kono 2007, p. 747). It is noteworthy that the arbitral procedure set out in Chapter 17 seems to provide more detail than in the other FTAs agreed between the PA members. For example, under Article 17.14 (3) a long list of the guarantees that the procedure must safeguard can be found,[13] which is not found in similar agreements (i.e. Article 16.12 of the Chile–Colombia FTA, and Article 16.9 of the Chile–Peru FTA) or that is drafted in a superficial way in other agreements (e.g. Article 18-10 (1) of the Chile–Mexico FTA, Article 19-12 of the Colombia–Venezuela–Mexico FTA, or Article 15.10 (1) of the Peru–Mexico FTA).

Likewise, Chapter 17 is more specific regarding the elements that a decision must contain. Most of the FTAs provide guidelines on this matter; however, the Additional Protocol's provisions (Articles 17.15 and 17.16) try to broaden the basis of the decision by including the arguments presented by the parties in the arbitrator's award draft.

In conclusion, if FTAs follow a model, and the procedure has been "so well established" so far (Jo and Namgung 2012, p. 1049), this raises a question regarding the continued use of the same model, as there is no substantial differentiation or an effective mechanism that is tailored to solve the violation of the obligations of the system in which was conceived. On the particular issue of the DSM, it does not provide a suitable instrument to protect the system from treaty breaches in a more effective way, considering the number of similar DSMs that the parties can resort to in case of dispute. The only reason to opt for one of them, rather than for the WTO's DSB, is the nature of the decision, considering that a judicial scheme operates under the principle of *stare decisis*, whereas under the scope of the FTA it does not. Although a pronouncement rendered by a DSM like the one in Chapter 17 would not imply a precedent in the strictest sense (Busch 2007, p. 741), it is a source – even a subsidiary one – that enhances the trade system and solves the particular problems that the economic bloc entails.

[13] Article 17.14 (3) sets a list of guarantees for the procedure, such as: each party has the opportunity to present on written, at least, the initial considerations as well as a rejoinder; each party is entitled to of, at least, one hearing before the arbitral tribunal, and in the same sense, they are entitled to present their case orally; the hearing in front of the arbitral tribunal should be open to the public, unless the information under debate is considered confidential or there is an agreement between the parties that there are justifiable reasons to not make public the hearing; the Tribunal's deliberation process is confidential as well as the documents classified as confidential by any of the parties; all the information presented to the Tribunal must be made available for the counterparty; the information classified as confidential has to be protected.

13.3 A Relationship Between Systems: WTO and the PA

To connect the diverse international institutions that shape the international trading system, it is necessary to take into account mechanisms that enhance the harmonization process and allow the achievement of trade liberalization (Aksar 2014, p. 187; Koremenos 2007, p. 209). In this regard, counting on a DSM means that the trading system has a tool to homogenize the application of its principles and rules in order to synchronize the different economic blocs that work at different levels. However, the question that arises is whether the existence of numerous DSMs, although similar to each other, guarantees homogeneous and consistent decisions, not only considering that the parties can choose which DSM to call upon, but also that most of them are not able to enforce their decisions (Bown 2016, pp. 7–8).[14]

In the first instance, it is important to underscore that the FTAs include provisions that bind their members to implement these agreements in accordance with the WTO guidelines, an obligation that is bolstered if all the members belong to the WTO. For example, the PA Framework Agreement recognizes that this Treaty is based on the existing obligations assumed by the parties at a *"bilateral, regional and multilateral level"*. With this in mind, the decisions made by the DSM have to respect the obligations that the Members have regarding not only their FTAs but also as part of the WTO.

Ideally, regardless of the forum chosen by the parties, they have to be consistent with the obligations adopted in all these scopes (Bown et al. 2014, p. 8), and as a result the decisions made by each DSM should lead every subject of the trading system to act in a synchronized way through which the whole structure gains strength (Culot 2008, p. 17). The PA's Chapter 17 is no exception. Article 17.4 allows the choice of forum in order to solve the disputes that might arise, and such a privilege is undoubtedly based on the premise that it is necessary to ensure a comprehensive application of international trade rules. As the PA rules follow the guidelines established in other trade agreements as well as the WTO, a DSM decision on the application and interpretation of these rules would be set into the international trade framework (Gao and Lim 2008, p. 903). Nevertheless, although trade liberalization is the common goal, each system is conceived to be enforced and applied in accordance with its own needs (Busch 2007, p. 740).[15] There might, however, be certain variations on the decision-making process that a DSM adopts which could

---

[14] "One clear policy implication arising from the new RTAs is that introduction of competition among different trade agreements in the area of dispute settlement will not work. Two different trade agreements covering the same economic (market access) jurisdiction with competing court systems would inevitably render inconsistent legal rulings. Such fragmentation of international trade law and juris-prudence would increase policy uncertainty that would discourage firms from investing in international commerce."

[15] "The complainant's choice of forum depends on whether it prefers to set a regional or multilateral precedent, or no precedent at all. By setting a precedent, I mean adding to an institution's body of case law that is followed by its judicial bodies when ruling on subsequent disputes."

affect the interpretation of certain concepts and lead to overlapping obligations (Aksar 2014, p. 189; Kwak and Marceau 2006, pp. 467–468).

On the other hand, regarding the enforceability of the decision, it is important to reiterate that the DSMs set out in FTAs – the one on Chapter 17 being no exception – are not endowed with an institution or the coercive power to enforce the decisions intended to resolve the disputes between members. It is undeniable that the WTO's DSB is one of the most important contributions to international trade (Davey 2006, pp. 345–347; Hayter and Edenhoffer 2014, p. 632). The DSB was conceived with the purpose of granting predictability and consistency to the implementation of the multilateral trade system (Brewster 2006, p. 253; Elsig et al. 2012, p. 491; Creamer and Godzirinska 2016, p. 277), especially by moving from a diplomatic–political system to a judicial one, in which the decisions can actually have effects (Guzman 2002, p. 305).

Bearing this in mind, it is important to consider that the DSB already has a set of rulings and concepts for interpreting diverse topics covered by different trade agreements that are part of the WTO system, such as tariffs, trade barriers, anti-dumping measures, etc.; in this sense, what is the point of implementing small systems that are going to approach the same issues when the tools already exist. This does not mean that it is not possible to get different perspectives or even to find different answers to questions already formulated, but it would be better to count on a centralized organization that enhances consistency, where such developments can actually be implemented and would benefit the whole international trade system (Gao and Lim 2008, p. 911).

However, the concepts set out under the scope of the DSB are insufficient to meet all the needs of international trade. As the Marrakesh Agreement does not cover all the issues that modern FTAs and preferential trade agreements (PTAs) do (Crawford and Laird 2000, p. 4) and the Doha round is not expected to conclude any time soon (Jovanovic and Damnajovic 2015, pp. 42–43), the issue that arises is how to harmonize and unify the new trade topics. The only practical solution is that when a dispute is considered WTO+ or WTO-X, its natural forum will be a DSM, such as the one conceived in Chapter 17 of the Pacific Alliance Additional Protocol. Nevertheless, the issue of unified concepts remains, as there is no guarantee that DSMs will harmonize the interpretation of those new topics. This is because, there are no multilateral guidelines for new WTO+ topics and the DSMs decisions should respond to different kinds of needs and relations (Bown 2016, pp. 3–4).

In conclusion, it is evident that DSMs, such as Chapter 17, are aimed to respond to the singularities that the DSB cannot. However, the existence of different DSMs that lack binding force and are not capable of guaranteeing consistent decisions that enhance the international trading system is not the appropriate solution to move forward to harmonizing the obligations that trade liberalization implies.

13.4 Conclusion

This chapter reviewed PA Chapter 17's DSM, which is a replica of a model that many FTAs have followed before. Even though its function is to solve the disputes that might arise among PA's members, it clearly has an impact on the implementation of the PA as well as on the obligations its members have acquired through other FTAs and multilateral agreements (Davis 2009, p. 29). In view of this, the DSM model should be a tool that guarantees the enhancement of trade liberalization, but questions regarding the effectiveness of the decisions it renders, lead to the conclusion that there are no incentives for members to bring their disputes before this forum.

Looking on the bright side, a strong effort is being made within the DSM under the framework of the PA to achieve a more transparent system. It provides for more procedural guarantees and tries to make available a larger amount of information to PA citizens. Nevertheless, as the aspects of efficiency and effectiveness entail the same problems as all the other agreements that have so far followed the NAFTA model, the predictability pursued through transparency is only valuable on paper, as long as the implementation depends on the will to negotiate of the parties.

The PA DSM in Chapter 17 does not provide any solution to the lack of effectiveness of the decisions it adopts. One of the premises used to justify it is that its decisions will satisfy the economic needs of its members (Bown 2016, p. 6); but then again, from a pragmatic perspective, it is clear that as long as those decisions cannot be implemented the needs of the PA cannot be fulfilled, and the progress of international trade might be affected (Davey 2006, p. 353).

If the goal is to guarantee and enhance the application of PA obligations, or even further, to harmonize the international trading system, then it is better to count on a scheme that has a judicial organ and provides enough power to set a precedent that members can follow in order to fulfil their obligations according to the international trade framework (Aksar 2014, p. 190; Álvarez 2005, p. 151). This should not mean that the system would remain static based on absolutes, or even that the decisions would not respect the particularities of each economic region (Caichiolo 2016, p. 5).

References

Statutes

Additional Protocol to the Economic Complementation Agreement N°24 (Colombia and Chile Free Trade Agreement) entry into force May 8th 2009.

Additional Protocol to the Pacific Alliance Framework Agreement, entry into force May 1st 2016.

Economic Complementation Agreement N°33 (Colombia, Mexico and Venezuela Free Trade Agreement), entry into force January 1st 1995.

Economic Complementation Agreement N°41 (Mexico and Chile Free Trade Agreement), entry into force August 1st 1999.

Free Trade Agreement between Chile and Peru, entry into force March 1st 2009
Pacific Alliance Framework Agreement, signed on June 6 2012.
Trade Integration Agreement between Mexico and Peru, entry into force February 1st 2012.
Treaty Creating the Court of Justice of the Cartagena Agreement, entry into force on May 28 1979. Modified on May 28 of 1996.

Books

Bertola, L., & Ocampo José, A. (2013). *The economic development of Latin America since independence*. Oxford: Oxford Uniersity Press.
Bhagwati, J. (2008). *Termites in the trading system: How preferential agreements undermine free trade*. Oxford: Oxford University Press.
Lester, S., et al. (2012). *World trade law*. Portland: Hart Publishing.
Matsushita, M., et al. (2015). *The World Trade Organization. Law, practice, and policy*. Oxford: Oxford University Press.
O'Keefe, T. (2008). *Latin American and Caribbean trade agreements: Keys to a prosperous community of the Americas*. London: Martinus Nijhoff.
Trebilcock, M., Robert, H., & Antonia, E. (2013). *The regulation of international trade*. London: Routledege.

Official Publications

Álvarez, J. (2005). *Recomendaciones de Bogotá para la negociación de un tratado de libre comercio con Estados Unidos:* asuntos constitucionales, institucionales, solución de diferencias, inversión y competencia (Alcaldía de Bogotá).
Crawford, J., & Fiorentino, R. (2005). The changing landscape of regional trade agreements (Discussion Paper N° 8).
World Trade Organization. *World Trade Report 2011. The WTO and preferential trade agreements: From co-existence to coherence.*
WTO. "SINGAPORE WTO MINISTERIAL 1996: MINISTERIAL DECLARATION" (WT/MIN(96)/DEC). 18 December 1996
WTO. "Doha WTO MINISTERIAL 2001: MINISTERIAL DECLARATION" (WT/MIN(01)/DEC/1). 20 November 2001

Book Chapters

Aksar, Y. (2014). Towards global dispute settlement mechanisms in international economic law. In Y. Aksar (Ed.), *Implementing international economic law* (pp. 187–191). Leiden: BRILL.
Baldwin, R., & Freund, C. (2011). Preferential trade agreements and multilateral liberalization. In J.-P. Chauffour & J.-C. Maur (Eds.), *Preferential trade agreement policies for development* (pp. 121–141). Washington, DC: The World Bank.
Baldwin, R. (2012). Preferential trading arrangements. In M. Daunton, A. Narlikar, & R. M. Stern (Eds.)., (eds.) *The oxford handbook on the world trade organization* (pp. 632–654). Oxford: Oxford University Press.

Davey, W. (2006). Dispute settlement in the WTO and RTAs: A comment. In L. Bartels & F. Ortino (Eds.), *Regional Trade Agreements and the WTO Legal System* (pp. 343–358). Oxford: Oxford University Press.

Elsig, M., et al. (2012). Dispute settlement mechanism. In M. Daunton, A. Narlikar, & R. M. Stern (Eds.), *The Oxford handbook on the World Trade Organization*. Oxford: Oxford University Press.

Kwak, K., & Marceau, G. (2006). Overlaps and conflicts of jurisdiction between the World Trade Organization and regional trade agreements. In L. Bartels & F. Ortino (Eds.), *Regional Trade Agreements and the WTO Legal System* (pp. 465–524). Oxford: Oxford University Press.

Whalley, J. (1998). Why do countries seek regional trade agreements? In J. Frankel (Ed.), *The regionalization of the world economy* (pp. 63–90). Chicago: University of Chicago Press.

Journal Articles

Barbee, I., & Lester, S. (2014). The TPP and the future of trade agreements. *Latin American Journal of International Trade Law, 2*, 207–225.

Brewster, R. (2006). Rule-based dispute resolution in international trade law. *Virginia Law Review, 92*, 251–288.

Busch, M. (2007). Overlapping institutions, forum shopping, and dispute settlement in international trade. *International Organization, 61*, 735–761. https://doi.org/10.1017/S0020818307070257.

Caichiolo, C. (2016). International law and dispute settlement mechanism. *Meridiano, 47*(17), 1–10. https://doi.org/10.20889/M47e17016.

Creamer, C., & Godzirinska, Z. (2016). (De)Legitimization at the WTO dispute settlement mechanism. *Vanderbilt Journal of Transnational Law, 49*, 275–321.

Davis, C. (2009). Overlapping institutions in trade policy. *Perspectives On Politics, 7*, 25–31. https://doi.org/10.1017/S1537592709090045.

Gao, H., & Lim, C. L. (2008). Saving the WTO from the risk of irrelevance: The WTO dispute settlement mechanism as a 'common good' for RTA disputes. *Journal of International Economic Law, 11*, 899–925. https://doi.org/10.1093/jiel/jgn036.

Guzman, A. (2002). The cost of credibility: Explaining resistance to interstate dispute resolution mechanisms. *The Journal of Legal Studies, 31*, 303–326.

Hayter, R., & Edenhoffer, K. (2014). Trade disputes, dispute settlement mechanisms, and local development. *The Professional Geographer, 66*, 631–640. https://doi.org/10.1080/00330124.2013.826559.

Holbein, J., & Carpentier, G. (1993). Trade agreements and dispute settlement mechanisms in the western hemisphere. *Case Western Reserve Journal of International Law, 25*, 531–569.

Jo, H., & Namgung, H. (2012). Dispute settlement mechanisms in preferential trade agreements: Democracy, boilerplates, and the multilateral trade regime. *Journal of Conflict Resolution, 56*, 1041–1068. https://doi.org/10.1177/0022002712445731.

Jovanovic, M., & Damnajovic, J. (2015). Saving multilateralism in a higgledy-piggledy trading system. *Journal of Economic Integration, 30*, 29–65.

Keohane, R., & Others. (2000). Legalized dispute resolution: Interstate and transnational. *International Organization, 54*, 457–488.

Kono, D. (2007). Making anarchy work: International legal institutions and trade cooperation. *Journal of Politics, 69*, 746–759.

Koremenos, B. (2007). If only half of international agreements have dispute resolution provisions, which half needs explaining? *The Journal of Legal Studies, 36*, 189–212.

Vazquez López, R. (2011). Integración económica en América Latina: la visión teórica de la CEPAL confrontada con la evolución del proyecto en la región. *Journal of Economics, Finance and Administrative Science, 16*, 107–118.

Other Print Sources

Bown, C. (2016). *Mega-Regional Trade Agreements and the future of the WTO*. Council on Foreign Relations (CFR).

Bown, C., & Others. (2014). *What do we know about Preferential Trade Agreements and temporary trade barriers?* (Policy Research Working Paper- World Bank 6898).

Chauffour, J.-P., & Maur, J.-C. (2010). *Beyond market access. The new normal of Preferential Trade Agreements.* (Policy Research Working Paper-World Bank 5454).

Crawford, J.-A., & Laird, S. (2000). *Regional trade agreements and the WTO*. Nottingham: Centre for Research in Economic Development and International Trade, University of Nottingham.

Culot, H. (2008). *OMC et accords régionaux: les relations entre les mécanismes de règlement des différends* (Working Papers Series 2008/5). Université Catholique de Louvain.

Websites

Foreign Trade Information System, Organization of American States. http://www.sice.oas.org/agreements_s.asp. April 29 2016.

The Pacific Alliance. https://alianzapacifico.net/documentos/. May 29 2017.

Chapter 14
Concluding Remarks: The Pacific Alliance – Stocktaking and the Way Forward

Craig VanGrasstek

14.1 Introduction and Summary

The Pacific Alliance (PA) is a regional integration initiative that was officially established on 28 April 2011 by Chile, Colombia, Mexico and Peru. One of the PA's principal objectives is to build – in a participatory and consensual way – an area of deep integration to move progressively towards the free movement of goods, services, resources and people.

It bears recalling at the outset that the PA is still very much a work in progress, a fact reflected in both the substance and scholarship of this initiative. As such, this chapter is built not around conclusions or consensus about the initiative, but is instead presented as a series of questions concerning the establishment, status and future of the PA. Apart from some purely empirical matters, it was too early at the time of the conference in late 2015 to reach definitive conclusions regarding the nature of – and prospects for – the PA. That may be even truer in late 2017, given the recently turmoil that the trading system has been confronted with. Several of the chapters of this volume offer answers to some of the questions presented below, and a few of them take notably different approaches. There remains, to be sure, some important questions that this volume does not fully address, or to which the answers are as yet unknowable. All of this suggests that the PA is a dynamic undertaking for policy-makers as well as for analysts and advocates, and that there remains considerable room for further investigation.

What motivates the creation and evolution of the PA?

Most of the analyses contained in this edited volume take the negotiations of the PA as an established fact, but there are important practical reasons for considering why this agreement came into being in the first place. Knowing why the initiative

C. VanGrasstek (✉)
Harvard Kennedy School, Cambridge, MA, USA

P. Sauvé et al. (eds.), *The Pacific Alliance in a World of Preferential Trade Agreements*, United Nations University Series on Regionalism 16,
https://doi.org/10.1007/978-3-319-78464-9_14

developed in the first place can help us to understand the extent of its achievements thus far, as well as its prospects for further development. These are seemingly academic questions, but could ultimately be the most significant insofar as they implicitly address the question of the initiative's sustainability.

What economic trends contribute to the creation of the PA?

This question might be answered with reference both to internal and external developments. Or in other words, one may examine the origins of the PA by looking from the inside out, or from the outside in.

Looking from the inside out, Rodrigo Corredor (Chap. 11)[1] emphasizes the importance of countries' transition from resource-based to services-based economies as a motivator for the creation of the PA. The desire to move that transition forward can encourage the negotiation of agreements with deep-integration provisions (e.g. on the protection of intellectual property rights).

Looking from the outside in, the answer might also be traced to the rise of new economic powers. Ana María Palacio Valencia (Chap. 1)[2] notes that the PA represents a new emphasis on countries' relations with the Asia-Pacific region. This is a topic that would benefit from much more detailed examination (as is discussed later in this chapter). Another important trend is the emergence of global value chains (GVCs). Iza Lejárraga has addressed the place of the PA in a world trading system that is increasingly dominated by GVCs (Lejárraga, Chap. 4).

Why have these four countries opted to negotiate widely and deeply, and why have some others not made that same choice? Globally, there would appear to be a correlation between economic success and countries' decisions to negotiate RTAs, but which is cause and which is effect?

While this issue is addressed head on in this volume, it is arguably one of the most significant issues in the trading system today because it concerns the division between the countries that are and are not willing to conclude agreements and make binding commitments. It would be interesting to explore in a comparative way why there are some countries like the PA members that are more enthusiastic about trade liberalization than some other Latin American countries at comparable levels of development. Put another way, several of the contributions to this volume compare *what* different PTAs do, but do not address the foundational question of why some countries do and some countries do not engage in this kind of liberalization. This issue is worthy of deepened analysis along political economy lines.

Is the division between developing and developed countries still valid when it comes to trade agreements?

The world may increasingly be divided not so much along North–South lines, but instead between the eager and the sceptical countries with respect to new trade agreements. PA participants appear to be in a category of their own in this regard.

---

[1] "The Pacific Alliance: Adding Value to The Global Intellectual Property Rights Regime?"

[2] "The Pacific Alliance: Building a Pathway to the High-Hanging Fruits of Deep Integration."

José Toro Valencia, for example, places the PA in the context of South–South trade agreements and the notion of development. He argues for the capabilities approach to understanding trade and trade agreements, and asked whether the PA presents a new model for development in trade agreements (José Toro Valencia 2015).

What role do political or social considerations play in the creation of the PA?
José Manuel Álvarez addresses this question from a constructivist[3] and critical perspective coupled with concepts stemming from the international law and economics school of analysis. He stresses the shared political objectives of the South American members of the PA, which he attributes to those countries' similar responses to the realities of a neoliberal and post-hegemonic environment (Álvarez Zárate and Beltrán, Chap. 13).

Although some chapters refer to the external political objectives of the democracies that form the PA, none explore it in depth. When the PA was first established, it appeared that for several of the founders the objectives were as much political as they were economic, including the desire to create a counterweight to the Bolivarian Alliance (or ALBA) led by Venezuela. With the great majority of the analyses approaching the PA from either a legal or an economic perspective, these political issues warrant greater analytical scrutiny.

Are the motivations behind the creation of the PA, as well as the negotiation of other trade agreements, permanent or transitory? For example, is the apparent success of these countries in recent years principally (and perhaps deceptively) a consequence of high commodity prices?
A detailed examination of the origins of the PA initiative may also speak to its sustainability and potential vulnerability to political changes in the member states. Several chapters stress the importance of presidentialism in the creation and development of the PA. As discussed in the next section, however, the reliance on presidential leadership may create a potential hazard. And to the extent that the PA's origins may largely be traced to economic causes, changes in the economic environment may likewise pose risks. One may well ask whether the recent decline in commodity prices will make these countries less confident about trade and investment liberalization in general. These issues too should command greater scrutiny. These apparent *lacunae* may well be understandable, however, insofar as one may only speculate on possible future developments in national politics and global price levels.

What are the procedural and institutional characteristics of the PA?
Two themes run through many of the chapters in this volume: *presidentialism* and *pragmatism*. Thus far, the PA initiative has taken a top-down approach dominated by the four countries' presidents. Their rule-making style has stressed pragmatism and the creation of soft law over formalism and hard law or institutions. There are

[3] In contrast to the competing school of realism and liberalism, constructivism is based on the contention that significant aspects of international relations are historically and socially constructed, rather than inevitable consequences of human nature or other essential characteristics of world politics.

both advantages and risks inherent in these two characteristics. The advantages stem principally from the relative ease with which decisions are made while the disadvantages relate chiefly to the equal ease with which these decisions might potentially be reversed in the future. Subsequent events in the United States, for example, have offered ample illustration of just how quickly and thoroughly a country's trade policy can be changed if the electorate chooses a new leader who does not share the perspectives of his or her predecessors.

How susceptible is the PA project to a slowdown or even a reversal as a result of changes in its members' leadership?

Álvarez noted that the creation of the PA appeared to the presidents of the member countries as a natural extension of reforms that they had been pursuing for years, including domestic reforms, more active participation in the World Trade Organization (WTO), and the negotiation of preferential trade and investment agreements with numerous regional and extra-regional partners (Álvarez Zárate and Beltrán, Chap. 13).

Other participants also emphasized the role of presidentialism in the creation and advancement of this initiative. The leaders in the PA countries treat the group as a policy platform that can deal with issues pragmatically. Palacio voices concerns over a decision-making process that depends so heavily on presidential involvement. That could make the prospects for future progress overly dependent on national election cycles and possible changes in domestic agendas and priorities (Palacio Valencia, Chap. 1).

Does the reliance on soft law make the PA more susceptible to a slowdown or a reversal than is the case for other regional arrangements that rely more on hard law?

Lejárraga noted that most PTAs in other regions are based on hard law, being subject to the dispute-settlement provisions of their respective agreements. It has also been argued that unless commitments are anchored in hard law they may be more susceptible to that aforementioned change in domestic agendas. It may, however, be a mistake to underestimate the difficulties that may be encountered if the system moves from its current and successful approach to one that more closely replicates the processes that has been tried and failed in earlier negotiations (Lejárraga, Chap. 4).

Does the PA provide for the right balance between regulatory convergence and autonomy?

This question underlies an interesting debate as to where "soft law" is situated along the spectrum between "policy space" and regulatory convergence by way of hard law. Here contributors maintain differing expectations regarding how specific and binding trade agreements should ideally be. These are issues that may be impossible to resolve on an empirical basis, insofar as the positions that people adopt on them may ultimately be traced more to first principles than to matters of objective fact.

Rodrigo Polanco and Pierre Sauvé have addressed the question of regulatory convergence in the PA. In their view, the issue comes down to the tension between policy space and policy duty. The concept of policy space, they argue, can be dangerously flexible and could result in the opposite of regulatory convergence. Regulatory convergence will always be incomplete, but may be preferable to leaving too much wiggle room. Convergence can also be susceptible to change over time. The PA provisions on this issue sometimes may well suffer the fate of best-endeavours clauses (Rodrigo Polanco Lazo and Pierre Sauvé 2017).

Markus Wagner (University of Warwick) took a very different approach, arguing that the PA members are missing an opportunity in this treaty to achieve the proper level of regulatory autonomy (Markus Wagner 2015). Countries' perceptions of the issue have been changed by shifts in the direction of investment capital and by rising concerns over negative externalities (e.g. in environmental protection). The case of cigarette plain-packaging laws offers an example of the evolution of the legal regime, and the ways that trade and investment tribunals are examining measures that are based on considerations in other fields of public policy (e.g. health).

Does the PA need a more concrete institutional foundation?

Several contributors are concerned that the PA as yet has no secretariat or other permanent institutional foundation. If there were to be a secretariat or institutional foundation this might lead to less reliance on top-down presidentialism and represent a step towards harder law.

Palacio nevertheless observes that it would be damaging to over-produce regional bodies. The PA needs an appropriate level of institutional development. Several other contributors advance similar points, sometimes citing the institutions of the European Union (EU) as an example that members of this group could not or should not seek to replicate (Palacio Valencia, Chap. 1).

Can international institutions fill the gaps in regional institutions by providing public goods?

Soft-law institutions such as the International Monetary Fund (IMF), the Organisation for Economic Co-operation and Development (OECD) and the Inter-American Development Bank (IDB), as well as the *Mercado Integrado Latinoamericano* [Integrated Latin American Market] (MILA), can provide regional or global public goods[4] in the form of technical and other assistance in support of such specific regional public goods.

Joaquin Tres Viladomat (Inter-American Development Bank – IDB) addressed the PA as a regional public good (RPG), a sub-topic in the field of public goods that has recently received increased attention. The study of RPGs is a field of investigation implicitly based on the proposition that countries in different regions can learn from one another's experiences. Most of the RPGs involve regulation rather than

[4]As first described by Paul Samuelson in 1954, public goods share two special characteristics: They are non-excludable (i.e. no one can be prevented from enjoying them) and are non-rivalrous in consumption (i.e. any one person's use of that good does not diminish its availability to others). (Paul A. Samuelson 1954)

infrastructure. IDB research shows that these RPGs can create regulatory convergence at high levels, such that the quality of regulation in the weakest country in a group might be brought up to the level of the most advanced country rather than the other way around. He argues that the absence of supranational institutions within the PA creates a greater need for assistance from international institutions such as the IDB, citing such programmes as the IDB's support for single-window systems as examples of the types of initiatives in which the PA members can benefit from external assistance. Palacio also notes the need for technical support (Palacio Valencia, Chap. 1).

Manuel Monteagudo (Pontifical Catholic University of Peru) stressed the value of the reviews conducted by the IMF, noting that they have helped to transform the region's financial institutions. Even so, he argued that this form of soft law is not sufficient. In his view it is still necessary to prepare for supranationality (Manuel Monteagudo Valdez 2015). The question then is whether the outsourcing of some functions to regional and international institutions should be seen as a substitute for – or a complement to – the development of institutions that are specific to the PA. This topic was among the more interesting and valuable issues reviewed at the conference, but for which it is likely too early to reach definitive conclusions.

III. What has the PA achieved thus far on substantive matters, and what more needs to be done?

The emphasis on soft law and on goodwill seems to have produced some impressive results, insofar as the PA and its early-harvest approach has moved farther and faster than most previous integration schemes in the Latin American and Caribbean region. Many of the conference participants expressed agreement with that point, but were nonetheless concerned that the PA may need to switch to a more hard-law approach in progressing towards the achievement of its aims.

Taken as a whole, what is the level of ambition and achievement of the PA?

Alma Castro Lara and Camilo Pérez Restrepo seek answers to the question of whether the PA is WTO-plus (i.e. goes beyond what is in the WTO) or WTO-X (i.e. covers issues for which there are no WTO agreements) on distinct topics. In their comparison of traditional issues of market access and others, the predecessor agreements to the PA were not deep, but the PA itself is. The comparison for trade in services reveals the same pattern. On intellectual property rights, the PA is heading towards a Trade-Related Aspects of Intellectual Property Rights (TRIPS)-plus system. As for WTO-X issues, with varying degrees of ambition and completion, the PA also goes beyond the existing commitments of the members with respect to the Singapore issues of competition policy, investment, government procurement, and trade facilitation. On all these topics, however, the PA tends to be a work in progress (Pérez Restrepo and Castro Lara, Chap. 3).

What has the PA done on trade in services?

José Durán and Daniel Cracau point out that services trade among the PA members is relatively larger than goods trade among them (Cracau and Durán, Chap. 2). Angélica Corvalán, Dorotea López, and Felipe Muñoz observe however that the nominal level of services trade to non-PA countries is far smaller than that of exports of goods, and especially natural resources, among the PA countries. As a group they make a small contribution to global services exports, with Mexico by far the largest services exporter within the group. The PA countries make deeper services commitments in their PTAs than they did in the General Agreement on Trade in Services (GATS), even if they tend to take exceptions for national treatment. The analysis of countries' applied measures may be more revealing and relevant than a comparative review of commitments in different trade agreements (López, Muñoz and Corvalán, Chap. 7).

In his contribution, Eric Leroux argues that there is basically nothing new in the PA when it comes to trade in services. The PA's provisions on this subject follow the models of the GATS and the North American Free Trade Agreement (NAFTA). This in his view is inadequate to achieve the stated aim of free movement of services. This critique is not unique to the PA, but rather relates to the shortcomings of existing negotiating templates as these are no longer well-adapted to the reality of the marketplace. Agreements on trade in services have not kept up with the changes that have taken place since the 1990s. Mode 3 (investment) restrictions are not as great an issue as they once were. Mode 1 (cross-border trade) is gaining importance owing to the rapid development of e-commerce and digital transactions. This analysis might be extended by providing a more detailed set of suggestions as to how the PA might try to establish a new model (Leroux, Chap. 8).

Monteagudo recalls that the PA is only a point of departure in the possible creation of a common financial market among its members, pointing to the convergence in the expanded autonomy of central banks in the region (Manuel Monteagudo Valdez 2015). Leroux argues that mutual recognition and the harmonization of regulations are now the key issues for trade in services (Leroux, Chap. 8). Likewise, Monteagudo argues that mutual recognition is necessary in the field of financial regulation (Manuel Monteagudo Valdez 2015). There is no consensus on this point, however, with several conference participants expressing deep scepticism about the ease with which mutual-recognition agreements may be reached, and the commercial utility of these instruments even after they have been negotiated and implemented.

What has the PA done on intellectual property rights?
Strong intellectual property protection is needed in order to promote the transition from resource-based to services-based economies, but to date the only step in this direction is a 2013 declaration that a PA working group be established to study the issue. Corredor advocates a much more active role in promoting regional science and technology policy, and research and development (Corredor, Chap. 11).

What has the PA done on agricultural trade?
Meryl Thiel expressed strong scepticism regarding the capacity of the PA to achieve real reforms in the area of agricultural trade, which is a sector of even greater importance in Latin America and the Caribbean than in most other regions (Meryl Thiel 2015). As taken up in a later section of this chapter, this is an issue where regional agreements generally have less capacity to achieve progress than do multilateral negotiations (which have problems of their own).

What has the PA done on e-commerce?
María del Carmen Vásquez notes that the PA countries already have many of the necessary laws in place, but the existing agreements among these countries do not. This is therefore a *lacuna* that the PA can help to fill. The PA countries follow a hybrid between a US and an EU model of data protection, and considerable room remains for deeper integration (del Carmen Vásquez Callo-Müller, Chap. 10). In her presentation, Carolina Solano offered a detailed picture of the legal basis for e-commerce in the group through its various modes (i.e. business-to-business (B2B), business-to-consumer (B2C) and consumer-to-consumer (C2C)). Although e-commerce is the subject of an entire chapter of the PA, as with many PTAs, the agreement overall creates few concrete obligations (Carolina Solano 2015).

What has the PA done on investment?
The key question for Victor Saco is whether the PA needs an investment protocol. After reviewing the landscape of existing commitments and agreements, they conclude that the group's members must choose between allowing the overlapping of treaties or terminating the old ones and negotiating via the PA (Saco, Chap. 9).

What has the PA done on competition policy?
Ulf Thoene and Loly Gaitán-Guerrero use the EU experience as a possible model for the PA countries to follow. Observing that a lot can be learned from the EU if one thinks of benchmarks, they note that there is as yet nothing on competition policy in the PA, much less any supranational institution to enforce such a policy. Their analysis suggests several ways in which the EU's achievements might be emulated (Thoene and Gaitán-Guerrero, Chap. 12).

IV. How does the PA relate to the other agreements and negotiations in which its members have been or are engaged, and its members' relations with third parties?
Several conference participants and contributing authors spoke to the traditional tension between open regionalism and closed regionalism, and the question of whether the strategy of competitive liberalization failed or was ahead of its time. Some of them argue that the PA builds significantly on the existing bilateral agreements to which these countries are parties, examining the various ways in which the agreement's provisions relate to other negotiations in which the members are involved. These include the various agreements whose membership (at the time of the conference) is charted in Fig. 14.1.

Even if they are not formally multilateralized, how can agreements like the PA be made global-friendly?
Lejárraga stressed the importance of ensuring that the terms of an agreement do not work against the formation of GVCs, and should be devised in ways that do not work towards the exclusion of value chains with third parties. Her chapter identifies key features that GVC-friendly agreements should contain with respect to tariffs, rules of origin, trade facilitation and infrastructure, a services–investment–knowledge nexus, and regulatory cooperation. Some areas have greater homogeneity than

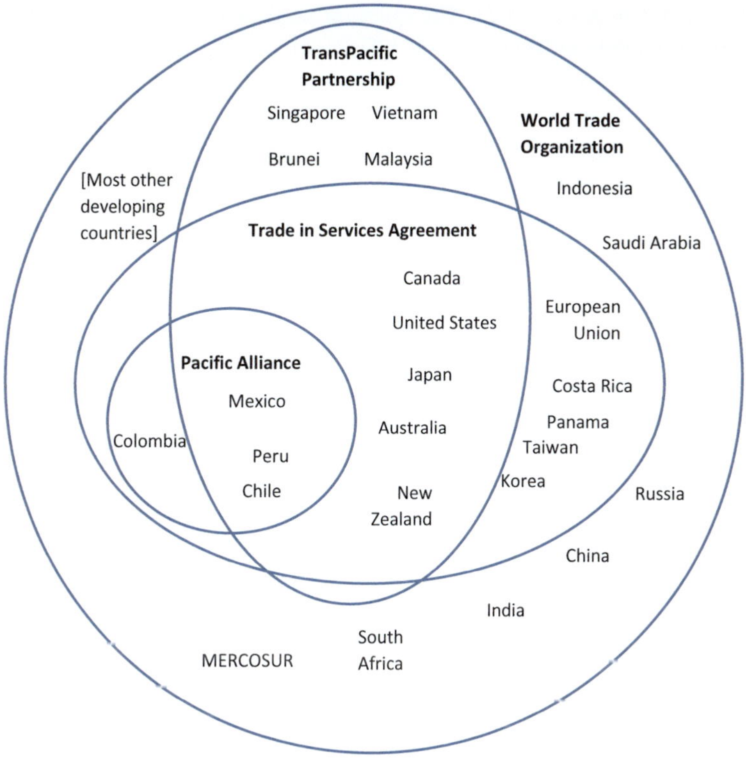

Fig. 14.1 Overlapping membership of four organizations or negotiations (Memberships for sets other than the PA and the TPP are not comprehensive)

others. She offered advice on the building blocks that an agreement should have in order to make it multilateralizable (Lejárraga, Chap. 4). Similar analyses with respect to other issues would be welcome.

Can the PA set precedents for other agreements?
Polanco and Sauvé have noted that the Trans Pacific Partnership's (TPP) provisions on regulatory coherence seem to have largely been taken from the PA (Rodrigo Polanco Lazo and Pierre Sauvé 2017). The observations made with respect to this topic suggest that it would be fruitful to undertake a more detailed comparison between these two agreements so as to determine (a) the extent to which the PA members may need to make further adjustments in their national laws to come into compliance with a prospective TPP, but also (b) the extent to which the PA may have served as a precedent-setting exercise for the TPP.

What are the implications of the PA-plus provisions of the TPP?
This question arises, for example, with respect to intellectual property rights. Corredor recalls that there is no intellectual property chapter (as yet) in the PA (Corredor, Chap. 11). It is, however, covered in the TPP, which includes all PA

members other than Colombia. The question nonetheless remains as to how the exclusion of Colombia from a possible TPP would affect the balance of commitments among the PA members. (It must of course be stressed that this issue was being discussed at a time when the United States had not yet pulled out of the TPP).

Should other countries accede to the PA? Or would those same countries be better advised to join the TPP or similar agreements?
None of the presenters dealt with the question of whether the PA and the TPP can be considered substitutes. Susana Wong and Carolina Palma discuss the experience of Costa Rica as a candidate member of the PA. Panama is the only other country that presently has the same status in the group. They stress the readiness of Costa Rica for membership, based on its similarity to the incumbent countries and its existing agreements with these and other partners. Nevertheless, there are some sensitive agricultural products that will need to be dealt with carefully (Wong Chan and Palma, Chap. 6). Durán and Cracau recalls that there are numerous Asian observers in the PA, and that some of these partners have been invited to form bilateral fora in which to explore issues of mutual interest (Cracau and Duran, Chap. 2).

What are the aims of the PA members with respect to their trade relations with third parties, especially major traders such as China, Japan, the EU and the United States?
This may well be the single most important topic for future analysis. While Álvarez alludes to the post-hegemonic nature of the current environment (Álvarez Zárate and Beltrán, Chap. 13), and Palacio discusses the orientation of the members towards the Pacific (Palacio Valencia, Chap. 1), both topics merit closer examination at both a high level of abstraction and at the detailed level of specific trade and investment flows, agreements, barriers and disputes. Among the questions largely left untouched by the volume is the relationship between China and the PA members. China has PTAs with Chile and Peru. One is under consideration with Colombia, but none with Mexico. What impact does this differing set of relationships have for the Pacific orientation of the PA?

What is the relationship between the PA and negotiations in the WTO, whether through the Doha Round or other initiatives such as TiSA?
One conference participant characterized the PA as "the little sister of the Cairns Group" and as being incapable of achieving real progress on agricultural trade issues. AT the time of the conference, all four PA members were engaged in negotiations towards a plurilateral Trade in Services Agreement (TiSA) that have since been suspended and whose fate remains uncertain. It would be interesting to see a closer examination of the roles that TiSA and the PA may play in one another's negotiations.

Johannes Bernabe (International Centre for Trade and Sustainable Development, Geneva) presented a multilateralist's perspective on a world of mega-regional agreements. What is the potential risk for discrimination against outsiders? He examined the WTO-plus and WTO-X aspects of mega-regional agreements. Some experts conclude that these agreements will create new discrimination, but this may not be very large. The potential for discrimination is limited by the relatively low level of most-favoured nation (MFN) tariffs and by the *de facto* MFN treatment of commitments made on services (Johannes Bernabé 2015).

Can the PA learn from the models of other regional arrangements, and vice versa?

Two recurring themes in the discussion involve a comparison between the PA and past initiatives in Latin America and the Caribbean, by which standard the PA may be judged a success, and a comparison with integration initiatives in other regions, by which standard the PA appears more like a work in progress. Some contributors note the asymmetry in the aims and achievements of the PA, especially by way of comparison with some other regional groups. The PA has achieved deep integration in legal principles that is not reflected in actual levels of intra-regional trade and investment integration.

Why is intra-regional trade lower among the PA countries, and more broadly in Latin America and the Caribbean, than it is in other regions such as Asia?

This comparatively low level of intra-regional trade might be attributed in the first instance to the lower level of complementarity in the region's economies. This is partly a consequence of the countries' resource endowments, especially their similar endowments of natural resources such as petroleum and minerals. That point generally holds true for Latin America and the Caribbean and specifically for the PA members. For instance, Durán and Cracau points out that parts and components account for only 7% of intra-bloc exports, much lower than the level achieved in other, more integrated PTAs (Cracau and Duran, Chap. 2).

In the more specific case of the PA, another explanation for the relatively low level of actual integration is the geographical distance of these countries. Other regional groupings typically bring together countries that are in close proximity to one another, often sharing economically active borders and major transportation routes. The only borders shared by countries in the PA (i.e. Colombia–Peru and Chile–Peru) are relatively remote from the main economic centres of the two countries, and the capital cities of the two most distant members (i.e. Chile and Mexico) are separated by 6586 km.

Can the PA members learn from the experience of other regional arrangements? For example, what aspects of the European model are applicable, and which are not?

No contribution to this volume advances the idea that institutions comparable to those of the EU would be appropriate for the PA. Leroux observes that the EU system offers an interesting model, but there is not sufficient will in the PA to replicate the European experience (Leroux, Chap. 8) and its origins in high politics (i.e. as a response to the two world wars), a view seconded by Thoene and Gaitán-Guerrero (Thoene and Gaitán-Guerrero, Chap. 12). The general view seems to be that the PA will evolve in response to its own internal dynamics and political DNA and remain a looser, less institutionalized, forum for promoting integration among a group of like-minded countries sharing a broad number of views on the optimal development path of their economies and the region and its links to the rest of the world, especially the Asia-Pacific region.

References

Bernabé, J. (2015). *Trade and sustainability in the Pacific alliance presented at the Pacific alliance in a world of preferential trade agreements: Lessons in comparative regionalism*, November 19, Universidad Externado, Bogotá, Colombia.

Polanco Lazo, R., & Sauvé, P. (2017). The treatment of regulatory convergence in preferential trade agreements. *World Trade Review*, 1–33. https://doi.org/10.1017/S1474745617000519.

Samuelson, P. A. (1954). The pure theory of public expenditure. *The Review of Economics and Statistics, 36*, 387.

Solano, C. (2015). *The Pacific alliance: Moving forward on e-commerce?* Presented at the Pacific alliance in a world of preferential trade agreements: Lessons in comparative regionalism, November 19, Universidad Externado, Bogotá, Colombia.

Thiel, M. (2015). *What can the Pacific alliance achieve in agricultural trade?* Presented at the Pacific alliance in a world of preferential trade agreements: Lessons in comparative regionalism, November 19, Universidad Externado, Bogotá, Colombia.

Valdez, M. M. (2015). *Financial and monetary policy perspectives on the Pacific Alliance presented at the Pacific Alliance in a world of preferential trade agreements: Lessons in comparative regionalism*, November 19, Universidad Externado, Bogotá, Colombia.

Valencia, J. T. (2015). *The Pacific alliance and the notion of development presented at the Pacific Alliance in a world of preferential trade agreements: Lessons in comparative regionalism*, November 19, Universidad Externado, Bogotá, Colombia.

Wagner, M. (2015). *Regulatory autonomy in the Pacific Alliance: A missed opportunity?* Presented at the Pacific Alliance in a world of preferential trade agreements: Lessons in comparative regionalism, November 19, Universidad Externado, Bogotá, Colombia.

MIX
Papier aus verantwortungsvollen Quellen
Paper from responsible sources
FSC® C105338

FSC
www.fsc.org

If you have any concerns about our products,
you can contact us on
ProductSafety@springernature.com

In case Publisher is established outside the EU,
the EU authorized representative is:
Springer Nature Customer Service Center GmbH
Europaplatz 3, 69115 Heidelberg, Germany

Printed by Libri Plureos GmbH
in Hamburg, Germany